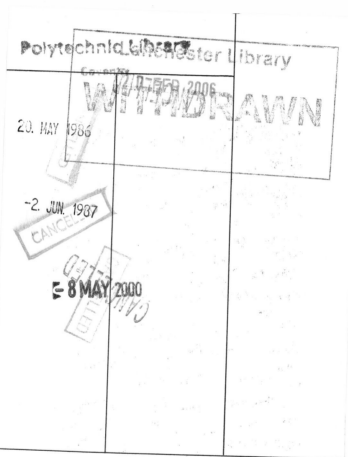

MODERN AMERICAN HISTORY ★ A

Garland
Series

Edited by
FRANK FREIDEL
Harvard University

ANGLO-AMERICAN RELATIONS AND COLONIALISM IN EAST ASIA, 1941–1945

John J. Sbrega

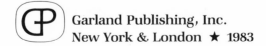

Garland Publishing, Inc.
New York & London ★ 1983

Library of Congress Cataloging in Publication Data

Sbrega, John J. (John Joseph), 1941–
  Anglo-American relations and colonialism in east
Asia, 1941–1945.

  (Modern American history)
  Bibliography: p.
  Includes index.
  1. World War, 1939–1945—Diplomatic history.
2. United States—Foreign relations—Great Britain.
3. Great Britain—Foreign relations—United States.
4. World War, 1939–1945—East Asia.   5. World War,
1939–1945, Japan.   6. Japan—History—1912–1945.
I. Title.   II. Series.
D753.S37   1983   940.53'22'410973   82-49078
ISBN 0-8240-5662-0

All volumes in this series are printed on acid-free,
250-year-life paper.
Printed in the United States of America

ANGLO-AMERICAN RELATIONS AND COLONIALISM

IN EAST ASIA, 1941-1945

JOHN J. SBREGA

DEDICATED TO

JULES DAVIDS

FRANK FREIDEL

WALDO HEINRICHS

WITHOUT THEIR INTEREST, ENCOURAGEMENT, AND ADVICE

THIS BOOK WOULD HAVE REMAINED "SIDEWAYS-CASEY"

TABLE OF CONTENTS

FOREWORD

Through a glass, darkly, is how historians have
perceived the Asian/Pacific phase of the Second World War.
That clouded vision resulted from many factors. To start
with, the Pacific War was more than just a military
struggle, it was also a clash of cultures. Europeans and
Americans saw the Sino-Japanese conflict of the 1930s as a
mere imitation of the wars of expansion and conquest that
had characterized European politics for centuries. But to
the Japanese and Chinese, their confrontation was but
another step in a pattern of give and take that had begun
long before Europe had coalesced into nation-states. The
fight for balance between China and Japan had been cultural,
social, intellectual, and economic. The political-military
phase of that struggle, as it developed during the Twentieth
Century and culminated with the Second World War, was one of
the least important chapters, at least from the vantage of
Tokyo and Peking. It was not until some three decades after
the Pacific War that American, European, and Japanese
scholars began to exchange ideas and evidence in a serious,
organized fashion, and studies began to appear that tried to
consider the cultural as well as the political aspects of
the conflict.

But other problems muddied the waters for scholars as
well. For most of the era of World War II, Anglo-American
historians and players alike viewed the crisis from the same
perspective as Secretary of State Cordell Hull; a threat to
Western Civilization was posed by Axis encirclement,
beginning with Hitler's Germany in Europe, Mussolini's Italy
in the Mediterranean, and somebody's Japan in East Asia.
That Americans never found a Japanese equivalent to Hitler
or Mussolini--Tojo and Hirohito never quite fit the bill--
should have suggested that there might be a basic difference
between European dictators and Japan's leaders, but the
emotions of war worked against such an analysis. By the
1960s, however, scholars had begun to treat the war in the
Pacific as almost a separate, distinct entity--a distortion
in the opposite direction.

Historical vision has been obscured by another factor, the cherished myth of an Anglo-American alliance that was free of the normal tensions, jealousies, arguments, and betrayals that have characterized alliances since the beginning of nations. Wartime patriotism took precedence over any public airing of such disputes, and that fellowship-of-battle continued well into the postwar era. And there are still those scholars who bristle at the idea of viewing World War II from the perspective of Anglo-American emnity, insisting instead that alliance triumphant is the only valid interpretation. The massive industry that has grown up around World War II books, movies, plays, and paraphernalia has never seen any commercial advantage in Anglo-American conflict beyond an occasional bar room (or pub) brawl scene quickly followed by the inevitable "we're in this together" comment from some senior officer.

But the mass of evidence that became available in 1972, when both the United States and Great Britain opened the bulk of their World War II archives, has enabled scholars to see the Anglo-American alliance for what it was--a remarkably successful coalition, but one in which the partners consistently sought to protect and expand their own national interests, even at the expense of the other. Early evidence of just such a relationship was always there, as a look at Robert Sherwood's Roosevelt and Hopkins demonstrates. But Cold War rhetoric replaced tension with an idealized version of Anglo-American selfless cooperation.

Perhaps the greatest tension between the two allies came over the question of the future of European colonialism in general and the British Empire in particular. As difficult as it is to pin down any aspect of Franklin Roosevelt's thinking, when one mulls over all his speeches, comments, and correspondence that touch on the issue of colonialism, it becomes evident that the President was well ahead of his two partners in the Big Three in realizing that European-style colonialism was doomed. Roosevelt's thinking was not consistent--he proposed during the war that Australia purchase the Portuguese colonies of Timor and Macao--and he did not foresee the sudden explosions of nationalism that would punctuate the immediate postwar world, thinking instead that Europe had thirty-odd years to get out of the colonial business. But he did believe that attempts by Europeans to hold on to their empires posed a greater threat to world peace than Soviet-American tensions, and events since World War II have proven him correct.

That is not to say that British diplomats and bureaucrats were unaware of the realities they faced. Churchill himself, while a staunch defender of empire, recognized the force of nationalism when he warned that the Japanese conquest of Singapore threatened all European colonies in Asia; hence his persistent pleas for a military re-conquest of Malaya as a way to reestablish British prestige. But despite warnings from various levels of government in Britain, the leadership of both the Tory and Labour Parties remained committed to the maintenance of empire. After all, one does not fight a war in order to lose territory, and politicians remembered well how the British public responded after World War I when Lloyd George proposed squeezing the Germans "until the pips squeak."

This, then, is the broad canvas upon which John Sbrega paints his picture of <u>Anglo-American</u> <u>Relations</u> <u>and</u> <u>Colonialism</u> <u>in</u> <u>East</u> <u>Asia</u>. This is not virgin territory, far from it. There have been a number of pathbreaking, important works on or close to the subject. But there is room for many more. The mass of fascinating documentation available continues to grow, and scholars need to continue to search for the kind of comprehensive thesis that can explain, or at least accommodate the contradictions that crop up. To understand American and British attempts to deal with nationalism in the immediate postwar world, we must understand the wartime assumptions and events that set the stage. What follows goes a long way towards accomplishing that task.

Warren F. Kimball
Rutgers University
Newark College

PREFACE

This study centers on Anglo-American relations during World War II and the issue of Western colonialism in East Asia. Specifically it develops two major themes. First, by comparing and contrasting American and British attitudes regarding colonialism, certain insights emerge about the coalition effort against Japan. To the extent that Washington and London remained skeptical about each other's motives and intentions, the strength of the coalition suffered. Some Americans believed that imperial interests dominated the British war effort, which, these critics felt, was geared almost entirely to recovering all prewar possessions. Conversely, some British observers suspected that American criticism of British colonial practices was unreasonable and uninformed, or, perhaps even worse, a ruse to conceal intentions in Washington to supplant prewar European imperialism with a postwar American version. These mutual suspicions, accordingly, weakened the effectiveness of the coalition. The second question to be explored is how the United States and Great Britain reconciled their ideas about the future of colonies with their concerns for security, especially in East Asia where Japan would no longer be powerful and where the Soviet Union would be expanding. The British--and the other colonial powers-- expected no major difficulties about reimposing their imperial authority after the victory. Americans struggled to reconcile their democratic, anti-colonial sentiment with perceived security requirements and national interests.

Documentary material in both the United States and the United Kingdom has been open to an appreciable extent for general research only relatively recently. A new synthesis is possible through a combination of this primary evidence with a judicious mixture of published sources. Of the latter, two seem particularly worthy of mention for this study: Christopher Thorne, Allies of A Kind (NY: Oxford University Press, 1978) and Wm. Roger Louis, Imperialism At Bay (NY: Oxford University Press, 1978). Each takes a somewhat different objective and framework from those in this study. Thorne's remarkable survey touches on colonialism only as part of the larger complexities affecting the Anglo-American relationship. His term "Allies of a Kind" is used, in particular, to call attention to shared racial assumptions in the United States and Great Britain. Louis' important book adopts a much narrower focus, namely, the evolution of the concept of trusteeship as developed during the war in Washington and London. Louis makes no attempt (as is made in this study) to set the Anglo-American controversy over colonialism against the backdrop of the Allied war effort against Japan. He carefully analyzes every nuance in the development of British policy regarding dependent areas and uses his broad scholarship of this question to trace this progress from the late Nineteenth Century. As illustrative of the difference, Louis makes extensive use of Colonial Office records, while this study emerges chiefly from papers of the Prime Minister and the Foreign Office. Thus, there is room, conceptually speaking, "between" the pathbreaking work of Thorne and Louis.

Another motive for this study stems from the complex nature of diplomatic history as interchange across international boundaries and international intercourse. Even the most valuable efforts of the early British and American "Official Historians" remain limited because they incorporated only their own national archival material. These studies, while important in their own right, tend to belie the richness and multiplicity that provide the essence of diplomatic history. Many of the earlier secondary works are more vulnerable in that the authors' access to primary sources has been greatly restricted until recently. Consequently, these efforts can be likened to a report of a telephone conversation by a reviewer observing only one of the participants. (Of course, the value of these works is even further limited if the observer has already decided--as some writers on World War II and the origins of the Cold War do--what both of the participants in the hypothetical telephone conversation should have said.)

Finally, despite the voluminous studies of the Second World War, a treatment of Anglo-American relations in East Asia regarding regionalism, colonialism, the Allied war effort against Japan, and planning for the postwar era still lacks an examination rooted in the primary sources of both countries.

The major premise of this study is that the strengths and weaknesses of the Anglo-American alliance are brought into sharper focus by examining various issues that arose throughout the war. In this case, several questions affecting colonialism, the wartime alliance, and postwar planning have been selected. These include the formulation of war (peace) aims, the controversial origins of the war against Japan, the effectiveness of the Far Eastern Allied coalition in the face of mutual suspicions regarding the selfish motives of the partners, French Indochina as a test case of Anglo-American policies with regard to the postwar restoration of prewar Western colonies (in East Asia), trusteeship, the structure of East Asia in the postwar era, and some unintended consequences of the decision to use the atomic bomb. By analyzing each of these questions and by tracing each in chronological development from 1941 through 1945, this study seeks to illuminate important elements of the Anglo-American wartime relationship.

PRÉCIS

The first chapter examines the progressive development of the close personal relationship between Roosevelt and Churchill. Of paramount importance is the context within which that unique friendship evolved. The embattled British sought to elicit American guarantees in the Far East while striving for survival against the European Axis Powers. In addition to the integrity of the British Empire, London worked to establish a joint Anglo-American underwriting of other European colonial possessions in the Far East as well as the independent sovereignty of Siam against Japanese encroachment. Conversely, the United States refused to be drawn into commitments carrying such enormous implications. Washington balked at venturing beyond the already perilous policy of providing the arsenal for democracy. The mushrooming Far Eastern crisis in late 1941 contributed to the explosive atmosphere in which tragic misunderstandings seemed inevitable until Japanese forces rendered that probability academic.

The next two chapters reflect Anglo-American tensions directly related to colonialism, or at least mutual perceptions of that controversial issue. Almost as soon as the grand principles of the Atlantic Charter surfaced, British and American interpretations of that document diverged. In particular, British attempts to qualify and restrict the scope of applicability of the Atlantic Charter elicited an extreme reaction in the United States. Americans harbored a certain distrust of British parochialism. These misgivings took on an added dimension with the controversy surrounding American entry into the war. Despite the Japanese initiative at Pearl Harbor, there lingered an uncomfortable, intuitive feeling that scheming Britain had somehow manipulated American leaders into the position of saving the British Empire. Unconcealed British delight at the new partnership only exacerbated American suspicions. Therefore, both sides indulged in a re-examination of the circumstances leading to American involvement in the war. Allegations about salvaging British chestnuts and Churchillian trickery serve to underline the direct connection of colonialism in these investigations.

Chapter Four traces some of the complex issues springing from British colonialism that hampered Anglo-American wartime cooperation. Most Americans failed to recognize that the interests of Great Britain and the interests of the British Empire were identical. The loud affirmations by Churchill in upholding imperial concerns enflamed American sensibilities as anachronistic sentiment in behalf of an outmoded concept. Indeed, a major American objective held that the war was being waged to destroy unwarranted restraints on the development of self-government for all peoples. Yet, if American critics confused the broader aspects of British interests it is also true that London relied too often on an unthinking, knee-jerk response in defense of British colonial administrations. This tendency revealed a parochialism that is somewhat surprising given the breadth of vision otherwise articulated by many British leaders, of which Churchill was only the most prominent. Those historians who subscribe to the stereotype of British "realism" overlook this disturbing element of British policy.

In Chapters Five, Six, and Seven emerge some of the complicated interplay between the colonial powers and American intentions to effect the removal of imperial administrations. In particular, the British sponsored the prompt return of French colonial authority in Indochina, whereas President Roosevelt promoted his concept of international trusteeship guiding that dependent area to eventual independence. Indochina, therefore, presents an interesting case study of this confrontation. Anglo-American relations and the politics of colonialism are clearly reflected in this unfolding story of France and her own imperial interests. Like the Dutch and the Portuguese, the British espoused the French cause in the belief that such policies strengthened the case for the restoration of British rule, too. Faced with this solidarity of the colonial powers (surprisingly slow in maturing), the United States gradually retreated from early ambitious projects about the global application of the Atlantic Charter. The noble premises of trusteeship also floundered upon the undisguised intentions of the American Service Departments to gain postwar control over the League of Nations Mandated Islands in the Pacific as well as other territories detached from Japan. Thus, the postwar visions of world order in London and Washington carried the dangerous potential for serious discord. Roosevelt acquiesced in compromises to salvage his first priority of institutionalized cooperation among the World Policemen (the exact number fluctuated from two to five) after the war. But the British managed to evolve a substitute structure of regional groupings should the idealistic scheme for an international organization fail. The inordinate British emphasis on Europe in contrast to the more broadly based American project neglected postwar realities and, again, indicates the fallacies of the historical clichés of British "realism" and American "idealism." The unfortunate sequel in the Far East, ironically, earned impetus largely from an important decision taken basically to relieve the terrible human sacrifices in the Far Eastern war. Two atomic bombs represented the perceived means of ending Japanese resistance. Whatever the historical judgments accompanying that fateful decision, the immediate Allied concern was realized. Yet, the abrupt termination of the war by Tokyo carried severe implications for the character of the Far East in the postwar era. The sudden surrender (also brought on, in part, by the entry of the Soviet Union in the war against Japan) prevented the United Nations from carrying out the measured liberation of Far Eastern territory in planned increments according to the Allied resources available. Moreover, this immediate case of indigestion was aggravated by the continued inability of the victors to complete expeditiously the reponsibilities of occupation. During this deadly interval, indigenous aspirations, previously held in check, were released and are in some cases still affecting Asian affairs.

The concluding segment deals with the general context of Anglo-American relations and the anticipated growth of the "Special Relationship." This study does not, however, venture into the murky historiographical waters of the origins of the Cold War. In addition, the extent of responsibility shared by Anglo-American wartime leaders for the subsequent explosion of coalition unity appears minimal, especially in view of the fact that neither Roosevelt nor Churchill remained in power until the completion of the war effort. That the wartime coalition failed to produce a trouble-free world pales dramatically beside the overriding consideration that the Allies succeeded in the primary task which had brought them together: achieving unconditional victory. Nevertheless, an apparently genuine opportunity to effect an enlightened new order of peace and justice, such as rarely occurs in history, dissolved. Thus, Anglo-American dreams during World War II remain a postwar challenge.

ACKNOWLEDGMENTS

Without the constant advice and encouragement of my mentor, Jules Davids, I would never have completed this study. My intellectual debt to Professor Davids can never be repaid, for he has guided my development throughout my graduate career. Similarly, Waldo Heinrichs and Frank Freidel have also become my intellectual creditors not only through their own work but also through their active interest in my possible contributions. Their valuable criticisms and suggestions immeasurably strengthened this study. Special thanks also goes to Warren F. Kimball who consented to critique the manuscript and to write the Foreword.

A Fulbright-Hays grant in 1972-1973 enabled me to explore many rich primary sources in the United Kingdom which would otherwise have been inaccessible. The United States-United Kingdom Education Commission in London greatly assisted my work by providing important liaison functions as well as administering the details of the Fulbright Scholar program. Professor D. C. Watt of the London School of Economics and Political Science made significant contributions in his capacity as my Fulbright academic supervisor. In addition, I must acknowledge the helpful services of the archival staffs at King's College Liddell Hart Centre for Military Archives, London; the British Museum, London; Nuffield College, Oxford University; Churchill College and University College, Cambridge University; and the Imperial War Museum, London. Special credit must go to Albert Harrington and the staff at the Public Record Office for their inexhaustible patience in guiding me to the most valuable portions of a seemingly endless supply of documents. Moreover, I want to express my gratitude collectively to the individuals mentioned in the bibliography for allowing me to impose upon their lives through correspondence and interviews. Their thoughtful reflections served to enhance my own understanding of the war years.

Professors Thomas Helde and Joseph Sebes, S. J., performed yeoman duties in serving as readers for an early version of this study. Others who influenced my development and strengthened this manuscript include Professors Dorothy Brown, Michael Foley, Richard Duncan, Wayne Knight, Josephine Holcomb, and John Ambrose. Also, financial assistance made available through Georgetown University Fellowships and a special research grant from The Center for Strategic and International Studies during the 1973-1974 academic year allowed me to pursue my research relatively unencumbered by excessive financial burdens. I am grateful, too, for assistance provided by the American Historical Association (Albert J. Beveridge grant) and the Virginia Social Science Association (research grant). Two summer grants from the National Endowment for the Humanities brought me under the influence of two outstanding historians. At Temple University, Waldo Heinrichs led me through the intricacies of "United States-East Asian Relations, 1937-1954," and, at Yale, J. H. Hexter revealed some of the challenges in "The Writing of History." Both professors showed remarkable patience and understanding (which I tested to their limits).

Staff members at the Franklin D. Roosevelt Library, the Library of Congress, the Sterling Library at Yale University, the Lauinger Library at Georgetown University, the Houghton Library at Harvard University, the Alderman Library at the University of Virginia, the George C. Marshall Foundation, The Citadel, Clark University, and particularly at the National Archives (including the Washington National Record Center in Suitland, Maryland) brought many important sources to my attention as well as relieving the day-to-day drudgery of protracted archival research.

In the editing, typing, and proofreading of the manuscript, exceptional service was performed by Bill Riley, Sandy Woodward, Debbie DiCroce, the McCormick sisters (Catherine and Ruth), Debi McNeilage, and Teri Holdridge. Despite this formidable array of readers, editors, typists, and proofreaders, however, it remains for me to assure them and you, the reader, that I alone am responsible for any errors or weaknesses in this book.   Finally, I reserve this traditional place of honor for all my family and friends who have helped me, for better or worse, to realize this objective. These people provided an inexhaustible reservoir from which I continue to draw nourishment. In particular, I want to single out my mother for her continuing support. I only regret that my father is not here to receive the credit that is due him and to see me put this history book on the shelf next to his math book. But most especially, there is my wife, Jo-Anne, and our two children, Daniel and Christianne. For all those "single-parent" outings, missed meals, and shouts for quiet while "Daddy is working," this book seems to fall far short of the cost. I deeply appreciate the love and understanding they showed throughout this shared adventure.

To all these, and to many others I could not mention individually, may I offer a sincere, if inadequate, "Thank You."

John J. Sbrega

Holyoke, Massachusetts

8 July 1983

CHAPTER I

ROOSEVELT AND CHURCHILL BEFORE PEARL HARBOR

With the spectacular events of September 1939, the "special relationship" between the United States and the United Kingdom entered a new phase. Predictions of extraordinary Anglo-American ties began almost as soon as the colonial connection had been severed in 1776, and despite continuing mixed reactions, that vision endured through the uneven evolution of the two countries down to the final moments of the inter-war years. Yet, even as the Old World leaders steered resolutely towards the precipice during the 1930's, Anglo-American relations were strained.

In 1937, Prime Minister Neville Chamberlain delayed two months before responding to a cautious overture in July from the President of the United States which suggested a meeting of the two leaders. Pointing to the deteriorating international situation, particularly in the Far East, Chamberlain informed the President: "I am afraid that I cannot suggest any way in which the meeting between us could be expedited."[1]

President Franklin D. Roosevelt, nevertheless, maintained at least infrequent contacts with the British Prime Minister. A member of Parliament, Colonel Arthur Murray, visited Roosevelt at Hyde Park 16-24 October 1938 and later conveyed a personal message from the President to Chamberlain. Roosevelt asked that he be quoted: "I will help all I can" with the proviso "as far as I am able." Privately, the President gave assurances that Chamberlain had "the industrial resources of the American nation behind him in the event of war with the dictatorships." For public consumption, Roosevelt suggested that the Prime Minister might say, "Great Britain, in the event of war, could rely upon obtaining raw materials from the democracies of the world." Murray stressed in his report that the President remained acutely aware of the strong noninterventionist-isolationist sentiment in the United States.[2]

Immediately after the circular declarations of war

during the first week of September 1939, Roosevelt invited
the Prime Minister to contact him "personally and outside of
diplomatic procedure" about any problems the British Cabinet
desired to discuss. Chamberlain replied very coolly that,
as yet, no need existed for such consultation, but he did
acknowledge that evidence of American support produced "a
devastating effect on German morale." Later, almost
apologetically, the reserved British leader, in a personal
letter to the President, admitted, "I cannot forebear from
sending you a private line of thanks and congratulation on
the great development of the last weekend. The repeal of
the arms embargo, which has been so anxiously awaited in
this country, is not only an assurance that we and our
French Allies may draw on the great reservoir of American
resources; it is also a profound moral encouragement to us
in the struggle upon which we are engaged."[3]

Although the overtures to Chamberlain withered,
Roosevelt remained undeterred in his efforts to establish a
line to London. On 11 September 1939--the same day he had
written to Chamberlain--the President greeted the new
British First Lord of the Admiralty: "It is because you and
I occupied similar positions in the World War that I want
you to know how glad I am that you are back again in the
Admiralty." In a fateful passage, Roosevelt promised, "I
shall at all times welcome it if you will keep in touch
personally with anything you want me to know about."[4] Thus
began the historic wartime exchanges between the President
and the recently appointed First Lord of the Admiralty,
Winston Spencer Churchill. Emerging from the British
political wilderness (he later admitted to being "decisively
discarded" and summed up almost a full decade of his life:
"I was awkwardly placed in the political scene"[5]), Churchill
recognized the significance of the opportunity and eagerly
seized this Washington connection. He arranged a telephone
conversation with Roosevelt on 5 October, warning the
President that the U.S.S. Iroquois, then en route to New
York, might contain a time-bomb planted during a stopover at
Queenstown. The First Lord authorized the President to
publicize the plot and to cite the Admiralty as the source
of information. The same day, Churchill, signing himself as
"Naval Person," wrote to Roosevelt, "We quite understand
natural desire of the United States to keep belligerent acts

out of their waters. We like the idea of a wide limit of, say 300 miles, within which no submarines of any belligerent country should act." Churchill promised that the British would comply with such an arrangement, and he asserted, "We wish to help you in every way in keeping the war out of American waters."[6]

When the Admiralty flashed its signal: "Winston is back," the appointment to the new War Cabinet created a mild sensation in some British circles. As First Lord, Churchill was returning to a position he had held during World War I. His earlier record will forever be tarnished by the notorious Gallipoli campaign, perhaps the most striking of the many controversies scattered throughout his public performances. Excluded from the Coalition Government in 1931 by Ramsey MacDonald and later from Stanley Baldwin's over the India question, Churchill remained outside the pale until receiving the call to the Admiralty in 1939 by Chamberlain. Churchill's work as head of the Admiralty attracted much concerned attention, especially from his many critics. Yet he not only displayed his administrative talents effectively but also managed to get along--as well as anyone could--with the aging First Sea Lord, Admiral of the Fleet, Sir A. Dudley R. Pound. "I find Winston admirable to work with," the irascible First Sea Lord reported to another "old salt," Admiral of the Fleet Sir Andrew B. Cunningham.[7]

Startling German military successes in Denmark and Norway during April 1940 precipitated a political crisis for the Chamberlain cabinet. Sir Samuel Hoare took note of a telephone message on 9 May from Leo Amery: "H. M. G. must go."[8] Amery had substantially abbreviated his stirring eloquence against Chamberlain in the House of Commons two days earlier, when he quoted the charge of Oliver Cromwell to the Long Parliament: "You have sat too long here for any good you have been doing. Depart, I say, and let us have done with you. In the name of God, go."[9] Chamberlain appealed in vain to his "friends," and, Hoare observed later, "The debate came and was managed badly. Winston ought to have spoken on the second day and Neville was not in good form."[10] On 10 May Chamberlain resigned and advised the King to summon Churchill to form a new government, apparently only after an unsuccessful attempt to marshal support behind Lord Halifax. Thus Chamberlain, the tragic and pathetic figure with the umbrella--a symbol of ridicule for his hapless efforts to bring peace in his time--gave way to the overriding need for a resolute, unyielding defiance that he could not summon. A comparison with his successor seems almost ludicrous now; one official British historian, Sir L. Llewellyn Woodward, mercifully concludes, "The personal influence of Mr. Churchill was so immense, foursquare and noble that it is unnecessary to try to heighten it by disparaging his predecessor."[11]

Five days after ascending to the Premiership, Churchill asked the American Ambassador, Joseph P. Kennedy, to deliver a message to the President. Adopting the pseudonym of "Former Naval Person," Churchill explained, "Although I have changed my office, I am sure that you would not wish me to discontinue our intimate private correspondence." The beleaguered Prime Minister commented somberly that "the scene has darkened swiftly." He then outlined the assistance that the United States could provide in a lengthy list which revealed the deepening dimensions of the crisis. In what must have been a humiliating experience for the proud leader of the British Empire, Churchill pleaded, "We shall go on paying dollars for as long as we can, but I should like to feel reasonably certain that when we pay no more, you will give us the stuff all the same." Finally, Churchill turned his attention to the Far East: "I am looking for you to keep that Japanese dog quiet in the Pacific, using Singapore in any way convenient."[12]

Roosevelt, in his response, expressed regret that he could not take immediate action on the urgent British requests. In retrospect, however, the deeper significance of this letter emerged with the President's affirmation: "I am most happy to continue our correspondence as we have in the past."[13] The considerable difference between carrying on a saucy exchange with a political renegade in the Admiralty and encouraging a similar relationship--often outrageous in its frank impertinence--with the head of a belligerent power risked political jeopardy for Roosevelt, given American isolationism and the 1940 election. Churchill obtained little satisfaction in his immediate requests, but more important in the long run, he earned increasing support from the President of the United States.

Teetering on the brink of defeat, the British faced at least three major obstacles in securing American assistance:

1. a still-powerful isolationist impulse running through American public opinion with special animosity toward His Majesty's Government associated with alleged British scheming to involve the United States in World War I;

2. an American bureaucratic labyrinth which made it difficult even to identify avenues of access in the Washington decision-making process; and

3. a deeply rooted hostility to colonialism in general and the British version in particular that clouded the motives behind virtually every proposal put forward by the British.

A considerable body of American opinion rejected repeated calls that America assume a greater responsibility in the world crisis. This influential segment, embracing both rational and irrational perceptions, spread a blanket of caution and hesitancy over official American behavior. "An old fossil like you with one foot in the grave should be ashamed of yourself for wanting to betray our American boys," thundered an irate "American Gold Star Mother" to an astonished Secretary of War Henry L. Stimson, who had issued a radio appeal for increased American aid to the Allies. "Shame on you and may the Devil take you."[14] Earlier, Roosevelt related to an English visitor to Hyde Park the story of a hypothetical query he had put to his cabinet about Japan attacking the Canadian Pacific coast. The whole cabinet agreed such an invasion would mean war for the United States. When the President next asked the same question about Japan menacing Australia and New Zealand, one cabinet officer replied, "Gosh! That's a hell of a long way off."[15] Senator Burton K. Wheeler made his infamous comparison of Lend-Lease to the Triple-A of the New Deal-- where every fourth American boy would be plowed under; while another senator, Ernest Lundeen of Minnesota, accepted the national chairmanship of the newly created Make Europe Pay War Debts Committee.[16] "Why pay taxes for England's War?" Donald Shea, Director of the National Gentile League wired Hull. "Don't be tax slaves for Jewish Rothschilds and

England."[17] And the mayor and the Board of Assessors in Detroit insisted that the local agency of the British Purchasing Commission file the required personal property assessment statement.[18] Rumors that the English Royal Family would move to Canada alarmed some Americans, who believed that the emigration either constituted a violation of the Monroe Doctrine or was part of a British plot to embroil the United States in the conflict.[19] Joseph P. Kennedy conducted his own public opinion poll in the movie theaters he owned throughout the country and announced that eighty percent of the American people were antagonistic to England.[20] Moreover, speeches by prominent--and popular-- politicians, such as Thomas Dewey, Robert Taft, and Arthur Vandenberg, added credibility to the mindless rantings of xenophobic extremists in American society.

In retrospect, the size of the isolationist bloc seems less important than the fact that a considerable element in the society (for whatever reasons) opposed America's entry in the war during the months prior to Pearl Harbor. Regardless of whether or not, for example, the administration could have somehow skillfully maneuvered a declaration of war through the Congress in this period, the problem remained from a leadership standpoint of how to ensure a united and wholehearted war effort. Existing disenchantment at such a policy would have crippled attempts to marshal American capabilities against the Fascist powers. Until Admiral Nagumo and his force attacked Pearl Harbor, American leaders felt the need to deal circumspectly with the perceived power wielded by the isolationists- noninterventionists. Meanwhile, His Majesty's Government interpreted American policy as a process of maddening gradualism. Two months before Pearl Harbor, Ambassador Halifax declared:

> [Roosevelt said] his personal problem was to steer
> a course between the two factors represented by:
> (1) The wish of 70% of Americans to keep out of
> war; (2) The wish of 70% of Americans to do
> everything to break Hitler. . . . He said that if
> he asked for a declaration of war he wouldn't get
> it, and opinion would swing against him. He
> therefore intended to go on doing whatever he best
> could to help us, and declarations of war were out
> of fashion.[21]

A second, lesser consideration for the struggling British proved to be the sheer mystery and inefficiency of the American governmental system coupled with the elaborate checks and balances prescribed by the United States Constitution. Sir Robert Vansittart, Chief Diplomatic Adviser in the Foreign Office, singled out the President and Undersecretary of State Sumner Welles for their "amateurishness."[22] But British concern reached more general levels. One special representative advised that "it was impossible to press more than one subject at a time in the United States Administration."[23] Halifax observed, "Every day that I am here makes me see how terribly disjointed is the whole machine of government." Complaining that "the Government Departments . . . might almost as well be the administration of different countries," His Majesty's Minister in Washington identified a main source of British frustration: "The result is I suspect that individuals like [Harry] Hopkins try to do too much and have no means of following up their activities, and that a great deal of what we try to do from the outside seems like hitting wads of cotton wool."[24]

In addition, the elaborate checks and balances positioned throughout the American democratic process made it even more difficult for the British to elicit a prompt response to their growing needs. Thus, at a time when decisive--and extensive--American action was required by London, constitutional considerations exacerbated the already ponderous workings of bureaucratic red tape and administrative inefficiency in the United States. Furthermore, British officials remained keenly aware of the comparison with their own ministerial system, which afforded considerably more latitude for action to them than that enjoyed by their American counterparts. The Prime Minister and his Cabinet accepted final responsibility; they might fall in a vote of no confidence, but while they held the reins of power they could be assured of voicing the official, united policy of His Majesty's Government. How different were affairs in Washington!

Consequently, the British in their perilous time had to accept a relatively passive role in dealing with Americans: instructing without appearing to interfere, warning without providing occasion for offense, and waiting for a broadly based consensus of support to crystallize.

Some British wartime practices even worked against courting American assistance. The blockade, the restriction of agricultural exports, the inspection of ships, the censorship of the mails, and questionable behavior by British intelligence agents in the United States served only to raise American anger. Twice Hull called in then-Ambassador Lord Lothian for reprimands that His Majesty's Government "was not mindful of our legitimate interests."[25] Lord Lothian warned then-Foreign Secretary Halifax about the "latent dangers" of arousing American antagonism. "It is due to the feeling that we have been needlessly inconsiderate of American interests, both public and private; that we have been trading upon her good will and more important perhaps in the long run," the Ambassador explained, "the U.S.A. is beginning to feel the old irritation against the way we use our 'command of the seas,' which has been the constant source of often unreasonable protest to us for the last hundred years."[26]

In general, however, London played a waiting game. "Between you and me we are not frightfully clever about propaganda," Lord Hankey revealed to an American friend, adding, "I believe that your own publicity people are doing it better than we should have done it."[27] Lord Beaverbrook, a close adviser to Churchill, relied on his unerring sense as a newsman to recommend abandoning the slogan "Aid to Britain" in favor of trying to educate Americans about their own interests. "Fear of Nazi power is good propaganda," he counselled and concluded that, overall, the best British approach would be "to let the news run."[28] The efficacy of this advice received reinforcement from Halifax, who noted the gradual awakening of American perceptions and exulted, "The Germans are certainly good producers of effects."[29] Perhaps the best explanation of the situation in the United States came from the discerning President himself. By early February 1941, Roosevelt apparently had set the general outlines for the course he wished to pursue. His instructions to the newly appointed Ambassador to London indicated the White House's conception of the American role in the international crisis. John G. Winant stated:

He wanted me to keep Winston Churchill and the British Government patient while the American people assessed the issues which faced them. He further instructed me to make plain to the people of Great Britain that we believed in their cause, that Nazism and Fascism were incompatible with the American way of life, and . . . that military training under the Selective Service Act had begun, American industry was keying to war production, Lend Lease was pending before Congress, and the transfer of fifty destroyers had already been accomplished.[30]

In addition to American isolationism-noninterventionism and the perplexing workings of the United States Government, a third formidable hurdle in the British quest to gain complete American support sprang from the deep-seated mistrust of British imperialism. In fact, some Americans believed that imperial concerns lay at the heart of all British actions and ideas. This enduring perception not only reinforced traditional American suspicions of perfidious Albion but also hindered the development of a true Anglo-American spirit of cooperation even after Americans joined the Allies. Japan and Germany erased two of the major obstacles confronting His Majesty's Government by declaring war on the United States, thereby undermining isolationist rhetoric and disposing of constitutional restraints against aiding the forces opposing totalitarianism. But even after the United States entry, this third problem would not disappear. American questioning of British motives and colonial interests continued throughout the Second World War and, indeed, persisted long into the postwar era.

One of the most revealing illustrations of how colonialism infected Anglo-American relations emerged in the wake of the Japanese attack at Pearl Harbor. In his exuberance over the significance of the event, Churchill broadcast a speech on 15 February 1942, in which he spoke of his having "dreamt of, aimed at and worked for" American involvement. The disquieting image of contrivance and perhaps nefarious deed immediately created a controversy. Many Americans believed that once again the British had tricked them into war; talk of pulling British imperial chestnuts out of the fire returned to plague His Majesty's

Government. An obviously disturbed Halifax reported the furor including provocations from "certain evilly-disposed sections of the press." The Ambassador warned, "I have doubt that it is being and will be used, and will be kept in cold-storage for sharper use against us later. . . . It is the words 'worked for' that are troublesome, and give the idea that a simple innocent people have been caught asleep by others cleverer than themselves." Eden shared Halifax's concern. The Foreign Secretary pointed out, "It is possible, I think, that a vivid passage of Max's [Beaverbrook] describing how you, at a council of war at the White House, pressed for an A.E.F. in Great Britain, will also be used later on to vindicate the Isolationists' slogan against us 'First our arms, then our money, then our boys.'" Both Eden and Halifax worried that Churchill's words would stir an anti-British, anti-colonial current in the United States. They urged the Prime Minister to try to make amends in some public declaration, but their efforts failed to move the unrepentant Churchill, except for the response:

> Qui s'excuse, s'accuse
> Qui s'explique, se complique.[31]

This sudden storm did aba'te, but an underlying tension always remained between indignant British defense of colonial arrangements and determined American vigilance against being drawn into unintended support for Old World imperialism. Despite the rise of the special relationship between the two countries and despite the 1939-1941 growth of what one perceptive observer has called the "Common Law Alliance,"[32] colonialism and all that the concept entailed carried the seeds of skepticism, if not dissolution, to the Allied coalition and prevented a true Anglo-American accord. Misunderstanding and mistrust on both sides further distorted each's perception of the other. Nowhere during the war would this potential discord be more likely to explode than in the Far East. For it is in that region that the war years produced dangerous tension among American idealism, imperial interests, and indigenous aspirations.

CHAPTER II

THE ATLANTIC CHARTER: PRINCIPLES AND PROMISES

Quite apart from the military effects, the embarrassing defeats inflicted against British interests early in the Far Eastern War produced severe political shock waves throughout the Empire. These intensified the already acute crisis in Europe which flowed from a Niagara of disasters--Denmark, Norway, the Low Countries, France, Greece, Dakar, Libya, the Hood, the escape of the Scharnhorst and the Gneisenau, and Tobruk. The beleaguered Empire was in danger of falling apart.

As Churchill returned in January 1942 from the first Anglo-American wartime conversations (ARCADIA), the Japanese had overrun the British colony of Malaya[1] and had imposed grievous losses on British and Dutch naval forces. Before mid-March Hong Kong, Singapore, and Java surrendered, while the abandonment of Rangoon opened the whole of Burma to the invaders. Japan enjoyed complete command of the Bay of Bengal, thereby threatening Ceylon and an India already beset with serious internal difficulties. John Curtin, Prime Minister of Australia, demanded, and of course received, the recall of Australian troops from the Middle East to prepare home defenses against the expected Japanese onslaught. In a move that might have salvaged the first Burma campaign, Churchill urged that the returning Australians--already en route--be diverted to Rangoon. The Australian Government, feeling bitter in the tragic sequence of military events and lacking confidence in the central direction of the war from London, refused abruptly. Also, New Zealand's Prime Minister, Peter Fraser, rebutted London's assessments of Japanese overextension. "We have in the course of this war seen tragic instances," Fraser charged, "in which the most competent opinion has been rapidly falsified by the event." Later, General Ismay sadly reflected, "No one had ever expected that retribution for our unpreparedness in the Far East would be so swift or so catastrophic."[2]

The surrender at Hong Kong and the series of progressive disasters leading to the fall of Singapore particularly jolted the flagging Empire. The Prime Minister revealed his awareness of the imperial implications in these fateful struggles. Emphasizing that "the eyes of the world are upon you," Churchill dispatched this doleful message to the beleaguered defenders of Hong Kong: "There must be no thought of surrender. . . . The honour of the Empire is in your hands." And from mid-ocean on his voyage to ARCADIA, Churchill cabled a warning back to the British Chiefs of Staff (COS) in London. "Beware lest troops required for ultimate defense Singapore Island are not used up or cut off in Malay Peninsula," he reminded the COS. "Nothing compares in importance with the fortress." Despite his broad experience, Churchill had never ventured farther east than India, nor did he seriously entertain any doubts that the far-flung imperial holdings could be supervised from London. His readiness to sacrifice Malaya on behalf of the fortress at Singapore merely reflected the prevailing British preoccupation with supposedly key strategic points in bolstering the security of the Empire. Singapore, after all, not only sat astride critical lines of communication in Southeast Asia but also represented a strategical springboard for operations against the Southwest Pacific area, including Australia and New Zealand. Yet London planners neglected the reverse side of this coin: Singapore lay just 1100 yards by causeway from the Malayan shore. "The policy adopted by H.M.G. was defensive to the verge of defeatism," C. A. Vlieland, the prewar Civilian Secretary for Malayan Defense, has alleged. Vlieland assigned "sole responsibility" to Churchill for the Far Eastern military disasters and charged that the Prime Minister "had the strangest ideas about the 'jungliness' and unimportance of the country called 'Malaya.'" Criticizing London's "imagination pictures of the geography of Southeast Asia and the relative importance of its parts," Vlieland pointed out that "the central feature of these pictures was a fortress and naval base called 'Singapore,' retention of which was supposed to be the one desideratum of importance in any way comparable with wide-ranging victory in the Middle East."[3]

Like the virtual evacuation of Malaya, the overemphasis on Singapore led to the questionable tactic of dispatching

two warships, the Repulse and Prince of Wales, to strengthen
the defense of the fortress. This decision is a measure of
the strategic contradictions and confusion in London by late
1941. On the one hand, the two ships, unaccompanied by a
support complement, amounted to less than sufficient
reinforcement to ensure Singapore's safety; on the other
hand, the two capital ships represented so much more of an
investment in seeking to deter Japan that they should not be
considered as mere symbols of concern expressed from the
helm of the Empire for one of its distant parts. Moreover,
the confusion was further compounded by the fact that the
two ships might have been used to great advantage against
Germany (which would have been more in keeping with
contingency plans for the grand strategy of "Europe-first"
should war come with Japan).

London thus felt the need to address imperial as well
as military priorities, and the two did not always coincide.
"The one lesson we have learned here is that it is essential
to have fighter protection over the Fleet whenever they are
in reach of the enemy bombers," First Sea Lord Pound
informed Admiral Cunningham in May 1940. Yet, the two
capital ships arrived at Singapore on 2 December 1941, more
as an expensive demonstration of colonial concern by His
Majesty's Government than as a sound military stratagem.
Vlieland described the two ships under Admiral Tom Phillips
as "outdated leviathans," whose destruction "followed
inevitably" the decision to assign them to the Far East.
General Sir Robert Brooke-Popham further confused the
imperial picture by denying the ships were for local
defensive purposes. "Warships must not be tied down to
their base; they must be free to operate to the full limit
of their range of action and know that they can still return
to a safe base when necessary," the C-in-C, Far East
announced at a Singapore ceremony celebrating the arrival of
the two ships. Curiously, he added, "These ships would be
of value to the Far East as a whole, but must not be
regarded in any sense as part of the local defenses of
Malaya and Singapore."[4]

On 10 December the fifth wave of an attack by Japanese
aircraft sank both the Repulse and Prince of Wales; on 14
January the General Officer Commanding III Corps ordered the
evacuation of Penang; on 15 February Singapore surrendered.

These disasters rocked Churchill. He anticipated even further setbacks in the Far East until the power of the United States could gradually become effective. "It is not easy to assign limits to the Japanese aggression," he told Roosevelt. "All can be retrieved in 1943 or 1944, but meanwhile there are very hard forfeits to pay." The critical Vlieland maintained that British arrangements for Malaya and Singapore amounted to "a set of paper plans, entirely devoid of physical backing, for the defense of an imaginary country against an imaginary enemy with imaginary resources in circumstances which were quite unimaginable." The former Civilian Secretary for Malayan Defense demonstrated the numerous fallacies underlying "an imaginary fortress 'Singraltar,'" and, at least on this point, his erstwhile antagonist, Brooke-Popham, agreed. The C-in-C, Far East recognized the crucial importance attributed to Singapore not only in London but also throughout the British Empire. The fortress was viewed as the strategical gateway to the Mideast as well as to India, Burma, and the sea passages extending to the twin Pacific Dominions of Australia and New Zealand. Brooke-Popham foresaw the widespread psychological damage that would follow the dire military consequences of the failure to safeguard this key strategic area--and symbol of Western colonialism. Could the colonial powers guarantee protection to their dependent areas? Before leaving London as Commander-Designate, he perceptively observed:

> But though carrying on even if reduced to a meagre diet of rice and rats and finally after firing one's last round, dying sword in hand in the innermost keep, may be romantic, it would be of little practical value towards the solution of the problem with which we have to deal.[5]

By the spring of 1942, the British Empire buckled under the continuing military defeats. One American intelligence report suggested the possibility that Germany might halt her assault on Russia at the Caucasus to mount a drive towards India. "At this time Germany could not be stopped at the present Indian frontier," this report warned. "If the Germans find the way to India open, they will surely not resist the temptation to strike for that country, which is

the world's most profitable imperial possession." An
unfortunate episode in December 1941 arose when General
Archibald Wavell, head of the new American-British-Dutch-
Australian Command (ABDA), twice refused Chinese offers to
provide troops for the defense of Burma. By doing so, he
aroused suspicions of British priorities that lingered
throughout the war. The British obviously preferred to have
imperial troops attending imperial interests. These
allegations were reinforced when the Governor of Burma, Sir
Reginald Hugh Dorman-Smith, upon hearing of imminent
Japanese air raids, ordered the sequestering of Lend-Lease
stockpiles, including important cargo aboard the U.S.S.
Tulsa, earmarked for China. The British were heavily
engaged in the defense of Burma at the time, and these
seizures at Rangoon assumed nefarious implications when
reported to Chungking. Generalissimo Chiang Kai-shek
delivered a stiff protest to Churchill (then in Washington).
The incensed chief of the American Military Mission in
Chungking, General John Magruder, relieved the American
military adviser at Rangoon and assailed the "arbitrary and
obtuse action" of the British. Churchill accepted the
explanations of the harassed Dorman-Smith, but the Prime
Minister frankly noted that "while declaring he had not
opened a single crate, he wanted to and very nearly did;
indeed, it would seem he may still."[6]

The list of incidents involving the British, such as
the Wavell and Tulsa episodes, during the early dismal
phases of the war swelled, and with it grew American
convictions of imperial scheming. General Joseph W.
Stilwell, the American commander with all sorts of
responsibilities throughout the China-Burma-India Theater
(C-B-I)--and an indefatigable anglophobe--accused Wavell of
being content to sit west of the Chindwin River lest "he be
criticized for not helping if the Japanese concentrate on
the Chinese and beat them up." Meanwhile in New Delhi,
General Benjamin Ferris complained that the British were
objecting to direct Lend-Lease aid by the United States to
India because of the political concern that India might
subsequently make exaggerated claims "at the peace table."
Next to the British Isles, the four Dominions (Canada, South
Africa, Australia, and New Zealand) lay at the core of the
British Empire. In a detailed examination of the Dominions,

the Office of Strategic Services (OSS) noted its great anxiety over the deteriorating military situation. The Dominions faced invasion and realized that the United Kingdom could no longer preserve the Empire (even with the help of the Dominions) without American assistance. "Coupled with this," the OSS study concluded, "there has been a growing dissatisfaction with British conduct of the war and an uncomfortable feeling that the heavy losses sustained by Dominion troops in Libya and especially in the Greek and Cretan campaigns are chiefly due to the mistakes of the British intelligence service and the mediocrity of British generalship."[7] Thus, the early defeats and apparent inaction upset those who envisaged a strong, united Empire marshaling all its resources to smite the aggressor foe. British central direction of the war attracted increasing criticism not only from within the Empire but also from other partners in the coalition of United Nations.

Ominous as the European defeats loomed, the military debacles in the Far East carried even greater adverse implications. The unexpected ease and thoroughness of the Japanese victories had called into question the whole concept of white supremacy and Western imperialism in Asia. The Japanese, eliminating the brutality which previously characterized their conquests, learned to exploit their newfound prestige. For example, the British Chiefs took anxious note of "new and extraordinary" Japanese methods, which included the encouragement of emerging nationalist aspirations, emphasis on religious themes (e. g., Catholic Japanese administrators began arriving in the Philippines), and the avoidance of efforts to transplant the ways of Japan[8]. Improved propaganda techniques and tempered administrative controls of occupied territories disguised the Japanese imperialism that was supplanting the Western version.

Indeed, so effective had been the Japanese methods that some Allied voices doubted whether total victory in the Far East could ever be achieved. In mid-1942, one State Department study declared gloomily, "Psychologically, Japan might well attain such a secure place as the leader of Asiatic races, if not of the colored races of the world in general, that defeat of Japan by the United Nations could scarcely be definitive."[9] Archibald MacLeish had earlier expressed similar views when he urged the President to counter "the intensive Tokyo propaganda that Japan is fighting for the cause of all races against the White race-- particularly the Anglo-Saxon race." He warned that the Japanese were effectively reaching many Asian people with this line and even exerting some influence on American blacks.[10]

The military and psychological significance of the British defeats appealed in particular to a developing Pan-Asiatic consciousness reacting against Western intrusion. The ubiquitous and historically heavy-handed presence of His Majesty's Government throughout the Far East led to the special attention--often distorted--focused on British setbacks at the hands of the Japanese. For example, a State Department paper certainly exaggerated in considering the crisis so great by mid-1943 that continued adherence to the original "Europe-first" strategy made victory over Japan "extremely difficult if not problematical."[11] But George M. Thomson, Beaverbrook's personal secretary, probably hit closer to the mark in observing that British prestige in Asia had dropped to zero. Thomson called attention to widespread criticism in Parliament and the press attacking "whisky-swilling planters, Blimp civil servants and exploiting rubber companies."[12]

If early military events promoted rising expectations among the Far Eastern peoples, the announcement of the Atlantic Charter acknowledged the need to address political changes. Churchill proudly pointed out that he had authored the first draft of the Atlantic Charter at the Placentia Bay meeting (ARGENTIA) with Roosevelt in August 1941. But his views on the British Empire, of course, were well known. About the Prime Minister, Sir Evelyn Wrench, founder of the Overseas League and the English-Speaking Union, remarked, "No one has a deeper conviction . . . that our Empire of free peoples is one of the chief buttresses of human freedom, order, and good government and has a supreme part to play in the future." Churchill set his own course in the famous pronouncement at the Lord Mayor's Day Luncheon on 10 November 1942:

Let me make this clear in case there should be any doubt about it in any quarter. We mean to hold

our own. I have not become the King's First
Minister to preside over the liquidation of the
British Empire.[13]

British concern about the applicability of the Atlantic
Charter and its far-reaching implications for imperial
possessions surfaced immediately after publication of the
document on 14 August 1941. The next day Clement Attlee
affirmed for the West African Students Union in London that
these principles "applied to all races." Speaking as Leader
of the Labour Party, the then-Lord Privy Seal explained, "We
have been glad to see how . . . the old conception of
colonies as places inhabited by inferior people, whose
function was only to serve and produce wealth for the
benefit of other people, has made way for nobler and more
just ideas." To the students' cries of "Hear, Hear," Attlee
continued, "You will not find in the declarations made on
behalf of the Government any suggestion that the freedom and
social security for which we fight should be denied to any
of the races of mankind." In early September, however,
Churchill advised the House not to apply "at this moment"
the broad principles of the Atlantic Charter to specific
instances. "The Joint Declaration does not qualify in any
way . . . the development of constitutional government in
India, Burma, or other parts of the British Empire," the
Prime Minister announced. "At the Atlantic meeting, we had
in mind, primarily, the restoration of the sovereignty,
self-government, and national life of the States and Nations
of Europe now under the Nazi yoke, and the principles
governing any alterations in the territorial boundaries
which may have to be made."[14] It will also be recalled that
at ARGENTIA the British protected their economic system of
imperial preference (by insisting on "due respect for . . .
existing obligations") and thereby evaded Roosevelt's desire
to end discriminatory practices in international trade after
the war. Thus, British qualifications to the Atlantic
Charter had begun; there would be more added later.

The September speech in Parliament by Churchill sparked
concern in West Africa that Attlee's assurances had been
misleading and unauthorized. The editor of the West African
Pilot demanded "clarification of the Atlantic Charter" and
inquired of the Prime Minister: "Are we fighting for

security of Europeans to enjoy the four freedoms while West
Africa continues in prewar status?" The obviously
distressed Colonial Secretary, Lord Moyne, informed the
Prime Minister that this newspaper was very influential in
Nigeria. He cautioned Churchill that "any attempt to gloss
over the fact--and there has in fact been some inconsistency
between the references to the Charter by the Prime Minister
and by Mr. Attlee" would be used to demonstrate British
insincerity. A Private Secretary in the Colonial Office
pointed out that "Lord Moyne has tried to find some way of
reconciling these two statements but has been forced to the
conclusion that any attempt to do so would fail to convince
the senders of the message who, it must be remembered, have
at times shown themselves suspicious of the good faith of
H.M.G." Nevertheless, the Colonial Office did submit a
draft reply for the Prime Minister to the direct challenge
from the Pilot. Churchill deleted an opening passage which
referred to the failure of Attlee to consult the Prime
Minister before delivering the pledge to the student
gathering. The actual response asserted:

> The declared policy of H.M.G. with regard to the
> peoples of the British Empire is already entirely
> in harmony with the high conceptions of freedom
> and justice which inspired the joint declaration,
> and the Prime Minister does not consider that any
> fresh statement of policy is called for in Nigeria
> or the West African colonies generally. To
> suppose, however, that the statement which the
> Prime Minister made is incompatible with the
> progressive evolution of self-government
> institutions in Nigeria or elsewhere shows an
> evident misunderstanding of his words, and any
> suggestion that this Empire's fight against Nazi
> tyranny is a fight for the security and freedom of
> European races alone is a suggestion which he
> feels confident all His Majesty's loyal subjects
> in Nigeria and elsewhere would unite in
> condemning.[15]

Yet, the ambitious rhetoric born at Placentia Bay
caused uneasiness for those directing the fortunes of the
British Empire. In particular, Point Three of the Atlantic
Charter pledged respect for "the right of all peoples to
choose the form of government under which they will live,"

but carried the awkward proviso that this right and sovereignty would be "restored to those who have been forcibly deprived of them." Despite the tacit understanding of the authors that this announcement was intended as encouragement for inhabitants of Axis-occupied countries, colonial peoples everywhere interpreted these grand principles in terms of their own aspirations. Two of the War Cabinet members most affected by these far-reaching implications grappled to reconcile imperial interests with the language of ARGENTIA. Leo Amery, Secretary of State for both Burma and India, notified the Cabinet that Burmese Ministers had fastened upon Point III as a promise of full self-government immediately after the war, regardless of domestic or international circumstances. In his dual ministerial capacity, Amery fell subject to similar pressures from India. He pointed out that he shared the wishes of the Viceroy to have an authoritative interpretation of Point III. The other War Cabinet member directly affected, Colonial Secretary Lord Moyne, was also troubled by the Point-Three phraseology, which he considered dangerously vague. "There are at least fifty governmental units in the Colonial Empire," Lord Moyne explained in a memorandum to the War Cabinet, "and, although the number might be reduced by federation, many would still remain too small, while others are strategically too important, for them ever to become completely masters of their destiny."[16]

Earlier drafts of Lord Moyne's memorandum prepared by the Colonial Secretary's Private Secretary, Christopher Gilbert Eastwood, reveal some official directions of British colonial thinking. Emphasizing the dangers of transferring institutions unmodified to people with entirely different histories and traditions, Eastwood had the Colonial Secretary declare, "I have been more concerned to expose the dangers of assuming that self-government with democratic institutions is the goal of all Colonies." The draft text applauded the desirability of fostering the growth of local institutions but pointed out that this process did not necessarily equal self-government. "Freedom and democracy are regarded almost as synonyms especially by our friends across the water," Eastwood commented; however, he added, "One of the morals of the present war is that the small unit can only survive by association with others." But the proposed solutions, official and otherwise, also reflected some of the prevailing ambivalences in British policies. For example, Eastwood argued, "Our aim must be so to mould the institutions of each Colony and so to fit them into the general Empire framework that they give to the people of that Colony the best expression possible in its particular conditions to our conception of freedom." And Lord Moyne, in the final version of his paper, observed, "We cannot admit a right of unfettered choice to those who, in the words of the League of Nations Covenant, are 'not yet able to stand by themselves under the strenuous conditions of the modern world.'" The Colonial Secretary concluded:

> I am sure, therefore, that we should be careful not to commit ourselves to fully responsible government as the goal for the whole Colonial Empire. As self-government often means the same thing in the popular mind, I should prefer not to mention self-government either. . . . We should avoid any implication that the free choice of the peoples of the Empire would necessarily be for self-government. . . . The Colonial Empire comprises peoples and territories of many different types and with a wide variety of institutions, which have evolved in accordance with the particular history and circumstances of each case. That evolution must continue on lines that accord with the British conceptions of freedom and justice.[17]

Leo Amery believed that Point Three of the Atlantic Charter embodied the spirit of British colonial policies and had not, therefore, introduced a new principle. Underlining the traditional British emphasis on developing self-government, the dual Minister was able to reconcile Point Three with the general thrust of both the "Declaration of August 1940," which dealt with Indian self-determination as soon as the war ended, and the "Governor's Address to the Legislature on August 26, 1940," which established the ultimate goal of complete self-government in Burma. Amery suggested that the rationale behind Point Three was:

> simply to give an assurance that we have no desire to impose against their will, either upon the peoples with whom we are at war or upon those whom we hope to liberate, any particular type of constitution. Though animated by the same spirit

of liberty as has guided the development of self-governing institutions in the British Empire--with regard to which both the general aim of our policy and our particular application in the case of India and Burma has been made abundantly clear --it has no direct reference to that process.[18]

Throughout the war His Majesty's Government grew increasingly sensitive to the rising international chorus of criticism, especially the American brand, directed against British colonialism and, indeed, Western imperialism in general. Speaking at Oxford in March 1943, the new Colonial Secretary, Colonel Oliver Stanley, bristled at "the great volume of friendly criticism and disinterested advice which came to us from America . . . directed to our Colonial Empire--or rather to the American conception of our Colonial Empire." Oliver reaffirmed his interest in what the British thought of the British Empire rather than what the Americans thought of it, and he asserted that the administration of the British colonies must remain the sole responsibility of Great Britain.[19]

This speech by Oliver earned much attention in Parliament. Churchill, under pressure, confirmed that Stanley's views represented official policy. When John Dugdale inquired whether the "truculent nature" of the speech had caused "misgivings" in the Dominions and America, each of whom "had hoped to see the Atlantic Charter implemented in our Colonial Empire," Churchill retorted, "We must equally beware of truculence and grovelling." The Prime Minister explained that British policies aimed at the broadest development of the colonies within the Empire and with friendly nations. Enough doubt had been created that Sir Percy Harris put the direct question: Did the Prime Minister still adhere to the principles of the Atlantic Charter? Churchill replied, "Yes, of course." But the Prime Minister balked when approached about a system of international mandates. "We should be opposed to the idea of condominions," he asserted, "which have always been found to bring about very bad results to the regions affected, but we naturally shall be in the closest touch and intercourse with our great Allies whose interests are closely connected with ourselves in some parts of the world." Churchill's response to a "supplementary" about the role of Commonwealth members in the future of British colonies bluntly affirmed, "They already have a considerable voice in the future of certain Colonies which come in their regions." This session revealed the depth of the emotion-charged issue of colonialism in Parliament. When one member demanded to know if occupied territory would be relinquished after the war "as Germany will have to do," the Prime Minister ended the stormy debate with the impatient rejoinder: "I think that it would be a very insulting parallel to draw."[20]

In the Foreign Office, attempts to reconcile the Colonial Empire with the Atlantic Charter proved equally difficult. Guy Wint expressed his concern about the postwar security implications of the eight principles. "Perhaps the public has reflected too little on the position of the British nation," Wint pointed out, "sandwiched between America and Russia and subject to their economic pressure if it weakly abandoned the territorial position in Asia and Africa which has enabled it to play the part, not of mere island traders but of a world power, devoted to the spread of peace." Wint feared that the old Wilsonian ideas disguised in the Atlantic Charter would strike idealist sympathies in the United Kingdom with far-reaching effects, such as "the virtual withdrawal of the tentacles of British influence all over the world." In particular, Wint warned against the "piecemeal dominionization" of British territory in the Far East, especially converging at the Indian Ocean-- "a British lake." He argued for a British confederacy in that region with collective military arrangements. From the British point of view, an added advantage of this proposal, which was designed primarily to promote a regional equilibrium, would be to forestall American criticisms, "the danger of which lies in the union of the sincere idealists with the more sinister groups using American Liberalism to undermine the sister Anglo-Saxon Empire." Wint concluded by recommending a vigorous role for the British in Asia which would not only appeal to British friends in the United States but also discourage outside interference because of its vitality.[21]

Reaction within the Foreign Office to the proposals by Wint illuminated the mixed ideas prevalent throughout the government on the controversial topic of postwar colonialism. Thomas E. Bromley felt that the memorandum described very real dangers. He doubted whether the Hindus would endorse the scheme but suggested that inclusion of the Netherlands East Indies would strengthen the confederation. Bromley cautioned, however, that the United States might interpret the new arrangements as a trick to preserve British hegemony in that region. Gladwyn Jebb ventured that the Moslems could manipulate such a system to gain control over the Hindus. Other criticisms of the proposed confederation pointed to the impracticality of the structure. C. K. Webster dismissed Wint's solution as "academic and unreal." The noted historian, working in the Foreign Office Research Department (FORD), believed that relations among the Great Powers would determine the extent of postwar security and questioned whether Asian people could adopt the Western concept of federalism. Security for the Indian Ocean, according to Webster, depended on the Mideast and Southeast Asia. M. E. Dening warned that the proposed scheme would only raise suspicions of British intentions. Linton Harry Foulds agreed with Webster's argument that a regional structure would be superfluous within the British Empire, which itself formed a confederation. Whether the imperial structure were strong or weak, Foulds pointed out, its parts would be the same. He declared that the support of British subjects, not American opinions, provided the key to the continuing viability of the Empire. Addressing the crux of the problem Wint had identified, Foulds stated, "We can believe in ourselves in our future imperial role without in any way being false to the principles of the Atlantic Charter, or backward in co-operating in a liberal manner in international affairs."[22]

Protection of the integrity of the Empire, of course, remained a paramount concern for the Churchill government. British officials were cautious about defining the scope of applicability of the Atlantic Charter. Ministers squirmed uneasily under awkward "supplementaries" in Parliament. Enthusiastic members of liberal persuasion led by Dr. Haden Guest, the Earl of Listowel, and the irrepressible Arthur Creech-Jones, objected to indications that British colonies were to be exempted from the ARGENTIA principles. The Chairman of the Research Advisory Committee in the Colonial Office, Lord Hailey, created some measure of official embarrassment with his persistent advocation of a "Colonial Charter," which would extend the general thrust envisaged in the Atlantic Charter to all dependent areas. The Colonial Secretary submitted a draft declaration on colonial policy to Churchill in July 1943 with the accompanying observation: "Various people . . . have made statements on this subject, going rather beyond what we actually have in mind, and I think it would be all to the good if the matter could be put in proper perspective." With the blessing of the Prime Minister, Stanley announced in the House that "His Majesty's Government would therefore welcome the establishment of machinery which will enable such [colonial] problems to be discussed and to be solved by common efforts." Specifically, the Colonial Secretary desired the establishment of regional commissions, which "would comprise not only the States with Colonial territories in the regions, but also other States which have in the region a major strategic or economic interest." Stanley pointedly emphasized that "each State would remain responsible for the administration of its own territory," despite more general arrangements "for consultation and collaboration." He did however, concede, "It should be possible, when designing the machinery of each Commission, to give to the people of the Colonial territories in the region an opportunity to be associated with its work."[23]

Apparently Americans placed more importance on a British statement of war aims, especially about colonial arrangements, than did the British. At the suggestion of Stanley K. Hornbeck, a leading influence within the State Department in Far Eastern policy, a special study group chaired by Leo Pasvolsky undertook a 1944 examination of announced British goals. The military objectives were unremarkable and similar to those of the United States-- unconditional surrender, disarmament, trials for alleged war criminals, return of Allied property seized, limited reparations, and self-determination for peoples of liberated areas. There were, nonetheless, divergent views about peace aims. Beyond security for Great Britain, equal status as a Great Power with the Soviet Union and the United States, and the bedrock determination to preserve the Empire, His Majesty's Government differed from American opinions regarding the structure of the projected international organization, the general security system to be established, administration of dependent areas, and postwar economic arrangements. American observers grew anxious about the British emphasis on regional arrangements and military enforcement agencies within the international organization. Moreover, the British, unlike the Americans, preferred to maintain controls over Germany and Japan (even after the enemies had been disarmed), flirted with recognition of Russian territorial demands, and positively excluded British colonies from any international schemes devised to lead dependent peoples to independence. The Pasvolsky group noted that British spokesmen tied any postwar economic collaboration to the financial resources available to His Majesty's Government at the time, while, as another State Department study demonstrated, British officials had taken care to remain relatively free from any shackling commitments regarding postwar promises and ambitions. Two major tenets, unconditional surrender and the Atlantic Charter (despite notable qualifications), emerged as the touchstones for virtually every British wartime statement of policy, including key addresses by members of His Majesty's Government.[24]

Significantly, one voice maintained a resolute silence--almost deafening in its impact--on the subject of postwar plans. Churchill steadfastly refused to enter the dialogue on peace aims. Upon taking up the Premiership, Churchill blunted inquiries about his objectives. "I can answer in one word," he thundered, "victory--victory at all costs, victory in spite of all terror, victory, however long and hard the road may be; for without victory there is no survival." His indomitable determination to concentrate single-mindedly on the war effort caused him to become greatly irritated at what he considered distracting proposals by his advisers regarding the postwar world. Eden, particularly, evoked stern lectures in phrases uniquely Churchillian. In May 1941, Eden pressed the Prime Minister for permission to deliver an economic statement prepared by John Maynard Keynes describing serious flaws in Hitler's "New Order" and indicating possible British postwar assistance for Europe. Only after receiving assurances from close advisers that no possible source of embarrassment lay in the speech (Brendan Bracken observed, "The stuff is alright, Keynes's points are wrapped in Foreign Office wool") did Churchill grudgingly consent to the speech. But he characteristically admonished his Foreign Secretary: "I should not have thought it was a very good moment to launch this economic manifesto when all our minds are concentrated upon the struggle. I do not think anyone knows what will happen when we get to the end of the war and personally I am holding myself uncommitted." A year later, when Eden proposed yet another statement on postwar promises, Churchill chastised him for taking his eye off the ball. Changing circumstances would automatically alter plans set down too early, the Foreign Secretary learned; furthermore, it was even dangerous to open such topics of potential discord within the coalition. "I hope that these speculative studies will be entrusted mainly to those on whose hands time hangs heavy," Churchill informed Eden, "and that we shall not overlook Mrs. Glass's Cookery Book recipe for Jugged Hare--first catch your hare."[25]

Yet, Churchill did not hesitate to plunge into speculation about postwar arrangements whenever he perceived hints that colonial links might somehow be pried loose. The broad spectrum of interpretations regarding the imprecise language in the Atlantic Charter proved particularly troublesome to the King's First Minister.

Three days after Pearl Harbor, the Foreign Office inquired about the possibility that the Prime Minister would now consider reversing his earlier deprecation of efforts to formulate war aims. This approach earned a predictable rebuke from Churchill, who dismissed the subject with the observation that "the general nature of our aims has already been made clear in the Atlantic Charter."[26] The United Nations Declaration of 1 January 1942 reaffirmed the "purposes and principles" of ARGENTIA. Perhaps its major significance rested in the positive appeal for unity in the war effort and in building upon Point Eight of the Atlantic Charter to establish the rationale for an international organization after the war. The Moscow Four Power Declaration, pledging postwar cooperation; the Cairo Declaration, disavowing territorial ambition in the Far East; the Tehran Communique, reinforcing the determination to cooperate in the war and in the peace that would follow; the Yalta agreements, scheduling the San Francisco

Conference to erect a general world organization and expressing (at least publicly) confidence about the character of the postwar structure; and the Potsdam Declaration, appealing to Japan to end her futile struggle so that "a new order based on peace, security, and justice" could begin--all these seminal statements acknowledged antecedents in the Atlantic Charter. Therefore, the reluctant Churchill, who played a major role in developing most of these documents, significantly influenced the guidelines and directions of postwar planning despite his protests to the contrary.

The scope of the applicability of the Atlantic Charter, however, proved quite a different matter for the Prime Minister. For example, he discounted any suggestion that the principles of Placentia Bay would forbid certain international boundary manipulations to punish foes and reward friends. When Stalin appealed for recognition of the territories added to Russia by the Russo-German Pact in 1939, Halifax labored "to reconcile your [Russian] security arrangements, and our common obligations under the Atlantic Charter," or as he later put it, between "our moral obligations and the forces of realpolitik." But Halifax possessed a poor track record in such matters, especially through his unfortunate association with Munich. Churchill, on the other hand, had earned a much different reputation concerning appeasement, yet significantly, he, too, advocated meeting some of the Russian demands. "We had never bound ourselves to apply the terms of the Atlantic Charter to ex-enemy countries," he protested to the War Cabinet. In his judgment, the United Nations coalition should make territorial changes in the Reich, and some of those changes might well be used to placate the aroused Russian bear.

For all its efforts, however, His Majesty's Government encountered heavy criticism from Washington, from enemy quarters, and even at home. American interpretations of the Atlantic Charter did not incorporate any such reserve clauses. Roosevelt offered general guarantees to Stalin about postwar security for the Soviet Union, but that was as far as the President would go in matching Russian desires against ARGENTIA designs. During the negotiations for the Russo-British pact in the spring of 1942, Halifax took soundings at the State Department about reactions to possible British acquiescence to some Russian territorial demands. He received a stern lecture from Sumner Welles about odious secret agreements. After reading Welles' account of this discussion, Adolph Berle, Jr. characterized the British scheme as tantamount to a "Baltic Munich." Shortly thereafter, the Foreign Office retreated by instructing Halifax to reassure Cordell Hull that the Russo-British Treaty of May 1942 did not conflict with the language of the Atlantic Charter; nevertheless, a separate State Department assessment concluded that the section of that treaty regarding postwar frontiers allowed for possible interpretation precisely along the lines of enemy propaganda allegations.[27]

Domestic suspicions and charges, especially from the left, about possible Allied collusion in secret territorial deals bothered Churchill in particular. "I am getting a little tired of being told by the Left Wing that we have fallen below their altruistic standards, when Britain seeks nothing for herself and the only cause of the trouble is the Soviet desire for territory," the Prime Minister confided to Eden in 1944. Earlier that year Churchill had warned the War Cabinet that "we were not free agents in the matter" because the Red Army was advancing and could undoubtedly enforce certain Russian requests. "You and I are being abused for our weak departures from the Atlantic Charter," Churchill again lectured the sympathetic Eden. "The only reason why we and the Americans are falling below the Atlantic Charter level is in order to try to keep in step with the Russian territorial demands--for the Baltic States, for part of East Prussia, for the Curzon Line, for Bessarabia and there may be more." The Prime Minister squirmed under accusations of perverting the spirit of the Atlantic Charter--first, by encouraging Allied territorial aggrandizement; and second, by prejudicing fair postwar treatment for the vanquished opponents, who might look to the safeguards of the ARGENTIA principles. "The Russian case is that they acceded to the Atlantic Charter (not as a Treaty but as a Declaration of Intention) because of their own resolved reservation that 'territorial aggrandizement' only began west of the Ribbentrop-Molotov Line," Churchill complained, sensitively attuned to the irony of criticism from the left. He pointed out, "Nothing would disturb the Russians more than the fact that it would have to be made public that they started from the Ribbentrop-Molotov Line, of which they are ashamed in principle, but which they are resolved to profit by in fact."[28]

Thus, one of Churchill's attempts to restrict the relevance of the Atlantic Charter landed him in considerable trouble. But in this specific instance he found a glimmer of hope from an unlikely ally. On 9 April 1944 Cordell Hull made clear that the postwar objectives of the United Nations crystallized on preventing aggression and providing world security. Consequently, Hull announced that "the Atlantic Charter did not prevent any step including those relating to enemy States to achieve these goals." Churchill's endeavors, therefore, to exempt ex-enemy territory and possessions from the protection of the Placentia Bay principles eventually received some slight reinforcement from Washington. In fact, Churchill believed that by interjecting this exception to the Atlantic Charter he had presented a strong argument for the controversial policy of unconditional surrender because of the obvious latitude of action now afforded to the United Nations coalition. A relieved War Cabinet responded to the Hull statement two days later, gratefully observing that "this clarification from a United States spokesman eased the pressure" on His Majesty's Government to issue an elaborate explanation of the official British interpretation of the Atlantic Charter.[29]

Another effort by Churchill to delimit the Atlantic Charter also provoked widespread criticism. Nothing could spur him to action more quickly than perceived assaults on his beloved British Empire. Elliott Roosevelt reported Churchill enlightening his audience aboard the Augusta at Placentia Bay with the affirmation that commitment to the Empire represented "the central tenet of his public and private life." He served as a guardian of the imperial system against any perceived encroachment, including the Atlantic Charter. A question arose in the House in 1944 as to whether Hong Kong or any part of the Empire was excluded (because of ambitious ARGENTIA rhetoric) from the Prime Minister's famous pronouncement not to liquidate the British Empire. The absent Churchill authorized Attlee to reply

with the uncompromising assurance: "No part of the British
Empire or Commonwealth of Nations is excluded from the scope
of the declaration referred to"; that is, he meant the
speech not the Atlantic Charter. Moreover, Churchill proved
equally adamant about restricting the applicability of the
Atlantic Charter to dependent areas in general. He seemed
peculiarly aware of his unofficial role as spokesman for the
other colonial powers, particularly France and the
Netherlands. A special American intelligence study of
official British reaction to this more general question
concerning colonialism and the Atlantic Charter pointed out,
"It appears that in virtually all [British] comments it was
assumed that the Joint Declaration was a document for
Europe, not for Africa or dependent areas."[30]

Given the attitude in His Majesty's Government that
what was good for the British Empire would also benefit the
international colonial system, the British differentiation
between applying the Atlantic Charter to British possessions
and to dependent areas in general seemed so subtle that it
dissolved to insignificance. But another criterion in
London regarding the scope of the Atlantic Charter
principles carried considerably more meaning. Churchill
insisted on a further qualification of the Joint
Declaration, even as it was being formulated, upon being
confronted with the prospect that imperial trade patterns
might be in jeopardy.

During the ARGENTIA discussions, Roosevelt outlined
American free trade predilections, while deploring
"artificial barriers." The Prime Minister bristled in
defense of the British imperial preference system
constructed in the 1932 Ottawa Agreements. At preliminary
talks with Sumner Welles on 9 August, Sir Alexander Cadogan
admitted he was "bitterly opposed" to this practice of trade
favoritism within the Empire. Welles, of course, pressed
for unrestricted economic intercourse after the war. The
following day Cadogan authored a working draft of what
became the Atlantic Charter, with the crucial Point Four
simply affirming the Anglo-American goal of "fair and
equitable distribution of essential produce not only within
their territorial jurisdiction but between the nations of
the world." Welles, in his revised text of 11 August,
incorporated in Point Four a pledge against discriminatory

practices. Apparently playing for time against the obvious
desire of the Americans to secure an immediate agreement, a
concerned Churchill allowed that he, too, had "alwavs
opposed" the Ottawa Agreements, but would require the
approval of the Dominions before consenting to the draft by
Welles; moreover, the Prime Minister estimated that the time
involved to obtain this permission would be "at least a
week." The American Under Secretary of State became
considerably exercised. He later related:

> I said that it was not a question of phraseology,
> that it was a question of vital principle which was
> involved. I said that if the British and the
> United States Government could not agree to do
> everything within their power to further, after the
> termination of the present war, a restoration of
> free and liberal trade policies, they might as well
> throw in the sponge and realize that one of the
> greatest factors in creating the present tragic
> situation in the world was going to be permitted to
> continue unchecked in the postwar world.[31]

Both Cadogan and Churchill concurred that the
difficulty revolved not about phraseology but about
principle, which presented "a material obstacle." Everyone
agreed to try to redraft the various problem area
statements, especially after the Prime Minister suggested
inserting the phrase: "with due regard for our existing
obligations" as a means of surmounting the obstacles in
Point Four. Later that day Cadogan presented to Welles what
became the final text of the Joint Declaration. The Under
Secretary of State raised no objection "inasmuch as point
four was broader and more satisfactory than the minimum"
which the President had authorized him to accept. Welles
then took the Cadogan draft to Roosevelt who approved in the
belief that "it was better than he thought Mr. Churchill
would be willing to concede."[32]

The qualifying phraseology in Point Four of the Charter
stirred American suspicions that were never completely
allayed. Prior to the 1944 Quebec Conference, Harry Hopkins
urged Roosevelt to complain forcefully to the British about
barriers to world trade. According to Hopkins, Churchill
believed that the assault against imperial preference was a
favorite project of Secretary Hull's but that Roosevelt

placed little importance on the matter. Hopkins encouraged the President to disabuse Churchill of this illusion and concluded, "I rather think that he thinks that the genius of this program in America lies with Secretary Hull, while the truth of the matter is that it is a program that, from the beginning, has been pushed by you." But the central issues revealed at Placentia Bay could not be lightly glossed over with a smile and the wave of a cigarette holder. For example, by the time of the Yalta Conference, the United States had approached the United Kingdom with a sincere offer to help its exhausted and flagging ally by continuing some form of Lend-Lease after the war. Even in its dire need, His Majesty's Government displayed a guarded wariness, which stemmed from a zealous desire to preserve imperial preference. Churchill would not yield even in preliminary discussions designed simply to set parameters for the necessary ensuing economic conversations. Roosevelt had tried to reassure Churchill. For example, as early as February 1942, the President declared:

> I want to make it perfectly clear to you that it is the furthest thing from my mind that we are attempting in any way to ask you to trade the principle of imperial preference as a consideration for lend lease. Furthermore, I understand something of the nice relationships your Constitution requires of your Home Government in dealing with the Dominions. . . . It seems to me the proposed note leaves a clear implication that Empire Preference, and say, agreements between ourselves and the Philippines are excluded before we sit down at the table. All I am urging is an understanding with you that we are going to have a bold, forthright, and comprehensive discussion looking forward to the construction of what you so aptly call "a free, fertile economic policy for the post-war world." . . . What seems to be bothering the [British] Cabinet is the thought that we want a commitment in advance that Empire Preference will be abolished. We are asking for no such commitment and I can say that article seven [Lend-Lease] does not contain any such commitment. I realize that that would be a commitment which your Government could not give now if it wanted to. And I am very sure that I could not, on my part, make any commitment relative to a vital revision of our tariff policy.[33]

Churchill, therefore, had carefully qualified the extent of the Atlantic Charter provisions by deflecting the applicability of its principles away from the economic system of imperial preference, away from the political ties of the British Empire, away from the international colonial structure in general as the Charter affected dependent areas, and away from the view that the boundaries of ex-enemy territories were inviolable. His task was made much easier by the President's amiability and apparent reluctance to confront obvious Anglo-American discrepancies resolutely. Despite the bold assertion by Welles aboard the Augusta in August 1941, in which the Under Secretary addressed the basic divergencies between Washington and London--and the fateful implications these differences entailed--Roosevelt would brook no confrontation that risked Anglo-American relations.

Roosevelt, like most of his countrymen, could not understand the Prime Minister's faith in imperial destiny, which, given the more immediate military crisis, seemed peripheral and provincial. The President expressed confidence that the supposedly outmoded ideas of Empire would fall of their own weight--as hopelessly antiquarian in the mid-Twentieth Century. The depth of British feeling, especially that born of Churchill's long experience, simply remained unappreciated by most Americans, who believed that the United States should promote indigenous movements for self-government among dependent peoples. Misunderstanding in the United States of the workings of the British Empire exacerbated American suspicions that some evil subsidiaries of the general war effort included extricating British chestnuts, underwriting international colonialism, and suppressing legitimate aspirations of awakening nationalism. After all, some of these fears touched on the very core of the whole antitotalitarian struggle.

British officials patiently endeavored to tutor Americans about the imperial process. Colonial Secretary Oliver Stanley recognized the danger of American misperceptions of British colonialism. In a major speech to the Foreign Policy Association in New York just prior to the Yalta Conference, Stanley ruled out any sharing of administrative responsibilities in the Empire, but welcomed criticism, "if that criticism is constructive and informed," he pointedly emphasized, adding, "Informed, that is the secret." And the Prime Minister once explained his own broad view to Walter Lippmann that "to think imperially . . . means always to think of something higher and more vast than one's own national interests." Churchill, in most American minds, embodied all that the very concept of colonialism entailed. The eloquent ex-subaltern of the Fourth Hussars employed his considerable talents to extol the virtues of the Empire and to rebuke outside interference. "'Imperium et libertas' is still our guide," he would thunder. "Without freedom, there is no foundation for empire; without empire, there is no safeguard for our freedom." His meaning of freedom clearly applied to "all states and nations within the circle of the Crown." Here was the stuff of legends--and American suspicions. Analyzing this point, Halifax perceptively concluded that Churchill

> was acclaimed not only as a war leader, but as a brilliant survival of a past age. Part of his greatness indeed was that he brought alive to the world of today the outlook and temper of the world of yesterday, making these singularly vivid and attractive. . . . the evident influence of his thought of great persons and great events of times long past helped to make easy the transition through the enjoyment of this resurrection of the past to a belief that his own outlook too belonged to those earlier days. The consequence was that by many Americans, and by many in high places, he was expected, if not assumed, to cherish sentiments which the American mind, priding itself on its progressive vigour and virtue, must inevitably judge reactionary. From such thoughts were born doubts and a lack of trust, of which we have not everywhere yet seen the end.[34]

But it would be a mistake to attribute American wariness solely to mischief created by Churchillian rhetoric. His considerable ability to give the roar for the British lion attracted the international spotlight to him. This personality cult, embodying the full range from adulation to hatred, however, distracted the attention of most observers away from the crucial consideration. He

spoke for the British Empire, but his efforts, however
eloquent, mirrored rather than molded imperial interests,
for it was the British colonial system--not simply the
elitism of Churchill--that aroused Americans, who, for their
part, at least voiced a commitment to less exalted and more
democratic inclinations.

CHAPTER III

"NEVER AGAIN": ONE MORE TIME

Widespread evidence of American misgivings about British colonialism surfaced throughout the war years. Within a week after Pearl Harbor, Leo Pasvolsky outlined possible areas of Anglo-American tensions for the Secretary of State. Hull's Special Assistant stressed that the United States would not accept the British system after the war, especially the economic discriminations inherent in imperial preference. Shortly thereafter, H. Freeman Matthews, at the Embassy in London, transmitted records of parliamentary debates on colonial reform and appended his own observation that the British "do not indicate much awareness of changing conditions or of the need of change." John Hickerson learned in early 1943 from a New York friend, "There is growing awareness in financial circles in this town that even the existing strained relations between our Government and His Majesty's will become worse before they are better." Also, a Princeton public opinion research poll suggested that throughout 1944 the view that Britain should "give more independence to its colonies" was endorsed by 69.2 percent of those surveyed with just 5.4 percent opposed. Asked whether the British treated their colonies fairly, only 26.8 percent of the Americans polled indicated approval. Unquestionably, the issue of colonialism plagued relations between the two Atlantic allies. Describing "distinctly chilly" conversations with British officials on the future of colonial areas, Isaiah Bowman declared, "The strength of the liberal church and missionary sentiment throughout the United States with respect to the treatment of dependent peoples is almost unknown to British officials."[1]

Perhaps the most telling barbs against British colonialism occurred in speeches and public declarations by prominent Americans, acting in an influential if not official capacity. For example, Vice-President Wallace and Sumner Welles particularly criticized the Empire structure, but as advocates in the public forum rather than spokesmen in behalf of the United States Government. Wendell Willkie, less troubled by the responsibilities of public office, vociferously championed self-government for dependent peoples. A concerned British Embassy in Washington reported in early 1942 "much loose talk" along the theme: "put an end to imperialism." Singling out the agitation by Wallace, Welles, and Willkie, British Attaché Sir Ronald I. Campbell lamented, "It now appears likely that opinion is tending towards the conclusion that as part of the postwar settlement, the existing Colonial Empires ought to be liquidated, or at all events greatly modified." Campbell recommended sending "a frank enquiry addressed to Mr. Welles" asking exactly what was meant by an end to imperialism. "We may find that they have nothing worked out," the British Minister observed. "Or the substitute may prove to be only American imperialism, open or disguised."[2]

Two episodes in particular raised British ire at American meddling in imperial affairs. During September-October 1942 Wendell Willkie made a much-publicized global tour as an unofficial ambassador of goodwill. While in Moscow, he relayed accusations heard there that the British had "stolen" Lend-Lease material intended for Russia. Also, Willkie heightened his self-styled campaign against colonialism in behalf of the dependent peoples in the world. From Chungking, he publicly endorsed Chinese complaints that the Allies failed to extend any meaningful aid, personally identifying British imperial designs as the major motive. Later, Beaverbrook informed Hull that the Prime Minister had been angered by Willkie's allusions not only on this trip but also in other public pronouncements by the erstwhile presidential candidate. Reporting this Beaverbrook-Hull conversation, Berle simply noted that Hull "somewhat dryly told a Tennessee story to indicate that Mr. Willkie was pretty well out of this and Mr. Churchill need not bother himself too much on Mr. Willkie's account." But Beaverbrook preserved the Hull allegory. The Secretary of State told of the farmer who shot a dog for killing sheep and then beat the body of the dead animal. Asked why, the farmer said, "Because I want the dog to know that there is a hell after death." Hull then explained that this tale portrayed Churchill's attitude toward Willkie, in that he kept on beating the dog after it was politically dead.[3]

A second brief but tempestuous furor arose from anti-British and anti-colonial remarks during September-October 1943 by five senators (Ralph O. Brewster, Albert B. Chandler, Henry Cabot Lodge, Jr., James M. Mead, and Richard B. Russell) after an apparently hurried and confused junket to the Far East. Lodge, for example, stated, "It has become plain as day and it is common sense to recognize" that Britain and Russia were pursuing narrow national aims. "One of them--Britain--frankly intends to maintain the Empire, and the other--Russia--has clear intentions regarding eastern Europe." Russell, as leader of the group, submitted a summary report to the Senate on 8 October 1943. The unfounded charges against British imperialism particularly enraged Churchill, who sent the text of his proposed rebuttal to Harry Hopkins on 13 October with the request that the President's views be ascertained. "Very strong feeling has been aroused here by the remarks of the five Senators," the Prime Minister explained, adding that if he had been in the United States he would offer to go before the Senate and "be confronted by those who made these charges." Hopkins showed the draft to Roosevelt and replied the following day with the disquieting (for Churchill) observation that it would be unwise to refer to the Senators since "there are many people over here who are saying the same thing." On 15 October he dispatched a more comforting (for Churchill) reassurance: "The inexorable events of the war are rapidly crowding the statements by the five Senators off the front pages and I therefore question whether you should feel inclined to say anything." Richard Law offered similar advice to the Prime Minister not to attack the critics, lest he "tend to arouse sympathy for them in the American mind." Roosevelt privately referred to the group as "the five fellow travellers" and underlined the unreliable sources of their information. After the Cabinet had determined that a detailed reply "would give this matter undue importance," the Prime Minister announced in the House that he would not take part in "wordy warfare" with the Senators, especially while British and American forces were fighting together. Thus, the incident deservedly faded into oblivion; however, the controversy had demonstrated the depth of suspicion in the United States about British colonialism and imperialism, and concerned London leaders acknowledged this potential source of friction. The minutes of the meeting at which the Cabinet counselled caution upon Churchill concluded, "At the same time, the War Cabinet recognized that, if statements such as those contained in the report by the five United States Senators continued to be given currency, it might, at a later date, be necessary for an authoritative reply to be made."[4]

Actually, some of the American suspicions during the war about unseemly British imperial motives stemmed from the controversial origins of American involvement in the conflict. Understandably, the obvious and unrestrained exuberance in London upon the news of Pearl Harbor at having a powerful Atlantic ally provoked American distrust. As previously noted, the ill-considered words of the Prime Minister at having "worked for" the entry of the United States landed him in unnecessary difficulty with the American public. From the British perspective, after more than two years on the brink, the participation of the United States now ensured ultimate victory--and preservation of the British Empire.

No one appreciated the meaning of American embroilment, certainly, more than the King's First Minister. "He is a different man since America came into the war," Lord Moran observed about his prominent patient. The physician described Churchill as an old man who had been carrying the weight of the world, but "now--in a night, it seems--a younger man had taken his place." Moran diagnosed the remedy: "Suddenly the war is as good as won and England is safe." Churchill confessed to Commander-in-Chief, India, General Sir Claude J. E. Auchinleck, "This is an immense relief as I had long dreaded being at war with Japan without or before United States. Now I think it is all right." The Prime Minister wired Roosevelt on 9 December suggesting a joint conference and that same day admitted to Jan Christian Smuts, "I am content with Sunday's developments in the Far East." Three days later, the Foreign Secretary, in Moscow, received the message from Churchill: "Accession of United States makes amends for all and with time and patience will give certain victory."[5]

General Sir Hastings Ismay wrote to the man who was a near approximation of his counterpart in America, Harry Hopkins, "I thought of you at once when the news arrived that the little yellow beasts had bombed Pearl Harbor; and my first thoughts were--'Anyhow Harry will be pleased that we are at any rate all in it together.'" Ismay later revealed that his own first reactions to the news amounted to "stunned surprise" and "thankfulness." He acknowledged, "Indeed, had I not been in a public place I would have shouted for joy." A few months later Phillip Holland, the American Consul at Liverpool, reported that "a vast number of the industrial workers are not pulling their weight" and described "the complacency which has permeated all classes since Americans entered the war." The British reaction, while understandable, had a dampening effect upon American public opinion, especially in view of the widespread feeling that London had somehow duped an unsuspecting United States once again. But British enthusiasm sprang from the recognition of a broader perspective. "No American will think it wrong of me if I proclaim that to have the United States at our side was to me the greatest joy," Churchill reminisced. "Many disasters, immeasurable cost and tribulation lay ahead, but there was no more doubt about the end."[6]

There existed an uneasy connection between the pragmatic admission by the Prime Minister that he would make a favorable reference to the Devil if an enemy of the Empire (Hitler) also declared war in Hell, and the disquieting image of his having "worked for" American entanglement. The implications of British intrigue, malevolence, and maneuver spurred the Americans to extraordinary lengths in investigating the minutest detail of the circumstances accompanying the entry of the United States into World War II.

Immediately after the Japanese attack, Congress launched a hurried inquiry to affix responsibility for the disaster. This committee--the Roberts Commission--attributed most of the blame to the failings of the two local commanders, Admiral H. E. Kimmel and General W. C. Short. In 1945-1946 Congress conducted a further investigation at the urging of Senator Alben Barkley in order to quiet a raging partisan debate. Congress published these results in October 1946--shortly before key elections--with the unwieldy title: "Report of the Joint Committee in the Investigation of the Pearl Harbor Attack,

Additional Views of Mr. Keefe, Together with Minority Views
of Mr. Ferguson and Mr. Brewer." Briefly, the majority
report exculpated Roosevelt, Hull, Stimson, and Navy
Secretary Forrestal by name. Kimmel and Short were
exonerated from charges of dereliction of duty, but were
deemed guilty of errors in judgment. In large part, Keefe
agreed with the majority, but criticized the supervisory
procedures of General Marshall. Keefe also pointed out that
Roosevelt had extended "war-like commitments" prior to Pearl
Harbor. The Minority Report asserted that a Japanese attack
was a certainty by 1 December 1941. Ferguson and Brewer
blamed the President for the lack of effective coordination.
Stimson, Knox, and Marshall (Hull's case was not explored in
this section) earned abuse and most of the responsibility
for the disaster from the two Republicans. (Postwar
disclosures of diary entries by Stimson later intensified
the belief that somehow America had been maneuvered into the
war through dark design.) The War Department had convened
an investigative board of its own in 1944, which
specifically requested the views of the State Department
about plans to have Japan initiate hostilities. Secretary
Hull explained (ironically to Stimson himself) that:

> it was not the policy of this Government to take
> provocative action against any country or to cause
> Japan to commit an act of war against the United
> States. At the same time . . . . there was nothing
> in this Government's foreign policy which imposed
> restrictions upon the taking of essential measures
> of national defense. As regards the statement
> mentioned in your letter that in the event of
> hostilities the United States desired that Japan
> commit the first overt act, nothing has been found
> in the Department's records bearing upon this point
> nor did this point arise in any discussion at which
> I was present or of which I have knowledge.[7]

With this climate of uncertainty and suspicion
prevailing in the United States throughout the war--indeed,
some Americans still feel the circumstances of the attack at
Pearl Harbor have never been fully revealed--the British
role could not escape attention. As the party most likely
to benefit from American involvement in the war, Great
Britain was the key suspect in various American inquiries

which sought either to ascribe British culpability or at
least to identify British machinations in arranging the
entry of the United States for the purpose of salvaging
imperial chestnuts. His Majesty's Government, therefore,
readily expedited the American investigations as much as
possible. For example, during the postwar Congressional
probe, Dean Acheson telephoned to Halifax a request for
official British permission to release certain 1941
telegrams between London and Washington. Acheson asked that
the British Government provide such approval within one day,
as Halifax explained, "Otherwise he feared possibility of
dangerous mischief, if idea could be started that we were
all trying to conceal some sinister skeleton." The
Ambassador reported to the Foreign Office that he had
talked with the Prime Minister (Attlee), who urged approval.
Halifax pointed out, "the Pearl Harbor business, as you may
guess, is looming up in ugly shape here, and PM would
naturally be glad to assist United States Government to
avoid embarrassment if possible." The Foreign Office
speedily endorsed the proposed action and referred the
telegrams in question to the Chiefs of Staff, who in turn
provided the necessary security clearances.[8]

Nor did every wartime British official adopt a friendly
position regarding the American entry. In June 1944 the
Minister of Production created a mild sensation with his
assertion that "it is a travesty on history ever to say
America was forced into the war." Oliver Lyttelton
maintained that the United States had provoked Japan to such
an extent that "the Japanese were forced to attack the
Americans at Pearl Harbor." An indignant Hull promptly
retorted, "Lyttelton was entirely in error as to facts and
failed to state the true attitude of the United States."
The President, however, took the news with surprising calm
and the offhand dismissal: "I suppose Lyttelton was tight."[9]
But despite the highly publicized American investigations,
the British, too, expended some effort to re-examine the
circumstances surrounding the origins of the Far Eastern
war.

In January 1943 P. H. Gore-Booth, at the British
Embassy in Washington, relayed "some gossip linked with our
unregenerate Japanese past" to the Head of the Far Eastern
Department at the Foreign Office, H. Ashley Clarke. He had

lunched that day with Wilfrid Fleisher, Far Eastern affairs correspondent in Washington for the New York Herald-Tribune, who bitterly resented the impression being created by Joseph Grew that he "foresaw what was coming" and had warned the State Department of the Japanese strength and intentions prior to Pearl Harbor. Gore-Booth explained, "Actually, according to Wilfrid, newspaper people had the utmost difficulty in persuading the American Embassy to take Japanese militarism seriously right from the beginning of the China incident, and he went so far as to say that even up to October, 1941, the situation was being represented by the American Embassy as slightly improving rather than the reverse." The British Counsellor found it "rather amusing" that this "comparatively knowledgeable discordant note" occurred among the present chorus of praise for Grew. "It is particularly interesting," Gore-Booth, who had been in Tokyo, observed, "because the American Embassy were always inclined to accuse us of panicking whenever we began to try and convince them and inform you that the situation had taken a turn for the worse." Gore-Booth reported that he had recounted Fleisher's story to Sir George Sansom (British Counsellor, Washington) who remarked, "Actually a number of better informed people in Washington think that Grew is going too far." Sansom passed along the statement by news commentator Raymond Swing that "Grew was more for appeasement than Craigie" in the period before August 1941. "When I look back to the troubles we had with the United States Embassy, especially with Dooman & Co.," Sansom continued, "I feel rather sore about Grew who is converting hindsight into foresight in a most disingenuous way." In the Foreign Office, M. E. Dening hailed the letter from Gore-Booth and concluded, "We seemed rather inclined to regard Mr. Grew as sometimes too wonderful and to forget that he was a pernicious influence in blinding the U. S. Administration to realities until very late in the day."[10]

Actually, Grew believed that a policy of cooperation among the Great Powers in the 1930's would have averted Sino-Japanese hostilities. Yet his own version of what course the powers should pursue was cloaked in decidedly pro-Japanese trappings. In June 1945 Grew extracted a 1935 memorandum, written by the ex-Minister to China, John V. A. MacMurray, and endorsed those views to Secretary Stimson.

MacMurray argued that Japan had tried to adhere to the Washington Treaties in the face of "Chinese intransigence and the selfishness of the signatory powers." Grew supported the charges in the memorandum that the American attitude worked "to condone the high-handed behaviour of the Chinese and to encourage them to a course of further recalcitrance."[11]

Chinese "behaviour" before December 1941 also greatly concerned the British. At the time (and in retrospect) London believed that the recalcitrant attitude of Chiang Kai-shek had the baneful effect of dissuading the United States from meaningful efforts to accommodate Japan through a modus vivendi. British observers before the war entertained no illusions about Japanese intentions. The Balliol College research group at Oxford had traced the ominous implications of Japanese ambitions in a 1940 report, "Japan's Plan For Greater East Asia." As early as 1931 the head of British Intelligence at Shanghai, G. P. V. Steward, reported, "There is no doubt that the Japanese has dreams that waft him." He noted that Japan considered herself robbed of the fruits of earlier victories and "is chary of diplomacy that does not seem to pay so well as soldiering." Steward described Japan as "the most imperialist nation of the earth," but also identified China as "a close second," possessing "an individualistic, instinctive imperialism." The Intelligence Officer criticized China for openly threatening and challenging Japan.[12] Nevertheless, the focus of Anglo-American concern about China soon shifted to whether or not the Heavenly Kingdom could sustain resistance to Japanese aggression.

By 1940 the possible collapse of China had become an increasingly worrisome problem for Washington and London. The Generalissimo accelerated his strong requests for Anglo-American assistance. Urging his friends "to recognize the fact that only on the foundation of a free and independent China can peace be built in the Far East, and normal and orderly relations be established between nations in the whole Pacific," Chiang Kai-shek presented an extensive bill of particulars described as "Concrete Measure for Mutual Assistance." In return for continued Chinese resistance, the Chinese leader wanted considerable supplies, credits, loans, and a joint affirmation by the Western Powers to uphold both the Nine Power Treaty and the principles of the Open Door. The Churchill Cabinet fretted about the preponderant Chinese influence in Washington, yet also recognized the dangers of unbridled Japanese hegemony in China. On 26 November 1941, an anxious Prime Minister acknowledged the cable from the President on the previous day elaborating the terms of a projected American modus vivendi prepared by Hull.[13] Unaware that this counter-project had been replaced by a less accommodating memorandum given to the Japanese negotiators that same day, Churchill told the President, "Of course it is for you to handle this business and we certainly do not want an additional war." He ventured, "There is only one point that disquiets us. What about Chiang Kai-shek?" The Prime Minister inquired, "Is he not having a very thin diet?"[14]

These prewar views earned closer scrutiny during an "in-house" British debate which re-examined the origins of the 1941 outbreak of hostilities in the Far East. In September 1943 William Hayter, Financial Counsellor at the British Embassy in Washington, sent a lengthy personal letter to H. Ashley Clarke revealing his reconsiderations "about the question which has often worried me, namely whether there was anything different which we ought to have done in the days before Pearl Harbour, and in particular whether there was any justification for Hull's and Hornbeck's suggestion that our lukewarmness was in some way responsible for the failure of Hull's 'modus vivendi.'" Hayter played a prominent role during the final weeks of discussions with the Japanese. He still believed in retrospect that "it was perfectly obvious" that the reason for the failure of the three-month modus vivendi scheme devised by Hull lay in Chiang Kai-shek's dampening messages to the President. But Hayter had to consider why Hull and Hornbeck felt justified in rebuking the British.[15]

"I now think that . . . if we had shown enthusiasm for the modus vivendi and had warmly supported the proposal, the Americans might possibly have plucked up enough moral courage to defy the Chinese and insist on the modus vivendi," Hayter declared. Instead, the Foreign Office confined its comments to leaving the matter up to Washington. This response coincided with the message by Churchill referring to "Chiang Kai-shek's thin diet," and

Hayter reflected that, together, this combination of British views indicated to American leaders that London supported the Generalissimo's opposition to Hull's plan or at the very least would not challenge Chinese objections. Hayter stressed this later point, which necessarily meant that, to implement the modus vivendi, the United States would have had to overrule Chiang Kai-shek unilaterally. He considered that the State Department remained unlikely to take such solo action, given the general Chinese pressures and the press campaign T. V. Soong was stirring against appeasement. "But the [State] Department did not like to admit even to themselves that they had yielded to Chinese pressures," Hayter concluded, "and in looking for a scapegoat in their minds, found the traditional one in His Majesty's Government."[16]

In addition, Hayter thought the State Department grew alarmed at the "after-effects" of the substitute 26 November memorandum which, as British Ambassador in Tokyo Sir Robert L. Craigie stated, Washington knew would be unacceptable to Japan. Of this 26 November proposal, Hayter explained, "I have no doubt at all that this memorandum was put in in a fit of petulance caused by the failure of the modus vivendi ('We'll show them we are not appeasers') and almost entirely for the record." Informing the British of this project, the State Department "always treated it as entirely academic and indeed Utopian, as something which would constitute an ideal settlement for the Far East but which the Japanese would certainly not accept in the then existing circumstances." Moreover Hayter asserted that this description of "academic" had been used by the State Department as the reason for not immediately showing the 26 November memorandum to the British Embassy in Washington. "They put it in largely to keep their own record clean when the correspondence was published, which as you know is fairly typical of American diplomatic procedure, and probably with very little thought of its immediate effect on the negotiations," he elaborated. "But having put it in they may have had qualms about Japanese reaction to it (and if Craigie is right their qualms were more than justified) and this no doubt added to the nervous irritation which Hull and his advisers showed in the days between the dropping of the modus vivendi and Pearl Harbour." Hayter added, "Thus, we only learnt of the decision to drop the <u>modus vivendi</u> and present the November 26th memorandum (a snap decision if ever there was one) when Hornbeck telephoned to me on the evening of the 26th in his most professional manner ('Now mind you get this straight') to tell me that it had already been done." In conclusion, the British Counsellor pointed out it was important for historians to realize that although His Majesty's Government had been kept fully informed and consulted for its views, "final decision and action was still being taken by the United States Government on their own."[17]

Hayter refused to suggest that the British should have provided a more encouraging response to the <u>modus vivendi</u>. He felt that "the State Department's irritation was entirely unjustified," but indicated that his explanation did illustrate "the state of mind into which they got." This letter received much attention in British diplomatic circles. L. H. Foulds considered the information "as near the truth as we are likely to get." He dismissed false self-accusations with the revealing comment: "We have nothing with which to reproach ourselves since the final result was that the United States came into this war." Clarke agreed generally with the views offered by Hayter, but believed Roosevelt and Hull "were more fully conscious of what they were doing" than Hayter implied. The Head of the Far Eastern Department explained, "This is borne out by the now published memo of a convn. with Ld. Halifax on 27th Nov. in which Mr. Hull records that he had 'expressed the view that the diplomatic part of our relations with Japan was virtually over. . . .'" In addition, Halifax presented his own conclusions. The Ambassador observed:

> I think Mr. Hayter's letter is a very fair and true diagnosis. The United States Government's attitude through those final days was I think a compound of (a) the result of strong Chinese pressure. (b) Mr. Hull feeling that the British Commonwealth, though prepared to go along, did not greatly like the <u>modus vivendi</u> plan, and expressed their real feeling through criticisms of detail i.e. about oil quantities, etc. (c) Mr. Hull's own loss of temper! But I doubt whether it would all have made much difference, though it might have affected the Japanese method. Here though I think we definitely gained, as compared with what they might

have done![18]

Most of these British comments had been sparked by a cause célèbre that, surprisingly, remained relatively confined within Foreign Office circles and a limited section of the diplomatic corps. In October 1942, after a period of forced internment by the Japanese and in accordance with traditional British diplomatic practice, His Majesty's Representative to Japan, Sir Robert L. Craigie, submitted a necessarily delayed Final Report on his Ambassadorship. Craigie's sympathies were well-known even before the war. For example, Lord Hankey privately cautioned Nevile Butler in early 1941 about British policies in the Far East with the observation: "My own view during the last ten years has been that, apart from Leslie Craigie, the tendency of the British official mind has been much too anti-Japanese." In addition to his personal predilections--and these most assuredly were pro-British rather than pro-Japanese, despite some critics' charges--the mounting Japanese pressures made it doubly difficult to resist the inclination to seek some sort of accommodation with Japanese ambitions. Thus, Craigie, no less than his American colleague Grew, convinced himself that the increasingly belligerent tone of the Japanese militarists had to be met with some measure of acquiescence, given the realities of the international situation. In fact, it is interesting to note just how many ambassadors during these crucial years became virtually uncritical of the policies of their host while growing increasingly disenchanted with the attitude of their home government. In June 1941, the London Far Eastern Committee learned that Japanese "bitter complaints . . . have made a considerable impression on the Empire representatives in Tokyo."[19]

In his Final Report Craigie severely criticized British prewar policies toward Japan. He regretted the irretrievable damage created by the two-phased economic freeze imposed in mid-1940 and July 1941 by the Western Powers. In his opinion the second penalty stage should have been rescinded after the Japanese agreed to return to the status quo ante in Indochina. During the latter part of his assignment, Craigie labored under explicit instructions not to initiate discussions with the Japanese Foreign Ministry.

He complained bitterly that this order hamstrung any opportunities he may have had to ease the growing tensions. With His Majesty's Government deeply embroiled in the struggle for survival with Germany, Craigie had emphasized the pressing need to adopt an official policy of neutrality about the Sino-Japanese hostilities. Instead, much to his chagrin, British sympathies were interpreted in Tokyo as decidedly pro-Chinese. "Reacting to this," he explained, "the Japanese Army soon displayed their intention of using the campaign to undermine and, where possible, destroy British interests in China." The apparent British hesitancy over the abortive modus vivendi by Hull was particularly criticized by the repatriated Ambassador. He remained firmly convinced that London should not have allowed the United States to assume the leading role in the critical negotiations immediately prior to 7 December. In his mind the proposals in the modus vivendi, if accepted, would have gained a three-month grace period during which Craigie could persistently recommend caution to his beleaguered home government in the acute awareness that military embroilment with Japan might mean British defeat everywhere. He concluded that had London accepted his advice "war with Japan could have been postponed and perhaps averted."[20]

Most of the retrospective commentary in 1942 had been precipitated by the Craigie memorandum. H. Ashley Clarke noted that Craigie attacked the Anglo-American-Dutch economic retaliations "although he appears to overlook the cardinal fact that for the first time we thereby obtained a joint front in the Far East with these two Powers." Clarke pointed out that the Ambassador "had even less information than we" about the Washington conversations, "nor could he know precisely our policy towards the United States in relationship to the war as a whole." After reading the complete original dispatch, Sir Maurice Peterson did not find the arguments convincing. The superintending Under Secretary of the Far Eastern Department explained that it would have been impossible for the United States (without setting back the American "spirit of resistance to aggression" by five years) to reach an agreement with Japan "which would have turned a blind eye to the whole of the 'China incident' in return for the evacuation of southern Indo-China." Also Peterson stated that there existed no

evidence as to the sincerity of the Japanese proposals:
"Once the Japanese made their fateful decision to try to
absorb the whole of China, there was really no hope left
that that decision would not bring them into conflict with
the United States and ourselves and the best we could hope
for was that the Americans would be drawn in with us." Sir
Alexander Cadogan labelled Craigie's report as "a very
controversial disputation" which "debars him from print" at
least until the Foreign Office prepared a refutation. "The
whole of Sir R. Craigie's disp. is a plea that, if we had
'appeased' a little more, all would have been well," the
Parliamentary Under Secretary declared. Cadogan dismissed
this argument because "the Japanese went relentlessly and
steadily on." He remarked that the Ambassador "looks
wistfully back" with satisfaction at British handling of the
episodes over the 1939 Tientsin blockade (in which London
acquiesced), the closing of the Burma Road, and the release
of the Asama Maru. "But these were not bright pages in our
history, and availed us nothing." Cadogan concluded:

> I was an "appeaser," because I wanted to learn the
> truth, beyond doubt, and I wanted the truth to be
> forced on my countrymen, who were not all convinced
> of it, and in whose unity we depended. I didn't
> deny the truth when it was apparent to all. Sir R.
> Craigie still denies it.[21]

H. Ashley Clarke, in April 1943, submitted the lengthy
collaborative draft of the proposed reply by the Foreign
Office to balance Craigie's Final Report. Earlier he had
outlined a "short answer" as the basis for the official
study:

> (a) that while endeavouring to postpone war as long
> as we could, our major objective was not to enter a
> Far Eastern war without the United States, and (b)
> that the presentation on the 26th November to
> Messers. Nomura and Kurusu of the United States
> Government's maximum demands was a complete
> surprise to us, and the text was not even divulged
> to us in advance. Finally, the Prime Minister in a
> famous broadcast defended his Far Eastern policy by
> claiming that his objective was to bring the United
> States into the war.

In his covering letter of explanation about the Foreign
Office report, Clarke refuted the contention by the
Ambassador that "British sympathies were fully engaged on
the side of China" rather than pursuing a policy of
neutrality. The Head of the Far Eastern Department
declared:

> The implication here is that if British sympathies
> had not been engaged on China's side there need
> have been no difficulty between us and the Japanese
> military! But what about Article 1 of the Nine
> Power Treaty providing for the respect for the
> sovereignty, the independence and the territorial
> and administrative integrity of China? Are we to
> assume that it would have been prudent and
> acceptable to the people of this country that we
> should at that time have associated ourselves with
> Japan's views on the subject of the validity of
> treaty engagements and dissociated ourselves from
> the United States and others who still held the
> old-fashioned view that a country's word was its
> bond?[22]

Perhaps the strongest point Craigie argued was his
optimistic view of the abortive modus vivendi developed by
Hull. But Craigie's critics, as noted, rebutted this
argument by pointing out the inability of the British to
influence American thinking at the time of this proposal.
Attention in Washington was focused almost entirely on China
and Japan. Indeed, Churchill cabled his thoughts about the
modus vivendi unaware that it had been replaced with a less
compromising American proposal that same day.

Copies of the two reports had been sent to the British
Embassy on a strictly confidential basis by H. Ashley
Clarke. The receipt of these documents, in fact, had
spurred the lengthy letter by William Hayter. Before Eden
eventually recalled all distribution of the twin memoranda,
other valuable commentaries had been elicited from British
staff members in Washington. In September 1943, P. H. Gore-
Booth, who had served in Japan with Craigie from 1938 to
1941 and had helped the Ambassador prepare his Final Report,
described "a divergence of opinion" at the Embassy in Tokyo
about British policies in the Far East. He stated, however,
that the Embassy staff unanimously agreed on two key
questions regarding American behavior during the final

months of negotiations with Japan. First, they believed
that the United States either did not fully understand the
situation or felt adequately prepared for war with Japan.
Second, they agreed with Craigie that the final American
note of 26 November had made war inevitable in early
December. According to Gore-Booth, the Embassy staff
diverged on the issue of whether the modus vivendi would
have avoided or merely postponed the war. Craigie chose to
believe the more optimistic alternative; however, Gore-Booth
pointed out, "I should say that the majority (of whom I was
one) disagreed with this opinion and felt that things had
gone so far in Japan in the way of organisation for war and
the promotion of the war spirit that it was too late to turn
the machine into reverse." Significantly, Gore-Booth
concluded:

> We can, I think, take comfort from the fact that
> the principal objective of our policy was realised;
> we managed to play for time with the Japanese for a
> sufficient period to allow the Americans to assume
> the lead in the Far East in the conduct of what
> might be called "parallel" policy adopted by the
> various democratic nations. It was only because we
> had been able for different reasons to avert
> hostilities so long that the Japanese felt
> themselves ultimately compelled to attack both of
> us at once, instead, as one must admit to fearing
> right up to the end, of beginning by attacking us
> alone.[23]

William Hayter took issue with the unanimous opinion of
the Embassy staff in Tokyo that Washington either failed to
recognize the dangers involved or felt adequately prepared.
"I do not think," Hayter asserted, "that the U.S. Government
were under any illusions as to the imminence of a Japanese
attack; but they felt that there was nothing they could do
to avert it except ditch the Chinese, and this they were not
prepared to do." Also from the British Embassy in
Washington came the comment of Sir Ronald I. Campbell that
"we by chance struck the wrong note with the best
intentions." Referring to American doubts that London
strongly supported China, Campbell suggested that British
assurances on this point "that we would not be behindhand
with the Americans in refusing to sell China down the river"

finally arrived in Washington in "a different state of
affairs: i.e. that in which Mr. Hull had suddenly decided on
the modus vivendi attempt, impressed largely by the
knowledge of U.S. unpreparedness." After reading these
statements, H. Ashley Clarke endorsed the qualification
offered by Hayter and agreed generally with Campbell. But
Clarke made clear:

> Our hesitations about Mr. Hull's modus vivendi
> derived from no particular desire to put ourselves
> right on this score--we were perfectly sound in our
> attitude towards China all along. Our objection to
> the m.v. was principally based on the belief that
> (in its original form) it would give Japan a most
> dangerous advantage not only over China but over
> ourselves also. . . . The mystery is rather how the
> Americans ever allowed themselves to be caught out
> at Pearl Harbour.[24]

While a detailed analysis of the origins of the Far
Eastern War falls beyond the scope of this study, it is
noteworthy that a consistent theme in these retrospective
views--and therefore a valuable insight into a preponderant
British motive during the prewar diplomatic maneuverings--
identified British interests with the involvement of the
United States in hostilities. As demonstrated, most of the
British participants believed that by remaining aloof during
the critical Washington conversations they increased the
likelihood of American embroilment with Japan. This welcome
prospect became virtually certain, as the British officials
later reminisced, once Hull had delivered his bombshell of
26 November. Thus London, convinced that war with Japan was
assured, made no significant effort to relieve the crisis
after 26 November. The Foreign Office rebuttal to Craigie
explained, "To maintain the united front, leaving the
initiative to the United States, meant also that if war came
there were good prospects of having the United States by the
side of Great Britain; whereas to advocate a policy of
concessions might have the positive disadvantage of causing
misunderstanding with the United States and of discrediting
Great Britain with her friends generally at a most critical
juncture."[25] The relevant point to be drawn out of the
whole discussion is that His Majesty's Government acted on
its interpretation of the best interests of the British

Empire. Unfortunately, in late 1941 that perception equated with an American plunge into the war. And who better to determine imperial interests than the First Minister of the Crown?

"A more one-sided and pro-Japanese account of what occurred I have hardly ever read," Churchill remarked upon reading the Final Report by Craigie. The Prime Minister continued, "The total lack of all sense of proportion as between any British and American slips on the one hand and the deliberate scheme of war eventuating in the outrage of Pearl Harbour on the other shows a detachment from events and from his country's fortunes." He criticized Craigie's tone for describing "the breach with Japan as if it were an unmitigated disaster," yet acknowledged that this view was understandable for "an Ambassador whose duty it is to preserve friendly relations with a particular country, and whose judgment is naturally affected by this fact." But the leader who confessed to having "worked for" the American entanglement and the defender of the Empire did not fail in late 1943 to appreciate the virtues of British policy in 1941. "It was however a blessing that Japan attacked the United States and thus brought America wholeheartedly and unitedly into the war," Churchill announced. "Greater good fortune has rarely happened to the British Empire than this event which has revealed our friends and foes in their true light, and may lead, through the merciless crushing of Japan, to a new relationship of immense benefit to the English-speaking countries and to the whole world."[26]

Thus, the welfare of the British Empire surpassed all other considerations for the Churchill Government. Militarily, the British accepted the temporary loss of Burma rather than risk the introduction of an uneasy influence there by the presence of an uncomfortable number of Chinese troops. Diplomatically, His Majesty's Government encouraged the United States to deal unilaterally with an increasingly bellicose Japan in the virtual certainty that a rupture in the teetering Washington-Tokyo relationship would precipitate a Far Eastern version of the global conflict and thereby enlist American power in the defense of the Empire. War did come, but carried in its wake unexpected forces that acted against the Empire. The circumstances of World War II unleashed rising expectations and humanitarian concerns that knocked over most of the philosophical underpinnings of colonialism. As the leading spokesman for the imperialist-colonialist system, the United Kingdom suffered the brunt of these attacks. Before the ceremonies aboard the <u>Missouri</u> signalled the end of the proceedings of the Second World War, Churchill had ample cause to ponder and reconsider his exuberant declaration that "greater good fortune has rarely happened to the British Empire."

CHAPTER IV

THE ALLIED COALITION AND THE PROBLEM OF COLONIES

British sensitivity to American perceptions about the Empire remained keen throughout the war. Yet London policy was not simply a matter of stonewalling critics of the colonial system. British planners clearly understood the obvious problem, namely, that Anglo-American relations touched on virtually every issue throughout the Far East and that American misconceptions about British aims were unnecessarily complicating these issues. John Sterndate Bennett voiced the concern of the Foreign Office that the American misconceptions were due "in part to willful misunderstanding and partly to ignorance," but, whatever the cause, His Majesty's Government had to take the criticism in the United States into account.[1] Therefore, a key task facing the British was to educate Americans about the workings of the British Empire.

Attempts to correct American thinking about the Empire, as previously noted, had been a leitmotif in the speeches of Colonial Secretary Oliver Stanley. He, too, asserted that mistaken notions in the United States about the British system nourished most of the false charges. But Stanley also recognized that great room for colonial improvement existed, especially in the economic sphere. For example, he advocated the introduction of industries in the dependent areas, the development of secondary industries to complement local markets and resources, and the absorption through more effective methods of the native labor populations. From the American Embassy in London Harold Shantz dispatched regular press summaries to the State Department on the subject of colonialism. In April 1942 Shantz commented, "It is evident from the general tone of the published comment . . . that many thinking people of the country realize the absolute necessity for changes in the political and economic colonial policy." Thus, spurred on by the genuine efforts of Stanley to remedy structural defects, British officials closely scrutinized relations within the Commonwealth and tried to explain its machinery to critical observers. "It appears to be generally recognized that under the circumstances now prevailing radical or even general changes in the administration of the British colonies cannot be put into effect during the war," another Embassy officer, W. J. Gallman, reported from London in mid-1942 to the State Department. Describing the British realization that changes "will be practically mandatory in the postwar period," Gallman, the Embassy Secretary, concluded, "There is a definitely noticeable trend . . . toward a realization that the provisions of the Atlantic Charter must be extended to the British Colonial perspective." Two months later Gallman submitted an account of a new British advisory board instituted to deal with questions concerning the welfare of British colonial subjects residing in the United Kingdom. In one of the more obvious British efforts, a Secretary from the Embassy in Washington admitted to a State Department officer that "his particular job was to find ways and means of better acquainting American public opinion, especially influential opinion, with the exact facts and problems of the British colonial question." The American official, P. N. Jester, observed that this had been the second member of the British Embassy staff to come to his office within a week to discuss that subject. Jester surmised that "apparently the British Government is taking active steps to counteract in this country the growth of critical opinion regarding British colonial policy."[2]

Despite the universal condemnation of colonialism in the United States, a curious ambivalence existed in American opinion with specific reference to the United Kingdom and the British version. A late 1940 strategic assessment of priorities by the Joint Board listed first "the territorial, economic and ideological integrity of the United States" and the Western Hemisphere, but the second most important American need was identified as "prevention of the disruption of the British Empire." Americans distrusted the British influence in the Far East, but not the British role in Europe. Historian A. E. Campbell observed, "It is notable that those Americans who were outraged by almost any British activity in the Western Hemisphere and mistrustful of British activity in the wider world were entirely content to see Britain powerful and active in Europe."[3]

Politically, the State Department did attempt to come to grips with colonial-imperial issues, perhaps partially in answer to the charges of Oliver Stanley about American misconceptions of the British Empire. In early 1944 a special subcommittee of the Postwar Foreign Policy Committee considered a suggestion by Berle and Paul Blanshard to designate "Colonial Specialists" within the State Department. This Committee on Colonial and Trustee Problems rejected the idea of a separate Colonial Division for a number of reasons. To designate specialists, the Committee believed, might promote misperceptions among dependent peoples, would attempt inadequately to label the full scope of American policies in dealing with the colonial powers, and might even introduce "confusing divergencies" among officers in the State Department handling relations with the mother countries. Instead, the report recommended establishing colonial desks in appropriate geographical divisions (e.g., British-French-Dutch) as the nucleus for a continuing Committee on Colonial Problems at the State Department.[4]

One expert from the Department's Economic Section submitted a 1943 analysis of the economic importance of colonies. Melvin M. Knight criticized "misguided bookkeeping analogies" as popular but not useful in assessing the economics of colonialism; he mentioned, for example, the difficulty in measuring the cost of public works projects against their long-term effects. Knight suggested, as a general yardstick, that "cruder bases for judgment" might be more helpful, such as separate comparisons of independent, nonimperialist countries in significant standards (population, skills, equipment, living conditions) with those of imperial powers and of colonial areas. "The issue is brought nearer," Knight remarked, "by asking whether imperial countries are apparently as well off as they would have been if they had not colonized, considering the probable alternatives." Thus key "practical questions" and awareness of "the probable effects of choices still open" would provide a better understanding of any specific colonial relationship. Knight identified other general points to consider in studies of colonialism. "The technology of industrialism is much more adaptable to different types of social organization than has been assumed," he stated, and warned that "too many people assumed either (a) that Japan was culturally Europeanized because she was industrialized, or (b) that her industrial efficiency must be overrated because she was not culturally European." Notwithstanding the various types of natural or social resources, Knight reflected that "basic social reconstruction" may not be a prerequisite to absorbing sophisticated technology. He observed, "If it is assumed that all peoples have similar inborn capacities, and that personal ethics apply to group situations, the problem is one of tutelage." While American policy on tutelage consistently envisaged "maturity with political independence," European conceptions treated this problem "in quite a leisurely way" and focused on what German writers have called "an economic colony" even after political independence had been achieved. But Knight emphasized the indications of liberal, progressive changes taking place in colonial or dependent relationships. The British had described a "revolution in policy" which implied "partnership" and "less treasury-mindedness"; the French had invoked the idea of an "Association" coupled with "respect for native institutions."[5] The economist pointed out that the postwar world would be more settled "than the one under which our North-Atlantic style of economic organization evolved." Describing the "uneconomic long hauls" in transporting strategically important items, Knight demonstrated that "the changing pattern of raw resources, and of their sources, has made Western Europe a less and less economic nucleus of industrial concentration." Looking to the future international economic structure, Knight prophesied:

> It is likely that the choice between rational
> deflation of West-Europe's economic position and
> catastrophe is more urgent than we suspect. If the

situation is as critical as it may well be, a large
capital fund, simply donated by various states for
colonial development, may be indicated. British
"partnership" ideas point to this on a merely
imperial scale. The quid pro quo would consist of
expected trade advantages in the very long run. If
various governments, parties to an international
arrangement, are to donate their taxpayers' money,
they will inevitably have a considerable interest
in its use.[6]

Other American studies sought to explain the intricate
workings of the British Empire. A 1942 State Department
memorandum by James F. Green addressed the confusion over
the meaning of the term "British Empire," which seemed to
cover all types of associations with London. Actually, the
Statute of Westminster in 1931 had signalled the end of the
transition from Empire to Commonwealth, with the Crown being
what Green called "the constitutional linchpin" of the
entire arrangement. Green suggested the term "Commonwealth"
to describe "the relation of 'free association' of self-
governing countries and dependencies." In early 1944, the
OSS examined British attempts to enlighten American opinion
about the Commonwealth. According to the OSS, British
spokesmen stressed the voluntary (as opposed to coercive)
ties to London and the fact that exploitation was
disappearing as the concept of trusteeship developed toward
the ideal of partnership. The OSS reported that another
British point emphasized the need for cohesion "in a world
threatened mainly by disintegration" (unlike Knight's
forecast of a more settled world). Consequently, the
British were predicting that disintegration at the periphery
of the Empire (i.e., the colonies) would threaten world
stability. This OSS study concluded by noting that the
British were taking more positive approaches by calling
attention to their actual accomplishments in the development
of their colonies.[7] Through these and other studies,
Americans were trying to understand the British system.
Particularly confusing for Americans, however, was the
status of the Dominions in the structure. The Green
memorandum demonstrated that the Statute of Westminster
relied on the definition of Dominions by the Imperial

Conference of 1926. This Conference defined these political
units as "autonomous communities within the British Empire,
equal in status, in no way subordinate one to another in any
respect of their domestic or external affairs, though united
by a common allegiance to the Crown, and freely associated
as members of the British Commonwealth of Nations."
Furthermore, the 1931 pronouncement stipulated that no
future act of Parliament would extend to the Dominions
unless specifically requested by each home government. But,
as already noted, the events and issues of the war worked to
loosen imperial connections, especially with the Dominions.
One OSS report noted that among other demands, the Dominions
wanted more involvement in the determination of colonial
policies--historically regarded as the domain of the United
Kingdom. The memorandum concluded that if London
acquiesced, "this acceptance will presumably be dictated
less by the conviction that the Dominions have a real
contribution to make in this field as by the realization
that she needs the support of the Dominions to bolster her
own position as a world power in the postwar world."[8]

Washington maintained cordial but strictly correct
relations with the Dominions, undoubtedly in deference to
London's sensibilities. Nevertheless, the Churchill Cabinet
and other observers remained wary of American intentions
regarding the Dominions, "I sense in various Washington
areas a tendency to contribute to the breakdown of the
British Commonwealth," Paul Appleby complained to Dean
Acheson. The American Under Secretary of Agriculture added,
"There is here and there a sort of gleeful satisfaction in
building direct relationships with the Dominions, for the
sake of an ill-effect on the Commonwealth." Economic
considerations particularly attracted those American
officials who welcomed centrifugal pressures on the
Commonwealth. In November 1941 Wayne C. Taylor, the Under
Secretary of Commerce, privately advised Milo Perkins to
limit the "character" but not the amount of Lend-Lease
assistance to the Dominions and to India so that some
flexibility in American trade would be preserved. Wayne G.
Taylor recommended avoiding any unnecessary constrictions on
later options or trade patterns with the Commonwealth,

especially because of the uncertainties of the war and possible postwar changes. "The application of the Lend-Lease Act to supplies other than those of an orthodox military character carries with it longer range economic implications in that by fostering the United Kingdom's control of Dominion dollar funds we are supplementing the British Imperial Preferential Scheme for use in future, and supplementing by the most effective known method of control, namely, financial dominance," he explained to Perkins, Executive Director of the Economic Defense Board. Taylor added, "If the Dominions are encouraged to permit the United Kingdom to manage and control their dollar resources, the Mother Country is then in a position to manage and control even more effectively than in recent years their economic and trade policies."[9]

Unlike Taylor, the Under Secretary of Agriculture, Appleby, deplored American subversion (in varying degrees of subtlety) of the Commonwealth. Appleby stated, "I feel certain that the President's purpose is quite different: to establish steadily better relations with each Dominion, but not to break down the great existing unity which is more and more the kind of unity--a unity of sentiment and freedom--which can be an important beginning of a larger unity which we need to build for postwar ordering of the world." He declared, "To build on the basis of such an existing unity seems to me enormously more hopeful than to seek some wholly new unity by first destroying old unities." While Perkins learned from Taylor of the need to reduce nonmilitary assistance to the Dominions that simply alleviated United Kingdom responsibilities, Appleby described to Lend-Lease Administrator Edward R. Stettinius, Jr. "a complete abandonment of ordinary commercial considerations" in London, where the English had gone so far to comply with American Lend-Lease stipulations banning British exports of cotton goods "as to damage their war effort."[10]

Each of the four Dominions nursed independent grievances and nourished individual goals. In fact, one OSS study reported, "Competent observers foresee a radical change in the focal center of the Empire, and the possibility that in the future the Dominions rather than

London may have the deciding voice in imperial policy."[11] Disenchantment with the early military debacles and disillusionment at not having more influence in the central direction of the war reinforced separatist sentiments within the four Dominions. The twin Pacific Dominions, Australia and New Zealand, voiced particular uneasiness at the likely prospect of invasion, but the awareness spread throughout all the members of the Commonwealth that the British could no longer ensure their security without an underwriting from the United States.

Australian Prime Minister John Curtin repeatedly clashed with Churchill in asserting a more independent voice from Canberra. At a particularly dark period of the war Churchill felt compelled to lodge a personal appeal to Curtin. Disclaiming any responsibility "for the neglect of our defences and the policy of appeasement which preceded the outbreak of the war," Churchill stated, "We must not be dismayed or get into recrimination but remain united in true comradeship." The Prime Minister showed his difficult correspondence with Curtin to the President. "The matter is complicated by Australian party politics, which proceed with much bitterness and jealousy, regardless of national danger," he explained to Roosevelt. "The present Labour Government in Australia, with a majority of one, contains various personalities, particularly Evatt and Beasley, who have made their way in local politics by showing hostility to Great Britain." And Churchill admitted. "The failure of sea power to protect Australia from Japan brings this sentiment to a head."[12]

Similarly, the other three Dominions also advocated, if less vehemently than Australia, a greater share of responsibility in imperial matters. New Zealand Prime Minister Peter Fraser welcomed American postwar participation in the Far East as another bulwark of Empire security. In a much-publicized declaration on 10 March 1943, he refuted the idea of any degeneration among the white races and offered to negotiate mutual arrangements with the United Nations concerning a comprehensive security system throughout the Pacific area after the war. On 21 June 1944, New Zealand and Australia announced the signing

of "The Canberra Agreement" (ANZAC), which indicated
Australia would host an international conference on problems
in the South West Pacific, proposed a regional commission to
deal with dependent peoples in the Pacific, proclaimed the
rights of the Dominions to participate in all armistice and
peace settlements (especially those involving territorial
changes in the Pacific), and affirmed a willingness to erect
cooperative postwar systems for collective security. When a
subsequent ANZAC conference in Wellington called for more
international control of colonial areas, the War Cabinet in
London fired off an expression of its "strong exception" to
such pronouncements. Moreover, an OSS assessment of the
ANZAC pact identified some strong American hostility to the
untimely announcement of such an agreement and quoted
American Ambassador to Canberra Nelson T. Johnson's
description of the pact as an "ANZAC Monroe Doctrine,"
observing "it was the first time he had heard of two small
tails trying to wag four large dogs."[13]

The unique personal relationship between Churchill and
Jan Christian Smuts tended to overcome many of the
difficulties arising between their two countries. Yet,
problems pertaining to the Empire did occasionally stir
trouble. For example, the South African delivered a few
controversial speeches advocating more international control
of colonial areas and accelerated programs leading to self-
government. After one particularly vehement statement by
Smuts, Eden quickly directed Halifax to inform Hull that the
speech was not inspired by Great Britain. In October 1944,
Air Marshal Sir John Slessor visited Pretoria and returned
to London to draw up plans for the disposition of units of
the South African Air Force in the Mediterranean, Mideast,
and the Far East. Within two weeks the Dominions Secretary
requested that the offer from South Africa should be
accepted but the air organizations should be stationed
elsewhere in the Far East than in India as planned. Lord
Cranborne explained he had contacted the Viceroy of India
who advised that because of the recent difficulties in Natal
(involving prejudices and repressions) about the status of
Indian residents there, it would be best not to assign South
Africans to India. Later, in answer to a specific request

from Lord Mountbatten in Ceylon for South African technical
assistance in his South East Asia Command, the South African
Commanding General regretted "it is not possible to provide
South African engineer units at present for South East
Asia." The British Chiefs accepted the excuse and, mindful
of the previous problem with India, told Mountbatten "You
will realise that there are political objections to pressing
too hard in view of this and a former sympathetic
refusal."[14]

London-Ottawa wartime intercourse reflected the
traditional ambivalence about the Canadian identity crisis.
United States Minister Pierrepont Moffat relayed a complaint
by an American representative of the War Production Board in
Ottawa that "it has been very difficult to deal with the
Canadians as three days a week they want to be the forty-
ninth State, three days a week they want to be an
independent nation, and the seventh day they want to be a
member of the British Empire." Furthermore the Canadian
Government faced serious domestic problems. A 1944 State
Department memorandum on postwar international security
arrangements explained this dilemma: "Relative to every
such proposal the Canadian Government must ask: Would
Canada's participation satisfy both the French-speaking and
English-speaking Canadians? Would it accord with the
policies of the United States and Great Britain?" The
result was that neither Washington nor London could easily
predict Canadian reactions or policies. In December 1945,
when the exhausted British drained every possible source for
manpower to satisfy the demanding obligations of Allied
occupation of ex-enemy countries, London hit upon the scheme
of enlisting the Dominion forces. The Dominions Office,
however, warned the British Chiefs that such an appeal to
responsibility "is not likely to cut any ice with the
Canadian Government especially in their present frame of
mind, and to emphasise this line might do more harm than
good." Summarizing his own soundings of Canadian opinion on
postwar collaboration after a 1943 visit to Ottawa, James F.
Green of the State Department reported:

It was said that Prime Minister Churchill's
proposal of a "European Council" and an "Asiatic

Council" provoked an unfavorable response among many Canadians, on the ground that Canada would be left to play a minor role in an "American Council." The familiar thesis that only through membership in the British Commonwealth can Canada maintain its identity in North America thus receives a new emphasis: The Canadians do not want Britain to withdraw from the British Empire![15]

Problems within the Commonwealth, moreover, were not confined only to the four Dominions. Political turmoil seemed to touch all parts of the Commonwealth, particularly among its dependent areas. In general, British postwar planning (very little political development was expected during the war) for the dependent areas of the Commonwealth crystallized on both the preparation of a colonial charter and participation in Consultative Regional Councils. These efforts, however, failed to prevent political eruptions by dependent peoples in the Commonwealth seeking more significant and more immediate political gains. For example, increasingly vociferous demands for full independence from Ceylon and Cyprus diverted English attention from the war effort. Other dependent areas with similar political concerns included Singapore, Malaya (plans for a Malayan Union), the West Indies, Burma, and India.[16] Official pronouncements in 1940 had, in fact, set guidelines toward self-determination for both Burma and India, but any proposals regarding these two leviathans inevitably affected the entire Far East.

Circumstances in Burma presented His Majesty's War Cabinet with serious political and military problems. The Cabinet did not approve an important White Paper on the future of Burma until May 1945, after two years of deliberation and procrastination. Even then, this study imposed so many safeguards involving a series of leisurely paced stages that the Burmese accused the British of hampering the eventual goal of Dominion status. One result of the apparent British lassitude was that extremists in Burma formed a coalition with more moderate elements under the Anti-Fascist People's Independence League. This political bloc agitated for a temporary Burmese national government and creation of a Burmese National Army which would absorb units of the British Burma Army. American analysts criticized London's refusal to accept the recommendations of British officials experienced in Burmese affairs, especially Governor Reginald Hugh Dorman-Smith and the Conservative Committee. The Burmese wanted Dominion status but refused to accept any limiting conditions, while influential British business groups entertained no confidence in Burma's capacity for self-government. Mountbatten reported in September 1945 that the "immediate threat of a rising" in Burma had been averted, but he recommended expeditious restoration of civil government through the return of the Governor and his staff of European and Burmese advisers. Dorman-Smith did return on 1 October and urgently began work to establish an Executive Council and a Legislative Council as evidence of genuine British intentions.[17]

Imperial interests also affected British military considerations about projected operations in Burma. In his memoirs, Ismay revealed, "The Americans suspected, perhaps with reason, that we were not putting sufficient energy and drive into the prosecution of the campaign in Burma." [Emphasis mine.] Chiang Kai-shek deplored the 1942 refusal by Wavell to incorporate Chinese troops in the defense of Burma. "This obstinate attitude on the part of the British is as incomprehensible as it is regrettable," the Generalissimo complained to the War Department. Colonel Louis Johnson reported to Roosevelt that the British preferred to give up Burma rather than be indebted to the Chinese or make concessions to the Burmese nationalists. Indeed, Amery, in his dual capacity, maintained an alert vigilance over Chinese activities in both Burma and India. "The greater the part which Chinese troops play in the reconquest or the subsequent garrisoning of Burma, the greater the voice China will expect to have in the settlement of Burma's future," the watchful Minister declared in 1943. Not only would it be difficult to get the Chinese out of Burma once implanted, Amery noted, but he also pointed out, "The greater the Chinese force the greater the say which General Stilwell and the Americans, as patrons of the Chinese, will wish to have, not only in the conduct of the campaign but in Indian and

Burmese affairs generally." Thus India as well as Burma presented sensitive difficulties for His Majesty's Government. Both Amery and the Viceroy (Wavell) expressed "grave misgivings" about Sino-American proposals to accelerate the introduction of Chinese troops in India because the British feared the "Chinese may meddle in Indian politics."[18]

Chinese meddling notwithstanding, Indian politics remained a storm center throughout the war years. In early 1942 Churchill dispatched the widely respected Sir Stafford Cripps to attempt accommodation with the various political factions in India. The influential Congress Party, however, thwarted any significant reconciliation with its insistence upon the immediate formation of a national government. Most of the Congress Party leaders followed the total pacifism of Ghandi, who advocated an end to British responsibility in India. Cripps referred these unyielding demands to London with the sad commentary: "There is clearly no hope of agreement." Churchill extended his condolences and congratulations to Cripps for his yeomanlike efforts. "The effect throughout Britain and the United States has been wholly beneficial," the Prime Minister asserted. "The fact that the break comes on the broadest issues, and not on tangled formulas about defense, is a great advantage." The political turmoil dragged through the rest of the war, despite the increasing readiness of British officials to bestow Dominion status on India. On the eve of the end of the war Indian political factionalism continued to bar meaningful progress towards a settlement, and Amery summarized for the Cabinet: "It was common ground that India could not be given Dominion status now because the essential precondition, of agreement among Indians, would not be fulfilled."[19]

Domestic upheaval in India greatly worried American observers, particularly because it jeopardized the Allied war effort. Averell Harriman emphasized to Beaverbrook that the British "die-hard attitude" on India was damaging the Far Eastern campaigns against the Japanese. American proposals in May 1944 that a combined committee study the possibility of building up India as a base for South East

Asian Command (SEAC) operations bothered the Cabinet because such an inquiry "was likely to have a very wide range." But the British later seized upon the project to develop main support bases throughout India as a vehicle for relieving domestic economic ills. For London, Indian economic recovery conveniently equated with military contingency. Amery, for instance, argued that meeting economic shortages in India was "an essential precondition" for any military operation based there. A few months later, however, R. T. Peel, of the India Office, warned the Far Eastern Committee that Americans were taking "too much of an interest in constitutional matters in India." Churchill never disguised his attitude that the difficulties in India remained exclusively an Empire affair. "Yes, it's a fine thing, isn't it," he stated to one interviewer, "that we should be sending all these troops and equipment to India only to be kicked out at the finish when we have saved the country."[20]

Chiang Kai-shek's interest in the Indian political turmoil further complicated relations among the Far Eastern allies. Eden briefed the War Cabinet in late January 1942 on the forthcoming trip by the Generalissimo to India. The Chinese leader had expressed his desire to meet Gandhi and Nehru. An anxious War Cabinet approved the recommendation by the Foreign Secretary that the proper procedure would be for Chiang Kai-shek to visit the Viceroy and make all requests for interviews at that time. Eden confirmed that the Viceroy would arrange for the Generalissimo to meet "persons representative of a wider selection of communities and sections of opinion, in order that he might realise the diversity of India." Not entirely satisfied, Churchill directly intervened to instruct the Chinese leader on the required diplomatic etiquette. The Prime Minister took note of the pending journey in a February telegram to Chiang Kai-shek, but pointedly added, "However, I am sure that you will understand that such a visit could only be made as the guest of the Viceroy." He also warned that all conversations must be cleared by the Viceroy. "I must therefore beg that Your Excellency, with whom I hope to collaborate in the closest possible way in conjunction with President Roosevelt and Premier Stalin, not only in this war, but in the world settlement which will follow it, will be so very kind as to consider these serious words of mine," Churchill asserted. That same day the Prime Minister reported the Cabinet decisions to the Viceroy, including a copy of his blunt advice to Chiang Kai-shek. "We cannot possibly agree to Head of Foreign State intervening as a kind of impartial arbiter between representatives of King-Emperor and Messrs. Gandhi and Nehru," Churchill declared. "Nothing would be more likely to spread pan-Asiatic malaise through all the bazaars of India."[21]

Carefully monitored by worried British officials, Chiang Kai-shek did visit India later in February. "I was accorded a warm reception and kind hospitality by the authorities of India for which I am deeply grateful," he told the uneasy Churchill. In carefully chosen words laden with extra meaning, he added, "I am happy to be able to assure you that another step forward has been made toward closer military collaboration and solidarity between China and India." Actually the Generalissimo did receive permission to talk with Gandhi, who advised the Chinese leader about the British: "They will never voluntarily treat us Indians as equals; why, they do not even admit your country to their staff talks." The perceptive Congress Party leader, of course, had unerringly thrust to the heart of Chinese sensitivities and grievances about the Far Eastern coalition. Chiang Kai-shek next approached Roosevelt with a proposal for a pair of joint Sino-American appeals (a) to Gandhi not to plunge India into anarchy and (b) to His Majesty's Government to settle the India question to the satisfaction of Indians. The Generalissimo reported that the crisis in India had reached "an extremely tense and critical stage," which "in fact constitutes the most important factor in determining the outcome of the United Nations war." He was concerned that the British would regard Indian demands as taking advantage of the beleaguered wartime government in London, and, in turn, would introduce more repressive measures. Calling attention to the obvious detrimental effects of this unfortunate cycle upon the Far Eastern War, the Chinese leader suggested that the Sino-American offer would help Indians "regain their sense of proportion and strengthen their faith that there is justice in this world," while the British must "remove the causes which tend to aggravate the situation" through "extraordinary courage, forbearance, far-sightedness and resolution." In other words, Britain should restore complete freedom to India. The Generalissimo concluded:

> The war aims of the United Nations and our common interest at stake make it impossible for me to remain silent. An ancient Chinese proverb says: "Good medicine, though bitter, cures one's illness; words of sincere advice, though unpleasant, should guide one's conduct."[22]

An obviously embarrassed President passed along these remarks to Churchill and asked for suggestions "with regard to the nature of the reply I should make to him." Churchill's 31 July salvo denied the Chinese interpretation and charged that the Congress Party "in no way represents India." The President learned that the British intended to go no further than the "sweeping proposals" carried by Cripps which guaranteed self-government for India after the war "under constitutional arrangements of her own devising." Churchill tried to lighten his warning: "I earnestly hope therefore, Mr. President, that you will do your best to dissuade Chiang Kai-shek from his completely misinformed activities, and will lend no countenance to putting pressure upon His Majesty's Government." Roosevelt earned British gratitude for staving off the Chinese request as unwise and inexpedient. But with the August arrests of the Working Committee of the Congress Party (including Gandhi and Nehru), the Generalissimo urged the President, "as the inspired author of the Atlantic Charter," to take effective measures. "I take it amiss Chiang should seek to make difficulties between us and should interfere in matters about which he has proved himself most ill-informed which affect our Sovereign rights," Churchill countered, after the President had again requested his counsel. The Prime Minister explained that the arrests had been authorized by twelve unanimous votes in the Viceroy's Executive Council (which contained only one European member). He accused the

Congress Party of seeking only "Hindu supremacy" and wanted
the President to point out that Gandhi had been prepared to
discuss free passage across India with the Japanese if the
British had departed in early 1942. Churchill rejected a
suggestion by Amery to inform the Chinese via Washington
that Gandhi's nonviolence would not open the Burma Road.
But the Prime Minister did make the observation to
Roosevelt: "The style of his [the Generalissimo's] message
prompts me to say 'cherchez la femme' [i. e., Madame Chiang
Kai-shek]." His Majesty's Government launched a strong
counteroffensive against outside interference in the Indian
crisis, calling on the Foreign Office, Amery, and the
Embassies in Washington and Chungking to clarify the British
position. Moreover, to avoid any possible misunderstanding
in Chungking, Churchill contacted Chiang Kai-shek directly
with a cable on 26 August. The Prime Minister declared:

> I think the best rule for Allies to follow is not
> to interfere in each other's internal affairs. We
> are resolved in every way to respect the sovereign
> rights of China, and we have abstained even from
> the slightest comment when Communist-Kuomintang
> differences were most acute. . . . I should like to
> place on record the fact that no British Government
> of which I am the head, or a member, will ever be
> prepared to accept such mediation on a matter
> affecting the sovereign rights of His Majesty The
> King Emperor.[23]

Reflecting on Sino-British relations in late 1942, a
Chinese professor suggested to Sir Stafford Cripps: "The
Indian question was perhaps more responsible for the bad
relations between our two governments than the Burma
campaign."[24] The implication, of course, meant that one had
to select among other possible reasons for "the bad
relations." Although the Chinese-proposed mediation
engendered much rancor, the episode languished after a brief
flare-up. The undercurrent of Sino-British friction about
the status of Hong Kong, however, had preceded Pearl Harbor
and endured beyond the defeat of Japan.

Raymond O'Connor observed that "the anti-imperialist
tendencies of the Kuomintang government . . . held dire

implications for the key outpost of Hong Kong and threatened the entire British position in Asia." Another of the colonial jewels, Hong Kong, stood as a glaring symbol of Western intrusion in the Far East. Despite the assessment by O'Connor of Chinese anti-imperialism, clear evidence of the extent of Chungking desires to recover alleged "lost" territories, such as expounded in Chiang Kai-shek's 1943 book China's Destiny, indicated that the Chinese opposed the Western variety rather than imperialism per se. Chinese maps claimed all of North Burma for China, and the Kuomintang Government cast covetous eyes toward Tibet. Hong Kong, of course, provided an obvious target for China's ambitions. Ambassador Seymour reported that the Generalissimo recognized British rights there but had warned the British Ambassador that "the Chinese hope for an eventual settlement of the question." During the negotiations for the relinquishment of British extraterritoriality rights in China, Chungking urged the British to abandon the Kowloon Leased Territory as part of the agreement. London coldly rebuffed this suggestion, and when the entire negotiations fell into jeopardy as a result of the stalemate, the Chinese dropped the mater "at this stage."25

Roosevelt placed particular importance on the future of Hong Kong as a key to postwar relations among the United Nations. No State Department study, however, seriously recommended that the entrepôt remain under British control. The President often interrogated Halifax about the status of Hong Kong as a Crown Colony. Halifax denied the President's view that the colony was "a personal possession of the King," but the Ambassador also had to admit that Hong Kong was not self-governing. Typically, Roosevelt devised a scheme which he felt would satisfy all parties. He wanted the King to give Hong Kong to China "as a free gift in perpetuity." In gratitude, the Generalissimo would preserve existing British interests; moreover, "the port of Hong Kong would be declared and remain for all time a free port for the commerce of all nations." The President repeatedly offered his view that Hong Kong should be made a free port. Vice-President Henry A. Wallace quoted Roosevelt's words to

Chiang Kai-shek in June 1944: "Churchill is old. A new British Government will give Hong Kong to China and the next day China will make it a free port."[26]

But the British were equally insistent upon restoring prewar controls at Hong Kong. Preparing for the visit of the indefatigable de-colonizer, Patrick J. Hurley, Churchill's staff warned that Hurley "is known to have rather violent views about 'British Imperialism.'" J. R. Colville supplied Foreign Office and Colonial Office papers concerning Hong Kong, reminding the Prime Minister of the British past record there, "of which we have no reason to be anything but proud." Almost in disappointment Churchill recorded after the interview: "I took him up with violence about Hong Kong" but the docile Hurley remained content to confine the conversation "to civil banalities." Notwithstanding this fizzled attempt to reaffirm the intentions of His Majesty's Government to reclaim Hong Kong, other opportunities were seized to clarify British policy. An apprehensive British China Association approached the Colonial Office with the advice that "if we are to continue to have valuable commercial assets in the Far East, it would appear highly desirable to keep Hong Kong under the British Flag as a trade base and symbol of our Far Eastern interests." Reassuringly, the Colonial Office replied, "Any reference to the common interest would, of course, require to be carefully worded so as not to suggest any uncertainty as to His Majesty's Government's intention to resume their sovereign authority in the Colony."[27] But perhaps nothing more clearly demonstrated British determination to re-assert colonial controls in general nor revealed more about bedrock imperial motivations than the furor over the surrender and occupation of Hong Kong.

On 1 October 1943, the Combined Chiefs of Staff had directed that in any area formerly under American or British Commonwealth control freed from enemy occupation, the policies for civil affairs would be "formulated by the government which exercised authority over the territory before enemy occupation." The Foreign Office requested the British Chiefs in early August 1945 to prepare comprehensive plans for the recovery of Far Eastern possessions of the

Empire, whether liberated by the military operations of any
member of the United Nations or by a premature Japanese
surrender. While London pondered (after Japan had admitted
defeat) "the method by which it should be communicated to
the Japanese in Hong Kong that they should surrender to a
British force," Mountbatten was informing Wedemeyer that the
"British Government wanted to steer clear of political
difficulty with the Chinese Government, but that the British
Government had no intention of negotiation with the Chinese
Government concerning British entry into Hongkong."
Wedemeyer sympathized with the Generalissimo that the
unfortunate death of President Roosevelt had removed a
staunch supporter of China's claims, but the American
general noted that China would now have to accept the
British plan "since nothing physical could be done about
it." On 17 August, Ambassador Seymour put forward the
official British position on the matter and learned that the
Chinese considered the "high-handed" plan contrary to
General Order #1 by General MacArthur, "which did not
include Hong Kong among the places to be surrendered to the
Supreme Allied Commander of SEAC." The next day Attlee, now
Prime Minister, refuted the American argument that the Crown
Colony should be included in the expression "within China"
as employed in the MacArthur directive. Chiang Kai-shek
tried to salvage some face out of a situation he could not
control by indicating a willingness to delegate some of his
authority to the British in order that they might accept the
Japanese surrender at Hong Kong. Ernest Bevin, now Foreign
Secretary, coldly rebuffed this thinly-disguised
proposition. The Foreign Office explicitly clarified on 2
September that "the surrender at Hongkong will be to Admiral
[C. H. J.] Harcourt, without any attached condition
suggesting that he is acting on behalf of Chiang Kai-shek
alone." Wedemeyer complained to General A. Carleton de
Wiart (the Prime Minister's Personal Representative to the
Generalissimo), MacArthur vented his anger on General Ronald
Penney (of Mountbatten's staff), and Hurley proclaimed to
everyone that "the bar of world opinion" would indict the
British; however, His Majesty's Government proceeded with
the uninterrupted occupation of Hong Kong. A chastened

Generalissimo announced, "I now declare to the nation and the world at large that the status of Hongkong which is based on treaties will not be changed without going through negotiations with Britain."[28]

By hurriedly dispatching troops to accept the Japanese surrender at Hong Kong, the British effectively foreclosed the unpleasant prospect of having to negotiate a transfer of authority from Chinese occupation troops firmly entrenched there. But the whole issue of the British colonial presence in Asia remained a major irritant within the Far Eastern coalition throughout the war.

Despite the various logistical and tactical difficulties thwarting a vigorous British military campaign in the Far East, there seems little doubt that imperial interests largely dominated British strategic decisions. And to the extent that such motives were recognized and opposed by the other Allied partners, coalition cohesion eroded. "The impression is widespread that we are not playing our full part in the war," a concerned Beaverbrook wrote to Halifax after talking to Harry Hopkins in August 1944. Six months earlier Stettinius met with John P. Davies and General Haydon Boatner (Stilwell's Chief of Staff) during the AXIOM visit to Washington. The Lend-Lease Administrator frankly advocated an American policy striving "to avoid steps committing us to colonial imperialism lest we find ourselves aligned with an anachronistic system in vain opposition to the rising tide of Asiatic nationalism which may enjoy Russian support." The following month, a proposal within the State Department to form a joint Anglo-American Psychological Warfare Division (PWD) within the South East Asia Command was disapproved because the British would advertise such an agency "as indicating full United States concurrence in their propaganda." As Halifax noted in providing an account of these State Department views for Eden, "Mr. Wallace Murray explained that he did not see how any propaganda theme could be acceptable to both British and Americans when their long-range policies were so divergent." The British Ambassador also identified similar American sentiments at the Political Warfare Division and at the Office of War Information. Thus, the increasingly alarmed

Beaverbrook fretted over the "acute deterioration" of the British position in American eyes.[29]

Perhaps the most outspoken American harboring deep distrust of British motives was Joseph W. Stilwell. He usually could find very little room for agreement with the Generalissimo, but one area in which both leaders concurred wholeheartedly was their fierce opposition to British colonialism. A typical example of the American general's extreme anglophobia surfaced in a rancorous memorandum to his Chief of Staff Major General Thomas G. Hearn in January 1944. "Mountbatten is dogging on the Burma job," Stilwell opened his salvo. Criticizing a new sequence of war plans divised by Mountbatten and his staff (of which, it must be noted, Stilwell served as second in command), he observed acidly, "The limies have now shown their hand." Stilwell felt certain that British imperial motives shaped Mountbatten's strategy, including keeping China "powerless" and retaking prewar colonial possessions. The General concluded, "This pusillanimous and double-crossing program amply confirms all our suspicions."[30]

But Stilwell's acerbic style represented only the extreme of a fairly consistent anti-British undercurrent in the Far East among American and Chinese observers. The American juggernaut steamrolling across the Pacific invited unfortunate comparisons with British lassitude. "For over a month we only hear footsteps on the stairs," the influential newspaper Ch'iao Sheng Pao editorialized in late 1944, "yet strong British naval and air forces in the Indian Ocean have not done anything much." Another newspaper, the Sang Tang Pao, charged, "Only in the SEA theatre . . . an offense is slow in coming." The American Consul at Chengtu, James K. Penfield, provided a summary of local press sentiment for Washington. In addition, he reported:

> Articles as strongly and as openly critical of England as the enclosed do not appear very often . . . but in private conversation several high-ranking local Chinese are outspokenly and bitterly anti-British and there still seems to exist in most Chinese circles in Chengtu a distrust of Britain and British policy which does not diminish with the passage of time.[31]

Part--but only part--of the problem sprang from a lack of awareness, especially in the United States, about the true nature and extent of the entire British war effort. Two days after the invasion at Normandy, Halifax complained about the "amazing and deplorable ignorance--even among friendly and usually well-informed Americans--about the extent of British participation in the present operations." He urged the Prime Minister to "correct the perspective which is constantly, but perhaps not deliberately, distorted by American correspondents." Earlier, Halifax and Eden had exchanged similar feelings about the distorted view in the United States. "Americans have a much exaggerated conception of the military contribution they are making in this war. . . . and we are too polite to put them right," Eden protested. "The result of all this is that the Americans advocate the claims of Washington as the capital of the country making the major fighting effort, which it certainly is not." The Ambassador replied with his own condolences and complete concurrence. Halifax suggested, "One of the most valuable bits of education, when the time comes, would be for British troops and aircraft destined for the Pacific to pass in sufficient numbers across the United States."[32]

Some other factors besides distorted perceptions that help explain the uneven quality of the British military performance in the Far East include a sharp disagreement over basic strategy in Burma, the noticeable lack of a well integrated Allied effort, and an understandable--if unfortuitous--disinclination to engage the Japanese in jungle warfare.

Perhaps the major reason for Anglo-American clashes over basic strategy in the war flowed from differences in the fundamental hypotheses postulated in London and Washington. The British preferred to mobilize, launch, and deploy on the assumption that ensuing circumstances would then determine the timing and location of the decisive engagement, if indeed such a decision ever really were required. This planning pattern, therefore, led not only to endless British analogies about "closing the ring" and "tightening the noose" but also to impatience at American demands for detailed schedules and requirements concerning the exact nature of long-range operations.

Unfortunately for Anglo-American harmony, Washington worked from the opposite pole by first asking where the crucial engagement would occur and then marshaling the resources necessary for successful execution of that original (and progressively unalterable) decision. Of course, the capacity of American technology to implement this strategic approach had reached unprecedented levels, and the British could not be blamed for failing to appreciate the revolutionary American twists to the traditional, and often faulty, approach of gambling high stakes by forcing a military showdown.

Churchill, for instance, felt oppressed by the "American clear-cut, logical, large-scale, mass-production style of thought." Kent Roberts Greenfield has observed that "the English seem not fully to have grasped either the capabilities or the limiting conditions of the American system of industrial potential." But American leaders were also learning. General Marshall announced at Tehran that his military education had always been concerned with "roads, rivers, and railways," but recently he "had to learn all over again" about global amphibious operations and requirements. "Now landing craft . . . was a continued preoccupation." Implied in this admission was the need for skillful, long-range production planning; for, as Marshall characterized the modern approach to war: "The problem therefore resolved itself into one of shipping and landing craft." How striking the contrast with Churchill's impatient outburst that "the destinies of two great empires . . . seemed to be tied up in some god-damned things called LST's whose engines themselves had to be tickled on by . . . LST engine experts of which there was a great shortage."[33]

This disagreement over general strategy exacerbated Anglo-American friction over the fundamental approach in the Far East against Japan. Sino-American emphasis on the Burma Road and aid to China elicited few British sympathies. "Going into swampy jungles to fight the Japanese is like going into the water to fight a shark," the Prime Minister asserted. "It is better to entice him into a trap or catch him on a hook and then demolish with axes after hauling him out onto dry land." Churchill scorned the proposed Operation BULLFROG for 1944 "with nothing to show for it but Akyab and the future right to toil through the swamps of southern Burma." Moreover, he could not agree with the priorities suggested in Washington and Chungking. "We are to plunge about in the jungles of Burma," he criticized such Sino-American recommendations, "engaging the Japanese under conditions which though improved are still unfavorable to us, with the object of building a pipe-line or increasing the discharge over the 'hump.'" And in July 1944 he adamantly insisted to the Defence Committee, "Nothing could be worse than having our Armies bogged down in Northern Burma, and I have no intention whatever of giving way to the United States Chiefs of Staff in this matter."[34]

Moreover, the quality of the British effort in the Far East remained suspect. Stilwell and Chiang Kai-shek frequently emphasized this point, but significantly, some confidential British admissions have recently come to light. For instance, in May 1944, Churchill sadly noted to the British Chiefs, "What with our differences and the uncertainty of American action, we are not unfolding a creditable picture to history." Earlier, General Noel M. S. Irwin privately informed Wavell that "we quite obviously don't yet know how to" fight the Japanese forces. "I am left in no doubt that we are most weakly served by our relatively senior commanders and by the lack of training," Irwin confessed, "and, unpleasant as it is to have to say so, the lack of determination of many of our troops." In retrospect, the harassed Irwin again lamented his fortune. "It seems," he recalled, "that I was constantly trying to hold what I had." And from London, Ismay confided to General Sir Henry Pownall, who was serving in Kandy as Mountbatten's Chief of Staff, this damaging admission: "When history comes to be written, I believe that the waffling that there has been . . . over the basic question of our strategy in the Far East, will be one of the black spots in the British Higher Direction of the War."[35]

Thus, although it is true that some other very real problems plagued the British performance in the Far East, it would nevertheless seem fair to say that British colonialism evoked the major share of Allied suspicions and scorn directed against His Majesty's Government, especially during the Premiership of Churchill, from 10 May 1940 to 26 July 1945. Furthermore, the bitter feeling within the Far Eastern coalition generated by imperial motives outlasted the war. In fact, it is virtually impossible to exaggerate the harmful effect of the colonial issue, whether real or imagined, among the United Nations in World War II. Nor was there a dearth of evidence substantiating such suspicions and ill-will. Secretary of State Cordell Hull warned Eden and Halifax in 1943 that the British preoccupation with Empire problems was poisoning sentiment among the Allied nations, not just in the United States. And Hull's successor, Edward R. Stettinius, Jr., frankly described for Halifax the "ground swell of opinion" prevailing against British imperial ambitions. Halifax reported that Stettinius:

> was not only concerned with what might be held to be the general emotional public opinion in America, but also with the sort of stuff which was coming back from Americans in responsible positions in the Pacific, and of which the general colour was the British thought nothing about China and were only concerned to re-establish our own position and Empire. He was meeting much more of this than he liked and though he fought it all the time, it was dangerous.[36]

The truth is that imperial considerations and certain perceived requirements actually did influence British strategic policy recommendations. Mountbatten visited London in 1944 to make a special appeal for the recapture of Singapore by the end of 1945. "Otherwise our Far Eastern Empire is to be returned to us over the peace table, as a result of operations in which we have virtually taken no part," the SACSEA explained, in what he knew to be a telling argument. General Ismay outlined Churchill's insistence on particular Far Eastern target operations and concluded,

"Doubtless there lay at the back of his mind the desire that we should recover by our own efforts, not only the territories but also the prestige, which we lost in South East Asia." In fact, as soon as the South East Asia Command (SEAC) was established in 1943, the wartime hobby of creating acronyms took on a new irony: "Save England's Asiatic Colonies." Although Churchill was repelled by the northern Burmese terrain, his attitude warmed noticeably as he described amphibious landings along "one or more points of the crescent from Moulmein to Timor," or the many advantages of attacking Sumatra (Operation CULVERIN) and thereafter reclaiming Rangoon (Operation BULLFROG) "which at least gives us back one of our own capital cities and should further our advance on to the Malay Peninsula." He particularly favored CULVERIN and praised that project as "the TORCH of the Indian Ocean." But the Prime Minister pointedly deleted a request for American assistance contained in early plans for CULVERIN with the revealing explanation that he did not want a large United States force in that area. One year later he approved the assignment of a British naval support force to the main American operations in the Pacific but insisted on a separate British operation against Rangoon as a preliminary step in reconquering Singapore, which he called, "the supreme British objective in the whole of the Indian and Far Eastern theatres." Churchill pointed out, "It is the only prize that will restore British prestige in this region." Eden, too, agreed that strategy should reflect imperial needs. At a secret military meeting in 1944, the Foreign Secretary expressed his belief that "people here would understand the necessity for putting up with further hardships much better if they saw that we were engaged in direct assaults for the recovery of our own possessions, rather than in operations in distant parts of the Pacific in which they had no direct interest." Attlee immediately endorsed Eden's views and suggested, "It was in Malaya, Borneo and the Netherlands East Indies that our reputation had suffered and it was there that the world would expect to see it rehabilitated."[37] No one at the meeting questioned the basic premise that the postwar restoration of colonial controls would occur.

British strategists never lost sight of the broader
political implications of the war against Japan. Submitting
a formal assessment of Far Eastern options in May 1944, the
British Chiefs of Staff examined various alternatives for
the British role without specifically endorsing any one
course. The study emphasized that, whatever the final
decision, the British had "to play a vigorous part" in
defeating Japan and this was "as much a political as a
strategical objective." The Chiefs concluded that "not only
our influence at the peace conference but our position and
prestige in the Far East for many years to come will be
determined by the extent and effectiveness of the
contribution which we now make. . . ." Thus, it is quite
erroneous to imagine British military planners working in
watertight compartments, oblivious to outside concerns. In
October 1943 the original terms of reference for M. E.
Dening as Political Adviser to Mountbatten's new command
stressed the protection of imperial interests as one of his
major functions. Dening later complained that without a
drastic change in the British war effort against Japan,
which he characterized as "merely contributory" to the
predominant American effort, "it is no exaggeration to say
that the solidarity of the British Commonwealth and its
influence in the maintenance of peace in the Far East will
be irretrievably damaged." In early 1945 the perceptive
Dening made clear to London that "it does not look as if
anybody is going to help us set our own Far Eastern
territories in order and we shall get no reward if we help
China at their expense." Mountbatten, meanwhile, continued
to press the Generalissimo for Chinese support in retaking
Rangoon and clearing all of Burma. This imperial
gamesmanship received further impetus in a detailed
memorandum by Dening entitled "Political Factors Affecting
British Participation in the War Against Japan After the
Fall of Singapore." Composed less that two months before
the Japanese surrender, this document argued, "Ocular
evidence of the defeat of the hitherto all-powerful Japanese
in any given area is likely to have more effect than hearsay
evidence that British troops have taken a part in an attack

upon Japan proper." The SEAC Political Adviser explained:

> British participation in an assault upon Japan
> proper being based in political as well as military
> considerations, the extent of such participation
> should be governed by Great Britain's need to
> restore her influence and prestige in particular in
> that area of the Far East which lies south of the
> Tropic of Cancer, by the role which she expects to
> be able to play in the Far East after the war both
> from the point of view of her own interests and
> those of Far Eastern and world security, by the
> necessity of maintaining Empire solidarity, and in
> the light of the fact that the destruction of Japan
> proper without surrender will not guarantee
> cessation of hostilities in the outer areas under
> Japanese occupation.[38]

Occasionally the continual theme of anti-colonialism by Allied critics stirred the wrath of British officials, but more often than not these infrequent outbursts of petulance were confined to the private backlands of the Foreign Office. J. Thyne Henderson let loose one such salvo on an August 1944 report of Chinese complaints and suspicions. "Moral leadership directed towards cooperation & collective security has meant so far that the Great Powers do all the work & the others benefit & criticise," the frustrated Henderson raged. Yet the public British attitude usually displayed remarkable forbearance in the face of such anti-imperial adversity. Constantly aware of appearances, London grappled with the dilemma of reconciling imperial interests with Allied sensitivities. When Halifax suggested an intensified British propaganda campaign in the United States, Churchill abruptly cut short the idea with his own terse recommendation: "Deeds not words." In May 1945 Mountbatten requested changing the nomenclature of his land component from "Allied Land Forces, SEA" to "11th Army Group, SEA." The War Office refused with the comment that "a change of title might be construed by the Chinese and possibly the Americans as an indication of a change of policy, an impression which we do not wish to convey."[39]

Friction persisted within the Far Eastern coalition about extracurricular and peripheral British motives in the war against Japan. John Paton Davies, Jr. astutely pointed out that the British recognized that whatever assistance was given to China would contradict imperial interests, whereas the United States should remember that "to whatever degree she joined Britain in helping to restore colonial rule and white supremacy [she] would be acting contrary to American policy sentiment and future relations with the countries of Asia." Davies later pressed for "frank American propaganda to Southeast Asia" as part of the American "obligation" to explain that "we [were] operating on our own terms, unassociated with the reimposition of imperial rule." And in Washington, the War Department warily monitored SEAC activity, ever-mindful of the agreed policy to share American resources with Mountbatten "when this does not prevent the fulfillment of the primary objective of rendering support to China including protection of the line of communication." Yet the British Chiefs had managed to extract a pledge from the Joint Chiefs of Staff not to withdraw any American resources once they were committed to SEAC operations. Thus, American men and materials played an important role in the very maneuvers that hinted of British colonial intrigue. Ambassador Hurley tried to brace Washington vigilance in such matters with his advice: "We are not opposed to giving the British more credit than they deserve in this war against Japan, but we are opposed to the surrender of the principles of democracy that led America into the war for the purpose of destroying Japanese imperialism." Despite their guarded suspicions, American officials could not conceal a grudging admiration for British tenacity in safeguarding imperial interests. John Hickerson betrayed his better judgment with the admission to H. Freeman Matthews:

> I have a real admiration for the way the British
> know how to take care of their interests. It would
> be foolish to deny their skill and ability in this
> regard. . . . I frankly feel that we have a very
> long way to go before we can come anywhere near the
> British type of streamlined control.[40]

And at the center of this efficient machinery stood the

Prime Minister, delineating imperial interests and promoting the general welfare of the Commonwealth. Whether encouraging far-flung assaults across the Bay of Bengal, or cheering operations such as DRACULA (for Rangoon) designed to return "one of our capital cities," or hoping to see the United States lodged in the Philippines and the British reinserted in Malaya before Russia entered the Far Eastern war, or, less subtly, ignoring suggestions from some of his Allies about the disposition of Hong Kong, Churchill was difficult to believe when he disclaimed colonial ambitions and imperial interests as decisive factors in British policies. Despite significant logistical and tactical difficulties in the military sphere, political considerations colored much of British wartime thinking, particularly as the defeat of Japan loomed more apparent. The increasing attention to the character of the postwar world led the British into another ruse to disguise imperial concerns. By sponsoring the cause of other colonial countries such as France, Portugal, and Holland, the British indirectly advanced their own imperial status. London readily recognized that a united front among the colonial powers would decrease the likelihood of individual possessions being stripped; the welfare of all the empires was bound unmistakably to the degree of unity that could be forged against idealistic onslaughts. Some American observers seemed less inclined to grasp this connection, perhaps lulled into a false optimism based on the conviction that a new order would surface from this military ordeal by fire. For example, Hurley optimistically informed President Truman, "The defeat administered to Japan on the sea and on the land and the present attack on the homeland of Japan should indicate even to the casual observer that all the Southeast Asia colonial or imperial areas must fall like ripe apples as America approaches the heart of Japan."[41]

Yet, not all Americans suffered this political myopia regarding Far Eastern affairs. Max Bishop warned in late 1944 from Kandy that Chinese representatives in SEAC held no meaningful political or military functions in the SEAC organization. He stated, "This leaves the American side of SEAC the only significant non-colonial partner." Bishop expressed his fear that the United States was being "politically out-maneuvered" in becoming identified in Asian eyes with white imperialism. Emphasizing that the United States lay open to charges of abetting the return of the colonial powers, Bishop surmised, "In all probability full agreement has been reached among British, Dutch, and French officials at the highest levels with respect to basic policies for southeast Asia." In fact, London fulfilled Bishop's anxieties about camouflaging its ulterior imperial ambitions by advocating the return of French and Dutch civil administrations to their prewar possessions. If British colonial considerations weakened the Allied coalition in Asia, the implications of an unchallenged return by other imperial powers in that region represented no less a threat to American efforts at building an enduring peace and arranging a stable Far East in the postwar world. Consequently, much more was at stake in this issue than the mere question of localized political-economic controls in a few isolated dependent areas, for, as Max Bishop discerningly pointed out: "Asia and its peoples seem destined to present future generations with most difficult problems. This part of the world may easily become a malignant source of irritation and a threat to peace and stability."[42]

CHAPTER V

ANGLO-AMERICAN COLONIAL POLITICS: A CASE STUDY OF FRENCH INDOCHINA

Most of American thinking about Southeast Asia during the war focused on the idea of regional cooperation. Writing in September 1943 for the special Territorial Subcommittee on postwar planning in the State Department, Rupert Emerson described Southeast Asia as the "crazy-quilt product of ancient and modern imperialisms and of racial migrations." Emerson reflected American planning assumptions about postwar Southeast Asia by calling for the creation of a regional structure which would transcend narrow imperial interests to address generally common concerns. At a meeting of the Territorial Subcommittee two months later, Adolph A. Berle, Jr. noted that the members favored some type of regional control in Southeast Asia. He alluded to the responsibility of the United States to obtain the agreement of parties involved in that area, explaining that whatever happened there, "we are permanently bound up in the Far East."[1]

Implicit in the State Department plans for regional machinery in Southeast Asia loomed the integral component of international collaboration and consultation. The State Department and the OSS produced studies which emphasized the need to integrate the area both economically and militarily (security arrangements). Shortly after the Japanese surrender, John Carter Vincent looked to a full range of regional cooperation for Southeast Asia in a speech to the Foreign Policy Association. Vincent disavowed any intention to support the restoration of prewar colonial controls in the area but affirmed that the United States, if requested, would assist efforts to reach political agreements throughout Southeast Asia.[2]

Even in their buoyant optimism, American officials recognized how tenuous was such international teamwork. "It is apparent that the British are playing a very clever game in this area," Wedemeyer complained in December 1944. "They

are sending agents to various points and are watching
developments concerning the [Chinese] Communists and the
French Indochina situation." The following month an
exasperated special State Department committee debated the
question whether or not the United States should proceed
with an independent policy vis-a-vis Thailand, and perhaps
elsewhere in Southeast Asia, excluding further consultations
with the British. But a subsequent memorandum from the
State Department to the President apparently ruled out any
serious thought of formulating American policies without
regard to British (or Allied) concerns. This study declared
that American efforts to maintain a separate identity from
that of the colonial powers were not wholly successful.
Calling attention to effective Japanese propaganda linking
the United States with European imperialism, the State
Department urged the President to secure assurances from the
imperial powers for more liberal postwar policies in
Southeast Asia, analogous to American policies in the
Philippines. Thus, the American dilemma regarding postwar
planning for Southeast Asia unfolded. On the one hand,
there was the full understanding that new levels of
international collaboration would be required to arrange an
enduring peace. On the other hand, ominous signs indicated
a reversion to the pursuit of narrow self-interest which had
plagued the prewar years. OSS Director William Donovan
touched on this dilemma when he reported in November 1944:

> There can be little doubt that the British and
> Dutch have arrived at an agreement with regard to
> the future of Southeast Asia, and now it would
> appear that the French are being brought into the
> picture. . . . It would appear that the strategy of
> the British, Dutch and French is to win back and
> control Southeast Asia, making the fullest use
> possible of American resources, but foreclosing the
> Americans from any voice in policy matters.[3]

Ironically, at about the same time an important staff
study compiled for the British Chiefs by the Post-
Hostilities Planning Committee also advocated the need for
postwar collaborative machinery in the Far East. This
memorandum called attention to the common interests of both
the colonial powers and the United States in Southeast Asia

and proceeded on the assumption of mutual collaboration in
the postwar era. But the Post-Hostilities Committee also
introduced a significant caveat, which seemed to confirm
mounting American suspicions. After warning that political
considerations in the United States might obstruct American
cooperation in any regional machinery developed for
Southeast Asia, the Committee recommended establishing close
British ties with both the French and the Dutch.[4]

Thus, uncertainty about the reliability of the United
States to act resolutely (a lesson twice impressed upon
London within twenty-five years) led to hesitancy and
ambivalence in British policy. There existed no doubt about
the desirability of American cooperation, but binding
guarantees of American support, which were unrealized
prerequisites in British diplomacy during the inter-war
years, could no longer be required for the development of a
system of collective security. Consequently, the British
had to attract American collaboration, yet not at the
expense of alienating the other imperial powers. This
problem--not altogether dissimilar from traditional
quandaries of island diplomacy in British history--emerged
particularly in the highly personal diplomacy of Churchill.
For example, two days prior to OVERLORD the Prime Minister
met with Charles de Gaulle and warned the French leader that
His Majesty's Government would never separate from the
Americans. "This is something you ought to know: each time
we have to choose between Europe and the open sea, we shall
always choose the open sea," Churchill asserted. "Each time
I have to choose between you and Roosevelt, I shall always
choose Roosevelt." Yet, less than six months later at a
Paris luncheon arranged by de Gaulle to commemorate
Armistice Day, Churchill proclaimed:

> For more than 35 years I have defended the cause of
> friendship, comradeship and alliance between France
> and Great Britain. I have never in the course of
> my life swerved from this policy. These two
> nations have for so many years shared the glories
> of Western Europe that they have become
> indispensable to one another. It is a fundamental
> principle of British policy that the alliance with
> France should be unshaken, constant and effective.
> I have been able to see this morning that the
> French people are determined to walk "la main dans

la main" with the people of Britain.[5]

Therefore the Anglo-American war effort illuminated the whole question of the relations of the two Atlantic powers with France. During the darkest hours of 1940, the British diplomatic and military corps in Southeast Asia desperately sought some accommodation with the French colonial administration in Indochina. Within a month after the fall of metropolitan France, local British and French navalists agreed to refrain from hostile action in the China Station (Noble-Decoux Agreement, July 1940). As the Japanese influence permeated northern Indochina and extended ominously southward, British officials tried both to cajole and coerce cooperation from the beleaguered French administrators under the Governor-General, Admiral Jean Decoux. When Decoux, on orders from the Vichy Government, declared the prohibition of all exports to the British Commonwealth in his 5 October [1940] Decree, the British reaction was immediate and sharp. The C-in-C, China, Admiral Sir Percy Noble, suggested immediate retaliation and recommended an embargo of all trade with Indochina, especially the cessation of the deliveries of gunny bags from India which were absolutely essential to the handling and transport of rice. On 7 November, Sir Frederick Leith-Ross, Chairman of the Economic Subcommittee of the Far Eastern Committee, presented the conclusions of his group that all British exports to Indochina should terminate effective 15 November except as authorized under license. He confidentially revealed that all licenses would in fact be refused. But Leith-Ross argued against relegating the influential Banque de l'Indo-Chine to the punitive Statutory List. He explained that the Bank and the place occupied by it and its subsidiaries in the economic life of Indochina was so extensive that "to specify it would be tantamount to treating the whole Colony as an enemy." The Ministry of Economic Warfare reinforced this position with the observation that it would be anomalous to forbid British subjects to deal with the Bank and its many branches throughout the Far East while not treating Indochina itself as an enemy destination (for contraband imports/exports).[6]

Most of the restrictions on both sides, however, were conveniently circumvented. In fact, Admiral Percy Noble recommended to London that some trade restrictions be relaxed, and, in a particularly revealing commentary on colonial methods of control, Percy suggested that opium be provided to help Decoux "in keeping the Annamite population quiet." Collaborating secretly at Singapore with Decoux's Naval Chief of Staff, Admiral René Jouan, Noble sought to develop some pattern of accommodation. Decoux sent clear signals that he wished to separate himself from the Vichy anti-British policies which he felt grew out of not only bitterness over the Anglo-French clash at Oran but also pressures from both Japan and the Franco-German Armistice Commission. The secret negotiations at Singapore produced the Noble-Jouan Agreement of December 1940, which affirmed a broadly based modus vivendi focusing on two mutual needs: trade and the maintenance of a French colonial government in Indochina with some measure of independence from the Japanese.[7]

Unlike the British, locked in mortal struggle with the European Axis Powers, American officials could afford less of a sense of urgency about developments in Southeast Asia, although, of course, awareness led to concern. Moreover, the chain of causation from aggressive Japanese advances in Indochina to the subsequent freezing order in retaliation by the United States to the attack at Pearl Harbor makes essential an understanding of American foreign policies vis-a-vis France and her colonial empire.

Despite the relative noninvolvement in Southeast Asia of the United States compared to British activities, American interest quickened briefly over one of the State Department's favorite causes: the nonrecognition of territorial transfers brought about by force or threat of coercion. The Thais lodged certain territorial claims (mainly along the Mekong River) in late 1940 against an Indochina weakened and disunited by the disasters in metropolitan France. Decoux issued an appeal for support to the British, who immediately sounded out the State Department. Nevile Butler expressed some relief in discovering that he and Sumner Welles generally agreed on the need to strengthen the French in Indochina. Welles addressed the specific Thai demands by invoking the important statement by Secretary Hull on 16 July 1937, which reinforced the principle of nonrecognition developed in

1931-1932 by President Herbert Hoover and Secretary of State Henry L. Stimson. Unbeknown to either of them, Butler and Welles foreshadowed a fierce postwar Anglo-American argument when they discussed the firm view of the United States Government that the Thais should submit their territorial claims at the end of the war. In general, however, Butler reported that Washington was sympathetic to British concerns about French Indochina.[8]

By the end of January 1941, the Far Eastern Committee concluded that His Majesty's Government should attempt to settle the dispute even at the risk of annoying the Thais. But the British hesitancy had discouraged the despairing Decoux Administration and had confirmed Thai skepticism that the British would not interpose themselves to shield Bangkok from mounting Japanese pressures. One week after the Far Eastern Committee finally determined to pursue a positive policy, Ashley Clarke reported that both contestants had accepted the Japanese offer of "mediation," thereby predetermining resolution of the question in favor of the Thais.[9]

French (Gaullist) plans regarding the postwar status of Indochina never seriously considered any other course except the restoration of colonial control from metropolitan France. Foreshadowing plans to create a French Commonwealth of Nations, the Brazzaville Conference in February 1944 announced, "The aims of the work of civilization accomplished by France in the colonies exclude any idea of autonomy, any possibility of evolution outside of the French bloc of the Empire." Dispelling all doubt about French intentions, this declaration insisted that "the possible constitution, even in the distant future, of self-government in the colonies is to be dismissed." Nevertheless, the French National Committee did encourage Indochina with promises of postwar reforms as well as "a new political status within the French Empire." And the French Ambassador to China, General Zinovi Pechkoff, held a press conference shortly after the Brazzaville meeting to provide assurances that Indochina, as a member of the proposed Commonwealth, would enjoy a certain amount of economic autonomy. "She will establish commercial relations with her neighbors," Pechkoff stated, "and especially she will cultivate a bosom friendship with China."[10]

Anglo-American wartime deliberations concerning Indochina invariably played upon two themes: the status of the French colony and the larger question of the role of France in international arrangements to maintain global stability. During these debates, British and American assessments evolved along different lines.

His Majesty's Government preferred to deal with one French authority (if not a government) while the United States remained reluctant to make a commitment to any one French faction, treating simultaneously with various individuals, such as de Gaulle and General Henri Giraud. In addition, the American hope that Allied military forces would administer French liberated territory ran counter to British expectations that some French civil authoritative body would relieve the Allies of this burden as soon as practicable. Although the 1942 Declaration of the United Nations allowed for later adoption by "appropriate authorities which are not governments"--a device designed by Churchill specifically with the Free French in mind-- Roosevelt steadfastly refused to extend any form of recognition to the French Committee of National Liberation either on that occasion or after subsequent British overtures sponsoring the Free French cause. "Eden and Hull are locked in lengthy discussions," an exasperated Prime Minister reported to the War Cabinet from QUADRANT. "Hull remains completely obdurate about not using the word 'recognition' in respect to the French Committee." Churchill explained, "I have pointed out in the plainest terms to the President that they will certainly have a bad press, but he says he would rather have a sheet anchor out against the machinations of de Gaulle." More than a year later another possible presidential motive surfaced. The new French Ambassador, Henri Hoppenot, in Washington to promote official American acknowledgement of the French National Committee's legitimacy in metropolitan France, talked about Roosevelt's reticence regarding recognition with the British Ambassador. "According to Lord Halifax, Admiral Leahy had so often predicted to the President that the Liberation would be a signal to plunge France into civil war, that Mr. Roosevelt did not believe it possible that General de Gaulle had firm authority over France," Hoppenot informed the self-styled "Government in Paris."[11]

Despite the American hesitancy about dealing exclusively with the Gaullists, the United States Government early in the war undertook public commitments to restore the full integrity of the French Empire. Indeed, American officials on several occasions had expressed similar sentiments regarding both Indochina in particular and French imperial interests in general. Ambassador Joseph Grew in Tokyo protested in 1940 against any Franco-Japanese bargain in Southeast Asia. Also, Sumner Welles, in his capacity as Acting Secretary of State on 21 July 1941, denied that there existed any reason either for the Japanese to occupy Indochina or to establish bases there; moreover, Welles publicly upheld French sovereignty over its prewar possessions in a speech 13 April 1942, and again privately to Eden the next year. President Roosevelt re-emphasized this guarantee on 8 November 1942, announcing, "I need not tell you that the ultimate and greater aim is the liberation of France and its Empire from the Axis yoke." Also, State Department officer Ray Atherton affirmed the principle of complete restoration in a letter 14 October 1941, to Vichy Foreign Minister René Pleven. But perhaps the most explicit statements of American intentions were inscribed in two letters from Robert Murphy (Political Adviser under General Dwight D. Eisenhower) to General Giraud during preparations for the Allied landings in North Africa. "I am able to assure you that the restoration of France in its complete independence, in all its grandeur and the extent it possessed before the war, in Europe as well as overseas, is one of the war aims of the United Nations," Murphy pledged. "It is understood that French sovereignty will be re-established, as soon as possible, in all the territories, continental and colonial, over which the French flag flew in 1939."[12]

Yet, as the war progressed, these early American assurances eroded noticeably under the evolving determination in Washington, albeit vaguely conceptualized, to implement some form of international trusteeship over most colonized areas, particularly Indochina. In the meantime, London thinking about the French travelled in the opposite direction.

Curiously--given the mutual colonial connection--the British were not prepared initially to go as far as guarantees about restoring the French Empire. "The inherent vice about these documents," Eden commented about the Murphy pledges, "is that although signed by the President alone [sic] they purport to commit H. M. Government as well as the U. S. Government." At the time of the American commitment to Giraud, however, Eden had asserted to Ambassador Winant the British intention to restore "the independence and greatness of France" and disavowed any design to annex former French territory; nevertheless, the careful language (indeed, the subject itself) indicated that the British were at least considering certain postwar contingencies. The British apparently expected the peace conference to settle the postwar status of some (i.e., non-British) colonial territories. From the Cairo Conference, Churchill cautioned the Cabinet not to "prejudge" the postwar status of Indochina or the Netherlands East Indies. And when Eden cabled his view that definite decisions about some French colonial possessions should await the peace conference, the Prime Minister replied, "I agree."[13]

The French colonial issue proved particularly bothersome to London because it appeared that, while launching a steady volley of explicit threats about breaking the colonial arrangements of the British (who had not given up in the dark stages of the war), American officials seemed content, at least temporarily, with the idea of reestablishing the prewar imperial interests of the French (who had given up). But British annoyance dissipated when it became evident that the President's mind was turning away from complete French restoration. At the Casablanca Conference Roosevelt reproached Murphy for exceeding his authority. "You overdid things a bit," he told the Ambassador, "your letter may make trouble for me after the war." Murphy recalled, "That was the first indication to me that Roosevelt was planning to encourage extensive reductions in the French empire." More reassurances reached the British during 1943 about American postwar policy toward the French. "The President looks like he is getting himself into a bit of a jam with the promises that Murphy seems to have made to Giraud about the complete restoration of all French territory, etc.," Halifax notified Churchill in February. Remarking that "all your statements have been more general," the Ambassador added, "No one seems quite to know where Murphy got his 'complete restitution and restoration' letter for Giraud." Shortly thereafter, Eden recounted for the Cabinet a revealing episode during his recent visit to Washington. Roosevelt was describing his sketchy ideas to the Foreign Secretary for an international trusteeship over Indochina when Welles interrupted with a reminder about American guarantees to France. The President, however, indicated his own impression that the pledges applied only to French possessions in Africa. Later, from the Tehran Conference, Churchill assured the Cabinet that "the President contemplates change" in the status of Indochina.[14]

The changes Roosevelt contemplated for Indochina centered on the trusteeship system well known in the financial world. "France has had the country--thirty million inhabitants for nearly one hundred years, and the people are worse off than they were at the beginning," he pointed out to the sympathetic Hull. "The people of Indo-China are entitled to something better than that." Despite his strong humanitarian and anti-imperialist impulses, Roosevelt never specifically formulated his vague concept. In general, he envisaged some sort of international trusteeship in Indochina for about twenty-five years "till we get them on their feet." At Cairo he described for Stilwell a three-member supervisory commission (American-British-Chinese), while at Yalta the President pictured an international trustee agency involving "a Frenchman, one or two Indo-Chinese, and a Chinese and a Russian, because they are on the coast, and maybe a Filipino and an American, to educate them for self-government."[15]

Several State Department studies in the Postwar Policy Committee sought to focus the fuzzy views at the White House concerning Indochina. Isaiah Bowman explored alternative policies, such as independence, or a condominium, or restoration to the French, but finally advocated a multinational agency monitoring French administration. "It begins with international cooperation in the colonial field," Bowman explained. "It puts the minimum of blame for French sins on the United States as a participant in a general or world organization responsible for colonial progress." Arriving at similar conclusions, James Masland and Amry Vandenbosch argued, "This solution would probably

make for more conscious planning by the French for a more
rapid democratization of the French Indo-Chinese government,
would in all probability be acceptable to the French, and
would likewise go far to satisfy liberal opinion throughout
the world." In yet another State Department study, Rupert
Emerson endorsed the closely related concept of regional
machinery in Southeast Asia. "Particularly if it were made
generally applicable," Emerson maintained, "there is no
reason to think the establishment of international
guarantees would be in violation of the American pledge to
secure a restoration of French sovereignty." [16]

Like Roosevelt, most State Department officers
introduced their assessments of Indochina with the premise
of French negligence. Melvin M. Knight (in the Economic
Section) criticized the highly centralized political basis
of French colonialism. "While this system worked
satisfactorily from the French point of view," he informed
the Territorial Subcommittee, "it raised considerable
antagonism on the part of the Cochin-Chinese both because of
the financial burden which it was forced to bear and because
the French officials received all the benefits of this
system without sharing the expense." Expressing disapproval
of French economic policies, Knight observed that "Indo-
China is typically Oriental in its habits and levels of
consumption, and out of place in an Occidental empire which
ignores the 'costs of distance' in setting up trade
barriers." He illuminated the strikingly exploitative
practices of French economic imperialism in which "the
burdens fell particularly upon the populations whose
ancestors had held the countries." Adding that, "It does
not seem immoderate to state that French colonial economic
policy since 1892 has been unfortunate," Knight concluded:

> "Tutorship" implies pupils being prepared for
> maturity. But when the "pupils" referred to are
> peoples, and remain alien as they mature, a time
> comes when the privileged powers and incomes of the
> alien "tutors" are resented and these are asked to
> give an account of themselves. Back of the problem
> of who conspicuously has power and income in Indo-
> China is another question of who, less
> conspicuously, has income and power because of
> Indo-China. Even with the best of intentions,
> distance and unfamiliarity tend to make the right

and left hands of empire uncritical, if not incurious, of each other's doings.[17]

Throughout 1943 and 1944, American officials maintained a calculated coolness towards the French Committee of National Liberation, especially with regard to Gaullist aspirations about participating in Far Eastern military operations and claiming postwar administrative control over Indochina. Immediately after the Tehran Conference, Roosevelt promised representatives from Britain, China, Turkey, Egypt, Russia, and Iran that he was working "very hard" to ensure that Indochina would not return to French control. Repeating one of his favorite themes, the President told this diplomatic corps that the French had done nothing there for one hundred years. Earlier, Stettinius forwarded a French request on 21 October for participation in the Washington Pacific War Council with his own editorial comment: "If accepted, the Committee's representative would doubtless take the position that the Committee represented all French interests in the Pacific, including Indo-China, and that one objective of the Pacific campaign must be the reconquest of Indo-China and its return to France." It took the President three months to respond to this question as well as to another French request to dispatch a military mission to SEAC. Even then, his only comment was that both issues "should be left to the discretion of the Joint Chiefs of Staff." Stanley K. Hornbeck "demurred strongly" during his conversations in London that any Free French participation in the Pacific War Council "implied a right to the return of Indo-China after the end of the war."[18]

In truth, personality clashes also contributed to the measured aloofness in wartime Franco-American relations. Roosevelt's antipathy towards the French leader was widely recognized. One observer, Brendan Bracken, ventured his own opinion that "Roosevelt hates de Gaulle," and Lord Moran remarked that the French leader "gets on his [Roosevelt's] nerves." Hull, too, shared a strong dislike for de Gaulle, whom he once characterized as a "little squirt" built up by the British. American enmity created reciprocal feelings on the part of the Free French, for as de Gaulle later revealed:

> Franklin Roosevelt was governed by the loftiest
> ambitions. . . . [A] kind of messianic impulse now
> swelled the American spirit and oriented it towards
> vast undertakings. The United States . . . yielded
> in her turn to the taste for intervention which
> concealed the instinct for domination. It was
> precisely this tendency that President Roosevelt
> espoused. He had therefore done everything to
> engage his country in the world conflict. He was
> now fulfilling his destiny, impelled as he was by a
> secret premonition of death. But from the moment
> America entered the war, Roosevelt meant the peace
> to be an American peace, convinced that he must be
> the one to dictate its structure.[19]

De Gaulle correctly deduced that Churchill would never
risk an Anglo-American rupture over remote and contingent
French requests, such as participation in the Pacific War
Council or a Military Mission to Mountbatten's Headquarters.
From London, H. Ashley Clarke privately confided to John
Keswick at Kandy that "the atmosphere is unfavourable" in
the "highest quarters" concerning an official introduction
of French troops to SEAC operations. Indeed, Churchill had
already put off pressures from the Foreign Office on this
subject with the casual dismissal: "No need for action yet."
To confirm the obvious, he instructed Eden: "We should adopt
a negative and dilatory attitude." Even after the War
Cabinet approved a 1944 memorandum by the Foreign Secretary
outlining a conditional return of French sovereignty to
Indochina, Churchill stubbornly refused to press Roosevelt
on the issue. "I think it is a great mistake to raise this
matter before the Presidential election," he explained, "I
cannot conceive it is urgent."[20]
While relations between the French and Americans
steadily waned, those between the French and British
steadily warmed (Churchillian resistance notwithstanding),
especially during 1944. Eden and the Foreign Office
continually advocated extending formal recognition to the de
Gaulle group. An aborted draft telegram composed in the
Foreign Office to explain British policy with the Free
French managed to find its way to the British Embassy in
Washington via private channels. This revealing document
focused on the British attitude toward de Gaulle. "We never

chose him," the message stated. "There was no other choice."
Halifax and his staff learned that the Foreign Office had
considered breaking with the controversial French General
"more than once," particularly in the summer of 1942 over
Syria. "We could not abandon him, nor did we wish to," the
statement affirmed, despite American disapproval. "With all
his faults we believe him to be a sincere patriot, untainted
by 'collaboration,' and a good soldier who wishes to fight
the enemy and sees in that the only hope of salvation of his
country."[21]

One of the first thoughtful British proposals for the
restoration of former French possessions emerged in
September 1943 with a Foreign Office memorandum by Linton
Harry Foulds of the Far Eastern Department. He recommended
that both the reconstituted Government in Paris and His
Majesty's Government approach Washington about the principle
of providing postwar facilities for American bases in French
and British territories. Foulds argued that such
arrangements not only would ensure a major goal of French
and British interests by encouraging an American commitment
to collective security but also would increase the scope of
Franco-British cooperation. Foulds explained the need for a
close connection between Paris and London:

Such co-operation will presumably be a vital factor
in our post-war policy and it would be seriously
jeopardised if it could be represented to the
French that we had willingly connived at a plan to
despoil their Empire during their period of
temporary weakness. A France hostile to ourselves
might well be able to supplement her own strength
by diplomatic connexions of a traditional kind,
e.g., a revival of the French-Czechoslovak-Soviet
bloc. It would appear to be a British interest
that there should not be a continental European
block in contra-position to a group formed by the
United States and the British Commonwealth; and one
way to keep the French loose from such a bloc would
be to give them as far as possible a sense of
common interest with this country as an overseas
Colonial Power.[22]

The developing military situation after mid-1943 also
contributed to British acceptance of increased French
responsibilities. The British Chiefs of Staff decided to

permit the French greater administrative control in some liberated portions of their prewar possessions. Restricting its concern mainly to the wartime British military use of facilities throughout key reoccupied areas of France's global holdings, the Joint Planning Staff based its recommendation on the premise: "Unless French goodwill is assured, it is unlikely that any agreement which may be concluded according us facilities in French territory will in practice prove satisfactory." In addition, the impending Second Front through a cross-Channel attack (Operation OVERLORD) lent a new and urgent dimension to this question. "We consider that it is politically most important that at least one French division should participate in 'Overlord' and that it should be engaged at as early a date as possible," the Foreign Office advised the British Chiefs on 3 April 1944.[23]

Negotiating a delicate course through extraordinary logistical obstacles in outfitting the French (Leclerc) Division, American wariness, and extravagant French demands for control in liberated France, the Foreign Office managed to secure a measured French participation in the military operations stretching toward Germany. The British Representative to the French Committee of National Liberation, Duff Cooper, received instructions "to emphasise the very real difficulties" in making use of the Leclerc Division to René Massigli, de Gaulle's Commissioner for Foreign Affairs. Pointing out that Americans simply preferred not to deal directly or officially with the French Committee, Oliver Harvey observed, "While we do not think that the United States Chiefs of Staff mind about this from the military point of view, they are probably afraid of treading on the political coat-tails of the State Department." Two weeks after D-Day another Foreign Office paper argued, "The trouble is, of course, that for political reasons the Americans prefer to use the military channel wherever possible so as to avoid emphasising the governmental status of the French Committee." The author, William Mack, serving as Political Liaison Officer with the American forces in Great Britain, complained, "This is a short-sighted policy since the French naturally resent such treatment where the questions at issue are not of an exclusively military character."[24]

Significantly, the August 1944 treaties establishing Allied relations with the Free French saw Eden approving the Franco-British agreement at the political level but Eisenhower signing the Franco-American pact on military grounds subject to cumbersome American reservations and restrictions. And on 7 August Eisenhower's Chief of Staff, General W. Bedell Smith, finally acknowledged the understandings patiently constructed by Duff Cooper with de Gaulle and Massigli. "We accept the fact that de Gaulle will do everything possible to provide essential reinforcements and will have removed any restrictions in the active employment of the [Leclerc] Division in France."[25]

Military assistance in the Far East represented the next logical step for the Free French after securing a meaningful role in the European Theater. This military emphasis complemented French political strategy by earning British support and eliciting a grudging American acquiescence, however qualified.

As previously noted, this French tactical assault came on a variety of fronts. In March 1943 de Gaulle described Indochina as "incomparably" the best base for Asian land operations against the Japanese. He informed a skeptical American naval mission that the French troops there "were almost entirely gaullist and would rise at his bidding and massacre the Japanese garrison." The Foreign Office did agree, despite the American refusal, to admit French representation on the London Pacific War Council because "eventually we may be driven to set up some body that may be more inconvenient." The British Chiefs demurred about increasing French land forces in Southeast Asia but virtually undercut any opposition from a military standpoint by approving future French naval augmentations to the Eastern Fleet. Originally the French requests had been turned down since there existed no French force to warrant a mission to SEAC. But Dening outlined French plans for a "Corps Léger Francais en Indo-Chine," and commented, "It now looks as if they are creating a force in order to justify the Mission." In March 1944, Mountbatten reported that the French desired either the acceptance of a Military Mission under General Roger Blaizot (French C-in-C, Far East) or the appointment of General De Crèvecoeur (senior French military commander in India) to the SEAC Command Staff. "The firmly implied alternative," Mountbatten declared, "is that they will transfer all their activities to China and take their chance on an admittedly bad wicket." And a Special Operations Executive (SOE) intelligence study concluded that the elite Corps Léger d'Intervention under Blaizot provided "the best means of organising the resistance" in Indochina and recommended inviting the French commander to confer with Mountbatten, since "clearly . . . without General Blaizot's personal authority very little can be achieved."[26]

The politics of French participation in the war against Japan, however, negated the military arguments in favor of such assistance. The Foreign Office endorsed most of the French requests but the British Chiefs decided to obtain American approval before supporting any French role in the Far East. Meanwhile the Americans obstructed and delayed all the British efforts for a joint Anglo-American commitment about French military participation in Asia. As late as December 1944 First Sea Lord Cunningham complained that London still had not received "a definite acceptance" from Washington on the matter. Churchill, of course, refused to rush Roosevelt. "I am a little shy of overburdening the President," Churchill explained to the British Chiefs, who were urging him to intercede for more American support to Indochina. "I hear he is very hard pressed and I like to keep him as much as possible for the biggest things."[27]

Nevertheless, it required no great leap of logic to move from (a) the need for strategic bases and other facilities throughout French possessions accorded to the United Nations during the war to (b) the concept of international facilities for composite forces of some world security organization (the nature of which already had attracted much attention by 1943) in the postwar world. And herein lay the importance of the French connection for British planners.

"During the course of our examination of various postwar questions, we have been impressed by the frequency with which our relations with France appear to be a most important factor in determining our future strategic position," a Post-Hostilities Planning Subcommittee asserted in May 1944. Outlining the global scope of Franco-British proximity, including Africa and Southeast Asia as well as the "major British interests" of facing no hostile power on the Atlantic seaboard, this study stressed in particular the Far Eastern implications: "Our experience in this war has already led His Majesty's Government to decide that it will pay us to maintain not only a friendly but also a strong France in the Pacific, especially in Indo-China." The strategic interdependence, therefore, of French and British interests around the world brought home the need for close postwar cooperation. The group, headed by Gladwyn Jebb, concluded, "We consider it strategically essential . . . that our policy should aim at maintaining a strong and friendly France or that, even if she remains weak, she should at least be friendly."[28]

Unquestionably, British perceptions of imperial interests influenced the warming trend between London and Paris, a pattern noticeably lacking in the progressively chilling Franco-American relationship. The early hesitancy in London towards the French--almost inexplicable, given their common colonial cause--dissolved to cordial cooperation. Twice in 1944 the War Cabinet approved proposals by Eden to support the return of Indochina to France on the understanding that the French accept all security provisions required by an international security organization. Three months prior to OVERLORD, Sir Maurice Peterson explained to the British Chiefs that Foreign Office support for a greater French role in the war stemmed from "the desirability that France should be strong and friendly to us in Europe and that a friendly French policy should be reflected in the French overseas Empire." During the October ordeal of the French to induce official American recognition of the Provisional Government in Paris, another sympathetic Foreign Office paper pointed out that "whatever the circumstances of the postwar settlement friendly relations will continue between Great Britain and France, for Anglo-French co-operation must remain one of the chief aims of our foreign policy."[29]

In his 1943 memorandum Linton Harry Foulds argued that if the French like the British accepted international arrangements or facilities in their colonial possessions the United States could never justify restrictions on French sovereignty. Foulds believed that His Majesty's Government should discourage any move to deprive France of imperial holdings; furthermore, "the reputation of the United Nations for disinterestedness would be severely damaged if they were to treat France in a manner markedly different from that adopted towards the rest." The strong implication, not ever to be mentioned, was that no British territory would be lost, and, therefore, the other colonial empires would also remain intact. But another Foreign Office colleague, Victor Cavendish-Bentinck, also sought to guard the Empire from American encroachments. Of the Washington chapter of the Pacific War Council, he warned, "In fact it is rather dangerous, as President Roosevelt tends there to voice ill-conceived and typically American-wooly views on the future of other people's possessions in the Far East, which are nonsense to some but nectar to the Chinese and Filipinos who grace the Washington Pacific Council." For Cavendish-Bentinck, the logic was clear: the diplomacy of coalition warfare embraced imperial interests. "If the Dutch, French and ourselves do not stick together as regards the Far East," he declared, "we shall experience great difficulty in getting back our own possessions."[30]

Increasing exposure of the unaccommodating American attitude about restoring French colonies sparked serious concern within the Foreign Office, especially after the Cairo-Tehran conversations. An anxious Halifax fretted that "it might be well to take some opportunity of putting the brake on." And Cadogan urged Churchill to champion the French cause since "there is much to be said for the Colonial Powers sticking together." That indefatigable defender of the Empire, Cavendish-Bentinck, again leaped to the attack. He surmised that Roosevelt suffered from "megalomania" (similar to that which afflicted Woodrow Wilson and Lloyd George) and had "gathered a collection of heterogeneous brown and yellow men together" in Washington to wage an evil campaign. "I trust that we shall not allow ourselves to quarrel with the French, without being on very strong grounds, for the benefit of a United States President who, in a year's time may be merely a historical figure," he declared. Yet, Cavendish-Bentinck recognized the hidden threat to all colonial powers in Roosevelt's chastisement of the French colonial administration in Indochina. He cautioned that if the President criticized the education and living standards in that French colony, "the Dutch and

British may later be told that oil reserves in NEI and Borneo haven't been properly developed or that rubber [production] in Malaya or the education of natives don't meet 'Washington standards' and that these territories should be placed under 'United Nations trusteeship' (perhaps with U.S. oil and rubber controllers)." Emotional invective aside, this line of argument struck a responsive chord for British planners. In a January 1944 study, for instance, a Post-Hostilities Planning Subcommittee emphasized the strategic vulnerability of the British Commonwealth "resulting from Indo-China being in the hands of a weak or unfriendly power." Significantly, this memorandum applauded postwar collaboration with the United States in the Far East but strongly opposed risking the alienation of the French to obtain American support "since to do so would be to ensure against one danger at the cost of exposing ourselves to another, more immediate and vital to the Empire as a whole" (i.e., a hostile France facing the British Isles).[31] Thus, the case of imperial interest largely dictated British policy towards the Free French in the latter stages of the war--a rationale fully appreciated, if deprecated, in the United States.

During the deliberations of the 1945 San Francisco Conference to develop an international organization, a worried French Foreign Minister Georges Bidault approached Secretary of State Stettinius with the nervous French hope that the United States still supported the guarantee by Sumner Welles on 13 April 1942. Stettinius reported his indignant reply: "It was made quite clear to Bidault that the record is entirely innocent of any official statement of this government questioning, even by implication, French sovereignty over Indo-China."[32] Although the Secretary of State technically danced with the truth, the thrust of his response appeared deliberately designed to mislead his French counterpart, whose fretful inquiring had been occasioned by a quite different set of impressions in Paris regarding the American attitude. A brief review of American wartime thinking about Indochina reveals just how truthful Stettinius had been with Bidault.

After the first flurry of grandiose guarantees and baseless optimism, American statements about the French Empire in general and Indochina in particular remained relatively subdued until the 1943 summit meetings at Cairo and Tehran. In his conversations with Chiang Kai-shek (23 November) and Joseph Stalin (28 November), Roosevelt contented himself with eliciting from those two leaders at least what he interpreted as endorsements of his preliminary soundings about some form of international trusteeship for postwar Indochina. That same month the Foreign Office endorsed a request from the French Committee to establish an expeditionary force under General Blaizot at New Delhi. The French Committee sent an identical request to the State Department. Hull, in turn, included this development in a general assessment of the situation in Southeast Asia for the President on 17 February. Roosevelt seized the occasion to illuminate the direction of his thinking by insisting that no French forces should be used in the liberation of Indochina.[33]

In March 1944 Mountbatten recommended (a) the immediate assignment of a French Military Mission to SEAC Headquarters, (b) the dispatch of an operational force, the Corps Léger d'Intervention, to India (its sole liaison with SEAC to be carried out by the British SOE), and (c) a commitment to the eventual employment of a full French expeditionary force. Both the British Chiefs and the Foreign Office contacted their American counterparts suggesting Anglo-American approval not only of the three points recommended by Mountbatten but also of French participation in planning for political warfare "in areas in which the French are interested." Also, in early July the State Department requested the views of the President (then in conversations with de Gaulle) about the various French requests. To all these overtures, Roosevelt would offer no response except for a curt comment in late August that he would discuss the matter with Churchill at the Second Quebec Conference (OCTAGON). But even there the two leaders remained strangely silent on the topic of French participation in the Far East.[34]

While the President pursued a determined course to stonewall French requests and British pressures, the rapid march of events diminished his capacity to influence the character of postwar France and French control of Indochina. The White House silence made less likely the realization of American democratic hopes for Indochina (and other colonial areas) and acted to tighten the colonial bonds of Franco-British relations. For example, on 30 August 1944, the French Committee announced that "the fate of the Union of Indochina will be settled according to the wishes of all the peoples of the union, between the Government of the Republic and the Japanese Government and it will be done through armed force." The next day London declared that Blaizot and a small staff would be invited to pay a "temporary" visit to SEAC Headquarters. Moreover, by October Churchill had ruled that the French Mission should be retained there permanently. In addition, the State Department never received a presidential comment to a lengthy memorandum of 8 September, which outlined the full story of French requests. Nor did the White House respond to an October State Department inquiry (passed on from Max Bishop in Ceylon) about the awkward official status of the arriving Blaizot Mission. Indeed, the American Consul in Ceylon, Robert Lewis Buell, tried four times without avail during October to learn the official American attitude toward the French military presence at Kandy. The same month the State Department could only advise the Office of War Information to say nothing about the French role in the Far East, while Roosevelt ended a noncommittal interview with Admiral Ranône Fénard (Chief of French Military and Naval Mission in Washington) by affirming his friendship for France. He escorted the Admiral out with the revealing observation: "Do not be impatient."[35]

On three other occasions, Roosevelt did at least consent to reply to overtures about Indochina from frustrated officials. Elmer Davis of the Office of War Information (OWI) went directly to the White House with his dissatisfaction at the innocuous State Department guideline not to broadcast anything about the French in the Far East. But Roosevelt told him to limit such coverage to "factual news reporting" only and to avoid the subject of French rule in Indochina. A second opportunity arose when Stettinius sent a lengthy report on the evolving situation in Indochina, which explained the French appeals, the OWI issue, and the views of OSS Chief William Donovan that the colonial powers in Southeast Asia were "foreclosing the Americans from any voice in policy matters" there. On 3 November, the President replied by urging Stettinius (soon to succeed Hull as Secretary of State) to explain clearly that "we must not give American approval to any French military mission." Above all, Roosevelt directed that "all our people in the Far East" make no decisions on political questions with anyone, "especially the French." Insisting not only that the United States expected to be consulted on postwar arrangements for Southeast Asia but also that this view be communicated to the full international diplomatic corps in that region, the President concluded, "We have made no final decisions on the future of Indo-China." When Halifax delivered a second British Aide-Mémoire three weeks later at the State Department again recommending American approval of the various French requests as well as confirmation that SEAC might engage in "pre-operational activities" in Indochina, the White House reacted sharply and promptly. The very next day Roosevelt instructed Stettinius:

> It should be called to the attention of our British friends that Mr. Churchill and I do not officially recognize the French Military Mission at SEAC and furthermore, I have made no agreement, definite or otherwise, with the British, French, or Dutch to retain their Far Eastern colonial possessions.[36]

Whether for reasons of health, or exaggerated optimism about the rewards of the unconditional surrender policy, or a desire not to complicate further the normal turmoil of the presidential electoral process, the Rooseveltian reluctance to pursue the issue of Indochina vigorously throughout 1944 unhappily coincided with the liberation of metropolitan France, the warming of Franco-British relations, the growth of French suspicions about American postwar designs, and the general coalescence of the colonial powers. Certainly, if Roosevelt genuinely believed his famous remark to Stalin about the response of the Polish-American vote to the handling of the Polish question, then his reluctance before the election to make known his hardening attitude about stripping Indochina from France becomes more understandable in light of the predictable negative reaction from the numerous Franco-American voters. Yet the disturbing hesitancy to force the issue falsely implied uncertainty.

"I still do not want to get mixed up in any Indo-China decision," he told his new Secretary of State on New Year's Day, 1945. "It is a matter for postwar. By the same token I do not want to get mixed up in any military effort toward the liberation of Indo-China from the Japanese."37

Awkwardly placed because of the determined White House silence, the State Department nevertheless stoutly defended the apparent presidential policy of espousing no policy about either French participation in the Far Eastern war or postwar Indochina. Stettinius dutifully called in Halifax to relay the President's attitude "that any action concerning Indo-China, whether military or political, was premature and he would prefer to discuss the whole question with the Prime Minister."38 To its credit, the State Department did regularly venture soundings of White House views about the French-Indochina problems but the Department's easy acceptance of presidential silence as a license for inaction thwarted the thoughtful planning which long-range considerations demanded and which accelerating events in metropolitan France as well as the Far East made progressively urgent.

To be sure, State Department officials entertained personal preferences about these issues. Hull, for instance, wanted the colony restored to France after the war provided that all parties agreed on ultimate independence for Indochina. Welles generally accepted this view, but favored the establishment of a regional trusteeship council to monitor the development of self-governing institutions. Moreover, in early 1944 a special Territorial Subcommittee endorsed a policy paper calling for the return of Indochina to French administration "subject to international accountability."39

Yet, the State Department never presented a thoughtful analysis of the need for resolute action to prevent the foreclosure of American options by the strengthening coalition of the colonial powers. Electoral pragmatism notwithstanding, the long-term interests of the United States demanded preventive measures against a lapse back to prewar parochialism, for otherwise, what enduring remedy lay in military victory? Colonial-imperial intrigues, symbolized by the de Gaulle-Churchill meeting ("la main dans la main") within a week of the American election, threatened to make a mockery of tremendous wartime sacrifices. Instead of pointing to the urgency of the need, however, the State Department contented itself with obediently passing along the unexplained--and unchallenged--directives of delay and irresolution. Indeed, the American diplomatic corps evidently took pride in this function. "The attitude of the State Department has been, in fact, entirely consistent with that of the President as revealed in his memorandum of November 2 [sic,3],"[40] John Carter Vincent boasted, as if he were affirming the principles of the Declaration of Independence rather than underlining the lamentable pattern of drift and indecision. Thus, the dangerous passivity that plagued American policy had not sprung from unfortunate misunderstandings or distracting preoccupation, but--and here is the real tragedy--had been consciously cultivated at the highest levels of the decision-making process.

While the urgency of the matter lay more in formulation than implementation (results would have to await the Japanese surrender), this lack of forthright planning in Washington not only connoted a dangerous drift in American policy but also disrupted effective coordination within the Far Eastern coalition. Mountbatten, for example, repeatedly reminded the Combined Chiefs of the fast-approaching need to initiate clandestine pre-operational activities in Indochina as Allied military fortunes in Asia progressively brightened. But the American refusal both to define SEAC command boundaries and to allow special French forces to launch those operations severely hampered tactical planning in Southeast Asia. London, too, suffered from this climate of uncertainty. In contrast to American lassitude, British energy mounted plans about relations with France and the future of colonialism. Yet American indecision thwarted these efforts, especially because of the determination of His Majesty's Government not to contradict American desires unnecessarily.

Two examples illustrate the British problem. When Eden prepared his memorandum for the Cabinet in February 1944 proposing the restoration of French control in Indochina, the Foreign Office was naturally intent upon discovering the corresponding American views. Alarmed by reports of a private conversational opinion ventured by Roosevelt that "the French were hopeless," British officials mobilized an

intensive campaign to marshal Commonwealth support behind
the Cabinet endorsement of the Foreign Secretary's
recommendations. But Churchill cut this effort short. "I
do not consider," the Prime Minister cautioned, "that chance
remarks which the President made in conversation should be
made the basis for setting all this ponderous machinery in
motion." A second British dilemma arose when Roosevelt
indicated his "off the record" approval of special French
(Force 136) sabotage operations in Indochina to Halifax in
January 1945. The President, however, added a condition,
which Halifax reported: "He did not want in any way to
appear to be committed to anything that would seem to
prejudge political decision about Indo-China in a sense
favourable to restoration of French status quo ante which he
did not wish to see restored." Describing the British
quandary, the Ambassador pragmatically suggested "to let
sleeping dogs lie." Mountbatten, the Foreign Office, and
the British Chiefs all concurred. Halifax also warned
against any steps "which would call attention to these
[French] activities such as official establishment with
fanfares of the Corps Léger d'Intervention."[41] As these two
episodes demonstrate, the British found themselves virtually
forced into a policy of subterfuge: surreptitiously re-
introducing the French influence in Indochina because of
their inability to discuss or elicit American views at an
official (and therefore policy-making) level.

Indochina was much more a political rather than a
military concern to the Allies during the war. In fact, the
French militarily engaged the Japanese there on only two
occasions--both unsuccessful--during the entire war. The
first came on 22 September 1940, when Japanese troops moving
across the Tonkinese border attacked Lang Son and Dong Dang.
After a brief flurry, all French resistance crumbled within
three days. The second episode, coincidentally in the same
area, followed the complete takeover of Indochina by the
Japanese in the military coup of 9 March 1945. This late
maneuver by the Japanese surprised few knowledgeable
observers. As early as December 1940, the British Commander
in Chief, Admiral Noble, had warned, "Present situation very
difficult; any sign of Free French or de Gaulle movement
breaking out will give crucial excuse to overrun country."
And in July 1944 an SOE study observed, "There are now

definite indications that the invasion of Western Europe, the approaching disappearance of Vichy, and the rapid advance of American forces in the Far East are straining relations between the Japanese and French authorities in Indo-China." This memorandum pointed out that the French in Indochina "are not likely to place themselves in a position of being at war with the victorious Western Powers" and that the Japanese "are consequently contemplating the complete taking over of the country," especially since the French authorities there were expected to renege on their 1941 pledge to Japan to resist any invader.[42]

Military plans to reclaim Indochina languished at the end of the war. Even these plans heightened Anglo-American tensions. For example, the apparently simple decision of which military theater would include Indochina erupted into an Allied cause célèbre. The 1942 arrangements for the short-lived ABDA (American-British-Dutch-Australian) Command designated both Siam and Indochina under Chiang Kai-shek. This nominal authority lingered almost academically until the final plenary session at QUADRANT, which assigned operational control of Siam and "subject to further check, possibly Indo-China" to the newly formed SEAC under Mountbatten. The Generalissimo, however, had not been consulted. Thus, the ever-present problem of "face" required conciliation to Chiang. Aware that stripping even part of the command of Chiang Kai-shek would cause certain humiliation, Mountbatten astutely suggested a gentlemen's agreement concerning lines of authority that would need no formal or public announcement. The terms of this solution, generally outlined during Mountbatten's visit to Chiang Kai-shek in October 1943, took shape in a written understanding 8 November 1943, delicately phrased by General Brehon Somervell, an American observer at the Chungking conference. The gentlemen's agreement explicitly declared, "If the troops are landed in those countries [Siam and Indochina] the boundaries between the two theatres are to be decided at the time in accordance with the progress of advances the respective forces made." This sensitive issue had been skillfully detoured along the reasonable course that the actual character of the land campaigns would shape the ultimate command boundaries. "I pointed out what a young and relatively inexperienced officer I was for such a high appointment but if I could feel that I could lean on his vast wisdom and experience for help and advice that it would be of the greatest help to me," Mountbatten informed an anxious Roosevelt about the Chungking negotiations with Chiang Kai-shek. "This line went over very well with him."[43]

Unfortunately, the gentlemen's agreement did not settle the issue of jurisdiction over any political-intelligence activities in Southeast Asia prior to any launching of full-scale military operations. The British refused a proposal by the Generalissimo to have all political activities in the region approved by a combined American-British-Chinese committee in Chungking. After procrastinating for a month, London finally did concur (as did Washington) in the Chinese contention that because the SACSEA enjoyed control over all Allied forces in his command, the Generalissimo should receive similar authority regarding all British and American troops in the China Theater. The British were convinced that they had gotten the best of the gentlemen's agreement, for, as Mountbatten later pointed out, he already had intentions to move into the Siam-Indochina area "the moment I cleared Burma and Malaya and Singapore," secure in the knowledge that "Chiang Kai-shek hadn't got the capacity" to attempt to occupy that region.[44] Thus, British (and possibly French) forces would liberate Indochina and be in a position to reimpose French colonial controls there. Meanwhile, the Chinese, who probably harbored their own desires about gaining influence in Indochina, would be too busy elsewhere to prevent the return of French rule.

After the 1945 Japanese coup, France implored Washington to send aid to Indochina. Secretary of State Stettinius prepared a draft statement pledging American support to the resistance in Indochina "subject to current and planned Pacific operations." Roosevelt dismissed even this qualified proposal as "inadvisable." Also, the sympathetic British Chiefs of Staff could not provide any help. They unhappily described the melancholy situation of having sufficient aircraft to aid anti-Japanese forces in Indochina but "the manpower shortage rules out" such plans. The President did finally authorize the use of American airpower there on 29 March, but by then the hopeless, unattended cause of the resistance had collapsed. A few days later Stettinius explained to Ambassador Henri Bonnet that "Allied resources must be concentrated on and employed in attaining our main objectives."[45]

The gentlemen's agreement carried with it the seeds of Allied discord largely because of the lack of widespread American recognition. General Albert Wedemeyer, Stilwell's replacement, questioned Mountbatten's claims to pre-operational activities; in addition, the American Ambassador to China, Patrick J. Hurley, knew nothing of the 1943 understanding and accused Mountbatten of dark designs in trying to implement clandestine plans to control Indochina. Churchill warned Roosevelt, "This is a situation from which much harmful friction may spring." But Roosevelt, while acknowledging the existence of the 1943 working agreement, now insisted that all Allied activities "regardless of their nature" be cleared with Wedemeyer.[46] Yet, as already noted, the President further confused this issue when he informed Halifax "off the record" that French clandestine operations there could proceed.

Roosevelt did little to dissipate the confusion before his death. At Yalta he made merely a passing reference to stripping Indochina from France in a private conversation with Stalin on 8 February, and the next day in a plenary session the President quickly qualified his fuzzy vision of international trusteeship: it would apply only to the Japanese Mandated Islands except in the unlikely event that colonial powers voluntarily relinquished their administrative authority. It is significant to note that Roosevelt did not broach the topic at all to Churchill at the Crimea Conference. Undoubtedly the President understood the futility of doing so. In a private conversation at Yalta he said that Stalin and the Chinese liked his idea of trusteeship for Indochina but that the British disapproved. "It might bust up the Empire," he confided, "because if the Indo-Chinese were to work together and eventually get their independence, the Burmese might do the same thing."[47]

During the two months of his life remaining after Yalta, Roosevelt, as noted, seemed only half-heartedly interested in the French plight after the Japanese coup and created considerable mischief with his contradictory statements concerning French clandestine operations. The President still clung to vague views about an Indochina

trusteeship on 14 March during an interview with Charles W.
Taussig, but he retreated from earlier positions by
indicating that he could tolerate a return of French
administration if it promoted eventual independence for
Indochina. Nevertheless, Roosevelt continued to obstruct
French intentions to resume colonial controls there. On his
instructions the State Department pigeonholed a request from
Ambassador Bonnet to conclude an agreement on Indochina
analogous to the Franco-Allied Pact of 25 August 1944, which
affirmed French authority over civil affairs after
liberation. Yet this obstructionist American attitude, born
of idealistic pragmatism and crippled by a lack of bold
formulation, could not long be sustained, especially with
the death of its creator. Therefore, Gary Hess is
essentially correct in his conclusion: "The Indochina
trusteeship died with Roosevelt."[48]

After Roosevelts's death and with the quickening pace
of events in Europe, the French intensified their efforts to
earn a prominent part in the war against Japan. Moreover,
His Majesty's Government became less hesitant about openly
championing the French cause. The British Chiefs
effectively forced the American hand by authorizing the
French Corps Léger d'Intervention to take part in military
operations in East Asia. Despite the American military
point of view that "the use of French forces in that theater
has relatively little if any value," Acting Secretary of
State Joseph Grew advised President Harry S. Truman in mid-
May that the United States was preparing "to help all we
can" in the French projects. Truman declared shortly
thereafter to Bonnet that the United States welcomed in
principle the French offer to provide two divisions for
deployment to the Far East subject to the two conditions
that there be no diversions in the planned allocation of
Allied resources and that the French units be integrated
with "present and planned operations." Truman, therefore,
did not challenge the French proposals.[49]

The French meanwhile pursued vigorous political
offensives in Washington, London, and Chungking. With great
public fanfare, de Gaulle announced the appointments of
French Commanders for the Far Eastern theater, and later the
French Government appointed Admiral Georges Thierry
d'Argenlieu High Commissioner of France in Indochina with

General Jacques Leclerc as commander of the French forces there. Meanwhile, the French Counsellor at Chungking, Achilles Clarac, instructed Ambassador Hurley, "France cannot admit any discussion about the principle of her establishment in Indochina." And Washington regularly received official French complaints about various activities in Indochina. These included charges that Americans were encouraging an independence movement in Laos, refusing to aid French prisoners captured by Annamite revolutionaries, attempting to disarm French troops at Vientiane (on the basis that Allied reoccupation arrangements never authorized French participation), and bombing targets "which did not seem to have any military justification" (especially several strikes against the dikes along the Red River causing flooding and an 8 April attack on Hanoi even though Japanese military targets nearby remained separated from the city "by the whole width of the Red River"). In addition, the French explained with great care to the Foreign Office why they could not comply with British requests to coordinate clandestine and military operations within SEAC boundaries, thereby ensuring that French efforts to reestablish their influence proceeded on an unmonitored basis. Even more important, the French sought British and American assistance in rolling back the mounting Chinese presence in Indochina. In Washington, Ambassador Henri Hoppenot charged that nothing could more seriously hinder cooperation within the Allied coalition than to permit the liberation of Indochina by "Chinese formations which . . . would appear . . . not only as the advance guard of the hereditary enemy of Annam and Tonkin, but as direct descendants of the bands of pirates and Jolly Rogers ['des Pavillons noirs'] who have so long caused the threat of their exactions to weigh upon those regions."50

As for the Chinese, they seemed to move reluctantly from a measured hostility against any French return to a grudging acquiescence at that prospect. "Although earlier Chinese suzerainty does not justify Chinese dominion after the war, this historical association stirs in China a deep interest in the destiny of Indo-China," the Chinese provincial government voice, the Yunnan Jih Pao editorialized in March 1945. Advocating application of the Atlantic Charter to the Orient and holding France responsible "for delivering offhand" the people of Indochina to the Japanese, this government newspaper argued, "Continuation of French dominion is only a burden to France, a yoke to the Annamites and a danger to Far Eastern peace." This editorial undoubtedly summarized the Kuomintang attitude about the postwar status of Indochina. Despite several disavowals by Chinese spokesmen of any territorial ambitions in Indochina, observers in Washington, London, and particularly Paris remained suspicious and skeptical. Nevertheless, official deportment in Chungking carefully avoided giving any offense to the Western powers. In 1944 the Generalissimo promised French Ambassador Pechkoff that "we have no claims in Indo-China nor any of its territory." Foreign Minister T. V. Soong and Ambassador to France Tsien-tai conveyed similar sentiments directly to de Gaulle in a 1945 Paris interview. The Generalissimo instructed T. V. Soong to provide assurances that "China wished France to remain her neighbor in Asia."[51]

The British exhibited nervous acceptance of events in Southeast Asia. Ambassador Seymour and Mountbatten fired off separate warnings about the disturbing implications of potential Franco-Sino-American friction in that area. Shortly after the Japanese surrender, the British Chiefs instructed their Joint Planning Staff "to examine the whole question of boundaries and areas of responsibility in the Pacific." This directive stemmed from an expression of Foreign Office concern about the overall British position in Southeast Asia. "Unfortunately, we must recognize that the mere presence of our forces in Indo-China may involve us in difficulties with the Americans, Chinese, or French depending on the policy we pursue," Sterndale Bennett explained to the Chiefs of Staff. He pointed out that if the British suppressed anti-French activities by the native revolutionaries "we shall open ourselves to attack from American anti-imperialist opinion and no doubt from the Chinese, whereas a policy of complete non-intervention in domestic affairs would no doubt be interpreted by the French as a further step towards our alleged long-term objective of pushing them out of their colonial territories." Agreeing with the French that "the first troops in Indo-China should be white troops with modern equipment," the Foreign Office believed that "the first aim" of British policy should be

the reintroduction of French troops to southern Indochina
and the expeditious withdrawal of British forces. The
Foreign Office proposed that Mountbatten issue a statement
making clear that:

> While he has no wish to intervene in the internal
> affairs of southern Indo-China more than is
> necessary for the fulfillment of his tasks of
> implementing the surrender of the Japanese forces
> and of releasing and evacuating Allied prisoners of
> war and internees, he cannot tolerate any
> activities or agitation which may be detrimental to
> the security and orderly administration of the
> country and thus prejudicial to the fulfillment of
> his task.[52]

If any further undermining of the Rooseveltian concept
were required, at the Potsdam Conference the Allies agreed
to divide Indochina at the Sixteenth Parallel for purposes
of accepting the surrender of Japanese forces there. This
directive allocated the southern portion to SEAC and
northern jurisdiction to China. The British, consequently,
could shepherd French influence back into Indochina while
the frustrated Chinese (and Americans) remained legally
handcuffed north of the British shield. Ironically,
Mountbatten felt that the Potsdam decree reflected a desire
to acknowledge the ideas of Roosevelt and to appease Chiang
Kai-shek. Thus, although Stettinius astoundingly assured
the French at the San Francisco Conference that the American
record was "entirely innocent . . . even by implication" of
any challenge to French sovereignty in Indochina, the
unclear, unviable, and unformulated notions harbored by
Roosevelt in quite the opposite direction had, indeed, been
laid to rest by the end of the war. An apt description of
the wartime story of Indochina surfaced in Sterndale
Bennett's revealing comment that while the details of the
problem there were partially of a military nature, "they are
symptomatic of a fundamental difficulty which, as the COS
have themselves frequently recognised, is political."[53]

The tragedy of the American wartime policy towards
Indochina lay in the fuzzy ideas of trusteeship bandied
about at the White House. The lack of clear-cut planning
and the inexcusable procrastination betrayed whatever
potential value the concept may ever have held. The

American diplomatic corps, armed only with vague notions about a postwar trusteeship, proved hopelessly inadequate to counter the bold, purposeful thrust of the strengthening Franco-British colonial partnership. "Neither General Wedemeyer nor myself has ever been given a definite written directive on Indo-China political policy," Hurley complained, as he witnessed the re-imposition of colonial controls throughout Southeast Asia. Consequently the superficial quality of Roosevelt's views about Indochina virtually ensured the realization of Franco-British ambitions. If the abortive trusteeship idea died with Roosevelt, confusion over the direction of American policy persisted. Dismayed at the apparent indications by Stettinius at the San Francisco Conference that the United States welcomed the restoration of French colonial authority, Hurley pointed to "a growing opinion throughout Asia that America favors Imperialism rather than Democracy in Asia." And the disenchanted Ambassador unwittingly summarized the unfortunate American experience: "I had been definitely directed verbally by President Roosevelt in regard to his policy in Indo-China, but we in this theater have never received a written directive on the political policy of the United States in Indo-China." Perhaps the best epitaph for the Roosevelt concept emerged in the letter of resignation by de Gaulle in January 1946. "The period of transition is now over," he proclaimed. "France, after immense trials, is no longer in danger."[54]

Consequently, a significant opportunity to influence the course of events in Southeast Asia toward a more democratic path had eluded the United States. Unrealistically waiting until the last shot was fired before addressing urgent political considerations, Roosevelt virtually volunteered the surrender of the considerable leverage gained by the United States early in the war. By postponing recognition of the obvious authority of the French Committee of National Liberation and by blocking French requests to participate in the Far Eastern War, the President helped pave the way for a new Franco-British entente. The broader implications of his reluctance to admit the sovereignty of France over Indochina served to reinforce the common bonds of the colonial powers. "The United States expects to be consulted on any arrangements as

to the future of Southeast Asia," the President announced,
but then rejected all overtures from London and Paris for
negotiations on the topic. And the State Department,
divided[55] and awkwardly placed because of the White House
silence, nevertheless, stoutly defended the presidential
policy of espousing no policy about either French
participation in the war against Japan or the postwar status
of Indochina. Despite its numerous memoranda and meetings
about trusteeship and Indochina, the divided State
Department never presented an analysis of the need for
action convincing enough to prevent the gradual foreclosing
of American options by accelerating events in metropolitan
France and Southeast Asia. The commendable concept of
promoting self-government took a sharp turn from reality in
the naive assumption that the war involved only military
considerations. This suspension of political judgment in
Washington, therefore, effectively precluded the realization
of the laudable goals attending American dreams for
Southeast Asia. And in a final twist of irony, the United
States became identified with Western suppression of
legitimate Asian aspirations for self-government. "The
United States, as the dominant power in the Pacific War,
cannot in their [Asian] eyes escape a major responsibility
for post-war arrangements in the Far East,"[56] the State
Department alerted Roosevelt before Yalta. Yet the White
House allowed the situation to drift. While entertaining
completely different hopes for the dependent peoples of
Southeast Asia, the American "non-policy of determined
drift" contributed to the effective undermining of those
very aspirations. And the blurred distinction between
intent and effect later grew more academic to embattled
Asians seeking to affix responsibility for the bloody course
of postwar events. Nor was Indochina the only opportunity
available in the Far East during the war for the United
States to promote its professed democratic ideals and anti-
colonial impulse; the question of the postwar status of
dependent peoples in general was another such opportunity.

CHAPTER VI

TRUSTEESHIP AND THE STRUGGLE FOR "INDEPENDENCE"

One of the key issues that plagued Anglo-American relations during World War II stemmed from each partner's views about the future of dependent peoples and the necessary corollary to that thorny problem: colonialism. Consequently, some of the wartime friction between London and Washington touched on the postwar planning in each country for the restoration or divestiture of the Western colonial empires, particularly those imperial holdings throughout the Far East.

American voices loudly and frequently assailed the evils of colonialism. As self-styled "Defender of the Empire," the eloquent Churchill served as a lightning rod for American criticisms. Churchill and other British officials were often irritated by what they considered to be unfounded American allegations. Nevertheless, His Majesty's Government recognized the overriding long-term need for Anglo-American harmony and, therefore, set out to educate the American people on the actual workings of colonialism in general and the British Empire in particular. The focus for this educational program centered on efforts to arrive at a mutual understanding about the nature of postwar colonial controls.

The first major wartime statement of colonial policy by His Majesty's Government was approved by the Cabinet in early 1940. Malcolm Macdonald, Colonial Secretary under Chamberlain, proposed a new "Vote for Colonial Development and Welfare." The Cabinet allocated a small subsidy of sixteen million pounds for the period ending 31 March 1944. "The whole effort will be one of cooperation between the authorities in the Colonies and those at home," Macdonald promised. "From London there will be assistance and guidance, but no spirit of dictation." Other official declarations in 1940 held out the prospect of Dominion status for Burma and India. The following year, the Atlantic Charter represented the first serious attempt at

Anglo-American accord on the subject, but, as previously noted, fundamental problems about imperial preference and later qualifications by Prime Minister Winston Churchill on the scope of the Charter's principles for the Empire left that whole issue in doubt. Some British officials, nevertheless, revealed a genuine desire to introduce administrative reforms throughout the Empire. In March 1941, the new Colonial Secretary, Lord Moyne, established a special committee on postwar colonial problems chaired by Lord Hailey. And progressive ideas discussed in Parliament particularly sparked American attention. Colonial Under Secretary Harold MacMillan told the House in June 1942 that "we should think of our future relationship with the Colonies as a permanent not a transitory thing." Significantly, he stressed the interdependence of the colonial relationship, especially emphasizing military-economic interaction. Arthur Creech-Jones, a Labour Party specialist in colonial affairs, responded to MacMillan with a call for "a new relationship with the Colonial peoples which conveys the idea of equality and fellowship, the idea of service and practical assistance and which expresses it in dynamic and constructive terms." The enlightened statement from MacMillan also elicited the comment from H. Freeman Matthews in the State Department that the remarks "portray a definite trend towards effecting a real improvement in the economic and social positions of the colonies individually and in their particular relations to empire."[1]

Yet, American barbs, especially those emanating from government officials speaking in an unofficial capacity, continued to trouble British planners. The British Ambassador in Washington, Lord Halifax, explained, "Welles and Wallace may be regarded as President's right and left hands on post-war matters"; however, the quasi-official nature of their expressed views on British colonialism made it difficult for the British to measure an appropriate response. In one typical episode, Sumner Welles let loose casual references to racial equality and an end to imperialism during the soaring rhetoric of his 1942 Memorial Day address. Was this a formal statement of government policy? Anthony Eden promptly requested Churchill to approach the President about discouraging such statements.

"American position is becoming highly absurd," the Foreign Secretary asserted, "for while they apparently contemplate disappearance of Dutch Colonial Empire, and perhaps our own, they have guaranteed integrity of French territories which is more than we have done." And the Dominions Secretary, Clement Attlee, protested:

> The High Commissioners are considerably exercised in their minds as to the habit of prominent Americans including members of the administration of talking as if the British Empire was in the process of dissolution. It will be well for Americans whose knowledge of Dominion sentiment is not extensive to be aware that the British Colonial Empire is not a kind of private possession of the old country, but is part of a larger whole in which the other Dominions are also interested.[2]

British impatience at American misconceptions about the Empire not only spurred exasperated outbursts such as the famous "liquidation" utterance by Churchill on 10 November 1942, but also led to constructive overtures for reaching a true understanding of the issue. A splendid opportunity arose after an August 1942 conversation between Cordell Hull and Halifax, in which the Secretary of State suggested that "the attainment of freedom involved mutual responsibility of . . . parent States and of those who aspired to it." The British Ambassador revealed that the Colonial Office was in the process of preparing a policy statement mainly to ward off uninformed foreign criticisms and especially to warn Chiang Kai-shek against interfering in British imperial concerns (e.g., India). Hull pleasantly surprised Halifax by remarking that a joint declaration would carry more weight for that purpose. The Secretary proposed a possible American-British-Chinese-Dutch announcement embodying "a very clear expression against officious intervention from outside with affairs which were responsibility of parent State." After digesting the report of this discussion by Halifax, Colonial Secretary Oliver Stanley pointed out to the Prime Minister, "It struck me at once that if we could get a Joint Declaration in the spirit of Mr. Hull's words . . . it would be an admirable pendant to your Guildhall ['liquidation'] speech and could not fail to reinforce the effect of that speech both here and in the

U.S.A."[3]

With the approval of the Prime Minister and with the collaboration of Attlee, Eden, and Stafford Cripps, the Colonial Secretary submitted a memorandum on colonial policy which earned the endorsement of the Cabinet on 9 December, subject to the agreement of the Dominions. This memorandum indicated the important political motives behind American anti-colonial rhetoric and asserted, "It is, indeed, certain that much criticism is the result of almost complete ignorance regarding conditions in British colonial territories." Nevertheless, the attitude of the Secretary of State had been unexpectedly satisfactory, and the authors concluded, "We are afraid that if no response is made to Mr. Hull's proposal we shall be faced, in the near future, with some American initiative of a less friendly character."[4]

Explaining that the proposed declaration affirmed "all Colonial Powers should be regarded as trustees bound to take due account of the interests not only of the local population but of the world as a whole," the authors prepared two draft texts for Halifax. The first set out the general policy guidelines within the fundamental need to defeat the present aggression and to prevent its recurrence. This objective looked to conditions of security and prosperity for all, including dependent areas not yet ready to share these burdens. Thus, this first draft asserted, "It will be a clear responsibility for all parent states to enter into general defence schemes designed to ensure freedom from fear for all peoples." In addition, the authors felt that the administering authorities should shape and extend social and political institutions in their dependencies. Then, after a system of international security had been established, the parent states would continue to promote the social, economic, and political well-being of "peoples who are unable, without dangers to themselves and to others, to assume full responsibility for their affairs." The final draft declaration concluded:

> By this combination of defence and scientific and ordered development, the parent States will thus fulfill their responsibilities to those peoples and enable them to enjoy rising standards of life and to continue to advance on the path of progress. In pursuance of this policy the natural resources of

Colonial territories will be organized and
marketed, not for the promotion of purely
commercial ends, but in the best interests of the
peoples concerned and of the world as a whole.[5]

The second draft message to the British Ambassador
addressed the practical application of these principles and
was to be presented only if Hull agreed with the proposed
general declaration. In this section, the British desired
to explore the type of machinery for consultation and
collaboration that could be made available. "For this
purpose Regional Commissions composed of representatives of
such [parent] States should also be made for the
representation of nations which have a major defence or
economic interest in the regions concerned," the authors
wrote. Also they wanted it clearly spelled out that,
despite this international framework, each parent state
would retain administrative responsibility for its own
territories. The authors admitted deliberately avoiding the
reference Hull had made to "the necessity for fitness for
and willingness to fight for freedom" in order to skip over
the awkward positions of Spain, Portugal, and France.
Southeast Asia was suggested as the best region for early
efforts at Anglo-American agreement because (a) the Japanese
occupied the entire area, (b) the need for common defense
was most urgent there, and (c) the United States had some
practical experience in colonial administration in that
region.[6]

Soliciting the opinions of the Dominions about these
draft texts, Churchill appended a message stressing the
importance of the project to each of the four Prime
Ministers. "It is clearly important that we should encourage
the United States to look outwards rather than inwards and
to be a world power rather than a hemispheric power," he
pointed out. "For this purpose we should do well not to
resent but rather to welcome American interest in the
British Colonial Empire, and there would be advantages in so
arranging our affairs that the United States joins in public
acceptance of a line of policy towards Colonial peoples and
their development." Churchill believed that the proposed
Joint Declaration "should do much to clamp down the
restless, irresponsible and ignorant criticisms which have

been prevalent in America."[7] But the responses from the Dominion leaders fell below expectations in London.

Without exception the four Dominion Governments protested the undue emphasis on defense in the draft declaration. Jan Christian Smuts, in London at the time and immediately available for comment, indicated his general agreement, but wanted to play down the idea of defense ("the United States defending the British Empire") while re-asserting the Atlantic Charter. In combatting American prejudices, the South African Prime Minister favored a system of "Empire partnership," in which, he stated, "The multiplicity of small colonies should make way for larger units properly grouped, with somewhat extended authority given to such units." Peter Fraser expressed similar views from New Zealand.[8]

Canada and Australia also stressed political considerations that seemed central to the American attitude. "Greater emphasis might be placed on the rights of native peoples to participate as much as possible in the conduct of their own affairs," Canadian Prime Minister Mackenzie King pointed out, "and the opportunity might be taken to remove misgivings about the universality of the Atlantic Charter and to underline that the various declarations on the necessity of raising living standards after the war apply to Colonies as well as self-governing areas." Dissatisfied that the projected regional commissions would have membership limited only to parent states and nations with major interests in the region, King recommended enlarging the commissions to include nations without major interests in the region (to provide what King labelled "genuine third party opinion") as well as representatives of the dependent peoples themselves.[9]

In Canberra, John Curtin suggested, "Parent states (a better term would be mandatory, guardian or trustee states) should accept the principle of accountability for their trust to some International Colonial Commission operating through machinery analagous to the Permanent Mandate Commission, which, on the whole, was regarded as successful." Curtin, too, wanted wider representation on the regional commissions, including Dominions in the area and "native peoples who have reached or are approaching the stage of self-government."[10]

Lord Linlithgow, Viceroy of India, included his unsolicited views in a personal message to Churchill. While having no doubts about Churchill and Roosevelt working together on this issue, the Viceroy confessed his anxiety about Anglo-American cooperation in the long run. He explained, "A weak P.M. here and an indifferent or electioneering President in U.S.A. might put us badly at a disadvantage." Thus, the proposed statement on colonial policy fared poorly among the Dominions whose general reaction was perhaps best characterized by Prime Minister King: "We fear, however, that the approach will not achieve the desired results unless it is more comprehensive and explicit."[11]

In addition, the Dominions Office received the immediate reactions of the four British High Commissioners in the Dominions. Each also recommended less emphasis on security arrangements, warning that "Americans who don't want to fight to restore the British Empire would feel they were now being invited to guarantee it without receiving any definite new advantages in return." Eden alerted Halifax to these views and also the general consensus that "our proposals should be presented very much as our contribution in the working out of Mr. Hull's own ideas and as a practical application of the Atlantic Charter with perhaps some clearer emphasis on the fact of the continued enjoyment by all of free access on equal terms to raw materials." Halifax agreed that the proposed Joint Declaration contained too great an emphasis on defense; he desired more evidence for the British view that genuine security depended not only on military strength but also on improved social, political, and economic conditions in the less developed areas. The Ambassador explained that Americans believed inequity of these conditions led to exploitation and intervention. Completing his second year in the United States, Halifax revealed a perceptive awareness of the American character. Emphasizing that the "question of presentation is of the highest importance," the Ambassador pointed out, "Tradition leads the Americans to attach great value to general statements of rights and principles." Consequently, he advocated providing Hull with only the "broad heads of proposed declaration" because, according to Halifax, the "Preamble of any declaration in which we ask them to join

will in their eyes be of almost equal importance to the
articles which follow." Together with Lord Hailey, the head
of the special study group on colonial problems who had just
attended the unofficial Mont Tremblant Conference, Halifax
left the British draft version with the Secretary of State
on 24 December. During their brief preliminary discussion
the Ambassador noted, "Mr. Hull was, as I expected,
interested in the raising of social standards as a basis for
[group undecipherable] front fit for freedom and plainly
showed that he was opposed to a system of international
control though favoring international co-operation." Two
days later Halifax and Hailey apparently elicited the
approval of the President for the concept of Regional
Commissions, for at least that was the impression relayed to
London.[12]

On 5 January 1943, Stanley, Attlee, Eden, and Cripps
presented a revised draft of the proposed declaration for
Cabinet consideration. Citing the eventual aims of winning
the war and preventing future aggression, which in turn
required assurances to all peoples of "security, prosperity,
equal status and equal opportunity," this memorandum upheld
"the duty of 'Parent' States to guide and develop the
social, economic and political institutions of the Colonial
peoples until they are able, without damage to themselves
and others, to discharge the responsibilities of
government." This newer version embodied a call "to enter
into general defence schemes" but laid much more emphasis
than had the original draft statement on the "duty of
guidance . . . in the general interest of all nations." For
example, the authors declared that the resources of
dependent territories "should be organised and marketed not
for the promotion merely of commercial ends, but rather for
the service of the people concerned and of the world as a
whole." The proposed announcement suggested a broader base
for the Regional Commissions, to include "people of the
territories" as well as the Parent States and other nations
"which have a major strategic or economic interest" in the
area. The stated goal of this cooperative machinery was "to
promote the advancement of the Colonial peoples and the
general welfare of mankind." Two days later the Cabinet
approved this revised draft after striking out the
references to "equal status" and "eventual" aims and upon

substituting the term "Parent or Trustee States" in place of "Parent States" throughout the declaration. The reaction of the Dominions was generally favorable and echoed the delight expressed by Smuts that the text "seems substantially to meet the American point of view." Halifax, too, indicated his approval and promised to emphasize "the duty of guidance which will appeal to the Americans." After incorporating stylistic changes suggested by various readers, the four authors obtained the endorsement of the Cabinet and final authority from the Prime Minister (at the Casablanca Conference) for this third draft to be delivered to Secretary Hull.[13]

Halifax gave the British draft to Hull on 4 February 1943, but the State Department waited almost two months before answering with a draft of its own. Yet, despite the apparent lassitude on this issue, American views about dependent peoples had evolved to a fairly mature stage by the time of Eden's visit to the United States in March 1943. In mid-1942 Hull confidentially revealed that "the Department is endeavoring to follow closely (1) outstanding ideas both publicly and privately advanced, and (2) trends of thinking in the several United Nations on post-war problems, especially of an international character, and their solution." This monitoring system produced a steady feedback on the trusteeship question and the growing world opinion in favor of an international organization. For instance, from the American Embassy in London, Harold Shantz called attention to British newspaper editorials questioning traditional colonial practices and advocating reforms in colonial policies. Moreover, internal State Department discussions about the postwar status of dependent peoples began to guide American policies. A Territorial Subcommittee concurred in July 1942 that because the boundaries established in the Versailles Treaty had "acquired a certain prescriptive justification," the planning principles shaping American objectives would be "minimum change and minimum displacement."[14]

American thinking about the concept of trusteeship had emerged in an August 1942 interview with the President by Sir R. Campbell. Roosevelt declared that the "trustees for any specific territory should be those of the Big Four Nations which were most nearly interested in the territory concerned." He did not define his interpretation of "interested," but Campbell intuitively felt it "would include both geographical propinquity and old-established interests of other kinds." Understandably vague about specific arrangements, the President made the analogy along "the precise lines of ordinary trusteeship in private life," imagining an initial ten-year term with perhaps a possible renewal for another ten years.[15]

Studies in the State Department on dependent peoples and trusteeship revealed increasingly sophisticated conceptualizations. In late August the Political and International Organization Subcommittee submitted a detailed analysis of a system of international trusteeship for dependent peoples. The proposed arrangement vested final supervisory functions in an Executive Authority of the World Organization, with inspection and information-gathering powers. This agency would also determine when the goal of self-government had been attained. In addition, Supervisory Councils would oversee the trusteeships in each separate region. All members of the Supervisory Councils would be selected by the Executive Authority and would include representatives from the administering states, interested states, and independent states within the region. These Councils would submit periodic reports to the Executive Authority. As an interim working policy, the administering authority would remain with the present (prewar) colonial power over its territories but all administering officials would be required to take a loyalty oath to the International Organization. Each Supervisory Council would have a Secretariat, budgeted by the world agency and specially trained in various fields (health, nutrition, public works, justice, etc.,). Although this version and subsequent revisions failed to consider either enemy possessions or smaller states possibly rendered dependent because of regional security requirements, the planning at this stage persistently emphasized the important point that all colonial powers, while retaining administering authority, had to place their territories under international trusteeship. The supervisory and administrative guidelines stressed (1) preparation for self-government, (2) economic and social justice achieved by the natives, (3) equal economic opportunity established for all,

and (4) contribution to the general international security.
This memorandum explained:

> The final objective of international trusteeship is
> self-government. Its success may be judged partly
> by the rapidity with which it can be terminated.
> Realistically, a dependent people may never attain
> the same economic and cultural independence which
> might have been theirs had the colonial power never
> been there in the first place. Consequently, if
> certain colonial powers should grant partnership to
> their colonies of a kind comparable to free
> membership in the British Commonwealth of Nations
> or on a federal basis granting self-government, we
> should be satisfied.[16]

Hull and the State Department formulated a different
program in a memorandum to the President in November 1942
which examined the "Atlantic Charter in relation to national
independence." The document proposed a system whereby an
agency of the international organization would handle only
those areas now under mandate and any territories detached
from enemy states. "Existing colonial arrangements would
not be disturbed," the Secretary of State pointed out, "but
the colonial powers would undertake a pledge to observe
specified principles of administration and would publish
essential information regarding their colonial
administrations." Thus, despite Hull's admission to an
astonished Halifax that the proposal for a Joint Declaration
had been made entirely on the Secretary's own
responsibility, American plans about trusteeship had, in
fact, significantly matured by the time the British draft
statement was being considered and the conversations with
Eden had begun in late March 1943.[17]

On the basis of the British proposal, Hull modified his
November memorandum on 9 March to describe two other
alternatives for the President: (a) placing all dependent
areas under international trusteeship ("the most drastic")
or (b) establishing international controls over mandated
territories and other areas separated from the enemies while
allowing present colonial administrations to continue under
the general supervision of the International Organization.
Hull still preferred his original November proposal,
however, and suggested it as the "most practical solution

[which] . . . really offers a basis for a forward movement of immense importance to peoples seeking independence, and to our good relations with our present associates, and to the peace and progress of the world." He described the Atlantic Charter as "a monumental milestone on the roadway of man's quest for freedom and independence," which provided the foundation for a "fully cooperative relationship between those who possess independence and those who aspire to it." Harley Notter, moreover, indicated that State Department postwar planning policies were coming into sharper focus with his summary report to Welles of the progress accomplished by each of the specialized postwar planning subcommittees. "As a general principle the peoples of any Far Eastern country or territory under domination of European powers should be liberated after the war," Notter explained, "and such possessions should be placed under an international trusteeship to assist the peoples concerned to attain political maturity and to control the raw materials of the area in the interest of all peoples."[18] Basic principles, therefore, had been firmly established in the troublesome questions of colonial administration and international trusteeship even before Eden arrived in Washington.

Although the Secretary of State later discussed the 9 March memorandum with the President, Eden did not receive a copy until his last day in Washington (29 March). The American draft distinguished clearly between mandated or detached areas on the one hand and colonial possessions on the other. Only the former would come under the regional councils of the international trusteeship program; yet the statement also incorporated the British idea of regional commissions for the colonial areas. Hull stipulated that colonial peoples should be granted progressive measures of self-government and should be given complete independence in accordance with a fixed time schedule. Also, Hull spurned the British term "Parent State"; he preferred to recognize more explicitly that the administering authority must assume "a special responsibility, analogous to that of a trustee or fiduciary." The statement called upon the United Nations to cooperate with the dependent peoples in preparation for independence and charged the United Nations with the duty "to observe in the case of such peoples each of the policies, obligations and methods hereinbefore set forth for observance by independent countries toward their own colonial peoples."[19]

Although there had been no opportunity to explore this issue or the American counter project, Eden informed Hull that after reaching an Anglo-American agreement, His Majesty's Government wished to consult the Dominions, the Dutch, and perhaps other interested parties. Yet, Eden reported to the Cabinet that the American draft "contained a number of points which would be unsatisfactory from our point of view." In the main, the British could not accept the imposition of time schedules or deadlines, and the announced target of full independence implied criticism of fundamental principles of the British Commonwealth of Nations. Self-determination, not an unthinking separation in the name of independence, seemed a more progressive and stabilizing objective to British planners. Furthermore, as the Foreign Secretary pointed out, the American draft statement made no distinction between dependent areas and territories which had lost their independence.[20]

The American draft declaration remained the basis for proposals on international trusteeship by the President at QUADRANT, and by the Secretary of State at the Moscow Conference of Foreign Ministers; however, the topic was not formally discussed at either meeting. Eden had given an aide-mémoire on the subject to Winant on 26 May, but, to the subsequent confusion of everyone, the Ambassador apparently had neglected to forward the new British version to Washington. Meanwhile, official British statements on colonial policy dispelled all doubt as to the intention of His Majesty's Government to retain present Commonwealth arrangements. As already noted, Colonial Secretary Stanley (supported later by Churchill) declared on 5 March that "the administration of the British colonies must continue to be the sole responsibility of Great Britain." And on 13 July he announced, "We are obliged to guide colonial people along the road to self-government within the framework of the British Empire." A month later at Quebec, Hull managed to hold a brief unofficial conversation with Eden about the American draft statement. "Mr. Eden's position was absolutely unchanged at the end of the discussion of this subject," Hull recalled, "and it was perfectly clear that it was the word 'independence' which he found could never have a satisfactory meaning which would cover what various governments might have in mind by this term." W. J. Gallman had earlier emphasized this point in a dispatch from the American Embassy in London which explained that the British references to "self-government" should not be interpreted in the same context as that used in the United States. Another revealing insight into the attitude at the State Department surfaced in the resigned lament by Isaiah Bowman that "British opinion concerning colonial empires was not as advanced as the American." But, happily for the coalition, there were more meaningful attempts to understand the position of His Majesty's Government. In November 1943, a composite memorandum from the special Economic Subcommittee addressed British colonial policy. Examining the pronouncements by the Colonial Secretary, this study concluded that in London

> partnership is conceived as a development and extension of trusteeship. There are no sharp distinctions in meaning between trusteeship, guardianship, tutelage and mandatory. . . . A highly developed imperial, guardian, tutor or mandatory state is still regarded as holding in trust for "backward" peoples and for "civilization" and/or "the commerce of the world," areas insufficiently developed to take full responsibility for their own affairs. Hence the durability of the mandate, with "paramount" stress upon imperial responsibility for the welfare of dependent peoples but also with acknowledged responsibility to the rest of the world.[21]

Until more detailed--but unofficial--conversations on this issue took place during the Stettinius Mission to London in April 1944, which revealed a considerable degree of Anglo-American accord, planners in London and Washington seemed to be passing on different rails. Each group labored on the project tangentially and only dimly aware of the ideas of the other. (Official ministerial statements did, however, lend less flexibility to the British position.) The British emphasis continued to rest with the concept of "Commonwealth" and regional groupings to consult on common problems as well as security arrangements. Thus, these views complemented the planning in progress for a general world organization in that His Majesty's Government always had upheld the doctrine of accountability in its colonial policies. The proposed international machinery fit these British principles, for as Lord Hailey observed, "the power of supervision would still be detached from direct responsibility for administration and its consequences."[22]

Early American ideas lacked a similar overall integration. Americans accepted regional machinery under international trusteeship but strongly opposed the fragmentation of general security responsibilities spread over various regional arrangements. Leo Pasvolsky, special assistant to Hull, emphasized in mid-1943 that the United States could not be disinterested in questions such as frontier adjustments and regional groupings. He spoke of the disjointedness of American planning and argued for an overall United Nations coordinating agency. "There is rapidly being brought to a head the need for the following decision: Should the initial steps toward creating machinery for long-range international activities continue to be taken on an ad hoc basis?" Pasvolsky inquired. "Or should there be created now a coordinated basis for activities in this direction?"[23]

Pasvolsky had identified a key problem in American postwar planning, namely, the need for an overall integrated whole. At a White House meeting prior to the Moscow Conference, for example, the President praised the general concept of trusteeship. "We ought to lay a great deal of stress on the possibilities of the trusteeship idea and apply it widely to all sorts of situations," he theorized, alluding vaguely to the Baltic passages and the Persian Gulf. And Rupert Emerson, in the State Department postwar study group, characterized Southeast Asia as "a region which from many standpoints demands a rationalization that can be achieved only by the abandonment of many imperialist pretensions and by the creation of a regional structure." American policy preparations thus failed to shift out of early abstractions into more practical assessments without abandoning the desired goals ascribed to trusteeship. Indeed to do so, according to one State Department policy paper, "would run counter to public sentiment in this country; it would weaken the principles of the 'Open Door'

and of internationally recognized standards for the
administration of dependent peoples; and it would seem to
ignore the original pledges of the Covenant and the Allied
declarations made during the present war." The British were
equally lax in planning specific arrangements, but were less
at fault because part of the system they were advocating--
colonial administration--had already proved viable within
the British Commonwealth. A special State Department
Committee on Colonial Problems described the difficulty:

> It was noted that most of the policy statements are
> thus far confined to generalities; both the United
> States and Britain advocate the progressive
> development of dependent peoples toward self-
> government. The American spokesmen stress eventual
> independence, while the British appear to envisage
> ultimate self-government within the British
> Empire.[24]

Despite problems on some of the guiding principles for
the imagined trusteeship system, a fundamental Anglo-
American consensus eventually did evolve. The Committee on
Colonial Problems discovered one element of basic agreement
while studying the alleged divergence about the problem of
independence-vs-self-government in September 1943. The
group pointed out that "this difference is less apparent in
actual practice, since the United States Government--as in
the President's recent message to Congress concerning Puerto
Rico--also tends to view its dependent territories as
permanent adjuncts of the national domain." In addition,
the special Pasvolsky Subcommittee on war aims in March 1944
made a similar observation. "British policy with respect to
the administration of dependent areas is in agreement with
American policy," one of its special reports observed, "in
recognizing as the objectives of such administration the
improvement of economic, social, and educational standards
and conditions in colonial areas and the progressive
development of dependent peoples toward self-government."[25]
But the real breakthrough in the joint formulation of the
territorial trusteeship concept came during the visit to
London of a group of State Department experts headed by
Under Secretary Edward R. Stettinius, Jr. in April 1944.
Aware that the British regarded the draft declaration

of 9 March 1943 (which still represented the American position) proposed by Hull as "vague and impractical," the Stettinius Mission set out to settle specific questions such as Italian Somaliland, Libya, the Japanese Mandated Islands, and the possible location of military bases on certain French possessions. As these conversations progressed, the mutual suspicions on the topic of international trusteeship gradually diminished. Stettinius later reported to Hull it had become clearer that "we are actually dealing in an international way with dependent peoples, including colonies, when we undertake to form a general security system under which both military bases and economic matters may be agreed upon." The American delegation cut through the British reluctance to discuss international controls involving imperial affairs by pointing to the value of the Anglo-American Caribbean Advisory Commission, which had been established to deal with commercial relations in that area. The Americans simply inquired whether similar commissions could not operate in other regions. Colonial Secretary Stanley and Isaiah Bowman took the lead in gradually arriving at a common understanding by first exploring the possibility of regional machinery in Southeast Asia, the Mandated Islands, and Italian colonies. Stettinius exulted:

> We and the British found ourselves much closer in our thinking at the end of our several talks than we could have hoped. The need for entering the French colonial field was obvious to our British colleagues and the argument seems to have been accepted that this hope could be realized and the position of the United States in an international scheme clarified with respect to the Pacific islands, only if Great Britain were willing to have the question of dependent peoples brought into the area of international discussion.[26]

To be sure, not all disagreement evaporated. Stanley and his advisers again expressed the British distaste about setting a definite time schedule for the granting of independence. A subsequent State Department study accurately summarized the British attitude: "They regarded as inadvisable the formulation of any general statement of principles regarding the administration of dependent peoples, and stressed the undesirability, from a security standpoint, of multiplying small, independent political entities throughout the world." Yet the Stettinius-Stanley conversations had emphasized congruence rather than conflict on the trusteeship question. Bowman informed the Foreign Office that the State Department still preferred to issue a joint declaration, but one that stressed self-government and material well-being for dependent peoples instead of pressing for political independence. He admitted, however, that American opinion expected international supervision not just consultation. Stanley believed that "the time was past" for such a joint declaration to carry any political value. Instead, the Colonial Secretary suggested that a separate section on dependent peoples should appear in the charter for a World Organization. At the conclusion of these discussions, Stanley presented four guidelines which the participants agreed would serve as the basis for further exploration. He indicated: (1) any statement on colonial policy should become part of the structure for the World Organization and not a joint declaration; (2) "the principle of regional commissions is acceptable to the British if they are not executive in character but are set up to study, recommend and advise. On them should be represented not only parent nations but nations that have major economic and strategic interests in such areas"; (3) "functional branches" of the World Organization (health, nutrition, labor, etc.,) should be linked to the work of the regional machinery and (4) all colonial powers had "a definite obligation" to submit annual published reports "to a control body."27

Point Two, of course, undermined the hopes of the more idealistic planners in the State Department, but it did reflect the preference of Secretary Hull. In fact, American attention to trusteeship before the Yalta Conference stayed within the general framework erected by Stanley. Progressively, State Department drafts proposed that "dependent peoples upon determination of adequate capacity" should become self-governing "on the basis either of independence or of autonomous association with other peoples within a state or grouping of states." Also "regional supervisory commissions" were transformed into "regional advisory commissions" with the doctrine of trusteeship accountability vested in the World Organization. The regional agencies would deal "on an advisory and consultative basis with problems of transport and communication, trade and commerce, health, nutrition, agriculture, labor and education that are of common concern within a given region."[28]

To the surprise of the British, the State Department bypassed the opportunity for valuable consultations by eliminating the subject of trusteeship from the agenda for the Dumbarton Oaks Conference. The explanation lay in a Joint Chiefs of Staff memorandum forwarded to the Secretary of State by Marshall. The General pointed out that any discussion on trusteeship necessarily affected two major military considerations: first, "the incalculable importance" of an early Russian entry in the Far Eastern war; and second, "the very profound changes that will be found in the relative military strengths of the major powers of the world upon the conclusion of the present war." Anticipating the emergence of a powerful Russia in world affairs after the war and foreseeing the likelihood of a considerably weakened British Commonwealth, the Joint Chiefs, for the time being, desired to avoid the awkward situation that realistic and frank discussions of postwar security and trusteeship arrangements would bring. Furthermore, American military leaders were gradually coming to the belief that national security required American control, if not possession, of the Japanese Mandated Islands. Although Roosevelt maintained his "definite desire" that the principle of international trusteeship be affirmed, the original American concept had suffered considerable erosion by early 1945. Preparations for the Yalta Conference revealed that the State Department had retreated to an acceptance of the British demand that colonial powers retain administrative authority over their possessions. By October 1944, Halifax cheerfully reported, "I do not anticipate any serious difficulty with Administration or public over the question of continuance of administration of the Colonies by single power." Nevertheless, a pre-Yalta briefing paper managed to salvage the 1942 aims. Its author, Ralph Bunche, stated, "The broad objectives of policy with respect to dependent areas consistently have been to promote the advancement of dependent peoples through international collaboration in the interest of both the dependent peoples and of the world at large."[29]

His Majesty's Government, meanwhile, adamantly resisted all attempts to convert colonial possessions into international trusts. London unquestionably felt that the British position would best contribute to postwar stability, and that an effective education campaign would dissipate American opposition. "Misunderstanding and ill-informed criticism of our colonial policy as you know is one of the most obstinate irritants in Anglo-American relations," Halifax declared in October 1944. He regretted the lack of publicity for the important policy statement by the Colonial Secretary in the House on 13 July 1943. The Ambassador urged His Majesty's Government to maintain the offensive, "thereby calling the tune ourselves rather than letting the initiative pass entirely to the Americans." He proposed another official statement and stated that Washington would favorably receive the thesis that trusteeship supervision by "countries which have no knowledge of colonial problems and no direct interest or concern in social and economic progress of dependent areas, has proved to be an unsatisfactory conception which it is desirable to replace by a series of regional bodies composed of powers interested in the progress of areas concerned."[30]

Again in December, the Ambassador warned that Pasvolsky had raised the issue of trusteeship which might arise at the forthcoming United Nations Security Conference, although unscheduled for the agenda, in conjunction with the inevitable discussion about the Italian colonies and the Japanese Mandated Islands. "He felt strongly that the ball was with us in this matter now," Halifax asserted, "and that if we could get something moving before the United Nations Conference, it would be a very great advantage."[31]

Immediately after reading this December message from the Embassy in Washington, Churchill addressed the Foreign Secretary:

How does this matter stand? There must be no question of our being hustled. or seduced into declarations affecting British sovereignty in any of the Dominions or the Colonies. Pray remember my declaration against liquidating the British Empire. If the Americans want to take Japanese islands which they have conquered, let them do so with our blessing and any form of words that may be agreeable to them. But "Hands Off the British Empire" is our maxim and it must not be weakened or smirched to please sob-stuff merchants at home or foreigners of any hue.[32]

Eden promptly reassured the Prime Minister, "There is not the slightest question of liquidating the British Empire." He enclosed a copy of a Cabinet memorandum Stanley had drawn up on the basis of the four points produced with Stettinius. "This paper outlines a constructive policy of international co-operation in colonial development which fully safeguards the sovereignty and administrative authority of the responsible Metropolitan powers concerned," Eden observed. He explained to Churchill that "we are anxious to persuade the Americans not to go in for half-baked international regimes in any ex-enemy colonies they may take over, nor to advocate them for others, but to accept colonial responsibilites on the same terms as ourselves."[33]

Still unconvinced and preoccupied with more urgent matters, such as the unexpected German offensive and the perplexing Polish question, the Prime Minister refused to be rushed into an official declaration about his beloved British Empire. Obviously uncomfortable that he had not the time to study the implications of the Stanley proposal personally, Churchill referred to another trusted opinion-- that of his Principal Private Secretary, John M. Martin. "Pray give your mind to this matter and see if we really are being jockeyed out or edged nearer the abyss," he charged Martin on 10 January. The influential assistant replied the same day, "I do not think that the proposals now under discussion involve any danger to our Colonial Empire." In fact, Martin believed the contrary: "they seem to be the best scheme that can be devised" to secure international agreement in ending "the vexatious Mandate System" and "to allow foreign powers a means of expressing their reasonable and legitimate interest in Colonial territories without affecting our sovereignty and executive authority, or entitling them to meddle in constitutional questions, or establishing international bodies possessing powers of interference divorced from responsibility." The Private

Secretary pointed out that the actions of the Regional Commissions were consultative "without executive or supervisory powers." Moreover, Martin informed Churchill that the Regional Commissions would include only states with colonial possessions in the area as well as states with major or strategic interests there. The Stanley memorandum had carefully spelled out the purpose of this regional machinery to secure collaboration in such matters as public health, communications, agriculture, etc., while explicitly eliminating any concern with constitutional issues. "The international agencies will resemble the I[nternational] L[abor] O[rganization] and deal particularly with general questions such as Labour, Health, Dangerous Drugs, Penal Administration and the like and so progressively improve standards in such matters throughout the world," Martin remarked. In addition, although Colonial Secretary Stanley had mentioned a possible "International Colonial Centre" to process and interchange the required reports of the trustees as well as all other pertinent documents and records, Martin dismissed this organization as "simply a clearing house of information."[34]

Although the Prime Minister promised Martin, "I will take your word for it," he could not shake his concern. Outlining his understanding of the Stanley paper on the basis of the synopsis supplied by his Private Secretary, Churchill warily told Eden, "If you are satisfied that this is so and that these proposals involve no danger to our Colonial Empire, I have no objection to further consideration proceeding on the lines you indicate" (i.e., Stanley visiting Washington and the memorandum being sent to the State Department). Eden, of course, could not fail to be sensitive to Churchill's hesitancy on this matter. Therefore, he again discussed the matter with Stanley and relayed more soothing words to the Prime Minister. In a revealing summation of British policy on the eve of the Yalta Conference, Eden explained:

> I have now discussed the matter with the Colonial Secretary and we both feel that our proposals cannot possibly involve any dangers to our Colonial Empire. On the contrary, it seems to us that if they are generally adopted, the position of our Colonial Empire would not be endangered but

rather buttressed and reinforced. A further great
advantage in our now agreeing to present them to
the Americans would lie in the fact that we should
thereby gain the initiative and possibly succeed in
preventing the Americans from circulating schemes
of their own which, if adopted, would endanger our
Colonial Empire. . . . I think, therefore, that
should the President revert to this question during
the forthcoming conference (and only of course if
he does) you might very suitably add that we hope
very shortly to present to his Government a well-
considered plan for international collaboration in
these problems. You might add that you would
greatly hope that the Americans for their part
would not circulate any papers on this subject
until they had carefully studied our proposals.[35]

At Yalta the issue of territorial trusteeship, which
had seemed a potential powderkeg, sailed through to
unanimous agreement with surprising ease, save for a brief
explosion by the Prime Minister in behalf of the British
Empire. On 4 February, Gladwyn Jebb outlined the British
position to James F. Byrnes and Alger Hiss. Explaining that
a comprehensive memorandum already lay before the Cabinet
and Dominions, Jebb stressed the goal of international
collaboration, especially through regional councils, to
promote self-government among dependent peoples as well as
to develop their general well-being. Hiss believed the
concept was inadequate. He thought that all administering
authorities should subscribe to a general declaration of
principles regarding colonial policy, and both Hiss and
Byrnes wanted the subject thoroughly explored at the
forthcoming United Nations Conference. Four days later
Roosevelt and Stalin privately agreed that Korea and
Indochina should be categorized as trust areas. At a
meeting of the Foreign Ministers on 9 February, Stettinius
managed to incorporate in a report to the heads of state the
draft proposal by Hiss that the Big Five "should consult
each other prior to the United Nations Conference on the
subjects of territorial trusteeship and dependent areas,"
and that these issues would be discussed at the United
Nations Conference itself.[36] The presentation of this plan
provided the occasion for the chauvinistic flare-up by an
anxious Churchill.

That afternoon, when Secretary Stettinius read the

report of the Foreign Ministers to the plenary session, the
Prime Minister "interrupted with great vigor," according to
Charles Bohlen, to say that he did not agree "with one
single word" of the statement on trusteeships. Protesting
that he had not been consulted, Churchill shouted that
"under no circumstances would he ever consent to forty or
fifty nations thrusting interfering fingers into the life's
existence of the British Empire." The notes by Matthews of
this eruption have the Prime Minister declaring: "I
absolutely refuse to engage myself in that without
consultation with the dominions. I will not have 1 scrap of
the Brit. Empire . . . [lost] . . . after all we have done
in the war I will not consent to a repres of Brit. Em. going
to any conference where we will be placed in the dock &
asked to defend ourselves, Never, Never Never. . . . Every
scrap of terr. over which Brit flag flies is immune."
Bohlen, less colorfully, reported that the Prime Minister
"continued in this vein for some minutes." Stettinius tried
to explain that the trusteeship concept was envisaged for
the League of Nations Mandates and any territories detached
from the enemies but certainly not to be applied to the
British Empire. Churchill, only somewhat calmed, said it
would be best to specify that the statement did not refer to
the British Empire. He added that His Majesty's Government
desired no territorial aggrandizement, but would not object
if trusteeships were to be considered only for enemy
territories. Even after sitting down, the Prime Minister
continued to mutter, "Never, Never, Never." He suddenly
turned to Stalin and inquired how the Marshal would feel
about a suggestion to internationalize the Crimea for use as
a summer resort. Stalin calmly replied that he would be
delighted to give the Crimea as a place to be used for
meetings of the three powers. Fortunately, there was a
recess at this point.[37]

In fact, during this intermission the Secretary of
State asked Hiss to jot down a summary of the American
memorandum that had earned approval that morning from the
Foreign Ministers. Stettinius then showed this hastily
written note to Churchill who indicated his satisfaction
before the plenary meeting reconvened. The Hiss memorandum
affirmed, "Territorial trusteeship would apply only to: (1)
Existing mandates from the League of Nations. (2) Territory

to be detached from the enemy as a result of this war. (3)
Any other territory that may <u>voluntarily</u> be placed under
trusteeship." Hiss's version also left to subsequent
agreements the matter of identifying which territories
within the three categories would be placed under
international trusteeship, while making clear that no such
specific discussions were contemplated either at Yalta or at
the United Nations Conference. "Only machinery & principles
of trusteeship would be formulated at the Conference for
inclusion in the Charter," Hiss concluded. The wording thus
presented to Churchill was substantially embodied in the
final "Protocol of Proceedings."[38] For all the notoriety
surrounding the decisions made at the Yalta Conference, this
particular agreement has not received the attention it
deserves.

Consequently, by acquiescing in the idea of voluntary
submission to trusteeship authority, the United States had
virtually ensured that all colonial powers would retain
control over all their prewar possessions. But what caused
this retreat from the original American ideal of a
comprehensive system of international trusteeship to promote
independence for dependent peoples?

Actually the State Department had followed the path of
least resistance since the Hull memorandum of 9 March 1943,
which endorsed the continuance of existing colonial
administrations as part of the overall framework for dealing
with dependent areas. But Roosevelt did not abandon
entirely his earlier intention to thwart restoration of
colonial rule. At Cairo and Tehran he enlisted the support
of Chiang Kai-shek and Stalin, overriding Churchill's
objections with the observation: "Now look here, Winston,
you are outvoted three to one." Yet the President
characteristically delayed making a final policy decision
for so long that events virtually preempted his options. By
the summer of 1944 the early presidential firmness had
dissipated. The Joint Chiefs of Staff, as noted, argued
successfully to drop the trusteeship issue from the
Dumbarton Oaks agenda. Moreover, a State Department draft
plan for dependent peoples that had been intended for
consideration at that conference included three categories:
(a) League Mandates, (b) territories taken from enemy
states, and (c) "territories voluntarily placed under the

system by states responsible for their administration." On 15 November, Roosevelt revealed that he still definitely desired a system of international trusteeship, but within a week another State Department memorandum exempted existing colonial relationships from the applicability of international trusteeship, which was deemed suitable only for the administration of mandated and ex-enemy territories. In addition, the President, himself, became more inclined towards the British idea of international accountability rather than trusteeship as the guiding principle for administering colonial possessions. Zealous Americans pressed more idealistic notions of territorial trusteeship on the reluctant British at Malta and again at Yalta that were uncomfortably close to the early proposals of supervision by the World Organization; however, these notions died when Harry Hopkins intimated to Eden at Yalta that the President might not go as far as some of his subordinates hoped in connection with the trusteeship for colonial areas. "I have a line from Harry Hopkins that the President himself may not press this too hard, and I suggest we wait to see what proposal he makes, if any," Eden advised Churchill.[39]

Therefore, the Yalta Protocol brought the virtual demise of any hopes for a progressive readjustment in the treatment of colonial dependencies in the postwar world. The earnest efforts of the British, who truly upheld the doctrine of accountability within the Commonwealth, to develop a workable solution to the problems of colonialism had the unfortunate effect of removing undesirable practices by other colonial powers from direct international supervision through the World Organization. Accountability, consequently, was seriously undermined as one possible safeguard for dependent peoples. Also, the regrettable penchant for procrastination by the President served to erode liberal and humane aspirations concerning the international colonial system. Roosevelt pursued a "non-policy of determined drift," and to that extent, he unwittingly contributed to the progressive weakening of his original concept of international trusteeship.

The interests of coalition warfare, of course, partially dictated the attitude of each partner towards trusteeship. Herbert Feis pointed out, "Whatever the

President had in the past thought should be done about Hong Kong and other British and French imperial outposts, he did not now [Yalta] risk the whole United Nations project by challenging the Prime Minister."[40] But postwar planning also influenced British and American policies regarding colonial systems. Thus, the scheduled United Nations Conference at San Francisco might have provided an opportunity for shaping a more liberal international understanding on trusteeship. But the formula worked out in 1943-1944 and inscribed in the Yalta agreements virtually precluded any radical undertaking by the assembled representatives on behalf of dependent peoples. As the San Francisco Conference opened, Ralph Bunche observed that "the proposed trusteeship system will have little, if any, significance to the colonial world."[41]

Even before the United Nations Conference met, bitter exchanges had erupted between the State Department and the military-naval leaders about American control of strategic Pacific islands. Now the controversy took on a new dimension. The Interior Department entered this debate with its position that if the United States exerted trusteeship controls they should be administered by civilians. The divided American Delegation wobbled uncertainly on this issue at San Francisco. To get around libertarian sentiment about taking over the mandated area, the United States proposed further dividing the already limited applicability of trusteeship. Territories designated as "strategic" would be separated from the other areas. This provision, of course, advanced the desires of the Joint Chiefs in legitimizing American control of key locations in the Pacific. The American plan was to place "strategic" trusts under the Security Council while the General Assembly exercised supervisory functions for the other trust territories through a Trusteeship Council. British anxieties that this arrangement might jeopardize imperial defense arrangements were eased with the insertion of a clause allowing trust areas to remain outside the supervision of the Trusteeship Council if the territory fulfilled its responsibilities "in the maintenance of international peace and security."[42]

The American position became even more awkward when the Chinese on 8 May and the Russians on 14 May introduced draft amendments supporting the eventual goal of "independence" for the trusteeships. Russian delegate Arkady A. Sobolev dryly observed that the term "is very useful to the inhabitants of trust territories because it clearly recognizes, on behalf of these people, those principles and aims which are included among the basic purposes of the Organization."[43] Harold Stassen tried to thwart this maneuver by dismissing any notion about "eternal freezing" of these trusteeship administrations, but the British were much more determined in their opposition. Dominions Secretary Lord Cranborne expressed "full objections" not only to these proposals but also to other embarrassing suggestions about powers of inspection. Furthermore, he opposed an American face-saving call for guarantees of "non-discrimination" by colonial and trusteeship administrating powers.[44] In London, meanwhile, Colonial Secretary Stanley recommended to the Cabinet, "If our essential objectives were not accepted in the present discussions, His Majesty's Government, though willing to adapt themselves to the new machinery that would replace the League of Nations, could not agree to any modifications of the terms of their present mandates."[45]

The Chinese and Russian proposals further divided the American Delegation, which met at the Fairmont Hotel to discuss the problem on 18 May.[46] Stassen asserted that the draft statements on trusteeship being offered by the Americans, British, and French favored the phrase "progressive development toward self-government," and he criticized "independence" as a "provocative word" damaging to Big Five accord. Taussig claimed that the Chinese and Russian proposals would more accurately reflect the views of the late President,[47] while Notter pointed out, "if we maintained the present position we would be spearheading for the British, Dutch and Belgian colonial empires." But Stettinius supported Stassen as did John Foster Dulles, who confirmed that the church groups were satisfied with the term "self-government." Isaiah Bowman darkly referred to the "inevitable struggle" between the United States and Russia. And in that context, he declared "the question would be who are our friends?" Bowman's position in support of the British and French attitude was heavily weighted by that consideration. Despite some unflagging determination

to insert the goal of "independence," the delegation finally
decided to oppose the Chinese and Russian suggestions.
Stassen argued that the position of the United States had
always been that "self-government" included "independence."
Pasvolsky proposed "dressing up" the rhetoric to put more
emphasis on the idea of independence without actually using
that word. Stettinius reminded the group, "The amendments
that we had supported on human rights and on equal rights
and the self-determination of peoples were directly related
to the peoples of dependent areas."[48]

An eventual compromise formula was worked out to avoid
the peculiar awkwardness of the term "independence." The
final draft on trusteeship incorporated the language of the
Atlantic Charter in aiming for "the freely-expressed wishes
of the people concerned." The Russians had persisted in
their reluctance, but after a frank personal approach by
Stettinius to Andrei Gromyko, in which the Secretary of
State reported "I did not mince matters at all," the
Trusteeship Committee reached agreement on 8 June. Twelve
days later, this section of the United Nations Charter
passed "without objection" through Commission II (under
President Smuts) acting in behalf of the full membership.
Lord Cranborne informed this distinguished group that the
declaration on trusteeship represented "the most remarkable
achievement of this Conference."[49]

Thus, the original American ideals of international
trusteeship to guide all dependent peoples toward the
realization of their freely expressed wishes had
considerably eroded by the end of the war. Ambitious
American projects to prevent a continuation of prewar
imperial exploitation proved no match for the skilled
maneuvering of those with a vested interest in colonialism.
Next, even the limited concept of international controls for
mandated areas and territories detached from the enemy
failed to stand against expanding concepts of imagined
security needs formulated by American military leaders in
what became a continuing element of United States postwar
policies. By encouraging the aggrandizement side of the
American domestic debate, the British strengthened the
position of the colonial powers while undermining the
idealistic American position. Churchill correctly
foreshadowed this pattern of events when as early as January

1942 he reassured the War Cabinet that Americans "were not above learning from us, provided that we did not set out to teach them." The United Nations Charter indicated that lesson. The tortuous path from Placentia Bay led almost relentlessly to the ludicrous position of the United States at San Francisco. There, abandoning the ideals Roosevelt had insisted upon in 1941, the American Delegation persuaded itself into a narrow parochialism similar to that which had been so often ridiculed in Washington as an outmoded British imperial weakness. Nor, unhappily, would the journey end in San Francisco. The sad saga of American postwar planning during the war vindicated all too fully a general warning issued by the Foreign Office in early 1942. Describing efforts to devise a world organization, a Foreign Office memorandum advised:

> In considering any plan for the organization of international security it should be accepted as fundamental that human beings are not exclusively guided by high motives or by long and wide views of their own best interests. . . . Many ambitious schemes for the regulation of international affairs stand condemned precisely because they make excessive demands on the wisdom and morality of human nature.[50]

Ironically, a tragic postwar twist would see the United States gradually become identified with the other Western colonial powers as suppressors of legitimate native aspirations for independence. In the absence of strong, clear leadership from either the White House or the State Department, American wartime policy concerning dependent peoples floated almost aimlessly. The ill effects of this uncertainty proved even more harmful in the face of resolute action by the colonial powers to protect their imagined imperial interests. Indeed, the praiseworthy objectives that had marked American efforts early in the war were submerged in a "non-policy of determined drift."

CHAPTER VII

WORLD POLICEMEN AND OTHER POSTWAR VISIONS

Four major reasons explain the gradual weakening of the American objective of international tutelage looking towards independence for all dependent peoples. The first was the absence of any notable support elsewhere for the American attitude which at the same time gave rise to the determined opposition of the British, French, and Dutch. The lukewarm almost passive acquiescence indicated by Chiang Kai-shek and Stalin (at least until the San Francisco Conference) paled beside the formidable counterattacks of the imperial powers, who had vested interests in preserving their colonial controls.

Two other reasons were the need to preserve the cohesion of the coalition and the need to encourage united action in establishing postwar security arrangements. The military necessity of the former remained obvious; the latter gained reinforcement from the growing concept of a world organization. For some American leaders it seemed the height of folly to jeopardize the entire project for international cooperation by alienating the colonial powers. Indeed, these leaders rationalized that the development of an effective international organization meant almost by definition attention to the advancement and well-being of dependent peoples. The benign participation of the opponents of the American trusteeship scheme was deemed vital to the success of the projected world organization. "Our prime difficulty generally with regard to Asiatic colonial possessions, of course, was to induce the colonial powers--principally Britain, France, and the Netherlands--to adopt our ideas with regard to dependent peoples," Hull later declared. "But we could not press them too far with regard to the Southwest Pacific in view of the fact that we were seeking the closest possible cooperation with them in Europe." He identified the American dilemma: "We could not alienate them in the Orient and expect to work with them in Europe."[1]

-154-

A fourth main influence in determining American policy towards dependent areas was the desire of the Joint Chiefs to retain control over the strategic Pacific islands that the League of Nations had mandated to Japan after World War I as well as other dependencies or outlying parts of Japan. The Japanese Mandates were the Marshalls, the Carolines, and the Marianas, which together comprised Micronesia, and the Japanese possessions most often mentioned in American planning sessions included the Izus, the Bonins, and the Ryukyu Island groups. Hull explained, "We [Roosevelt and the State Department] encountered resistance from our own War and Navy Departments, which felt that our ideas conflicted with their desire to acquire sovereignty of Japanese islands in the Pacific for use as United States bases." As early as October 1942 E. D. Hester, Economic Adviser to the High Commissioner of the Philippine Islands, alerted Interior Under Secretary Abe Fortas to the need for beginning preparations for civil government of the Pacific islands. Hester observed that studies for military administrations were already in progress both at an Army school in Charlottesville, Virginia, and in Washington under the Far Eastern Section of the OSS Division of Special Information. State Department analysts favorably reviewed the record of American colonial administrations in Guam (the "unselfish administration" of the Navy), Wake Island (under jurisdiction of U. S. District Court at Hawaii), and American Samoa ("the American people may well be proud of the administration of American Samoa by the U. S. Navy"). By late 1944 the steamrolling American drive across the Pacific had left a problem of considerable concern in its trail: over one-half million Japanese troops still controlled the bypassed areas and eventually would have to be uprooted. Because of the critical manpower shortage of the colonial powers, it appeared that American troops would have to backtrack in order to prevent the Japanese from gaining control through breeding of those islands they had failed to conquer by force. In a personal letter to Admiral Ernest R. King on the eve of the San Francisco Conference, Russell Willson (Vice-Admiral, Retired) commented on the security aspects of the various issues on the agenda for that meeting. Among his concerns, Willson specifically mentioned the Military Staff Committee (United Nations

Organization), international bases, arms control, and "the International Trusteeship System, a question of particular importance to us and one which will require considerable vigilance on the part of our military people to counter the utopian ideas of the International Welfare Group."[2]

Officials and associates in State Department planning circles, of course, represented the bulk of these utopian dreamers that caused the military leaders such great concern. A special Inter-Divisional Area Committee on the Far East considered and explicitly rejected in December 1944 "after a long discussion" the proposal that the United States attempt to gain postwar sovereignty over the mandated areas. The next month Colonial Secretary Stanley visited Washington and encouraged American planning experts to assert control over the Japanese Mandated Islands, but the matter was left to future study. In general, the State Department would go no further to meet the views of the Joint Chiefs than a recommendation that the United States be appointed sole trustee for the mandates within an international system. For instance, just prior to the Yalta Conference, George H. Blakeslee submitted a memorandum on the subject which identified the best interests of the United States with "the principle of international trusteeship for the Mandated Islands modified by incorporating in the instrument or instruments establishing such trusteeship provisions designating the United States as administrator and giving it control over bases which it desires to establish in the islands." Notwithstanding the disenchantment of the military, even this position represented a considerable departure from the idealist spirit of the Atlantic Charter. And Roosevelt himself indicated a similar shift when as early as October 1943 he instructed Hull to lodge a request at the Moscow Conference of Foreign Ministers that the Japanese Mandated Islands be placed under international trusteeship[3]--an arrangement inconceivable without American involvement.

Stimson presented the American military attitude in a detailed memorandum to Stettinius, 23 January 1945. He pointed out that the 1943 Four Power Declaration at Moscow envisaged a General International Organization and an interim consultative organization of the Four Powers, which Stimson believed would act "to maintain the security of the world which they have saved during the time necessary to establish a permanent organization of the whole world." The fulfillment of this task, the Secretary of War felt, encompassed "the settlement of all territorial acquisitions in the shape of defense posts which each of these four powers may deem necessary for their own safety in carrying out such a guarantee of world peace." President Woodrow Wilson had a similar purpose in mind when he proposed a joint covenant of guarantee by Britain and America of the security of France, but, according to Stimson, Wilson had erred in not securing that tripartite arrangement "before the second step of creating the League of Nations whose safety was in large part to be dependent upon such a guarantee." The Secretary of War discerned the same mistake in present American policy "by attempting to formulate the Dumbarton organization before we have discussed and ironed out the realities which may exist to enable the four powers to carry out their mission." Thus, any effort to launch a world organization "will necessarily take place in an atmosphere of unreality until these preliminary foundations are established," for, as Stimson explained, "The attitude of the numerous minor nations who have no real responsibility but plenty of vocal power and logical arguments will necessarily be different from that of the large powers who have to furnish the real security."[4]

Addressing the specific question of the Japanese Mandated Islands, the Secretary of War argued that the trusteeship system would be inappropriate. "Acquisition of them by the United States does not represent an attempt at colonization or exploitation," he asserted. "Instead it is merely the acquisition by the United States of the necessary bases for the security of the Pacific for the future world." Urging that the United States obtain "absolute power to rule and fortify" the mandates, Stimson provided the justification: "They are not colonies; they are outposts, and their acquisition is appropriate under the general doctrine of self-defense by the power which guarantees the safety of that area of the world." He warned that "you will get into endless mazes" by trying to organize trusteeships in these areas "before the necessity of their acquisition by the United States is established and recognized." Stettinius learned from Stimson that the military anticipated a similar problem with regard to basic Russian interests. "She will claim that in the light of her bitter experience with Germany, her own self-defense as a guarantor of the peace of the world will depend on relations with buffer countries like Poland, Bulgaria, and Rumania, which will be quite different from complete independence on the part of those countries," declared Stimson. He concluded by reiterating the familiar attitude of the Joint Chiefs that the subject of territorial adjustments, including trusteeships, should be avoided at least until Russia entered the war against Japan. Otherwise, he stated, such discussions "are almost certain to induce controversies which put at risk a united and vigorous prosecution of the war itself." Dismissing as "fanciful" the notion that discussion of the subject of trusteeship at a general conference could be contained to the overall form of the system, Stimson predicted that the introduction of the topic would "provoke a welter of opinion and great jockeying for position." And he tried to extend some solace to the State Department:

> I think we should not put the cart before the horse. . . . We should endeavor to secure a covenant of guarantee of peace or at least an understanding of the conditions upon which such a general undertaking of mutual guarantee could be based. If there is a general understanding reached among the larger powers I do not fear any lack of enthusiasm on the part of the lesser fry to follow through with the world organization whenever a general meeting may be called.[5]

Stimson, of course, tried to guide the State Department through the awkward discomfort of espousing a policy which seemed to flirt with naked aggrandizement. Apparently this was a new version of the "Never Again" refrain which had been popular during the interwar years. Now, instead of an American foreign policy based on isolationism-noninterventionism, the United States would be actively involved in a general security system--but under conditions that seemed to contradict the fundamental American principles of self-determination. Senator Tom Connally characterized this American dilemma during the San Francisco Conference. "I don't want to be morally in the wrong," he declared during a discussion by the delegation of the Mandated Islands, "but I want to keep the islands." Roosevelt was not insensitive to the apparent conflict between military realities and political ideals, and, as in the case of his attitude toward Indochina, he navigated a gradual retreat. En route to the Cairo Conference he lectured the Joint Chiefs on international trusteeship, pointing out that "this form of administration presents itself to a very satisfactory solution of the government of ex-enemy territory." Exactly one year later the President upheld his belief that the international organization should develop the trusteeship machinery. In fact, he told State Department officials that the military views ran counter to the Atlantic Charter. Nor did Roosevelt think outright American control of the mandated areas was necessary; he cautioned, "All that we would accomplish by that would be to provide jobs as governors of insignificant islands for inefficient Army and Navy officers or members of the civilian career service."[6]

By the time of the Yalta Conference, however, it became clear that the President envisaged unilateral American control of the strategic Pacific islands while reconciling the principles of the Atlantic Charter with the requirements of the American Chiefs under the disguise of international trusteeship. In late December 1944 Roosevelt informed Richard Law that, although he remained "unalterably opposed" to annexing the Japanese Mandated Islands, "from the point of view of military security alone there would have to be something done about them." The President wanted the islands reverted to the supervisory authority of the United Nations with the United States assuming responsibility for actual control. Upon learning of these remarks, the British Cabinet eagerly announced support for the general principle that "a dependent area should be administered and defended by the same power." Sterndale Bennett surmised that the President "was seeking some moral cloak" to cover ulterior motives.[7]

The idea of unilateral American authority (in practice) over the Japanese Mandated Islands did not arise at Yalta, but given the latest views in Washington and London, every discussion of these islands must have carried that implicit assumption; moreover, the Russians entertained similar ambitions under the convenient rubric of international trusteeship.

During a private conversation at Yalta about trusteeships, Stalin indicated a desire for some of the Italian colonial possessions. Byrnes later commented, "He [Stalin] wanted territory--indicating his conception of a trusteeship." In addition, Roosevelt surprisingly endorsed Stalin's claims as a quid pro quo for eventual Russian entry into the Far Eastern war. For the first time the President made a commitment on territorial changes prior to the peace conference. Robert Sherwood labelled this agreement "the most assailable point in the entire Yalta record."[8]

Uncharacteristically, Roosevelt surrendered some of his cherished "freedom of action." Furthermore the Yalta discussions or tacit understandings, as already noted, virtually ensured the return of colonial administrations (including the French in Indochina) via the "voluntary" escape clause in the trusteeship agreement and promoted a serious compromising of the spirit of the Atlantic Charter by allowing for sole American control over the Japanese Mandated Islands. But the historic Yalta decisions in general and the evolving American and British attitudes about international trusteeship in particular defy comprehension without an understanding of the overall conceptualizations of the postwar world in both Washington and London. An exploration of these American and British views illuminates the whole complex issue of dependent areas, including colonialism and trusteeship.

Even before the United States became embroiled in the worldwide conflagration Roosevelt had formulated tentative ideas about the character of the postwar structure. Welles described the President's cherished hope: "If any good came out of the Second World War, it would be the opportunity afforded the Americans and the British to bring order out of the resulting chaos and, in particular, to disarm all those powers who in his belief had been the primary cause of so many of the wars of the preceding century." After the entry of the United States in the hostilities, the postwar conceptualizations of Roosevelt crystallized on the elitist scheme of the four superpowers maintaining international law and order. In April 1943 he confided to his trusted aide William Hassett that "the policy of policing the world was not insurmountable." And he criticized the League of Nations for sidestepping its responsibilities. The Moscow Conference and the Four Power Declaration of 1 November 1943 envisaged a two-staged process, whereby the four great powers would keep the international peace during the interim period before a more sophisticated system under the auspices of a new world organization assumed that obligation. Returning from the Cairo and Tehran Conferences, Roosevelt informed a group of diplomats in Washington that the "peace must be kept by force," and he pointed out that the "World Policemen" would need bases in strategic areas around the globe. Moreover, the President recognized that the areas most likely to spark international friction were the dependencies, especially those possessing critical natural resources and raw materials. He told Admiral R. Fénard in October 1944 that the position of the white race in the Far East would have to be different after the war. "Ideas of independence have become familiar to all the populations who up to now submitted to the authority of the European countries," Roosevelt lectured the uncomfortable Chief of the French Military and Naval Mission. The President announced that he was seeking "a general formula" to deal with tensions between the white and yellow races, the traces of which were already foreshadowed in the American call for a timetable for independence. Summarizing Roosevelt's attitude on this point, Foster Rhea Dulles and Gerald E. Ridinger declared, "He believed wholeheartedly that the future peace of the world would never be assured until the Powers were prepared to recognize the rights of people everywhere--in Asia quite as much as in Europe--to take their place in the international community in freedom and self-respect."9

Naturally, the perceptions of the Joint Chiefs of Staff colored American postwar planning. The military leaders seized the occasion of a British policy paper on the disposition of Italian overseas territories to examine the larger issue of future relations in Europe among the Big Three Powers. "From the point of view of national and world-wide security, our basic national policy in post-war settlements of this kind should seek to maintain the solidarity of the three great powers and in all other respects to establish conditions calculated to assure a long period of peace, during which, it may be hoped, arrangements will be perfected for the prevention of future world conflicts," Leahy asserted in presenting the JCS views to Hull in May 1944. Emphasizing the significance of "the fundamental and revolutionary changes in relative national military strengths that are being brought about in Europe as a result of the war," the American Joint Chiefs considered that any subsequent great conflict would see the great powers aligned on opposing sides. "Since it would seem in the highest degree unlikely that Britain and Russia, or Russia alone, would be aligned against the United States, it is apparent that any future world conflict in the forseeable future will find Britain and Russia in opposite camps," Hull learned. Working from the premise that American intervention in any Anglo-Russian war could only prevent a British defeat without gaining a military victory over Russia, the Joint Chiefs recommended an American policy to cultivate harmonious Big Three relations. "So long as Britain and Russia cooperate and collaborate in the interests of peace," Leahy concluded, "there can be no great war in the foreseeable future."[10]

Nor did the Joint Chiefs of Staff neglect Far Eastern considerations in their postwar planning. "It is imperative that Japan be prevented from controlling the sea and air routes across the Pacific," Leahy advised the Chairman of the Subcommittee on General Security as early as September 1942. Chairman Norman H. Davis discovered from Leahy's report that the Joint Chiefs preferred the United States to make no commitments on "any territory suitable for air and/or naval bases" held by Japan pending further study. And at a meeting of the Security Committee in June 1943 the naval representative, Captain H. L. Pence, stressed the strategic value of the Japanese Mandated Islands which the Japanese referred to as "aircraft carriers." Pence outlined the Navy's plans for an extensive American presence in the Far East after the war, describing the Pacific Ocean as "our lake." Another revealing display of American military projections for the postwar era emerged in the JCS request that international trusteeship be deleted from the Dumbarton Oaks agenda. Anxious that the topic might create a rift in Allied unity, the American Joint Chiefs underlined the importance of continuing great power cooperation after the military victory. "Assuming the effective disarmament of Germany and Japan, nations other than the United States, Russia, and the British Empire may be potential sources of breaches of the international peace and security, as conceived by the General International Organization, but even collectively they will not possess sufficient military power to involve the world in a global war against the concerted will of the three great powers,"[11] the military leaders asserted, reinforcing the underlying theme supporting the President's vague concept of "World Policemen."

One severe complication for advocates, like Roosevelt, of a greater role in international affairs for the United States after the war was the lingering isolationist impulse that had poisoned American diplomacy in the interwar period. The President had to steer a delicate course in patiently guiding public opinion towards an acceptance of the responsibilities of a world power.

"Indications are plentiful that majority opinion in the United States has broken loose from its traditional moorings on the subject of national security from war through isolationism, but that the allegiance of American opinion to any alternative policy has not been secured," Joseph Jones informed the Postwar Planning Committee in March 1943. Actually, at that time there existed considerable evidence that the isolationist anchor had not been cut loose. Within one month of Jones' report, Thomas Dewey refused to come out in favor of simply the idea of a new League of Nations, while a special survey by the Associated Press revealed that exactly one-third of the Senate opposed "committing the United States at this time to post-war participation in an international police force for the preservation of peace" (another forty Senators remained undecided or unresponsive). Moreover, at Yalta the irony was not without significance when Roosevelt admitted that American occupation forces would have to be withdrawn inside of twenty-four months. "I can get the people and Congress to cooperate fully for peace but not to keep an army in Europe a long time," the President declared in an apparent self-contradiction. Thus the leading American advocate of the World Policemen concept could not provide a simple guarantee to fulfill occupation obligations. Reflecting the persistent strain of isolationism in American society, Senator Arthur Vandenberg explained his interpretation of the issue of collective security measures by the international organization. In a private letter to Hull on 29 August 1944, the Senator pointed out:

> It is my view that when our Delegate casts his affirmative vote at such a moment it is a clear commitment on the part of the United States to promptly engage in the joint military action. Therefore it is tantamount to a Declaration of War. I believe our Constitution clearly lodges the exclusive power to declare war in the Congress. I do not believe the American people will ever agree to lodge this power anywhere else.[12]

But Roosevelt moved cautiously within his design, as one 1941 State Department report put it, to "grow" a League of Nations instead of trying to "make" one. Eden was convinced after his 1943 mission to Washington that "it is through their feeling for China that the President is seeking to lead his people to accept international responsibilities." During these conversations he became aware of the general thrust of Roosevelt's thinking about a postwar international organization. The President repeated these ideas to Churchill at the first Quebec Conference. The Prime Minister reported Roosevelt's views about three separate levels: (a) "a General Assembly of all the United Nations in which, presumably, respectable neutrals might find their place. This would provide opportunities for the ventilation of opinion and would be able to pass resolutions but would enjoy no executive power"; (b) an Executive Council, eventually totaling eleven states; and (c) the four great powers, who would "guarantee by force the maintenance of peace and order and the enforcement of Armistice conditions."[13]

Gradually, indications of a growing acceptance within the United States of participation in some form of international security organization began to emerge, despite the significant exceptions of influential isolationist-noninterventionists. Somewhat surprisingly, two public opinion polls in late 1942 estimated that almost three-quarters of the American people favored the Allies starting immediately to plan a world organization. The Fulbright Resolution passed easily on 21 September 1943, and an analysis of the House voting of this call for United States participation in "the creation of appropriate international machinery with power adequate to establish and maintain a just and lasting peace" revealed that "the partisan character of the [negative] vote appears to be less significant than its sectional distribution." A similar measure in the Senate, the Connally Resolution, sailed through to overwhelming endorsement (85-5) on 5 November 1943.[14]

The State Department, of course, responded to the guidance of Hull in support of the President. "It is clearly impossible for us to play the world role now required of us unless the Executive achieves a new responsibility in the conduct of world affairs," Joseph Jones argued in early 1943. The postwar planning effort supervised personally by Hull consistently advocated American involvement in a world organization. A progress report to the President at the end of 1944 explained, "Our policy is to join with other peace-loving nations in assuming the maintenance of international security and peace, both in the interests of our own security and that of all other nations."[15]

Gaddis Smith claimed that Roosevelt "abandoned" the concept of world policemen "in response to the rising enthusiasm in the United States for the formation of a universal collective security organization, the United Nations." Actually, it can be argued that the policemen ideas simply went underground covered in the trappings of the proposed postwar organizational machinery. Thus the "Security Council" served as a euphemism for the elitist ideas of a Big Two or Three or Four or Five, while placing overall (but nominal) authority in the cumbersome General Assembly granted a certain legitimacy to the earlier and cruder presidential conceptualization. Whatever disguise assumed, the basic ingredient of a few great powers underwriting world security persisted in American postwar planning. Identifying this fundamental premise, the special committee studying an international security organization pointed out, "If the three powers develop fundamentally divergent policies and persist in pursuing them at the

expense of the effort to work together to preserve
international peace and security, no arrangements can
finally preserve the peace whether they are of a bilateral,
regional, or universal character."[16]

Some implications of this fundamental, overriding
premise exposed certain inconsistencies with the principles
of the Atlantic Charter. For example, it seemed clear that
the interests of the few great powers, as determined by
themselves, in maintaining international order would eclipse
the lofty political-economic jargon of the Charter. The
American military and naval arguments against international
trusteeship for the Mandated Islands stemmed from the basic
motive of ensuring harmony among the policemen. Moreover,
American discomfort at the glaring contradiction between
claiming control of the Japanese islands and criticizing the
evils of colonial administration was aggravated in light of
the fact that both policies, in part, sprang from the world
policemen concept. That is, apart from the genuine
praiseworthy motives, previously noted, spurring American
anti-colonialism, that stance was also prompted by an effort
to promote postwar cooperation among the great powers. The
Joint Chiefs had made clear their belief that a future war
with Russia was unthinkable and that the key to postwar
stability lay in encouraging Anglo-Russian cooperation. And
Roosevelt drew an important connection between colonialism
and international unrest. "Don't think for a minute," he
told his son Elliott en route to Casablanca, "that Americans
would be dying tonight if it had not been for the short-
sighted greed of the French, British, and Dutch." The
concept of the World Policemen, therefore, served as the
linchpin for prewar ills and postwar remedies. Gaddis Smith
perceptively pointed out:

> From 1944 onward Roosevelt and his advisers were
> fully committed to the early establishment of the
> United Nations as the only way to lasting peace.
> They became increasingly suspicious of Churchill's
> ideas. Ironically, many Americans came to believe
> that British imperialism and continued adherence to
> the idea of the balance of power were greater
> threats to security than anything Soviet Russia
> might do.[17]

Like Woodrow Wilson, Roosevelt firmly believed that once cooperation among the Great Powers had been institutionalized and legitimized within the framework of an international organization, postwar problems could be resolved working through that organization to ensure world stability. The elementary logic held that while all difficulties, of course, would not automatically disappear, the combined might and resources of the Great Powers, acting in unison, would discourage other states from interrupting international peace. "Under this protective umbrella," Raymond O'Connor observed, "nations were to work out their problems without resort to war, and aspiring 'criminals' would be chastened by the overwhelming military superiority of the great powers." Thus, against this backdrop, the actions of the President at Yalta are brought into sharper focus. "Mr. Roosevelt believed that, if handled tactfully, and brought within the legal arrangements of the International Security Organization, the Russians would be no danger to European stability," Woodward asserted. "Hence on almost every point in the discussions at the [Yalta] Conference where the Prime Minister and Mr. Eden were prepared to resist Russian claims or to insist upon concession for concession the President gave only half-hearted support or took the Russian side."[18]

Consequently, to salvage his highest priority item, the postwar international machinery, Roosevelt felt justified in abandoning his precept about no territorial changes before the peace to meet the Russian price for fighting Japan; moreover, he refused to jeopardize the project by colliding with the notorious British inflexibility over the issue of voluntarily placing colonial areas under the trusteeship system. In a related vein, Roosevelt was even prepared to gloss over an obvious compromising of his principles in order to accept the argument of the Joint Chiefs of Staff that unilateral American control of the Japanese Mandated Islands would contribute to international stability. Unquestionably, by the time of his death Roosevelt believed he had succeeded in charting the cherished postwar collaboration of the Big Three, and this conviction induced his rosy interpretation of the Crimean Conference. "Never before have the major Allies been more closely united," he exulted in a message to Congress about this momentous meeting. Roosevelt described his "firm belief that we have made a good start on the road to a world of peace." What did it matter if certain inconsistencies survived Yalta? The postwar structure would remedy any injustices. The Great Powers would guarantee stability, and as O'Connor explained:

> Within the context of this pacific world the peoples could strive for political, social, and economic reform in inaugurating a new era in the history of mankind. An impossible dream perhaps, but this is what Roosevelt believed America was fighting for, and in his pragmatic way he subordinated other considerations to its realization.[19]

Similarly, an understanding of the British expectations about the general postwar structure leads to some insights into the attitude of Churchill at Yalta and into the context of British policy regarding trusteeship arrangements for the Japanese Mandated Islands. Churchill strongly upheld the traditional British faith in the balance of power concept. He seemed not to question the assumption that European stability would lend itself to a general global well-being. Although the Prime Minister impatiently dismissed detailed considerations about the postwar world, he did indulge himself in August 1940 by privately describing his vision of a Council of Europe with a Supreme Judiciary, Economic Council, and common air force. Churchill outlined a nine-member unit including great states of Britain, France, Italy, Spain, and Prussia, as well as four confederations, geographically arranged with capitals at The Hague, Warsaw (or Prague), Vienna, and Constantinople. Russia, he felt, would have to fit into an eastern confederation, and characteristically, Churchill virtually ignored the Far East.[20] But, for the most part, he concentrated on the war effort and counselled his advisers to do the same.

Yet in October 1942 Eden submitted a lengthy proposal based on the vague American notions about "Four Great Powers." The Foreign Secretary concluded that "China apart, . . . the Four Power Plan is thus a practical conception provided its real if not its declared object is to hold down Germany and Japan for as long as possible."

Eden also urged that the system should provide "for regional organizations, for the sharing of bases, for the establishment of certain international technical services, and for new arrangements for the development and disposal of colonial resources." Undaunted by a sharp rebuke from the Prime Minister ("First catch your hare"), Eden presented a much briefer version of his paper to the Cabinet to elicit a wider range of views. Offering "no special proposals," the Foreign Secretary explained, "I would wish to be free, in conversation with our Allies, great and small, and if necessary in public speeches to develop the idea that the world organization of the future must be based upon the close co-operation of the Four Powers within a framework of the United Nations." Receiving some encouragement, Eden added another memorandum in January 1943 emphasizing the idea of regionalism as part of a global security network and suggested that "in the period after the war it will be necessary for the Great Powers to undertake obligations on behalf of the World Council until the latter can be fully organized."21

During his March 1943 visit to the United States, Eden exchanged his own ideas of postwar arrangements with prominent Congressmen and State Department officials. Also, in a particularly enlightening conversation with Roosevelt, the Foreign Secretary gained some valuable insights into the trend of American thinking on that subject. So emphatically did Roosevelt insist on the inclusion of China as one of the Big Four that Eden, as noted, believed the President was employing the sympathy of the American people for the Heavenly Kingdom as a means of leading the United States to accept greater international responsibilities. Roosevelt outlined his view that the international machinery would consist of: (a) a General Assembly, to "blow off steam"; (b) an Advisory Council, including the Big Four plus six or eight other states; (c) an Executive Council of the Big Four, entrusted by the Advisory Council with "pretty wide powers"; and (d) a Moderator, or officer, who could convoke the Advisory Council and Executive Council for consultation. The Foreign Secretary agreed generally with these views except "the extent of the powers which it was hoped might be entrusted to the Executive of the three Great Powers and China" as well as the idea of ranking France below China.

Roosevelt agreed to drop one of his favorite proposals, namely, that only the Big Four would retain national armed forces, when Eden argued that neutrals could not be forced to disarm, that military service represented an "essential feature of national life" in Europe, and that the international organization would be given control over some forces from each country.[22]

Eden returned home impressed with the persistent American warnings "to organise all these United Nations organs on a world-wide and not upon a regional basis." He delivered his report to the Cabinet on 13 April, and the same day Sir A. Cadogan presented a related memorandum to Churchill describing the critical importance of obtaining continuing cooperation among the Great Powers. Everything depended upon their determination to use force to restrain future hostilities, Cadogan stated, and once this agreement had been secured the Allies could then design "all the outbuildings of the future Palace of Peace."[23]

Churchill had responded acidly that Roosevelt's plan "shows the dangers which will attend any attempt to decide these matters while the war is raging." He pointed out, "A proposal to rank France lower than China even in matters affecting Europe, and to subjugate all Europe after disarmament to the four Powers, would certainly cause lively discussion." Yet, in spite of his distaste for spending time in postwar planning, the Prime Minister could not resist revealing his own dreams. In January 1943 he dispatched some "Morning Thoughts" on the subject from Turkey. Calling for "the total disarmament of the guilty nations" and acknowledging the impossibility of trying to make the vanquished pay for the war, Churchill predicted that all countries would be devoting "full energies" for many years to the tasks of "economic reconstructions and rehabilitation." He described the efforts of the United Nations to build a world organization which, in his mind, would include a Far Eastern Council and "an instrument of European government" comprising the larger states as well as at least three confederated blocs (Scandinavian, Danubian, Balkan). He expected that "the most intense effort will be made by the leading Powers to prolong their honourable association, and by sacrifice and self-restraint win for themselves a glorious name in human annals."[23]

When Eden returned from the United States, the Prime Minister took the occasion to address once again the subject of postwar arrangements. His conceptualization included a War Council of Asia "borne forward on the comradeship of the common struggle." But he declared, "It is the Council of Europe which is after all the crux of the matter and of supreme importance." With Russia and China likely to be long preoccupied with reconstruction tasks and with the American presence gone within "four years after the cease firing," Churchill anticipated that "Europe must be a self-governing entity, capable of managing her own affairs, and the assistance given by the United States should be of a soothing and stabilizing character." Later, while in Washington for TRIDENT, the Prime Minister repeated these general views during an informal conversation with leading American officials. Churchill envisaged powerful American, Pacific, and European organizations working under the supervisory authority of a World Council. To avoid unfortunate connotations, the World Council would consist of the Big Four plus other states added by election in rotation from the regional bodies. He attached great importance to the regional principle: "The central idea of the structure was that of a three-legged-stool-- the World Council resting on three Regional Councils."[25]

But the Prime Minister's insistence on regionalism met resistance in many quarters. For example, when His Majesty's Government broached the idea as part of the discussions about a Four Power Declaration at the forthcoming Moscow Conference of Foreign Ministers, Roosevelt dismissed a regional approach because "it smacked too much of 'spheres of influence' policies, the very thing which it was designed to prevent." Ironically, the overall British design did not differ markedly from the American concept. Rather, the London emphasis on regionalism represented almost the sole source of concern in Washington--and among the Dominions. In fact, despite Roosevelt's rebuke, British officials generally agreed with the American idea of a Four Power Declaration. "My first impression is that we would be well advised not to make too many difficulties in regard to this document, which seems to me very much on the right lines," Eden reported after being handed the draft "Four Power" proposal by Hull at QUADRANT. Also, Stettinius discovered during his April 1944 conversations in London about a world organization that "in general, British thinking on this subject seems very similar to our own." But the Under Secretary warned Hull, "In conversation it was clear that Mr. Churchill has not thought out the operations and complexities of regional councils."[26]

Stettinius had discerned that, unlike Churchill, some British officials (notably in the Foreign Office) preferred to "put the weight of world security upon the World Organization rather than upon regional councils." This London fissure became more pronounced the following month at the Conference of the Dominion Prime Ministers. Eden counselled caution to Churchill during these May meetings. "Mr. Hull has committed himself publicly to a world organization of a quite different kind," Eden declared, "and we have been repeatedly warned by Mr. Hull and others that any attempt to organise the world on continental lines before the world organisation itself is set up would probably cause the United States to refuse any permanent responsibility outside its own hemisphere." Churchill learned that a stubborn adherence to his position "might mean abandoning the whole project and with it the best chance that we possess of associating the United States permanently with the British Commonwealth in the maintenance of world peace and security." Yet, the Foreign Secretary felt that these same objectives could be attained "by indirect means so far as possible inside a world organisation based on a drastic reorganisation of the League of Nations." Churchill's vehement support for regionalism, moreover, was unanimously opposed by the Dominion leaders.[27]

Voicing the strong opinions of his three colleagues (Curtin, King, and Smuts), Peter Fraser pointed out their objections to dividing the world into three continental blocs. First, the plan "will encourage the reluctance of States to take part in sanctions against an offending State which is not located in their regions." Second, "it is not a suitable foundation" for the eligibility of states to membership of a World Council. In other words, the Dominion Prime Minister believed that a small country would not be selected as one of the few representatives of its region in the larger body and, consequently, would soon lose its identity even in the regional organization. Third, a Pacific or Asian Council "is an unreal conception." The New Zealand Prime Minister complained, that "we see in an Asiatic region no 'equivalent' to the common racial and cultural background and interests which could conceivably form the basis of unity for the nations of Europe." He listed two other related arguments: the proposed system "might tend to increase rivalries and conflicts between one region and another. . . . [and] might therefore introduce an element of potential discord between the members of the British Commonwealth situated, as they would be, in different regions." Finally, Fraser identified perhaps the most compelling argument against regionalism in that "we know in advance" the United States would reject the idea.[28]

Thus chastened, Churchill accepted the spirit of the criticisms. "Yes, I feel that the idea of Regional Leagues is full of dangers," he admitted to Dominion Secretary Lord Cranborne. "I hope however to rescue 'The United States of Europe' from the midst of them." The Prime Minister preferred a regional approach for many reasons: the advancing Red Army, the weakened condition of France, the unreliability of American resolve to stay the course after the war, and, as Roosevelt believed, "Churchill does not like China." The King's First Minister could not tolerate the idea of Asian intrusion in the family affairs of his beloved Europe as the President's policemen scheme seemed to imply. The notion of Chiang Kai-shek wielding an influence within the British Commonwealth of Nations could render Churchill positively apoplectic. "As to China, I cannot regard the Chungking Government as representing a great world power," he had complained in chastising Eden in 1942 for working on a Great Power postwar design. The Prime Minister revealed some of his more substantive concerns about China with the remark: "Certainly there would be a faggot vote on the side of the United States in any attempt to liquidate the British Overseas Empire."[29]

The Foreign Secretary shared this concern; in his January 1943 recommendations for postwar arrangements, Eden declared that "we must assume that all the Four Powers (with the exception of China) are in principle equally interested in maintaining the peace everywhere in the world." When Eden reported the American ideas to the Cabinet, Churchill ridiculed the concept of Four World Policemen. "The idea that China is going to have a say in the affairs of Europe 'other than ceremonial,' or that China should be rated for European purposes above France or Poland or whatever takes the place of Austria-Hungary, or above even smaller but ancient, historic and glorious States like Holland, Belgium, Greece and Yugoslavia--has only to be stated to be dismissed," he exploded.[30]

Often Churchill incorporated a slap at the Kuomintang regime while referring to other subjects. For example, in sending his congratulations to Eden on the news of the Four Power Declaration at Moscow, the Prime Minister included a critical aside: "It is remarkable that the Russians accepted China." When John Martin called his attention to a July 1941 Gallup Poll which estimated that only thirteen percent of the American public disapproved United States membership in a World League, Churchill minuted: "Good, but only on condition China should be the head of it." And while cabling his views on various proposals to the British Delegation at Dumbarton Oaks, he indicated his agreement with a Russian plan to include the Big Four in a Security Council "subject of course to the fact that China will be in great disorder by that time." But Churchill presented perhaps the most revealing explanation of his criticisms against Roosevelt's postwar concept in a memorandum to Eden at the close of the London Conference of Dominion Prime Ministers. He pointed out:

> As I see it, the Big Three or Big Four will be the trustees or steering committee of the whole body in respect of the use of force to prevent war; but I think much larger bodies, and possibly functional bodies, would deal with the economic side. You should make it clear that we have no idea of three or four great Powers ruling the world. On the contrary, their victory will entitle them to serve the world in the supreme respect of preventing the outbreaks of more wars. We should certainly not be prepared ourselves to submit to an economic, financial and monetary system laid down by, say Russia, or the United States with her faggot vote China. The Supreme World Council or Executive is not to rule the nations. It is only to prevent them tearing themselves in pieces. I feel I could argue this very strongly from the point of view of

derogations of national sovereignties.[31]

But against this backdrop, the Prime Minister worried that a world security system, including the projected Big Two or Three or Four or Five, would collapse in the face of a revival of some form of American isolationism. He believed that American occupation troops would withdraw within four years, in other words before Europe had recovered and while the Red Army might still be at least as far west as Berlin. Consequently, although Churchill was willing to support the concept of a world organization, he began to hedge that bet. "The underlying thought is to embody all that was best in the League, while remedying its defects," the Prime Minister declared in designing a world organization. In particular he wanted more leeway for the Great Powers, authorized to act "without a too precise definition of the circumstances." Yet he was clearly uncomfortable in dragging out the frustrations associated with the League of Nations. Resolved to remain prepared against a similar disillusionment after this war, Churchill journeyed in October to Moscow to draw figures with Stalin and in November to Paris to re-establish the traditional French connection.[32]

On 25 November the Prime Minister notified Eden, "I think we should have a talk in the Cabinet pretty soon about the Western bloc." Noting the prevailing "hopeless weakness" of that area, he asserted, "That England should undertake to defend these countries, together with any help they may afford, before the French have the second army in Europe, seems to me contrary to all wisdom and even common prudence." But Churchill realized the risks involved. "I cannot imagine," he stated, "that even if we went on with taxes at the present rate, which I am sure would be ruinous for economic revival, we could maintain an expeditionary Army of 50 to 60 divisions, which is the least required to play in the Continental war game." He argued instead that "with a strong Air Force and adequate naval power the Channel is a tremendous obstacle to invasion by Armies and tanks." That same day the Prime Minister cabled to Stalin: "There has been some talk in the Press about a Western bloc. I have not yet considered this."[33]

Eden responded in complete accord. The Foreign

Secretary agreed that Western Europe "behaved very foolishly between the two wars," but he pointed out that the record of His Majesty's Government was not entirely praiseworthy either. "It has always seemed to me that the lesson of the disasters of 1940 is precisely the need to build up a common defense association in Western Europe . . . pursuing what you have so aptly called the policy of 'one by one.'" Describing the bloc scheme as a British "defense in depth," the Foreign Secretary advocated that France and the smaller Western European states "agree to organise their defenses together with us according to some common plan." Similar views to those of Churchill and Eden had surfaced earlier. The Dumbarton Oaks Conference looked forward to the "establishment of regional security associations within the framework of the World Organisation." And on 20 October, a special Foreign Office group interpreted this Dumbarton Oaks statement as a "green light" to launch preliminary discussions with a view to a multilateral, Western European security association. The British Chiefs, too, had made clear during that conference that they anticipated the formation of regional sub-committees of the Military Staff Committee of the World Organization. But by playing all these options--which London considered only prudent--the British ironically reinforced familiar American suspicions about dark motives and parochial interests. Leahy concurred when Joseph E. Davies criticized the Prime Minister for "being 'first, last and all the time' a great Englishman . . . more concerned over preserving England's position in Europe than in preserving peace." The Admiral affirmed that the American Joint Chiefs felt the same way "throughout the war." Indeed even a month after the German surrender, as Brian Gardner pointed out, "This impression of Churchill as a greedy, imperialist ogre, straight out of a Chicago Tribune cartoon, munching up praiseworthy little Balkan states, was still firmly lodged in the minds of American statesmen and service chiefs."[34]

Therefore it is clear in an examination of the trend of thinking by Roosevelt and Churchill prior to February 1945 on arrangements for a World Organization, international trusteeship and colonial administration, that at least on those issues the Yalta Conference represented a continuation of existing patterns rather than an abrupt turning point.

Similarly, the United Nations Conference at San Francisco reinforced previous decisions on the limited scope of the trusteeship concept, especially as applied to colonial areas and the Japanese Mandated Islands.

Reporting to the President in January 1945 on events at the Institute of Pacific Relations Conference in Hot Springs, Philip C. Jessup revealed, "In general it seemed to me that the British view insisted on hanging on to the colonies in the Pacific area--first for economic or trade reasons; second (but a close second) to re-establish and maintain the prestige of the British Empire in Asia; and only third for security." Roosevelt learned from Jessup that the French and the Dutch both supported British efforts to reestablish the colonial system "without embarrassing international interference." But the trusteeship formula, worked out in 1943-1944 and set down in the Yalta agreements, had already precluded such interference unless voluntarily requested by the administering power. And, as noted, Ralph Bunche had sadly concluded even before the San Francisco Conference opened that the proposed trusteeship system would not affect Western colonialism.[35]

It is a general characteristic of war that military fortunes impress themselves directly onto the political scene. Therefore, the fact that scheming or maneuvering for postwar position occurred in World War II is not unusual. What is sadly ironic, however, is that one of the last major military decisions of that conflict--the decision to drop the atomic bomb--taken in the full confidence that hundreds of thousands of lives would be saved in the long run, contributed to three decades of subsequent tragic warfare and untold human suffering as well as political turmoil. Moreover, the use of the atomic bomb, while leading directly to the surrender of Japan, also played an important, if indirect, role in the concluding chapter on the issue of the restoration of Western colonialism in the Far East.

CHAPTER VIII

HIROSHIMA-NAGASAKI:
SOME UNINTENDED CONSEQUENCES FOR WESTERN COLONIALISM

One of the most significant factors dominating the course of events in the Far East after the Second World War was the presence on the Asian mainland (including Southeast Asia) of unconquered Japanese forces. The unexpectedly sudden termination of hostilities, brought about largely through the two uses of the atomic bomb, signalled the start of a grim race to liberate Japanese-occupied territories. Although historians continue the controversies intertwined with the dropping of the atomic bombs on Hiroshima and Nagasaki, the connection between the two atomic bombings in August 1945 and the protracted postwar struggles endured by indigenous nationalist movements in the Far East remains relatively unappreciated.

Allied planners worried about the prospect of eliminating Japanese resistance commensurate with the war aim of unconditional surrender. As late as VE-Day several problems of the United Nations, including the growing war-weariness, the psychological letdown after the German surrender, the ubiquitous burden of logistics, and the increasing intrusion of political considerations, made it very difficult to foresee accurately the end of the war against Japan. Perhaps the overriding consideration lay in the severe sacrifices anticipated in an invasion of the Japanese home islands (Operations OLYMPIC [later named MAJESTIC] and CORONET) in addition to the heavy tolls expected in simply attaining the general tactical positions necessary to launch the final stage. No other factor in analyzing the strategic decision to use the atomic bomb compares in importance to the unhappy--and politically unacceptable--assessment that over one million casualties would be exacted as the Allied price to occupy Japan. Even then, victory would not be certain, for the frustrating prospect seemed likely that the Japanese authorities would shift to secure strongholds on the mainland, like Manchuria, and prolong hostilities virtually indefinitely.

Indeed, the determined Japanese resistance encountered throughout the war consistently affected fundamental Allied military planning. The Allied approach to fighting in the Far East was colored by the character of the opposition in a way not reflected in European strategy. Only eighteen months after Pearl Harbor, Winston Churchill warned, "All we have seen of the Japanese shows that they fight to the death to an extent not equalled by any other race possessing modern weapons." Later at OCTAGON, Franklin D. Roosevelt worried about the "fanatical Japanese tenacity,"[1] recounting for the British the recent ordeal at Saipan where Japanese soldiers and civilians chose suicide rather than surrender.

Repeatedly, the Japanese demonstrated their fixed purpose not to yield any territory to the Allies voluntarily, thereby providing shocking previews of what lay ahead for those who dared to violate the homeland. For example, of the three thousand Japanese troops at Tarawa in November 1943, only seventeen surrendered; and in February 1945 at Iwo Jima, two hundred Japanese prisoners were taken of the original twenty-one thousand defenders. This stark Pacific scenario compelled Allied strategists to seek other means to end the grueling process of the war. Russia could not be persuaded, but might voluntarily join in; moreover, the strategy of encirclement and blockade (including offensive naval-air operations) was not guaranteed to achieve unconditional surrender. Suddenly another factor entered the planning equation that presented an alternative to a costly invasion. Critics who in retrospect flail the decision to use the atomic bomb against Japan unrealistically lose sight of the situation in mid-1945 by focusing on subsequent postwar developments. The two atomic bombings had, as Henry L. Stimson later affirmed, "saved hundreds of thousands of Americans, British, and Japs who would have perished if the invasion that we were setting on foot had taken place."[2]

On 20 August 1945, the Supreme Commander of the Japanese Army announced in a Domei broadcast monitored in Australia that "America has disregarded all principles of humanity" by using "a most deadly inhuman weapon" against the civilian population "mercilessly," and therefore Japan had accepted the terms of the Potsdam Declaration. But this

statement emphasized the significant point that the homeland
as well as other Japanese-occupied areas were still
"unchallenged," and despite the recent official decision to
surrender, "the dignity of the Imperial Nippon Army remains
supreme." Indeed, the sudden abbreviation of the war
stranded millions of Japanese troops in units intact
throughout the Far East. Many of these units held positions
of great strength, capable of prolonging hostilities far
beyond mere procrastination, and bewildered at the
inexplicable acquiescence of Tokyo to Allied demands. For
example, the attitude of the Japanese forces in Burma
particularly reflected an inability to comprehend the
imperial order to lay down arms. "They do not consider that
they have been defeated and say so quite openly," warned M.
E. Dening, British Political Adviser to Lord Mountbatten,
after returning from the surrender ceremonies at Rangoon.
Dening informed the increasingly concerned Foreign Office
that "the situation is still fraught with danger."[3]

Separate American and British estimates of the Japanese
Order of Battle described ground forces in excess of 6.5
million, with over two million of that total guarding the
home islands. Even though the Philippine Islands had been
retaken, there remained 44,000 Japanese troops there at the
end of the war. In addition, there were 55,000 in Thailand
(plus 90,000 Thai troops); 60,000 in Burma; 110,000 in
Indochina; 100,000 throughout the Mandated Islands; 116,000
in Malaya; and over 490,000 in the Netherlands East Indies
(NEI). One revealing indication of the confusion reigning
on the Asian mainland after the abrupt Tokyo surrender
emerged in the fact that almost three million Japanese or
puppet troops were still actively engaging the Allies in
China (including Formosa) and Manchuria. Remarkably, no
major incidents in China arose during the interim period
between the imperial announcement of acquiescence on 14
August and the surrender ceremony at Nanking on 9 September.
Near-chaos prevailed in China for a month, and it is largely
to the credit of Japanese discipline that no significant
trouble erupted. Enclosing a report about the proceedings
at Nanking by the Commander of British Troops in China, Sir
Horace Seymour explained, "The situation described by
General [Sir Eric C.] Hayes must indeed be unique in the
history of warfare." Japanese forces protected the railway

between Nanking and Shanghai. "Public order was . . . being maintained entirely by the powerful and undefeated Japanese Army," the British Ambassador to China continued, not only in Nanking but also Tientsin and Shanghai. Seymour relayed Hayes' belief that law and order in eastern China "depends almost entirely on the Japanese and when they are disarmed one cannot help wondering what will happen."[4]

Similar conditions existed throughout the South East Asia Command (SEAC), where Mountbatten as Supreme Allied Commander (SACSEA) apparently had no other choice in preserving law and order than to authorize Japanese troops for policing duties. He remained alert not only to the dire implications of such short-run exigencies but also in the long run to the myth-making potential inherent in the absence of decisive Allied military action against all Japanese forces in the Far East. In a letter to General Douglas MacArthur shortly after the Japanese notice of surrender, the SACSEA declared:

> I am sure that your views coincide with mine, namely that it will be the greatest mistake to be soft with the Japanese. The fact that you have been prevented from inflicting the crushing victory which OLYMPIC and CORONET undoubtedly would have produced and that I have been prevented from carrying out ZIPPER and MAILFIST [Malaya-Singapore, NEI] will, I fear, enable the Japanese leaders to delude their people into thinking they were defeated only by the scientists and not in battle, unless we can so humble them that the completeness of defeat is brought home to them. Normally I am not a vindictive person, but I cannot help feeling that unless we really are tough with all the Japanese leaders they will be able to build themselves up eventually for another war. . . . Although everyone must be delighted at the early termination of the war, nevertheless, I cannot refrain from expressing my feelings to you on realising that the tremendous operations that you were to command will not now take place.[5]

Mountbatten had good cause for concern at the nature of the Allied victory because most of the areas allocated to his command still belonged to the Japanese as of 14 August 1945. Suddenly, SEAC forces faced the need to occupy Malaya, the Netherlands East Indies, Indochina, Siam, and much of Burma as soon as possible rather than by planned stages through a series of gradual military operations. A severe case of indigestion afflicted the Allies. The unplanned military victory not only brought enormous problems for the necessary occupation-liberation tasks but also carried serious political ramifications.

In virtually every country throughout the Far East the Allies encountered a nationalist, left-wing, politico-military association aspiring to independence. These indigenous groups received encouragement either from the Japanese (Indonesia, Indochina, Burma), from the local resistance that had risen to oppose the Japanese (Philippines), or, indeed, from a curious admixture of both influences (Malaya). Nor did it go unnoticed that the only independent entity in Southeast Asia--Siam--had managed largely to avoid devastation in a war that inflicted great suffering on colonial areas supposedly under the protection of European imperial powers. Moreover, the Japanese experience shattered most of the underlying principles of colonialism and exploded the myth of white supremacy.

In Malaya the startling Japanese triumph exacerbated the marked social cleavages that historically divided that country. Native Malayans tended to welcome the Japanese invader as a means of ridding themselves of economic domination by the Chinese population. To avoid the cross-firing persecution of the Malays and the Japanese, many of the Chinese fled to the safety of the jungle. There the more militant Chinese Communist element formed the nucleus of the resistance: the Malayan People's Anti-Japanese Army (MPAJA); and while not all Chinese refugees in the jungle were communists, these squatters universally entertained anti-Japanese, pro-MPAJA sympathies. Thus, the classic elements of the "fish-water" syndrome in guerilla warfare had been established.

Despite an agreement with Mountbatten to fight the Japanese in return for SEAC supplies, the MPAJA maintained essentially a defensive posture. Immediately after the Japanese surrender, however, communist propagandists convinced much of the population that the MPAJA deserved the credit for expelling the invaders. Their success stemmed from a combination of factors, such as the lack of outside communications, the abrupt end of the war, and the interim delay before SEAC reoccupation. Also, the MPAJA maneuvered to consolidate its position and sought to transform lingering anti-Japanese sentiment into a broader anti-foreign attitude. The Malayan population, meanwhile, had risen to new heights of political awareness under Japanese tutelage. Retreating from their own ambitions of aggrandizement to a more realistic policy of "Asia for Asians," the Japanese encouraged the nationalist aspirations of the Malayan population, while simultaneously fanning anti-Western antipathy. Thus, under quite different influences and motivations, the two major segments of the population in Malaya anticipated an end to prewar colonial ties.

Before the British authority returned, communist leaders Lai Teck and Chin Peng conducted a brutal campaign of retribution against the Malayan element of Japanese sympathizers. The Malays, of course, retaliated not only out of self-defense but also in the determination to avoid returning under the Chinese economic yoke. In this escalating process, the distinction between Chinese who were communists and Chinese in general blurred, just as the entire Malayan population--not simply the collaborating element--fell victim to the militant communists. After stockpiling arms and ammunition in jungle caches, Lai Teck finally agreed to cooperate with the British occupation forces. Each MPAJA guerilla received $116, a ration of rice, a promise of employment, British medals, and a copy of Mountbatten's speech at the formal reoccupation ceremony; moreover, Chin Peng--the number two communist--was flown to London to receive the Order of the British Empire and to lead the Malayan contingent in the Victory Parade. It is a matter for idle speculation as to what might have happened if the planned, gradual liberation of Malaya through ZIPPER and MAILFIST had taken place, or if SEAC occupation forces had arrived promptly. There can be little doubt, however, that in the interval between the Japanese surrender and the Allied return the fuse had been lit to ignite another fifteen years of upheaval in Malaya.[6]

Similarly, social disorder in the Netherlands East Indies and Indochina at the end of the war promoted political agitation that had endured from prewar antecedents. Under Japanese occupation the two countries became, at least in name, sovereign, independent states.

Japanese conquerors in the NEI set free many of the political prisoners who had been detained by the Dutch. Those released included nationalist leaders Mohammed Hatta and Achmed Sukarno, who were opportunistically willing to collaborate with the Greater East Asia Co-Prosperity Sphere program. Tokyo proclaimed--and initially treated--the NEI as Japanese territory. In doing so, Japanese leaders hoped to create a diplomatic bargaining chip. They expected the Allies to be eager to compromise for peace, and this newly acquired territory (as part of Japan) might prove useful to them in negotiating for that compromise. But Allied military successes eventually forced Japan to modify this position. In September 1944 Tokyo promised eventual independence for the NEI. Also, the Japanese established the Investigating Committee for the Preparation of Indonesia's Independence (DOKURITSU JUMBI CHOSAKAI) during the summer of 1945. With the flurry of events in August, however, Hatta and Sukarno accelerated their plans. Upon notifying the Japanese occupation commanders of their intentions, the two nationalist leaders declared the Indonesian Republic just two days after the unexpected Tokyo capitulation. Once again, a relatively long and fateful period intervened before the prewar colonial power could begin any meaningful program of reoccupation. The relatively untested Japanese forces in the NEI (notwithstanding some notable Allied inroads) openly supplied the Indonesians with arms and permitted the nationalists to assume administrative functions, which even included the replacement of selected Japanese forces guarding the Dutch military and civilian internees.[7]

Sukarno gave some indication of the extent of indigenous dreams for a "Pan-Indonesia" on 11 July 1945. "I have never said that Indonesia comprised only those areas that were ruled by the Dutch," he declared to the sympathetic Japanese Investigating Committee. "When I look at the islands situated between Asia and Australia, and between the Pacific and Indonesian [sic] Oceans, I understand they are meant to form a single entity." This ambitious rhetoric, reflecting strong anti-colonial motives, pointed to a postwar collision with the Dutch. Dutch officials, meanwhile, suffered the added frustration of uncontrollable circumstances. Despite assurances that the British Foreign Office "strongly favors closer association" with the Dutch in the Far East, logistical difficulties, shortages of Allied shipping, SEAC priorities in Burma, and the determined Japanese resistance had all combined to thwart the prompt return of the Dutch to the NEI. To complicate matters even further for the Dutch, the uneven liberation of Holland by the Allied forces in Europe (because of the race for Berlin) had also hindered the organization of comprehensive civil-military reoccupation teams. Many important colonial administrators and other key officials remained under detention in German-occupied areas of Holland.[8]

Dutch leaders voiced displeasure at the apparent lack of Anglo-American responsiveness to their needs. "In view of the very different war records of the Dutch and the French in South East Asia," the Dutch Minister for Overseas Territories, J. H. A. Logemann, argued that "Java should have a much higher priority than Indo-China and that, if necessary, the release of ten to fifteen thousand men from the Far East should be delayed so that the maintenance of law and order could be ensured until the arrival of an adequate number of Dutch troops." On 25 May 1945, Dutch Colonial Minister Hubertus J. von Mook (also Governor-General of the NEI) complained to the State Department requesting "urgent action" be taken to provide not only the transfer of Dutch marines to the United States for training before undertaking the liberation of the NEI but also the transport of troops and civil affairs personnel to Australia for the required preparations before actually administering the liberated areas. "Both projects are of the highest importance for the future of the Kingdom," von Mook explained. He cited the "unexpected slowness" in freeing Holland completely from German influence. Since 1940, the Colonial Minister pointed out, all Dutch shipping had been placed at Allied disposal, and he particularly referred to the "grievous losses" suffered by the Dutch Navy during the bleak stages of the war. Thousands of volunteers were now clogging Dutch ports, awaiting duty in the Far East. Von Mook warned, "The Netherlands Government cannot possibly acquiesce in this state of affairs." And in London, Dutch Minister P. J. Gerbrandy expressed similar concerns, even going so far as suggesting that the Pacific War Council be revived to explore Dutch needs.[9]

Actually, Washington and London--for different reasons--welcomed the reintroduction of Dutch influence in the Far East. The United States interpreted the wartime Dutch pledge about developing self-government in the NEI as a stabilizing influence in the postwar Pacific; the British attempted to shield their own imperial interests by championing the return of another Western colonial administration. H. Freeman Matthews forwarded the complaints of von Mook to the State-War-Navy Coordinating Committee with the observation: "The Department of State considers that it is politically desirable that the Netherlands should participate in the liberation of the Netherlands East Indies to the fullest extent permitted by military considerations." Another State Department memorandum reminded the President that the French had given no guarantees about an enlightened colonial policy after the war. "The State Department perceives no political objection to Netherlands participation in SEAC," Roosevelt learned from this memorandum, "except in so far as it may have a bearing on French participation." Similarly, the British provided assurances of their support. Churchill promised Gerbrandy, "I will not lend myself to any trickery to deprive the Dutch of their territories." Ironically, the same day as the Nagasaki bombing, Mountbatten worked out detailed arrangements for the full Dutch civil-military complement with H. R. H. Prince Bernhard, Commander-in-Chief of the Dutch Forces.[10]

Allied assurances notwithstanding, the deteriorating situation in the NEI rapidly worsened after the sudden Japanese surrender. Dutch determination to reassert imperial authority clashed with the Indonesian people's aspirations for independence--well nourished by the Japanese occupation forces. Concern for a colonial partner's troubles led the Foreign Office to abandon previous caution. In October 1945 Foreign Secretary Ernest Bevin ordered a draft statement prepared for Mountbatten, emphasizing that "while he has no wish to intervene in the political affairs of the NEI more than is necessary . . . he cannot recognize any authority not approved by the sovereign Power; nor can he tolerate, so long as he is responsible for the NEI, any

activities or agitation which might be detrimental to the
security and orderly administration of the country." Two
months later the Chief of the Imperial General Staff,
General Sir Alan E. Brooke, underlined British anxiety about
the NEI by travelling to a Singapore meeting with
Mountbatten. Their communique called for "a more active
[SEAC] policy for Indonesia."[11] But, as in Malaya, the
situation in the NEI on 14 August 1945 virtually ensured
active indigenous resistance against Western efforts to
reimpose prewar colonial controls. Nor would the
circumstances in Indochina alter this melancholy pattern.

An almost identical dilemma developed for the French.
The fall of metropolitan France had exacerbated the problems
of the French colonial administration in Indochina. As
already noted, from 1940 to 1945 the Governor-General,
Admiral Jean Decoux, struggled to negotiate a course through
Japanese demands, Siamese designs, Allied requirements,
Vichy regulations, French imperial interests, and indigenous
aspirations.

Relations between the French and the population groups
of Indochina, never smooth, were particularly stormy in the
early years of the war. Pragmatic French diplomats played
upon known Nazi-racist predilections to appeal with fair
success during the June 1940 armistice talks that Germany
not only maintain a foothold in Asia for the white race by
sustaining the French colonial administration but also
persuade its Far Eastern Axis partner, Japan, to ameliorate
the severe pressures on Decoux. Unlike in Malaya and in the
NEI, in Indochina Tokyo did refrain from overt control (until
9 March 1945). The French colonial administration, however,
enjoyed only nominal independence. Moreover, the people of
Indochina remained unconvinced of the benefits of colonial
status. At the end of 1940, the French Administration
ruthlessly suppressed local uprisings at Lang Son (executing
the veteran revolutionary Trang Tung Lap), Do Long (northern
Annam), and My Tho (Cochin China). Yet rising expectations
persisted in Indochina; one State Department briefing paper
for the Yalta Conference informed Roosevelt, "There is
considerable independence spirit among the Annamites."[12]

The Japanese took complete control of Indochina on 9
March 1945, chiefly because of the unconcealed growth of
pro-Gaullist sympathies among the French population. On the

day after the Japanese coup, President Kuniaki Koiso
disavowed any territorial designs there and promised to
support indigenous movements for independence. Under
Japanese pressures, King Norodom Sihanouk of Cambodia,
Annamese Emperor Bao Dai, and Laotian King Sisavang Vong of
Luang Prabang abrogated their treaties with France to
proclaim independence. A Japanese-sponsored "National
Federation of Tonkin" at Hanoi promised to participate in
the Japanese Co-Prosperity Sphere. Also, a civilian
Japanese governor assumed authority in Cochin China (a
French colony, not a protectorate). General supervision
throughout Indochina, however, rested in the hands of the
Japanese Commander-in-Chief, Field Marshal Juichi Terauchi.
Nevertheless, some resistance groups, such as those under Ho
Chi Minh, refused to collaborate with the Japanese and
actively engaged them until the sudden announcement of the
Japanese surrender.

Unlike the 1945 circumstances in the NEI where Allied
liberating efforts had at least begun successfully, military
operations to reclaim Indochina languished barely out of the
planning stage. Surprisingly, despite the intense
controversy generated by the theater boundary dispute and
subsequent "gentlemen's agreement" misunderstandings, the
participants at the Potsdam Conference elected to divide
Indochina at the Sixteenth Parallel in efforts to spread
the load of occupation responsibilities. Ambassador Patrick
J. Hurley described this fateful decision as "purely an
expedient operational matter," while, enlightened by thirty
years of retrospect, Mountbatten dismissed that historic
demarcation as "crazy."[13]

The dropping of the atomic bombs and the unexpected end
of the war aborted the military operations designed to
absorb Indochina along gradual lines commensurate with
Allied resources. The failure of the Allies to reoccupy
that country immediately and thus ensure an orderly transfer
of authority away from the unconquered Japanese forces set
in motion a fateful chain of events. As was the case in
Malaya, the delayed process of reoccupation in Indochina by
the Allies strengthened the position of an indigenous,
leftist, military association. Bao Dai abdicated a week
after Tokyo surrendered. On 2 September, a Provisional
Government under Ho Chi Minh (which had been established on

29 August) issued a declaration of independence at Hanoi, consciously modeled after the American version of 1776. While de Gaulle railed at what he considered contrived Anglo-American delays (actually caused by severe shortages in shipping) in transporting French forces and administrators to Indochina, the British and Chinese struggled to fulfill their obligations of joint occupation south and north respectively of the Sixteenth Parallel as provided in the Potsdam Declaration. Once again, a deadly interval worked against the goals of the victorious powers. The Japanese military, undefeated in battle, represented the only stabilizing force in Indochina. The Japanese, furthermore, voiced sympathy for native dreams of independence. Admiral Decoux, imprisoned at Loc Ninh, could not persuade the local Japanese commander, General Tsuchihashi, to release him after the surrender announcement. Guerilla groups harboring expansive political ambitions expected to fill the void after the Japanese withdrawal. The French, of course, refused to admit any discussion about reestablishing their prewar authority in Indochina, but it was a claim they could not immediately enforce.[14]

At a conference in Saigon with the French and Annamites on 9 October, British officials disavowed any political ambitions in Indochina. The British purpose, they explained, was only to disarm the Japanese and then to evacuate expeditiously. The small French force would participate in processing the enemy troops. The Annamites indicated a desire to cooperate in the occupation, but the native representatives did not conceal their intention to oppose the French if necessary to gain their freedom once the British had departed. The following day, five British soldiers died when their patrol was ambushed by irregular native forces. Local SEAC commander, General Sir Douglas Gracey, as a result of this incident and numerous other similar clashes, suspended the official sanction of the Viet Minh to continue occupational duties. On 13 October, Gracey ordered all property restored to its "rightful" ownership, thereby ensuring the return of the preponderant French prewar influence. Gracey declared that the responsibility given to native leaders had "gone to their heads," but since they had ignored his orders, they would now be punished.

Several Annamite villages were burned, and local populations suffered from the harsh systematic searches conducted in attempts to eliminate what Gracey described as "pockets of resistance areas." Meanwhile the increasing French forces, sympathetic to the vociferous demands of the French civilians for death to all Annamites caught carrying arms, carried out brutal independent operations of their own.[15]

Despite their avowed desire to leave as soon as possible, the British experienced great difficulty in extricating themselves from the Indochina tar baby. In mid-October Mountbatten advised the Acting French Commander-in-Chief in the Far East, General Jacques Leclerc, that the British force commanders at Saigon would retain their civil as well as military authority but would work through the local French civil administrations as these agencies were established; moreover, the SACSEA delegated added responsibility in military matters (especially clandestine activities) to the French forces. The British Chiefs honored French requests for both "the rapid transfer of two Spitfire Squadrons to Indo-China" and accelerated movement of the Ninth French Colonial Infantry Division there from Marseilles. In December, Mountbatten confirmed Foreign Office estimates that he could not keep to his earlier premature assessment to withdraw by Christmas. The SACSEA promised that the British Force 136 in Indochina could terminate in another month, but "residue commitments" required the continuing presence of a special British unit of 569 men on an indefinite basis. He explained, "There is no doubt that these personnel are, at the moment, doing important work, especially insofar as the settlement of ex-guerilla forces is concerned."[16]

The mushrooming British role in Indochina alarmed some perceptive observers. General Sir William Slim, for instance, worried about the non-conciliatory French attitude as well as the grave implications of British involvement in reimposing the imperial powers. "The real and underlying danger is that the situation may develop so that it can be represented as a West versus East set-up," Slim cautioned the British Chiefs. "I need not point out how extremely dangerous this may be." The pattern of confrontation, in fact, had been established in the absence of planned military operations in successive stages allowing for the gradual liberation of Indochina by the Allies. Such operations were barely in the planning phase when Japan surrendered. On 1 January 1946, General Gracey and French High Commissioner Admiral Thierry d'Argenlieu finally reached accord on the termination date (4 March) for SEAC responsibility in Indochina in favor of the French.[17] The sad prologue included three decades of virtually uninterrupted hostilities.

A somewhat similar 1945 interregnum unfolded in the Philippines. American arrangements for the granting of independence to the Philippine Islands were in the Tydings-McDuffie Act of 1934. Anticipating a gradual program of development to independence in 1946, the Americans found their plans derailed by the swift Japanese conquests in early 1942. Japanese Prime Minister Hideki Tojo promised immediate independence to President Manuel Quezon, and there is no doubt that the prospect enticed a number of influential Filipinos. Quezon recommended that the United States grant immediate independence to forestall the Japanese offer. He also suggested that the embattled Japanese and American forces in the Philippines mutually withdraw as part of his compromise package. General MacArthur and High Commissioner Francis Sayre endorsed this proposal, but Stimson, Marshall, and especially Roosevelt, all disapproved. The President instructed MacArthur to hold out as long as possible. In addition, Roosevelt tried to bolster Quezon's morale by pointing to occupied China as a typical example of the Japanese concept of "independence." In March, MacArthur escaped to Australia on direct orders from Washington, while Quezon arrived in the United States.

The Filipinos suffered from brutal Japanese treatment despite the lip-service paid to their autonomy by Tokyo. After retaking Manila in February 1945, the victorious MacArthur handed over civilian authority to Sergio Osmeña (Quezon had died in the United States the year before) and the new Commonwealth Government. Perhaps fortunately, for the sake of political stability, the United States adopted a lenient attitude toward the disturbing evidence of collaboration with the Japanese by certain Filipino leaders. Overcoming their initial reluctance, American officials proceeded with plans to bestow independence as originally scheduled. Elections in April 1946 saw Manuel Roxas replace

Osmeña in time to preside over the proclamation of independence on 4 July 1946.[18]

Unlike the experiences elsewhere in Southeast Asia at the end of the war, military operations in the Philippines had succeeded in evicting most of the Japanese forces. Liberation plans were already being implemented when Tokyo capitulated. Furthermore, the presence in the Philippines of an influential leftist organization with a military nucleus arising out of the resistance movement was attributable more to local conditions on central Luzon than to a heroic struggle against foreign suppression. The Hukbalahaps continue to sustain an impressive influence three decades later by addressing domestic ills, such as widespread corruption and the need for extensive agrarian reforms, perhaps in spite of rather than because of their considerable communist tinge.

Siam (or Thailand) as the only independent entity in the region presents an interesting case study in contrast to the colonial territories in the region because of its fate during the war and immediately thereafter. A bloodless coup in 1932 brought a liberal, Western-educated group of militarists to power under Luang Pradit, succeeded in 1938 by Colonel Luang Pibul. Two years later Pibul concluded a non-aggression pact with His Majesty's Government. Almost immediately Thai-British relations deteriorated as the Japanese subjected Bangkok to increasing pressures. London, nonetheless, relied on the strength of economic ties to prevent trouble; as one Treasury officer remarked, "It looks as if it would be a somewhat expensive process for Thailand to quarrel with us."[19]

Yet, Thai territorial demands (supported in Tokyo) against the weakened French Indochina and the growing economic ties between Japan and Thailand caused considerable alarm to His Majesty's Government. "We are not at present strong enough in the Far East to impose our will," Sir Alexander Cadogan briefed Churchill in January 1941, "and we have only been able to do our best through His Majesty's Minister in Bangkok to warn the Thais against the danger of selling themselves to the Japanese." Four months later, the British Minister, Sir Josiah Crosby, observed, "Thailand is now at the parting of the ways." He added, "Thai Government never forgets that we are without adequate fleet based on

Singapore. . . . and strengthening of our defences in Malaya
is not sufficient to counterbalance Thai Government's fear
of Japan." Crosby's American colleague, Hugh Grant, echoed
British requests to Washington for a firm official statement
to help pro-Western Thai elements from "wavering between
going along with old friends or joining up with the Japanese
axis group." But the State Department dismissed such a
policy as "unwise" in feeding ammunition to Axis
propagandists about American interference in the internal
affairs of an independent country. These views were passed
on to London, where they earned a sharp rebuke from the
Foreign Office: "Until it is proved that the Thais (Siamese)
are past praying for we cannot afford to take a view at once
so pessimistic and detached as Mr. Hull of the position in a
country where our vital strategic interests are so much at
stake."[20]

Crosby tried to bring about some accommodation to
prevent the crucial tin and rubber supplies of Thailand from
going exclusively to Japan. The Americans had suggested
coupling Thai exports (in the free market) to Great Britain
with Western supplies to Thailand, but the British preferred
a strict quota system of allocations on the assumption that
"if rubber is to be free to everyone to bid for, it is
surely unreasonable to link our purchases of rubber with our
supplies to Thailand." Crosby, like so many other
ambassadors in these fateful years, grew virtually
uncritical of the policies of his host while becoming
increasingly disenchanted with the attitude of his home
government. "You are being unjust to the Thai Government,"
he complained in June 1941, protesting that a particularly
stiff Foreign Office telegram "wears something of a
tergiversation." Yet, during the flurry of activity in the
hours prior to the Japanese attacks, His Majesty's
Government revealed a genuine interest in aiding Bangkok,
quite apart from natural strategic concerns about the Kra
Isthmus. On 7 December Churchill sent an urgent message to
be delivered directly to Pibul. The Prime Minister stated:

> There is possibility of imminent Japanese invasion
> of your country. If you are attacked, defend
> yourself. The preservation of the full
> independence and sovereignty of Thailand is a
> British interest and we shall regard an attack on

you as an attack upon ourselves.[21]

Under pressure of the actual Japanese invasion under way, Pibul signed an alliance with Japan on 11 December 1941. The Thai Minister in Washington, Mom Rajawongse Seni Pramoj, repudiated that alleged alliance the same day. He signalled Bangkok, "I shall henceforth carry out only orders which in my opinion are of His [Thai] Majesty's Government's free will." Despite "significant changes" in the Thai Cabinet, London recommended not declaring war after receiving "convincing indications that the majority of Thai opinion is anti-Japanese if not pro-Ally, and it is likely to become increasingly anti-Japanese as the Japanese proceed to apply their usual arrogant methods and to infringe their agreement to respect the sovereignty of Thailand." Washington felt that the anti-Japanese sentiment in Thailand was not as widespread as the British believed, yet described American policy as "in substantial agreement" with the British views. Minister Pramoj announced formation of the Free Thai Movement, but the United States continued to recognize him only as Minister of Thailand.[22]

The issue of territorial settlements soon split the early Anglo-American unity regarding Thailand. While the American attitude insisted on the return of the illegal Thai amputations from Indochina (and in 1943 from Malaya), the State Department envisaged comprehensive negotiations after the war that did not rule out territorial readjustments under arbitration. Significantly, the previous American guarantee to restore the French Empire, as Sumner Welles indicated, "does not preclude the consideration of territorial claims presented by Thailand and French Indochina, and the arrangement of mutually acceptable boundaries between them." The British considered Thailand an enemy after the declaration of war from Bangkok (via an indirect, curious route) on 25 January 1942, while the United States maintained throughout the war that Thailand was an enemy-occupied territory.[23]

Strategic interests also colored the British view. The lessons of Indochina and Thailand falling into unfriendly hands had been dearly impressed upon the British Empire in 1941. London wanted more than friendly assurances from the postwar Bangkok government concerning mutual defense arrangements. "In view of the probable development of modern warfare," the British Chiefs declared in a 1945 memorandum that carried disturbing implications, "it would not be practical to restrict the facilities which we require, to some special arrangements in the Kra Isthmus." Thus, the British anticipated active participation in Thai affairs and resisted American efforts to elicit a statement of British support for a free and independent Thailand after the war. "The absence of a British statement of British intentions with respect to Thailand is causing considerable inconvenience to my Government," Ambassador John Winant pointed out in August 1944, "in that it delays decision on important cognate matters relating to Thailand and Indochina." But the British military advisers had earlier argued that "in making any declaration of this nature, His Majesty's Government should avoid using any form of words which might, by free interpretation, derogate from our freedom to obtain our minimum strategical requirements." Eden reinforced this position by explaining that the Thais had "betrayed" British friendship and "like other countries in like case 'they must work their passage home.'" American policy rejected the idea of soliciting prior commitments from Bangkok before endorsing the independence of Thailand; however, the British clung to the opposite view. The War Cabinet declared:

> Much will depend on the measures which Siam takes to contribute towards the expulsion of the Japanese from Siamese territory and towards the ultimate defeat of Japan; and on her readiness (a) to make restitution to His Majesty's Government and their Allies for the injury done to them in consequence of Siam's association with Japan and (b) to ensure security and good neighborly relations in the future.[24]

Obviously, the British expected Thailand to accept any military and economic arrangements required for postwar international security as well as British stipulations regarding the Kra Isthmus. As is so often the case in assessing British Far Eastern policies, colonial concerns played a dominant influence in shaping British attitudes. Imperial security required assurances about the Kra Isthmus that London no longer wished to leave simply to the reliance on Thai good will. In addition, the British early realized the implications of reoccupying colonial areas during the expected food shortages at the end of the war. H. L. Sanderson, Director of Rice at the Ministry of Food, warned in January 1945 that "as soon as the Asiatic rice consuming countries are liberated they will require very large imports of rice and it will be disastrous if our re-entry into them coincides with a shortage of essential foodstuffs." This forecast added another dimension to the importance of postwar controls over Thailand. "Owing to the lack of incentive and transport difficulties the Siamese (rice) surplus is believed to have dropped to little more than the pre-war one of 1-1/2 million tons," a group of economic experts advised in December 1944. "As the position in Indo-China is similar, and in Burma much worse, the importance of the Siamese surplus has greatly increased."[25]

In the case of Thailand, therefore, the abrupt end of the war brought a different kind of hardship on the Allies. The problem was one of food supplies rather than the difficulties of military occupation (despite the presence of 55,000 Japanese troops and 90,000 armed Thais). The inability to implement operational plans which would have incorporated Thailand--and, of course, control over the essential Thai rice supply--into the Allied sphere at a comfortable pace meant that an enormous crisis awaited the Western powers whenever they did manage to reassert colonial authority.

After the humiliating military defeats to Japan and the corresponding loss of prestige, the returning colonial powers could ill afford the additional complications associated with severe food shortages. Consequently, the British, although aware that the United States would regard their demands on Thailand "as savouring of reparations," insisted that the Thais "work their passage home." The subsequent Thai-British Treaty of December 1945 required the Thais to give the British Rice Unit in Bangkok any existing surplus of rice up to 1.5 million tons, plus all future surpluses until 1 September 1947. Washington monitored these negotiations but intervened only to influence the terms of the postwar security arrangements, which originally were "designed to secure for His Majesty's Government, if not a protectorate over Siam, then at least some special military position or rights." The Thai Government, nevertheless, regarded the treaty as "tantamount to an ultimatum."26

In summary, the momentous decision to use the atomic bomb set off another kind of chain--or rogue--reaction which entailed far-reaching, unintended political consequences in Southeast Asia. The use of the bomb helped bring about an abrupt end of the war;27 but this, in turn, prevented a process of gradual reoccupation by the Allies in stages carefully planned to match Allied capabilities and resources. The sudden demands for occupation forces throughout the Far East exceeded those capabilities and resources.

The inability to digest liberated areas in measured increments, including the overriding need to establish the legitimacy of Allied military and civilian personnel in maintaining internal order, meant that indigenous political groups with leftist tendencies, in most cases armed and under the spell of the powerful Japanese rhetoric of autonomy, remained unabsorbed and outside Allied control. These groups immediately sought to implement their political aspirations. The crucial interval between the unanticipated Tokyo announcement of surrender and the time it took the Allies to assume the staggering burdens of reoccupation provided these political groups with a priceless opportunity--an opportunity which they exploited in ways that have had an enormous significance for the stability of the postwar world.

The continuing historical debate has not sufficiently addressed these consequences of the use of the atomic bomb in 1945. Moral dilemmas and even the military necessity of dropping the two bombs to force Japan to surrender remain-- properly--open to value judgments. But another important dimension has thus far been less appreciated: the indirect military consequences of the use of the atomic bomb elsewhere in the Far East. While the decision to drop the atomic bomb did not by itself "cause" the unhappy Far Eastern epilogue to World War II, that decision unintentionally contributed to the complex pattern of circumstances that led to the political turmoil and military conflicts that in some cases have continued for three decades.[28]   Moreover, the direct connection of Western colonialism to this tragic story is so obvious that it requires no further indictment than on this charge alone.

CHAPTER IX

CONCLUSION: "ALL THOSE CATCHPENNY PHRASES"

During the war and in the planning of the transition for what Beaverbrook delightfully characterized as "the return from the pleasant profligacies of war to the grim realities of peace,"[1] the question of the restoration of Western colonialism in the Far East detracted from Anglo-American efforts not only to defeat Japan but also to promote postwar stability in the Far East. Furthermore, it hampered the development of the long-anticipated "special relationship" between the two countries. The politics of coalition diplomacy necessarily reflected the suspicions, schemes, and hostility of the Allied partners. Each distrusted the postwar intentions of the other, and that shared mistrust represented a major obstacle to the elusive goal of developing a truly united effort during the war and a purposeful commitment after the war.

Part of the problem lay in the vagueness of some of the moralistic-legalistic pronouncements of the Allies, especially those of the United States. The failure to be precise and specific encouraged a wide range of conflicting interpretations. Without exception, the various important wartime statements of policy contributed to some unfortunate misunderstandings. To the United States Government the words meant a gradual--and global--evolution towards international peace and justice. To American business circles the words meant virtual assurance of the predominance of their interests. To the Chinese the words meant foreign interference in Chinese and Asian affairs. To the British and other colonizers the words meant the same as their own idealistic interpretation of their imperial practices. To the colonized peoples the words meant yet another device to perpetuate Western control of their affairs. And to the Russians the words meant nothing.

"Those with recollections of internationalism, collective security, League of Nations, Kellogg Pact, and all those catchpenny phrases must feel in these days that the more practical we are the better," Lord Londonderry warned in 1943.[2] To a certain extent, the easy slogans that rolled out of Washington and London--"Atlantic Charter," "Open Door," "Unconditional Surrender," "Free Trade," "United and Democratic China," "International Trusteeship"-- held powerful meaning during the early phase of the war. After all, the war effort involved a battle for people's hearts and minds too. These kinds of phrases were important beacons of hope to people all over the world. The performance, however, failed to live up to the promise. The early wartime statements offered general guidelines about a better postwar world but needed concrete measures to implement those valuable goals. Anglo-American planners never moved beyond the easy generalizations--and exciting potential--of the slogans. The phrases became empty, devoid of meaning, largely because of their universal applicability.

In the face of Anglo-American suspicions and narrow self-interest, the rhetoric of idealism was adopted for contradictory purposes. For example, on one hand, the Atlantic Charter stirred noble sentiment and high expectations in the United States about a grand, new era in international relations, including an end to exploitative colonialism. On the other hand, the British, through careful qualifications and interpretations, supported the Charter in the sincere belief that its language reaffirmed traditional British colonial practices. Everyone voiced the same words; but the words meant different things to different people. This "Alice-Through-the-Looking-Glass" ambiguity plagued efforts to fulfill praiseworthy generalities through specific measures building for the postwar era. Thus, proponents of a wide range of motives along the human spectrum, from altruism through malice, invoked (and subscribed to) identical language. As one example of the many consequences of this curious circumstance, historians continue to debate the "ideals-vs.-self-interest" character of American foreign policy.

Indeed, the very question of whether or not the United States conducts a coherent foreign policy grows out of its uncertain language. Supreme sacrifices have been voluntarily made by some Americans in behalf of verbalized policies which some other Americans have skeptically scorned. "The astonishing feature of our foreign policy is the wide discrepancy between our announced policies and our conduct of international relations," one embittered American Ambassador charged in his letter of resignation.[3]

American slogans, moreover, increasingly became not useful descriptions of American attitudes but, rather, convenient pigeonholes or substitutes for substantive policies. That is, American war aims or trusteeship concepts or economic goals or views about China took on easy labels in lieu of detailed analysis. Somehow, for example, the general idea of self-determination for dependent peoples became confused with the concrete steps required to attain that objective. The United States suffered an imbalance between ends and means; the "ends" were formulated with relative ease, while the "means" of achieving those ends lacked purposeful leadership and commitment. As Tang Tsou effectively pointed out, American administrations consistently refused to "use military power purposefully to achieve political objectives."[4] Despite heroic measures in winning the war, and particularly in uprooting Japan's hold over most of the Pacific and Far East, Roosevelt failed, for the most part, to gain his larger goal. Whatever the degree of admirable content in the rhetoric put forth, Washington satisfied itself with the mere invocation of verbalized ideals without assuring their implementation.

This tendency particularly plagued Roosevelt's style of personal diplomacy because he tended to slide over real differences to cultivate momentary amiability. His cosmetic applications temporarily disguised ugly realities but could not in the long run make them vanish. At Placentia Bay, for instance, he avoided confrontation with Churchill over imperial preference, yet that fundamental issue surfaced again and again to disrupt Anglo-American harmony throughout the war. In addition, his easy compromises in order to get an international organization established eventually solidified what he considered only brief expediencies to such an extent that an effective system of consultative arrangements fell into peril. His willingness, furthermore, to retreat from his original ideas about territorial trusteeship not only ensured the reimposition of colonial rule but also brought the United States into closer association in Asian eyes with Western suppression of their

legitimate aspirations. His vaporous style too often proved
impenetrable. He preferred it that way and contrived to
avoid being pinned down. Gaddis Smith described a
"compulsion to be liked" in the Roosevelt character:

> In dealing with others he would feign agreement
> with an opinion rather than produce disappointment.
> In domestic politics this habit of trying to please
> everyone caused confusion but no lasting harm.
> When Roosevelt's final views on an issue emerged,
> the man who had been misled could resign. Many
> did. But this Rooseveltian technique had doleful
> results when applied to international affairs,
> where the favorable conditions that Roosevelt
> enjoyed at home were missing. The nations in
> uneasy coalition against the Axis disagreed not
> only on the means of winning the war, but also on
> fundamental objectives of the future. Differences
> were too profound to be dissolved by geniality, and
> disgruntled allies, unlike subordinates, could not
> be ignored.[5]

What could Roosevelt have done differently? Actually,
most of his problems appear to have stemmed from the buoyant
optimism that he nourished. This supreme sense of optimism
led Roosevelt on occasion not only to an innocent naiveté
(despite his rigorous experience in the rough-and-tumble
world of American politics) but also to an exaggerated self-
confidence, which sometimes bordered on the dangerous--
"naiveté" in expecting the imperial powers to accede to his
own impression that the era of colonial systems had ended,
"potentially dangerous" in miscalculating his ability to
manage both Stalin and the course of Soviet-American
relations.[6] Also, his buoyant optimism led him to what
Stimson called, "an impulsive nature and a mind which
revolts against the dry facts."[7] It led him to
overemphasize the personal equation in diplomacy; it led him
to substitute idle chatter in place of hard, realistic
decision-making; and it led him to a blind faith about
establishing stability and equity in postwar relations among
the "developed" and the "developing" where formerly
instability and exploitation had characterized those
relationships. If ever the term "Happy Warrior" described
anyone, it described Roosevelt.

The final analysis awaits the answers to what seem

unanswerable questions: Why did Roosevelt feel he could not be more explicit about these issues? What did he think would happen on other issues if he were to take a concrete position on a particular issue, such as decolonization or equal access to raw materials? The answers existed only in Roosevelt's mind. While historians can examine the tension and the consequence of a particular policy or decision, they can only guess at Roosevelt's deeper motivation. Ill health,[8] buoyant optimism, pragmatism, racism,[9] political concerns,[10] personal judgments--all these, combined somehow with the countless other elements of Roosevelt's world view, helped shape the way Roosevelt made his decisions. But who is to say exactly what mixture of these elements produced exactly which policy? Roosevelt, perhaps more than any other president, managed to conceal his deepest motives and reasoning from outsiders, including his family and closest advisers. The inner workings of Roosevelt's mind, protected by what Robert Sherwood has aptly called a "heavily forested interior,"[11] proved impenetrable to contemporaries--and remains so to historians.

Conversely, if Roosevelt adopted a tone of generality and abstractness, Churchill demonstrated a preference for a provincialism that seemed antiquated by mid-1945. The President looked to multilateralism and the spirit of international cooperation, while the Prime Minister preferred a much narrower base of bilateral or regional understandings grounded always in the interests of his beloved Empire and in the special relationship between London and Washington. Churchill is sometimes praised for his valiant, if futile, attempts to make Presidents Roosevelt and Truman realize the political dangers of the Red Army spreading throughout Eastern Europe by self-styled "realists" who, at the same time, overlook Churchill's actions in thwarting other postwar political issues, such as the hope held out in the Atlantic Charter for a more equitable sharing of global resources and the promise of an ambitious trusteeship system to address the dreams of dependent peoples.

"The qualities which produce the dogged unbeatable courage of the British, personified at the time in Winston Churchill," Dean Acheson declared, "can appear in other settings as stubbornness bordering upon stupidity."

Churchill's determined resistance to encroachments, real or imagined, against the British Empire blinded him to the important long-term implications of such a restricted view. He journeyed to Moscow in 1944 to buy off Russian ambitions; he felt China, holding tremendous promise, could also be dealt with if that potential ever came close to being realized. British interests for Churchill meant imperial interests, and this simple equation explains why the problem of colonialism arose so frequently in the diplomacy of the coalition. "It was the nation and the race dwelling all round the globe, that had the lion heart," he reminisced about his wartime premiership, "I had the luck to be called upon to give the roar." Even his renowned eloquence extolling the virtues of special relations with the United States stemmed from the conviction that the association would further safeguard imperial interests. He would agree with the British schoolboy, who when asked to name the three most important things in the world, recited: "God, Love, and Anglo-American relations." Prophesying an unprecedented postwar unity between the two English-speaking blocs, Churchill enthused:

> The British Empire and the United States will have to be somewhat mixed up together in some of their affairs for mutual and general advantage. For my own part, looking out upon the future, I do not view the process with any misgivings. I could not stop it if I wished; no one can stop it. Like the Mississippi, it just keeps rolling along. Let it roll. Let it roll in full flood, inexorable, irresistible, benignant, to broader lands and better days.[12]

Fairness demands a look at the other side of the ledger too. Often neglected in assessing the diplomacy of World War II is the one dominant fact that the United Nations successfully accomplished the fundamental purpose that had brought them together. Any retrospective dissatisfaction with the performance of the wartime leadership pales in significance beside that one overriding consideration. Once the association formed, the only hope for the Axis Powers lay in its disunion.

To their credit, Roosevelt and Churchill, each in his own way, subordinated all other interests to adhere to the lowest common denominator of coalition cohesion, for, after all, it did hold together until victory. The long and difficult path from Pearl Harbor to the Missouri presented a formidable journey that neither leader could complete. Consequently, it is difficult to see the justification in affixing responsibility to either Roosevelt or Churchill for the actual course of events after the war, especially when a new President and Prime Minister ascended to political power even before the war had ended. The unique Roosevelt-Churchill system did not last the war, let alone extend into the postwar years.

Moreover, none of the leaders of the coalition held any mandate to arrange a trouble-free world once victory had been attained. Indeed, their efforts, plagued with the inevitable human frailties, proved all the more remarkable in the magnificent achievement of total military victory. To require a simultaneous solution for the enormous postwar problems is to ask too much.

The benefits and evils associated with colonialism long predated Pearl Harbor. Whatever the judgments accompanying those particular legacies, to that extent Churchill and Roosevelt became historical captives. One sought to strengthen the traditional colonial ties while the other dreamt of a new order; both, in fact, were pressured to some degree by historical forces beyond their control. Historian D. C. Watt, for example, has pointed out that "where American policy-makers did not succeed in forcing their views through, it was much less, as some 'revisionist' historians have argued, from their fear of communism and consequent need for the friendship of the European powers, but simply that their power to act turned out in practice to be illusory."[13] Roosevelt astutely recognized that world peace and the security of the United States depended in part on the successful resolution of the aspirations of colonial peoples. He also perceived, with slight exaggeration, that some imperial powers had mishandled some of their dependencies. Above all, in this context, he foresaw-- perhaps better than any of his contemporaries--the postwar explosions of nationalism and decolonization that shattered the old order. His earnest anti-colonial attitude, in fact, flowed largely from his determiniation to defuse those mighty forces. By 1940 less than eight hundred thousand

European whites dominated four hundred fifty million Asians. That evolving situation was long in coming and difficult to reverse. Roosevelt and Churchill played varying roles--but comparatively small ones--in that continuing process.

Nevertheless, in the more immediate circumstances of wartime diplomacy, colonialism worked against a concerted Allied effort. Even the entry of the United States into the war carried a cloud of suspicion about the dark motives of the colonial powers. Virtually every strategic decision and political-economic discussion thereafter suffered some influence connected with colonialism; "suffered" because of the mutual wariness and hostility in London and Washington which invaribly accompanied all Anglo-American wartime deliberations. This is not the stuff of coalition cohesion. Colonialism, therefore, distracted from the primary purpose of winning the war. And, as victory neared, the distractions of real or imaginary imperial interests increasingly imposed themselves on the policy-making process. The postwar era witnessed a continuation of the suspicions and schemes--and bloodshed--associated with colonial arrangements.

Roosevelt, in particular, can be criticized for letting slip from his grasp the chance to use his position and tremendous influence to insist on qualitative changes in the planning of postwar international affairs. By refusing to discuss urgent political-diplomatic problems and detailed postwar arrangements until the last shot was fired, Roosevelt virtually forfeited his powerful diplomatic leverage in a way that other wartime leaders, like Stalin and de Gaulle, did not. For example, Roosevelt demanded, "We expect to be consulted with regard to any arrangements applicable to the future of Southeast Asia."[14] But he took no concrete measures to ensure such consultation--save to repeat vague, almost ritualistic, political incantations about "independence" and "international cooperation" as if his wishes, expressed often enough, would come true. Although it would be unfair, as noted, to blame the President for the actual course of postwar events, Roosevelt, with his "non-policy of determined drift," bears a large share of responsibility for the Allies' failure to plan--and implement--specific bold and progressive measures for the postwar era.

In addition, the anticipated special relationship never really developed after the war. "As you know, my preference would be to get the Empire and the U. S. together, around which any desired or desirable minor nations would crystallize," Lord Cherwell informed the deposed Churchill, after the stunning British electoral results in July 1945. "I think you and Roosevelt could have done this, but I doubt whether Truman and Attlee can or will."[15] And George Malcolm Thomson later described the transfer of British supremacy to "the smiling power beyond the Atlantic, the good friend who was also the impatient heir."[16] In effect a "natural" relationship--carrying with it the host of congruent interests shared by the two countries--supplanted expectations of an artificial "special" relationship. Meanwhile the Soviet Union continued a spectacular ascendancy, and the subsequent tensions and terror of the postwar era suggest that the four-year wartime alliance had been a brief period of forced cooperation--a necessary aberration in the otherwise uninterrupted pattern since 1917. A measure of Russian cooperation appeared with the dire totalitarian threat and then dissolved as soon as the danger subsided. And in the Far East, turmoil mocked the glowing prospects sketched during the early phases of postwar planning. For example, the sharply deteriorating relations between the United States and China destroyed any hopes, lingering from Roosevelt's wartime rhetoric, about Four World Policemen. "One could hardly find a more sobering example of the tragic results produced by a policy of good intentions and high ideals," Tsou concluded about the course of Sino-American relations, "which lacked the foundations of a correlative estimate of self-interest and which was not supported by military power equal to the noble tasks."[17] He might well have been describing the American experience generally in the Far East since 1941; a heavy toll continues to be exacted three decades later in Asia. As late as 1949 a prophetic report by Donald O'Connor, in the Office of Price Administration, stressed the overwhelming need to secure the China trade for the West. "If the direction of its trade is other than this," O'Connor warned, "it is worth at least a speculation that heavy U. S. military expenditures will be made in the lands adjacent to China."[18] The indigenous reactions in the postwar era against Western colonialism (which, ironically, came to include the United States in the pattern of Western suppression) virtually ensured the unhappy sequence in O'Connor's prophecy.

Thus, the sad prologue to World War II has clouded the purposeful pursuit with which the Anglo-American partnership originally undertook the task of unconditional victory. The momentous ARGENTIA meeting outlined a program of objectives that anticipated new heights of international cooperation. The subsequent erosion of the spirit of the Atlantic Charter, whether through design or misunderstanding or human frailty, does not diminish the promise held out in that historic document. Its principles retain an enduring, universal value and continue to serve as a guidepost for human progress. Therefore, the task of translating this noble idealism into international reality represents a dilemma--and a tragedy--not only of coalition diplomacy but also of subsequent efforts in the postwar era.

ENDNOTES

NOTES ON CHAPTER I

[1]Chamberlain to Roosevelt, 28 September 1937, PREM 1-261, Public Record Office, London, (Hereafter cited as PRO.) This file also contains Roosevelt's letter to Chamberlain, 28 July 1937.

[2]Murray to Chamberlain, 28 October 1938, PREM 1-367, PRO.

[3]Chamberlain to Roosevelt, 8 November 1939, PREM 1-366, PRO. Roosevelt's letter to Chamberlain, 11 September 1939, and Chamberlain's response, 4 October 1939, are attached.

[4]Roosevelt to Churchill, 11 September 1939, PREM 3-467, PRO. For a review of the developing Roosevelt-Churchill relationship, see Joseph Lash, Roosevelt and Churchill, 1939-1941 (New York: W.W. Norton, 1976); Roy Douglas, New Alliances, 1940-1941 (New York: St. Martin's, 1982).

[5]Winston S. Churchill, The Second World War, Vol. I: The Gathering Storm (6 vols.; New York: Bantam Books, 1962), p. 33. (Hereafter cited as Churchill, with appropriate volume title.)
cc

[6]Churchill to Roosevelt, 5 October 1939, PREM 3-467, PRO. The text of the telephone conversation is included.

[7]Pound to Cunningham, 30 March 1940, Andrew B. Cunningham Papers, British Museum, London, Vol. 52560.

[8]Hoare Diary, Viscount Templewood (Hoare) Papers, University Library, Cambridge University, file xii/3.

[9]The full minutes of this historic debate are in Great Britain, Parliament, Parliamentary Debates (House of Commons), 5th ser., Vol. 360 (23 April-13 May, 1940), pp. 1074-1366. The Amery Papers are closed. (Julian Amery to the author, 2 August 1973.) Clement Attlee, who felt that the Labour Party was not ready for a coalition government in September 1939, advised the Labour Party not to accept the motion of adjournment on 7 May. This rejection sparked the whole debate about the central direction of the war. Attlee noted that Churchill, to his credit, "vigourously supported" Chamberlain, and the Labour leader applauded the "remarkable effort" by Amery. See Attlee Papers, Archives Center, Churchill College, Cambridge University, file 1/16. Lloyd George warned Churchill on 8 May not to be an "air-raid shelter" for Chamberlain and on 11 May offered his

congratulations: "Best wishes for success in your efforts to liberate this country from the consequences of the great muddle into which it has been brought by your predecessor." (Lloyd George Papers, Lord Beaverbrook Library, London, file G/14/5/46). Admiral of the Fleet Sir Roger Keyes also made an outstanding contribution during these debates. See his notes in the Keyes Papers, Churchill College Library, Cambridge University. For a brief but valuable summary of the political intrigues during this historic debate, see Churchill, Gathering Storm, pp. 588-91. For accounts by Ambassador Joseph P. Kennedy to Secretary of State Cordell Hull of these May events, see Record Group 59, General Records of the Department of State, State Department Decimal File (hereafter cited as SD) 841.00/1472 and 841.00/1477, National Archives, Washington, D.C. (hereafter cited as NA). Unless otherwise indicated, all State Department Decimal File citations, including Office of Strategic Services Research and Analysis Reports (OSS R&A), refer to Record Group 59, NA.

[10]Hoare to the Hon. William Astor, M.P., 15 May 1940, Templewood Papers, file xii/4. Hoare served as Lord Privy Seal in the original Chamberlain War Cabinet, then as Secretary of State for Air after the reorganization of 3 April 1940. He temporarily lost all official standing when Churchill became Prime Minister. This caused him great concern, and he wrote to Chamberlain (who had become Lord President of the Council) of his fear of being judged weak and incompetent. "I alone of the four of us who went through Munich am left isolated to stand this unjust criticism. All this makes me ask you to press Winston to give me India." (Hoare to Chamberlain, 14 May 1940, ibid.) "India" went to the eloquent Amery, but Hoare did receive the Ambassadorship to Spain.

[11]Sir Llewellyn Woodward, British Foreign Policy in the Second World War (2nd impression; London: HMSO, 1972), p. xxix. Halifax commented on his own chances to become Prime Minister in his memoir, Fullness of Days (New York: Dodd, Mead and Co., 1957), pp. 218-26. Halifax asserted that he stepped aside mainly because he would have to remain in the House of Lords. This story is largely substantiated, though presented in third-hand version, by Lord Stamford who heard the report from A. J. Cummings and then passed it on to W. R. Crozier (editor of the Manchester Guardian) in an interview 12 November 1942. See W. R. Crozier Papers, Beaverbrook Library, London, file "Lord Stamford," Box 7. Crozier also interviewed Churchill on 26 July 1940, and the Prime Minister observed, "I owe something to Chamberlain, you know. When he resigned he could have advised the King to send for Halifax and he didn't. And he consented to serve under me as Premier--not everyone in his position would have done that. Asquith, for instance, wouldn't serve under Lloyd

George. But Chamberlain works very well with me and I can
tell you this--he's no intriguer," (Crozier Papers, folder
"Winston Churchill," Box 2.)

[12]Churchilll to Roosevelt, 15 May 1940, enclosed in
Churchill to Kennedy, 15 May 1940, PREM 3-468, PRO.

[13]Roosevelt to Churchill, 17 May 1940, PREM 3-468, PRO.

[14]American Gold Star Mother to Stimson, 18 June 1940,
Henry L. Stimson Papers, Sterling Library, Yale University,
New Haven, Connecticut, Box 134.

[15]Colonel the Hon. Arthur Murray memorandum, 21 October
1938, PREM 1-367, PRO. "In other words," the President
continued, "in the first instance there was no doubt in the
mind of anyone as to what the action would be; whereas in
the second instance there was a 'question mark.' Events, of
course, might tend to lay stress on the 'question mark'
attitude, and we can conceive events in which it might be
eliminated altogether." For a discussion of Chamberlain's
suggestion that Congress served as the "Mr. Jorkins" of
Roosevelt's foreign policy, see David Reynolds, The Creation
of the Anglo-American Alliance, 1937-1941: A Study in
Competitive Cooperation (Chapel Hill: University of North
Carolina Press, 1981), p. 165, 338. Jorkins was the dreaded
(but unseen) junior partner of a law firm in David
Copperfield. The senior partner used Jorkins as the excuse
for not being able to be more lenient in dealing with the
firm's employees.

[16]Frank Livesey (Economic Adviser to Hull) informed the
Secretary of State in letters 8 and 11 March 1940 about the
war debts group. See these and related materials in SD
711.4114/16. For Wheeler's remark and Roosevelt's disgusted
reaction, see New York Times, 15 January 1941. See also
Robert A. Taft to Harold Phelps Stokes, 20 May 1941, Harold
Phelps Stokes Papers, Yale University, file 113, Box 4.

[17]Shea to Hull, 5 January 1941, SD 711.41/493. For
another aspect of Shea's anxieties, see the undated
[September] 1941 letter from Dr. Chaim Weizmann to Churchill
urging that a separate Jewish fighting force be established.
Weizmann stated that the five million American Jews made up
"the only big ethnic group which is willing to stand, to a
man, for Great Britain. . . . From Secretary Morgenthau,
Governor Lehman, Justice Frankfurter, down to the simplest
Jewish workman or trader, they are conscious of all that
this struggle against Hitler implies." Weizmann claimed that
these people "tipped the scales" in the last war and would
be "keen to do it--and may do it--again." See WP(G)(41)95,
10 September 1941, CAB 67/9, PRO.

[18]The thick packet of material on the Detroit controversy during April-May 1941 may be found in SD 841.01B11/197-210.

[19]The debate about the Monroe Doctrine is traced in SD 841.001George VI/867 and SD 841.01/70-82. Generally, the State Department refused to comment on the hypothetical situation but Hull did point out to Representative Sol Bloom on 15 June that George VI was also "King of Canada and the constitutional head of the Government of Canada." (SD 841.01/71.) Churchill's close assistant, General Hastings Ismay provided some substance to these rumors by informing the Chief of the Imperial General Staff that the War Cabinet was considering evacuation of the Royal Family to Canada. Ismay to General Sir W. E. Ironside, 3 July 1940, General the Lord Ismay Papers (hereafter cited as Ismay Papers), Liddell Hart Centre for Military Archives, University of London, King's College, London (hereafter cited as Liddell Hart Centre), file V/I/2/1-2.

[20]Breckinridge Long memorandum of conversation with J. P. Kennedy, 15 February 1940, SD 711.41/463.

[21]Halifax to Churchill, 11 October 1941, PREM 4-27/9, PRO. Halifax continued, "He made the curious observation that public opinion here would accept American action against the Azores, but not against the Cape Verde Islands, the Azores being Western Hemisphere and the others not. I said: 'What about Iceland?', but that he said was clearly recognized by public opinion to be a possible jumping off ground for German approach round the Northern curve. They didn't yet appreciate that Dakar was equally a jumping off ground to the Southern curve, Brazil, and Panama Canal, etc."

[22]Vansittart memorandum, 14 March 1940, 1st Baron Vansittart Papers, Archives Center, Churchill College, Cambridge University, file VNST 1/27.

[23]FE(41)48, 13 March 1941, CAB 96/2, PRO.

[24]Halifax to Churchill, 13 March 1941, PREM 4-27/9, PRO. See also, "Note on the Working of the Central Executive Government of Great Britain and of the War Cabinet Office," enclosed in Ismay to Marshall, 3 July 1943, George C. Marshall Papers, George C. Marshall Foundation, Lexington, Virginia, file 52, Box 58. Marshall, attuned to the differences in American and British organizational machinery, requested a copy of the British model.

[25]Hull's two lectures to Lord Lothian came on 22 January 1940 (SD 641.116/2578) and 23 February 1940 (SD 711.41/456). Other descriptions of American grievances and

protests may be found in A. L. Moffat memorandum 25 January 1940, SD 841.711/3027; Herschel V. Johnson (Chargé, London) to Hull, 28 February 1940, SD 711.41/457; James C. Dunn memorandum, 6 March 1940, SD 711.41/465; Robert T. Pell memorandum, 6 March 1940, SD 711.41/458; A. A. Berle, Jr. memorandum, 10 March 1942, SD 841.20211/36. In a joint memorandum, "The Censorship of United States Mails," then-Foreign Secretary Lord Halifax and then-Dominions Secretary Anthony Eden justified the British practice "on the grounds that the examination made is not for censorship, but for contraband purposes." Nevertheless, they concluded that "there is abundant private evidence to show that the average American takes the strongest exception on grounds to any interference with his correspondence." See WP(40)85, 7 March 1940, CAB 66/6, PRO.

[26]Lothian to Halifax, 27 January 1940, WP(G)(40)30, 27 January 1940, CAB 67/4, PRO.

[27]Hankey to Arthur Hugh Frazier, 29 August 1940, CAB 63/93, PRO.

[28]Beaverbrook to Churchill, 24 June 1941, Lord Beaverbrook Papers, Beaverbrook Library, London, file D/126.

[29]Halifax to Churchill, 13 March 1941, PREM 4-27/9, PRO.

[30]John G. Winant, A Letter From Grosvenor Square (London: Hodder and Stoughton, 1947), p. 15.

[31]See in PREM 4-37/9, PRO: Halifax to Eden, 24 February 1942; Eden to Churchill, 30 April 1942; and Churchill minute, 30 April 1942. Also see Churchill memorandum, 22 November 1940, PREM 3-489/4, PRO. Churchill wrote, "Our object is to get the Americans into the war. . . ."

[32]Robert Sherwood to Ismay, 11 May 1948, Ismay Papers, file IV/HOP/28.

NOTES ON CHAPTER II

[1]The Japanese invasion of Malaya preceded (by forty-four minutes) the attack on Pearl Harbor. See Commodore G. R. G. Allen to Churchill, n.d., Ismay Papers, file II/3/119/1-2. Converting to Greenwich Mean Time, Allen stated that the attack at Pearl Harbor occurred at 6:30 P.M., G.M.T., 8 December 1941 (or 8:00 A.M., Local Time, 7 December); while the attack at Kota Bahru came at 5:46 P.M., G.M.T., 8 December 1941 (or 1:16 A.M., Local Time, 8 December). A detailed consideration of Allied strategical

and tactical decisions is outside the scope of this study, but some of the wider causes and consequences of military affairs, particularly as they relate to the issue of colonialism, will be analyzed.

[2]General the Lord Ismay, The Memoirs of General the Lord Ismay (London: Heinmann, 1960), p. 247. Fraser to Churchill, 12 January 1942, PREM 3-167/1, PRO. This volume contains the harsh Churchill-Curtin-Fraser correspondence in 1941-1942; also General Sir E. I. C. Jacob (Assistant to Ismay and the British Chiefs of Staff) interview with the author, 26 June 1973, Woodbridge, Suffolk; Churchill, Hinge of Fate, pp. 133-44; Sir Harry Batterbee (wartime High Commissioner in New Zealand) interview with the author, 3 August 1973, London. Jacob remained convinced that Burma would have been saved if the diversion of the troop ships had been approved but agreed that there was "no question" of overruling Curtin's vociferous demands. Batterbee shared similar feelings about the defense of Burma, sharply contrasting Curtin's leadership with the "quite genuine" concern for the integrity of the Empire held by Fraser.

[3]C. A. Vlieland, unpublished Memoir-Memorandum, n.d., Liddell Hart Centre; also Churchill to Sir Mark Young (Governor of Hong Kong) and General Sir Christopher M. Maltby (C-in-C, Hong Kong), 21 December 1941, Ismay Papers, file "PM's Personal Telegrams--1941; Churchill to Ismay (for Chiefs of Staff), 15 December 1941, ibid. Vlieland stated, "There was nothing in the least 'jungly' about the developed part of Malaya, which was the only part that mattered strategically." He noted that fighting did occur in "close country" but that the terrain was "more like the orchard and hop-garden country of Kent," especially the Japanese invasion route along the Kroh-Grik-Kuala Kangsar Road, which London had dismissed as "impractically bad." It should be noted that Vlieland was relieved in January 1941. He did not get along with the Commander-in-Chief, Far East, General Sir Robert Brooke-Popham. The C-in-C, Far East declared, "I should have liked to have made use of Vlieland, but it would have taken too long to wean him from his habits. He had a brain but it was only second-class and he failed to realise that though he had a certain facility for sarcastic phrase, he lacked the wit that converts irony into humorous criticism." See the Brooke-Popham letters to Ismay, 5 December 1940 and 6 January 1941, Papers of General Sir Robert Brooke-Popham, Liddell Hart Centre, file V/1/4.

[4]Brooke-Popham memorandum, HIST(DD)1, 25 June 1942, Brooke-Popham Papers, file V/II/17; "Notes on Prince of Wales and Repulse," n.d., ibid., file V/5/71; Pound to Cunningham, 20 May 1940, Cunningham Papers, Vol. 52560; Vlieland, Memoir.

[5]Brooke-Popham to Ismay, 26 October 1940, Brooke-Popham
Papers, file V/1/1; Commodore G. R. G. Allen to Churchill,
n.d., Ismay Papers, file II/3/119/1-2; Churchill to
Roosevelt, 5 March 1942, DO(42)21, 5 March 1942, CAB 69/4,
PRO; Vlieland, Memoir; Beaverbrook memorandum, "The
Evacuation of Penang," 20 January 1942, Beaverbrook Papers,
file D/130; Brooke-Popham notes, n.d., Brooke-Popham Papers,
file V/4/1-2; Brooke-Popham's correspondence with the Chiefs
of Staff in December 1941 concerning the naval disasters may
be found in ibid., folder V/8/49/3. For correspondence with
the official investigating agent, Air Vice-Marshal Sir Paul
Maltby, see ibid., folders V/8/12, V/8/18/2, V/8/23/2;
Maltby's report is in ibid., folder V/13. For an eye-witness
account of the sinkings, see the report by Captain W. G.
Tennant (Captain of the Repulse), COS(42)6, SSF, 6 January
1942, CAB 79/87, PRO. The Japanese later unsuccessfully
attempted to salvage the two ships. See Carl H. Boehringer
(Consul, Chungking) memorandum, 24 February 1944, enclosed
in Ambassador Clarence Gauss to Hull, 4 March 1944, SD
740.0011PW/3786.

[6]Churchill to Eden, 7 January 1942, PREM 3-90/2, PRO.
For more on the "Tulsa incident," see Dorman-Smith to
Secretary of State for Burma Leo Amery, 29 December 1941,
PREM 3-90/2, PRO; Beaverbrook to Harry Hopkins, 31 December
1941, Beaverbrook Papers, file D/28; Eden to Halifax, 2
January 1942, ibid.; Magruder to Adjutant General, 28
December 1941, SD 893.24/1510; Hull to Gauss, 29 December
1941, SD 893.24/1236; Roosevelt to Chiang Kai-shek, enclosed
in Hull to Gauss, 31 December 1941, SD 893.24/1246; A. C.
Brady (Consul, Rangoon) to Hull, 13 December 1941, SD
893.24/1240; Gauss to Hull, 29 December 1941, SD
893.24/1236; Lester L. Schnare (at Rangoon) to Hull, 29
December 1941, SD 893.24/1237; Maxwell Hamilton (Far Eastern
Division, SD) memorandum, 15 January 1942, SD 893.24/1266;
Troy Perkins (Consul, Kunming) to Hull, 17 February 1942, SD
893.00/14844; William Donovan (on inspection tour, Bombay)
to Hull, 27 May 1942, SD 893.24/1335. The American
intelligence report is enclosed in Office of Strategic
Services (OSS) Coordinator of Information, British Empire
Section, to Dr. William O. Baxter, 27 October 1941, OSS
Research and Analysis (R&A) Report Number 7, NA. Wavell's
refusals stemmed from "difficulties of supply and
communications" for the Chinese troops. But Churchill added
a new version of the imperial preference principle to this
controversy. "The Cabinet thought it would be a great
mistake at this moment," he told Field Marshall Sir John
Dill, "when heavy misfortunes must be expected [emphasis
mine] to put out a cry of this kind for help from China."
See Churchill to Dill (Head, British Joint Service Mission,
Washington), 12 February 1942, Ismay Papers, file "PM's
Telegrams--1942"; Dill to Churchill and Churchill to
Roosevelt, 12 February 1942, ibid.; Marshall to Roosevelt,

5 November 1942, Marshall Papers, file "The President, 1942--Nov. 2-13," Box 80; Wavell, Despatch By the Supreme Commander of the ABDA Area to the Combined Chiefs of Staff in the South-West Pacific: 15 January 1942 to 25 January 1942 (London: HMSO, 1948); John North, ed., The Memoirs of Field Marshal Earl Alexander of Tunis, 1940-1945 (London: Cassell and Company, Ltd., 1962), p. 94; Foreign Office to Halifax, 11 July 1942, FO 371.31811, F 4740/4/23, PRO. (Hereafter all British archival records with prefixes of PREM, CAB, and FO 371, unless otherwise indicated, will be taken from the PRO.)

[7]OSS British Empire Section, Special Memorandum Number 29, 15 January 1942, OSS R&A 49; Stilwell to General George C. Marshall, 20 December 1942, Record Group 332 (hereafter cited as RG 332), Records of United States Theaters of War: World War II (hereafter cited according to section--Stilwell Files or Wedemeyer Files), Washington National Record Center, Suitland, Maryland (hereafter cited as WNRC), Vol. 1, Box 1; also Ferris to Stilwell, 31 December 1942, RG 332, Stilwell Files, WNRC, Vol. 1, Box 1.

[8]Dewing memorandum, "Operations in South West Pacific Area," COS(43)362(O), 6 July 1943, CAB 80/71. See also OSS memoranda "Japanese Administration in Malaya," 8 June 1944, and "Japanese Domination of Thailand," 18 September 1944, Ralph H. Gabriel Papers, Yale University, file "Burma, Malaya, and Thailand Under Japan," Box 38; unsigned, undated memorandum, "Japanese Occupation and the Indonesian Revolution," Stimson Papers (Diary), film 6, reel 3.

[9]Unsigned State Department memorandum, 20 June 1942, SD 893.00/6-2042.

[10]MacLeish to Roosevelt, 19 January 1942, SD 893.00/14836.

[11]Unsigned State Department memorandum, "Accomplishments in East Asia Since December 1941 Claimed By Japan," 29 May 1943, Files of Leo Pasvolsky, RG 59, file "April-June 1943," Box 5.

[12]Thomson to Beaverbrook, 12 April 1942, Beaverbrook Papers, file D/68.

[13]Text of speech, New York Times, 11 November 1942; Wrench, "Churchill and the Empire," in Churchill By His Contemporaries, ed. by Charles Eade (London: Hutchinson, 1953), p. 200; Woodward, British Foreign Policy, p. 535; Churchill, Grand Alliance, p. 367; Great Britain, Parliamentary Debates, Vol 374, pp. 67-74. For an excellent account of ARGENTIA, see Theodore A. Wilson, The First Summit: Roosevelt and Churchill at Placentia Bay, 1941,

(London: Macdonald, 1969). Also see Richard R. Stokes (Parliamentary Peace Aims Group) to Lloyd George, 10 October 1941, Lloyd George Papers, file G/19/3/35; Dwight Lee memorandum, 26 October 1942, Dwight S. Lee Paper, Clark University, Worcester, Massachusetts, file "Council on Foreign Relation," Box 8. The complete text [see Appendix B] of the Atlantic Charter is in Samuel I. Rosenman, comp., The Public Papers and Addresses of Franklin D. Roosevelt (13 vols.; New York: Random House, 1938-1950), X, 314-17. For some misunderstanding about the corresponding need for a "Pacific Charter," see Clarence Gauss (Ambassador to China) to Hull, 3 June 1942, SD 893.00/1370; Welles to Gauss, 25 March and Gauss to Welles, 28 March, in FRUS 1942, China, pp. 730-1; Maxwell Hamilton memorandum, 7 April 1942, SD 893.24/1366; Professor E. Stanley Jones (Duke University) to Roosevelt, 10 June 1942, Franklin D. Roosevelt Papers, Franklin D. Roosevelt Library, Hyde Park, New York, President's Secretary's File, folder "Post-War," Box 175.

[14]Great Britain, Parliamentary Debates, Vol. 374, pp. 67-69. The text of Attlee's speech 15 August 1941 is in PREM 4-43A/3.

[15]See in PREM 4-43A/3: draft text of reply and Lord Moyne's views, enclosed in C. H. Thornley (Colonial Office) to John M. Martin (Principal Private Secretary to the Prime Minister), 20 November 1941; telegram from the Pilot to Churchill, enclosed in Sir B. Bourdillon (Governor of Nigeria) to Moyne, 15 November 1941; approved ammended text of reply, enclosed in Martin to Thornley, 24 November 1941; Moyne to Nigeria (also Gambia, Gold Coast, Sierra Leone), 25 November 1941; Thornley to F. F. Turnbull (India Office and Burma Office), 25 November 1941; Dr. C. Haden Guest, M.P. to Churchill, 9 December 1941; Anthony Bevir (PM's Secretary) to Guest, 16 December 1941.

[16]Moyne memorandum, "Interpretation of Point Three of Atlantic Declaration in Respect of the British Colonies," WP(G)(41)89, 2 September 1941, CAB 67/9; Amery memorandum, WP(G)(41)85, 29 August 1941, CAB 67/9.

[17]WP(G)(41)89, 2 September 1941, CAB 67/9. See the two earlier drafts by Eastwood: "The Constitutional Future of the Colonial Empire," 1 September 1941, PREM 4-42/9; and an enclosure in Eastwood to Martin, 1 September 1941, PREM 4-42/9. Eastwood described his paper to Martin: "I am afraid that it may appear a little bold and frightening to those whose thoughts have moved along conventional lines in these matters."

[18]WP(G)(41)85, 29 August 1941, CAB 67/9. Amery annexed his pertinent correspondence with Burma and India. He reaffirmed the pledge of Dominion status for Burma in the

House on 15 December 1943.

[19]Oliver Stanley, "No Outside Control of Colonies," 5 March 1943, PREM 4-43A/5. On 22 November 1942 Stanley succeeded Viscount Cranborne (who had replaced Moyne on 22 February 1942).

[20]Great Britain, Parliamentary Debates, Vol. 387. pp. 1181-82.

[21]Guy Wint memorandum, "the Atlantic Charter and the Indian Ocean," 19 May 1943, FO 371.35927 F 2116/1953/61.

[22]Ibid.; see attached minutes by Bromley, 28 April; Foulds, 28 April; Dening, 29 April and 1 June; Jebb, 14 May; Webster, 25 May.

[23]Great Britain, Parliamentary Debates, Vol. 391, pp. 142-45. Pertinent material, including the Churchill-Stanley correspondence, is in PREM 4-43A/5.

[24]Pasvolsky Subcommittee report, "British War and Peace Aims," Files of Harley Notter, RG 59, file "PC," Box 15. See also a copy of the 77-page compendium, "Statements on War and Peace Aims Made on Behalf of His Majesty's Government in the United Kingdom From January 1st to June 30th, 1942," prepared by the Foreign Office Research and Press Service, Balliol College, Oxford University, 1 December 1942, Pasvolsky Files, file "April-June 1943," Box 5. For more on this important research group, see C. K. Webster Collection, Imperial War Museum, London.

[25]Churchill to Eden, 18 October 1942, PREM 4-100/7; Great Britain, Parliamentary Debates, vol. 374, pp. 67-74. For the full correspondence about the Eden-Keynes speech, including Bracken's curt assessment and approving judgments by Frederick Lindemann (later Lord Cherwell) and Roy Harrod, see PREM 4-100/7.

[26]Victor G. Lawford (Administrative Assistant to the Foreign Secretary) to Martin, 10 December 1941, and Churchill's reply, enclosed in Martin to Lawford, 12 December 1941, in PREM 4-100/8. On 4 January 1942 Hull announced that the United States Government, as depository for the U. N. Declaration, would receive statements of adherence "from appropriate authorities which are not governments." This language was intended to accommodate the Free French, but Washington and London were immediately flooded with requests from would-be adherents. Churchill complained on 27 February to Roosevelt, "Applications have been received, among others, from Otto Strasser's Free German movement, the Basque and Catalan emigre movements, King Zog and the Latvian Minister at Washington." (Ismay

Papers, file "PM's Telegrams--1942.") The Prime Minister agreed with Eden, who was anxious to establish Britain's right to be consulted about future adherents. He advised the Foreign Secretary on 11 February: "Will you kindly meanwhile draw me up a list of the candidates for election and mark those you want blackballed? It is rather like Grillions, the other way round." (PREM 3-449/1.)

[27]The Foreign Office explanation and the State Department study are contained in Welles to Roosevelt, 29 May 1942, SD 741.6111/60 1/2. See also Halifax to Churchill, 11 January 1942, PREM 4-27/9; WM(44)34, 16 March 1944, CAB 65/41; Welles memorandum of conversation with Halifax, 30 March 1942, SD 741.6111/55/7; Roosevelt's reaction is contained in Welles memorandum, 20 February 1942, SD 741.6111/52/7; Welles memorandum of conversation with Halifax, 1 April 1942, SD 741.61/985. Welles' admonition is in Welles memorandum, 4 April 1942, SD 741.611/981. Berle's assessment is in Berle memorandum to Welles, 3 April 1942, SD 741.61/982. The Russo-British Pact of May 1942 built upon the Russo-British Agreement of 12 July 1941.

[28]Churchill to Eden, 1 April 1944, CAB 21/968-14/3/34 Part I; Churchill to Eden, 31 March 1944, CAB 21/1608-57/12; WM(44)11, SSF 25 January 1944, CAB 65/45; WM(44)34, 16 March 1944, CAB 65/41.

[29]WM(44)47, 11 April 1944, CAB 65/42. The text of Hull's speech may be found in PREM 4-27/10; also State Department Bulletin, 15 April 1944, pp. 335-42.

[30]OSS memorandum, "British and American Views on the Applicability of the Atlantic Charter to Dependent Areas," 30 August 1944, OSS R&A 1972; unsigned memorandum T-529, n.d., Notter Files, file "526-537," Box 39; Great Britain, Parliamentary Debates, Vol. 404, pp. 1352-54; FE(44)5, 24 November 1944, CAB 96/5; Elliott Roosevelt, As He Saw It (New York: Duell, Sloan and Pearce, 1946), pp. 35-46. The Conservative M.P. (Astor) who put the question to Attlee replied that he was particularly happy to have the leader of the Labour Party give that response. W. J. Brown (Labour M.P.) interrupted with the rejoinder: "Does my right Hon. friend recognise that whether the Leader of the Labour Party is right or not to-day, the ex-Leader of the Tory Party very nearly gave the Empire away for a pound of tea?"

[31]James H. Lewis (Commercial Policy Division) memorandum, "History of the Negotiations With Respect to Point Four of the Atlantic Charter," 16 January 1945, Notter Files, file "Atlantic Charter," Box 1.

[32]Ibid.

³³Ibid.; Roosevelt to Former Naval Person and Winant, enclosed in H. Freeman Matthews to Churchill, 11 February 1942, Beaverbrook Papers, file "Lord Privy Seal." Roosevelt suggested that nothing be excluded from the agenda because "things which neither of us now dreams of will be subjects of the most serious consideration in the not too distant future." He rejected the proposal to exchange preliminary notes, made by the suspicious Beaverbrook--that self-appointed guardian of imperial preference--observing that such an exchange would "dilute our statement of purpose with cautious reservations." See also Sumner Welles, Where Are We Heading (New York: Harper and Brothers, 1946), pp. 6-17; E. Roosevelt, As He Saw It, pp. 24-36; Churchill, Grand Alliance, pp. 366-80; United States, Congress, Joint Committee on the Investigation of the Pearl Harbor Attack, Investigation of the Pearl Harbor Attack (Washington, D.C.: G.P.O., 1946), Pt. 14. pp. 1269-99; Woodward, British Foreign Policy, pp. 433-35; Henry H. Adams, Harry Hopkins: A Biography (New York: G.P. Putnam's Sons, 1977, pp. 370-83; United States, Department of State, Foreign Relations of the United States, 1945: The Conferences at Malta and Yalta (Washington, D.C.: G.P.O., 1955), pp. 135-38, pp. 325-27, pp. 962-63; Reynolds Competitive Cooperation, pp. 278-79.

³⁴Halifax, Fullness, pp. 281-83. The remark to Lippmann is recorded in Nigel Nicholson, ed., Harold Nicholson Diaries and Letters, 1945-1962 (3 vols.; London: Collins, 1966), I, 403. 40. For the text of the Stanley speech (19 January 1945) and the Churchill speech (14 March 1945 at the annual convention of the Conservative Party), see Notter Files, Black Binder "Dumbarton Oaks (II)," Box 274. Brian Gardner states, "Americans' suspicions of Churchill had risen to a pitch that can only be described as idiotic." See Brian Gardner, Churchill In His Time: A Study In A Reputation, 1939-1945 (London: Methuen and Company, Ltd., 1968), p. 267; also Woodward, British Foreign Policy, pp. xxxiv-xxxviii; Winant to Secretary of State, 16 January 1945, SD 740.0011PW/1-1645; Great Britain, Parliamentary Debates, Vol. 407, pp. 31-32; Stimson Diary, 12 May 1943, Vol. 43, #55.

NOTES ON CHAPTER III

¹Bowman to Winant, 25 April 1944, Notter Files, file "International Org Exchanges With the British," Box 77; Pasvolsky to Hull, 12 December 1941, Pasvolsky Files, file "1941," Box 2; E. L. Crocker to Hickerson, 22 January 1943, SD 711.41/558. The public opinion poll was transmitted by Jack B. Fahy (Special Assistant to Secretary of the Interior Harold L. Ickes) to B. W. Theron (Director, Division of Territorial and Insular Possessions, Interior), 3 January

1945. See file 9-0-48, folder "1 Dec 44-31 Dec 45," Box 156, Record Group 126, Records of the Office of Territories, Department of the Interior, NA.(Hereafter cited as RG 126.) For more on American anti-British sentiment related to the colonial issue, see George Summer to Hull, 28 November 1942, SD 841.00/1621; P. W. Glidewell to Department of State, 1 September 1943, SD 711.41/549; W. G. Yerby to Hull, 27 October 1944, SD 841.00/10-2744; also reports from H. Freeman Matthews, 27 May 1942 (SD 841.00/1595) and 31 July 1942 (SD 841.00/1601).

[2]Campbell to Eden, 31 July 1942, PREM 4-42/9. During a March 1943 visit to Washington, Eden made a point of sounding out--and debating--Welles' views on colonialism. See Eden's account to the War Cabinet in WM(43)53, SSF, 13 April 1943, CAB 65/38. For various reactions to speeches by Wallace and Willkie, see W. J. Gallman (1st Secretary, London Embassy) to Secretary of State, 1 December 1942, SD 841.00/1615; and Ambassador William H. Standley (Moscow) to Hull, 12 March 1943, SD 711.61/877. Hull thought that the speeches went too far. See Cordell Hull, The Memoirs of Cordell Hull (2 vols.; New York: Macmillan, 1948), II, 1599, 1697; and Harley A. Notter, Postwar Foreign Policy Preparation, 1939-1945 (Washington, D.C.: G.P.O., 1949), pp. 387-90.

[3]Berle memorandum of conversation with Hull and Beaverbrook, 24 July 1944, SD 711.41/7-2444; Beaverbrook, "Notes on a Conversation," n.d., Beaverbrook Papers, file D/64. For more on Willkie's trip and his relations with Roosevelt, see Wendell Willkie, One World (New York: Simon and Schuster, 1943); Hull, Memoirs, II, 1599; Rosenman, Public Papers, XI, 436-37; Robert Sherwood, Roosevelt and Hopkins: An Intimate History (New York: Harper and Brothers, 1948), pp. 634-36. Churchill said that "Willkie reminded him of a Newfoundland dog in a small parlour, which had wiped its paws on a young lady's blouse and swept off the tea cups with its tail." See William Phillips memorandum, 28 October 1942, William Phillips Papers, Houghton Library, Harvard University, Cambridge, Massachusetts, OSS file, Vol. 28.

[4]WM(43)142, 18 October 1943, CAB 65/36. See the 1943 correspondence in PREM 3-476/6: Richard Law to Churchill, 13 October; Churchill to Hopkins, 13 October; Hopkins to Churchill, 14 October; Churchill to Hopkins, 15 October; Hopkins to Churchill, 15 October. For the report by Winant of Churchill's brief declaration in the House, see Winant to Hull, 21 October 1943, SD 711.41/604. Roosevelt's comments on 12 October are recorded in William D. Hassett, Off the Record With F.D.R. (London: George Allen and Unwin, Ltd., 1960), pp. 214-15. Hassett recalled that the President "showed rather forcibly that the senators, besides picking up some incorrect info, failed utterly to understand what

they had seen in their whirlwind flight." Hassett criticized
political motives which make "senators kneel for the
photographers by the graves of dead soldiers in order to win
the votes of the live ones." For Lodge's remarks, Russell's
report, and more on this episode, see United States,
Congress, Congressional Record, 78th Congress, 1st Session,
Vol. 89, Pt. 6, 8189; Pt. 11, 7919-24, A3205. Reporting on
this senatorial criticism from Santiago, Chile, Consul
Donald R. Heath indicated that the British Embassy there
expressed apprehension that "publicity for such statements
creates the impression of a rift and lack of confidence
between the Allies." (Heath to Hull, 9 October 1943, SD
711.41/602.) From La Paz, Bolivia, Consul Robert F. Woodward
summarized local attitudes about the episode: "Rivalry and
misunderstandings of this nature can grow until they reach
such proportions as to interfere seriously with the war
effort and the post war reconstruction." (Woodward to Hull,
5 November 1943, SD 711.41/608.) This affair even became a
cliché. For example, Halifax wrote to Eden that a visiting
Englishman in the United States (T. L. Horabin, M.P.) "was
doing far more harm than all the five senators put
together." Halifax to Eden, 18 November 1943, PREM 4-83/2.)
Also a Parliamentary Secretary in the Ministry of
Production, M. J. Garro-Jones, announced in a Liverpool
speech,"When we reflect that the blood of men of all nations
and the silent tears of their bereaved are shed in the
belief and consolation of a future better than the past, we
must feel contempt for any, whether American senators or
British critics, who, by pettiness, falsehood or
selfishness, sow new seeds and weeds of bitterness on the
earth." But Minister of Information Brendan Bracken called
this speech to Churchill's attention with the warning: "His
purple passage about the American Senators will be fully
reported in the Isolationist Press with headlines such as
'British Minister Attacks American Senators.'" Churchill
agreed, and he wrote to Garro-Jones' supervisor (Minister of
Production Oliver Lyttleton), "Such words . . . will of
course be given undue publicity in the United States and
help to make the mischief of the five Senators more
widespread." See the 1943 correspondence in PREM 4-84/1. For
more on the remarks of the senators, see New York Times,
8,10-13 October 1943; Stimson Diary, 4 October 1943, Vol.
44, #57. On 19 October, the Prime Minister announced in the
House that "there would be no advantage in His Majesty's
Government taking part in this wordy warfare, especially at
a time when the British and United States Armies are engaged
shoulder to shoulder." Great Britain, Parliamentary Debates,
Vol. 392, pp. 1211-12.

[5]See Churchill to Auchinleck, 7 December; Churchill to
Roosevelt, 9 December; Churchill to Smuts, 9 December; and
Churchill to Eden, 12 December 1941; all in Ismay Papers,
file, "PM's Telegrams--1941; also WM(41)125, 8 December

1941, CAB 65/20.

[6]Churchill, Grand Alliance, pp. 511-12; Ismay to Hopkins, 12 January 1942, Ismay Papers, file IV/HOP/7: Ismay, Memoirs, p. 241; Holland to Hull, 28 February 1942, SD 841.0071578a.

[7]Hull to Stimson, 23 September 1944, SD 740.0011PW/8-2644. (See also in this file: Acting Secretary of War John J. McCloy to Hull, 26 August; and Joseph Ballantine, Head, Far Eastern Division, to Hull, 21 September.) See the September 1944 Hull-Stimson correspondence attached to SD 740.0011PW/9-1444; also Stimson Diary entries in 1941 for 23 May, 21 July, and 25 November (Stimson Papers, file 9, Box 173). The 1942 Final Report of the Roberts Commission is in Senate Document #159, 77th Congress, 2nd Session. The postwar congressional investigation is published in Pearl Harbor Attack. (op. cit.) For some of the best sources on the circumstances and responsibility for Pearl Harbor, see Gordon W. Prange, At Dawn We Slept: The Untold Story of Pearl Harbor (New York: McGraw-Hill, 1981); Hans L. Trefousse, Pearl Harbor: The Continuing Controversy (Malabar, FL: Robert E. Krieger Publishing Company, 1982); Wayne Cole, "American Entry Into World War II: A Historiographical Appraisal," Mississippi Valley Historical Review, XLIII (March 1957), 595-617; Dorothy Borg and Shumpei Okamoto, eds., Pearl Harbor As History: Japanese-American Relations, 1931-1941 (New York: Columbia University Press, 1973); Roberta Wohlsetter, Pearl Harbor: Warning and Decision (Stanford: Stanford University Press, 1962); Sherman Miles, "Pearl Harbor in Retrospect," Atlantic Monthly, CLXXXII (July 1948), 65-72; Immanuel C. Y. Hsu, "Kurusu's Mission to the United States and the Abortive Modus Vivendi," Journal of Modern History, XXIV (September 1952), 301-7. For a convenient summary of the various American investigations of the attack at Pearl Harbor, see Bruce R. Bartlett, Cover-Up; The Politics of Pearl Harbor (New Rochelle, NY: Arlington House Publishers, 1978); Hanson Baldwin correspondence with General Marshall and Admiral Stark in April 1954, Hanson Baldwin Papers, Yale University, file 763, Box 15; National Security Agency record of interview with Ralph Briggs, 13 January 1977, American Committee on the History of the Second World War, Newsletter No. 24 (Fall 1980), 44-61. Briggs alleges that his radio intercept (4 Dec 1941) of the Japanese "winds execute" message, immediately transmitted to Washington, was subsequently suppressed and that he was expressly ordered not to participate in or cooperate with the subsequent investigation of the attack on Pearl Harbor.

[8]See enclosed in COS(45)294, 18 November 1945, CAB 80/51: Halifax to Foreign Office 16 November 1945; Foreign Office to Chiefs of Staff (enclosing the 1941 messages and

the statement of Foreign Office approval for release), 17 November 1945. Acheson wanted to provide ten messages to the congressional committee. Of these, the Foreign Office called the attention of the Chiefs of Staff to three in particular. First, a Foreign Office cable to Halifax, 11 February 1941, urged an Anglo-American declaration to Japan "that any attack on the Netherlands East Indies, or on British possessions in the F. E., will involve Japan in immediate war with both countries." Second, the Foreign Office instructed Halifax on 29 November 1941 to reveal that the British planned to occupy the Kra Peninsula if Japan attacked Thailand (as seemed likely) and to press for American support in the event of hostilities. Third, on 30 November 1941 the Foreign Office told Halifax that Thai permission to occupy the Kra Isthmus would be sought in view of the existing Anglo-Thai Non-Aggression Treaty. See all these released British documents as published in Pearl Harbor Attack, Pt. 14, pp. 1084-1300, Pt. 19, 3441-3487.

[9]Roosevelt and Hull are quoted in Hassett, Record, p. 254. See also John Hickerson to Hull, 20 June 1944, Records of John Hickerson (RG 59), NA, file "Memoranda 1944," Box 2; Dwight C. Poole (OSS Foreign Nationalities Branch) to Hickerson, 13 July 1944, SD 740.0011PW/7-1344; Stettinius to Hull, 20 June 1944, Edward R. Stettinius, Jr., Papers, University of Virginia, Charlottesville, Virginia, file "S-May 1944," Box 218.

[10]Gore-Booth (enclosing the views of Sansom) to Clarke, 26 January 1943, and the attached minute by Dening, 12 February 1943, FO 371.35957, F 751/751/23. Gore-Booth and Sansom were in Tokyo with Grew as was Eugene Dooman, while Dening served in Washington. See Wilfred Fleisher, Our Enemy Japan (Garden City, NY: Doubleday, Doran and Company, 1942); P.H. Gore-Booth, With Great Truth and Respect (London: Constable, 1974), pp. 108-09; Katherine Sansom, ed., Sir George Sansom and Japan: A Memoir (Tallahassee, FL: The Diplomatic Press, Inc., 1972), pp. 110-16.

[11]Grew to Stimson, 26 June 1945, Stimson Papers, file 7, Box 149. The MacMurray memorandum, dated 1 November 1935, may be found in the MacMurray Papers, Yale University (microfilm copy). Grew's alleged self-promotion campaign included the writing of a brief book in which he claimed, "During my mission to Japan I kept our Government informed. . . . I reported that Japan might strike 'with dangerous and dramatic suddenness.' This is precisely what happened. . . ." See Joseph C. Grew, Report From Tokyo: A Message to the American People (New York: Simon and Schuster, 1942), p.vii, p. 29. For more on Grew's views, see Grew, Ten Years in Japan (New York: Simon and Schuster, 1944); Waldo Heinrichs, American Ambassador (Boston: Little, Brown and Company, 1966); Walter Johnson, ed.,

Turbulent Era (Boston: Houghton Mifflin, 1952); Stimson to Grew, 11 May 1944, Stimson Papers, file 6, Box 145; Hugh Byas memorandum, Hugh Byas Papers, Yale University, file 11, Box 27; Grew diary entries for 1941 (see especially file 19, items 5631-32), Joseph C. Grew Papers, Houghton Library, Harvard University, Cambridge, Massachusetts.

[12]Steward to General J. W. Sandilands (in China), 18 October 1931, Papers of Major General Sir Ronald C. Penney, Liddell Hart Centre, file II/1-5; Foreign Office Research Department (FORD) memorandum, "Japan's Plans for Greater East Asia," 31 October 1940, and the minutes of the meetings pertaining to this continuing study (#1, 1 November 1940 through #17, 16 July 1941), C. K. Webster Collection, Vol. XVI/5.

[13]An examination of Hull's abortive modus vivendi falls outside the scope of this study. Briefly, the plan called for (1) Japan and the United States to affirm their mutual desires for peace; (2) promises that neither Japan nor the United States would advance into Southeast Asia, Northeast Asia, or southern and northern Pacific areas; (3) commitments by Japan to withdraw her troops from southern Indochina, to reduce the total number of her troops in Indochina to the level of 26 July 1941 , and to refrain from sending any additional troops, including replacements, to Indochina; (4) a promise by the United States to ease her economic restrictions against Japan including imports "freely permitted" from Japan and certain American exports (e.g., supplies for vessels in trade, food, raw cotton, medical supplies, and petroleum to meet Japan's civilian needs) in varying levels to Japan depending on the status of American-Japanese relations; (5) Japan to relax her economic freeze of American assets; (6) the United States to ask the Australians, British, and Dutch to undertake similar promises to those in #4 above; (7) Japan and China to begin discussions to resolve their differences based on the fundamental principles of peace, law, order, and justice; (8) a time frame of three months for this modus vivendi during which Japanese-American negotiations would continue (either to seek a comprehensive settlement for the entire Pacific area or to work out an extension of the modus vivendi). For different drafts of this plan (22, 24, and 25 November 1941), see FRUS, 1941, IV, 625-40, 642-46, 661-65. Although Churchill did not receive the full text of the final draft until late on 25 November, Hull had presented the basic outline in his first draft to the British, Australian, Dutch, and Chinese Ambassadors on 22 November. Later that day, Hull noted, "Each of the gentlemen present seemed to be well pleased with this preliminary report to them except the Chinese Ambassador, who was somewhat disturbed, as he always is when any question concerning China arises not entirely to his way of thinking." (FRUS,

1941, IV, 640.) Eden and the Foreign Office sent their comments to Hull on 25 November (ibid., 654-57) and Churchill explained his reaction on 26 November (see the following note).   Hull withdrew the proposed modus vivendi on 26 November. See also State Department to Grew, 26 November 1941, Grew Diary, file 78, items 6069-70; A. A. Berle diary entry, 1 December 1941, Adolph A. Berle, Jr. Papers, FDRL, file "Diary, December 1-11, 1941," Box 213; Stimson-McGeorge Bundy interview, 14 June 1946, Stimson Papers, file 9, Box 186; Lester H. Brune, "Considerations of Force in Cordell Hull's Diplomacy, July 26 to November 26, 1941," Diplomatic History, II (Fall 1978), 389-405.

[14]Churchill to Roosevelt, 26 November 1941, Ismay Papers, file "PM's Telegrams--1941."   For more on the 1940-1941 British attitude, see the memoranda and minutes of the Far Eastern Committee in CAB 96/1-4.   See Generalissimo's proposals, enclosed in Ambassador Nelson T. Johnson to Hull, 11 November 1940, SD 711.93/459; also Welles to Johnson, 18 November 1940, SD 711.93/453.   On 26 November, Hull explained to Roosevelt that the decision not to present the proposed modus vivendi to the Japanese was reached "in view of the opposition of the Chinese Government and either the half-hearted support or the actual opposition of the British, the Netherlands, and the Australian Governments, and in view of the wide publicity of the [domestic] opposition and of the additional opposition that will naturally follow through utter lack of an understanding of the vast importance and value otherwise of the modus vivendi." (FRUS, 1941, VI, 665-66.) On 27 November, Hull told the Australian Minister, "I did not feel that the communications from Churchill and Eden, with qualifications such as were in them would be very helpful in a bitter fight that was projected by Chiang Kai-shek and carried forward by all of the malcontents in the United States." (Ibid., 668.) That same day, Halifax asked Welles why the proposal had not been presented to the Japanese. When Welles gave one reason as "the half-hearted support" of the British, Halifax protested that he had communicated London's full support to Hull. Welles stated that Churchill's telegram was a "very grave questioning of the course proposed." Halifax then tried to explain that Churchill was only presenting objections likely to be raised by the Chinese. (Ibid., 666-67.)

[15]Hayter to Clarke, 18 September 1943, FO 371.35957, F 5068/751/23. See also Sir William Hayter, A Double Life (London: Hamish Hamilton, 1974), pp. 60-70.

[16]Hayter letter (see previous note).

[17]Ibid.

[18]Ibid. See attached 1943 minutes by Foulds, 12 October; and Clarke, 13 October. Clarke never got the opportunity to discuss this during Hornbeck's visit to London. (Clarke to Hayter, 19 October 1943, ibid.) Halifax's comments, dated 29 October, were enclosed in Hayter to Clarke, 2 November 1943, FO 371.35957, F 5766/751/23. For more on the stillborn plan by Hull, see Immanuel C. Y. Hsu, "Kurusu's Mission to the United States and the Abortive Modus Vivendi," Journal of Modern History, XXIV (September 1952), 301-7; Hull, Memoirs, II, 1073-82; Pearl Harbor Attack, Pt 14, pp. 1145-70. For the views of one State Department officer who arrived separately at conclusions similar to those of Hayter, see Edmund O. Clubb, Twentieth-Century China (New York: Columbia University Press, 1964), pp. 230-31.

[19]FE(41)126, 26 June 1941, CAB 96/4; Hankey to Butler, 21 April 1941, CAB 63/177.

[20]The author is grateful to the Ambassador's son, Robert, for permission to examine the original manuscript dated 23 October 1942, an unexpurgated copy of which is not deposited in the records of the Foreign Office. For edited versions, all dated 4 February 1943, see FO 371.35957, F 821/751/23 and FO 371.31811, F 7301/4/23; also author's interview with Robert Craigie, 4 July 1973, London. For excellent background material, see Nobutaka Ike, ed., Japan's Decision for War: Records of the 1941 Policy Conferences (Stanford: Stanford University Press, 1967); James W. Morley, ed., The Fateful Choice: Japan's Advance Into Southeast Asia 1939-1941 (New York: Columbia University Press, 1980); Richard J. Grace, "Whitehall and the Ghost of Appeasement, November 1941," Diplomatic History, III (Spring 1979), 173-191; Peter Lowe, "Great Britain and the Outbreak of War With Japan, 1941," in War and Society ed. by M. R. D. Foot (New York: Barnes and Noble, 1973), pp. 17-37; Akira Iriye, "The Ideological Background to Japan's War Against Asia and the West," International Studies, II (1982), 1-14; papers (Part I) in Ian Nish, ed., Anglo-Japanese Alienation, 1919-1952 (Cambridge: Cambridge University Press, 1982); Byas to Sir Frederick Leith-Ross, 23 December 1935, Byas Papers, file "Correspondence 1935-1942," Box 4. For more on the economic pressures Japan faced, see Appendix G.

[21]See the 1942 minutes in FO 371.31811, F 7301/4/23: Clarke, 25 October; Peterson, 27 October; and Cadogan, 31 October. Eden attached his reaction on 6 November: "I agree with these minutes in every detail. I have no time now for past controversies."

[22]Clarke minute (enclosing the draft text), 14 April 1943, FO 371.35957, F 2602/751/23. But Clarke conceded,

"The reason for holding it up in the first place was that it was liable to promote controversy and ill-feeling (e.g., with the Dominions): even if there were time for post-mortems of this kind, such controversy does not contribute anything valuable to the war effort." Attached comments reveal strong concern in the Foreign Office to limit circulation of the Craigie report. The printed Foreign Office memorandum, "From the Burma Road Crisis to Pearl Harbour," 23 April 1943, and an abbreviated version of Craigie's Final Report, are in FO 371.35957, F 821/751/23. L. H. Foulds attached his comment on 12 February: "The original has been taken away by Sir R. Craigie." Clarke provided the "short answer" in a memorandum dated 25 October 1942 (FO 371.31811, F 7301/4/23). Craigie learned just how limited the actual circulation had been when the King asked him much later why he had never submitted a final report. (Author's interview with Robert Craigie.) His son claims that Craigie was technically kept on active employment status at a partial salary without an actual assignment by the Churchill government and not allowed to retire to a full pension. (The Foreign Office has not responded to the author's inquiry on this point.)

[23]Gore-Booth memorandum, 28 September 1943, enclosed in Michael Wright (Embassy, Washington) to Clarke, 21 October 1943, FO 371.35957, F 5766/751/23.

[24]Clarke memorandum, 7 November 1943, attached to Michael Wright letter, ibid.; also attached were the comments by Hayter, 29 September and Campbell, 9 October. Campbell added that American "War and Navy Departments had become bellicose and it will be remembered that Hull told H. E. [Halifax] that he had dropped the modus vivendi and 'let the soldiers and sailors have their war then, and I hope they're better prepared than they seem,' or words to that effect."

[25]Foreign Office memorandum, "From the Burma Road Crisis to Pearl Harbour," 23 April 1943, FO 371.35957, F 2602/751/23.

[26]Churchill to Eden, 19 September 1943, ibid. [Emphasis mine.] The Foreign Secretary attached his comment on 22 September urging Churchill to read the Foreign Office report which, Eden said, "leads up to your own conclusions and is designed to show (a) that Japan was bent on our undoing; (b) that no measures of appeasement would have averted this; and (c) that our policy contributed to bring the British Empire, the United States and the Dutch into line in the Far East in time before Japan struck." Both agreed on an extremely limited circulation of Craigie's version.

NOTES ON CHAPTER IV

[1]FE(44)1, 15 November 1944, CAB 96/5. The Chairman of this Committee (dormant since 1941) was Parliamentary Under Secretary of State George H. Hall.

[2]P. N. Jester memorandum, 6 January 1943, SD 841.00/94; Shantz to Hull, 3 April 1942, SD 841.00/1581; Shantz to Hull, 9 April 1942, SD 841.00/1634; Gallman to Hull, 28 August 1942, SD 841.00/1604; Gallman to Hull, 12 October 1942, SD 841.00/1608; Gallman to Hull, 24 March 1943, SD 841.00/1634; text of Stanley speech, 4 March 1943, FO 371.35917, F 1589/877/61.

[3]A. E. Campbell, "The United States and Great Britain: Uneasy Allies," in Twentieth-Century American Foreign Policy, ed. by John Braeman, Robert H. Bremner, and David Brody (Columbus: Ohio State University Press, 1971), pp. 489-90. The 21 December 1940 Joint Board study on strategic priorities had two titles: (a) "National Defense Policy of the United States" and (b) "Study of the Immediate Problems Concerning Involvement in War." (See text in JB 325, ser. 670, 21 December 1940); also unsigned composite manuscript, "War Against Germany," JCS Files, Modern Military Branch, NA.

[4]"Report on Suggestion for the Designation of Colonial Specialists in the Department of State," CTP-120a, 8 March 1944, Notter Files, file "Committee on Colonial and Trustee Problems, CTP Mins.," Box 56.

[5]Of course, "respect for native institutions" did not necessarily connote entirely beneficial practices. Corporal punishment, "tiger cages," and widespread "corruption" (which may be regarded as a Western description for a native institution) were also thereby perpetuated in addition to local religious practices and quaint dress styles.

[6]Knight memorandum, "The Economic Importance of Colonies," T-134, 17 May 1943, Notter Files, file "T Docs 310-319," Box 34.

[7]OSS memorandum, "British Colonial Policy," 28 April 1944, OSS R&A 1398; Green memorandum, "British Empire: British Institutions," 9 December 1942, Notter Files, file "T Docs 171-198," Box 32; unsigned memorandum, "The British Empire: List of Territories," 10 December 1942, ibid.

[8]Green memorandum, ibid.; OSS memorandum, "Colonial Policy and the British Dominions," 24 April 1944, OSS R&A 1971.

[9]Taylor to Perkins, 15 November 1941, Record Group 40, General Records of the Department of Commerce, folder "L-L Bill," Box 957, 102517/36, NA; Appleby to Acheson, 9 June 1942, SD 711.41/539.

[10]Appleby to Acheson, and Appleby to Stettinius, 9 June 1942, SD 711.41/539.

[11]OSS British Empire Section Special Memorandum #29, 15 January 1942, OSS R&A 49.

[12]Churchill to Roosevelt, 23 March 1942, Ismay Papers, file "PM's Telegrams--1942," Churchill to Curtin, 19 January 1942, DO(42)5, 21 January 1942, CAB 69/4. For more on Australian sentiment, see in CAB 65/25 the 1942 Cabinet correspondence and minutes: WM (42)5, 14 January; WM (42)10, 22 January; WM (42)11 and 12, 26 January; WM(42)13, 29 January; WM(42)14, 2 February; WM (42)32, 9 March; also FE(44)1, 15 November 1944, CAB 96/5; WP(G)(39)92, 13 November 1939, CAB 67/2; WP(G)(39)76, 8 November 1939, CAB 67/2; WP(G)(39)91, 15 November 1939, CAB 67/2; FE(41)32, 31 January 1941, CAB 96/3; WM(42)11, 26 January 1942, CAB 65/25; COS(44)144(O), 5 March 1944, CAB 79/80; COS(45)12(O), 5 January 1945, CAB 80/90; COS(45)522(O), 8 August 1945, CAB 80/96.

[13]OSS memorandum, "The Canberra Agreement and Reactions To It in the United States and the United Kingdom," 7 July 1944, OSS R&A 2226; WM(44)149, 13 November 1944, CAB 65/44; Dominions Office to Foreign Office, 24 January 1943, FO 371.34027, A 6027/2832/45; WP(39)74, 5 November 1939, CAB 67/2; Halifax to Eden, 11 March 1943, FO 371.34207, A 2832/2832/45; author's interview with Sir Harry Batterbee, 3 August 1973, London.

[14]COS(44)1050(0), 26 December 1944, CAB 80/89; COS(44)922(0), 24 October 1944, CAB 80/88; COS(44)945(0), 3 November 1944, CAB 80/89; Hull memorandum of conversation with Halifax, 5 January 1943, SD 841.014/96; WP(G)(39)91, 15 November 1939, CAB 67/2; also see reports requested by the State Department on press reactions to a speech by Smuts on 23 November 1943, dated 28 January-8 February, 1944, contained in SD 741.00/271-79.

[15]Green memorandum, "Report on Conversations in Ottawa, November 27-29, 1943," 1 December 1943, Notter Files, file "Canada--Misc. Papers & Exchange," Box 284; P. Moffat memorandum of conversation with Joseph Tucker (WPB Representative in Canada), 21 October 1942, Hickerson Files, file "Memoranda--1942," Box 2; J. F. Green and E. H. Armstrong memorandum, "Canadian Policy Towards Post-War International Arrangements," 28 April 1944, Notter Files, file "Canada--Misc. Papers & Exchange," Box 284;

COS(45)70(0), 31 December 1945, CAB 80/98; WP(G)(39)119, 28 November 1939, CAB 67/3; W. J. Gallman to Hull, 10 November 1943, SD 841.01/108; WM(44)13, 31 January 1944, CAB 65/41; Ismay memorandum, "Canadian Participation in the War Against Japan," COS(44)434(0), 17 May 1944, CAB 80/83; COS(45)702(0), 29 December 1945, CAB 80/98; General Jacob memorandum, COS(44)236(0), 8 March 1944, CAB 80/81.

[16]Detailed analyses of these complex problems lie outside the scope of this study; they are cited merely to indicate the enormous political and imperial tasks imposed on London. For a lengthy report on Cyprus, see M. R. Malleson (Colonial Office) to J. H. Peck (PM's Secretary), 24 April 1943, PREM 4-43A/10. Details on administration of the colonies are in Stanley memorandum, WP(45)66, 3 February 1945, CAB 66/61 and WM(45)14, 5 February 1945, CAB 65/49. George H. Gater (Colonial Office) submitted a study of policy for Malaya in a letter to the COS 22 September 1945, outlining tentative plans and previous Cabinet decisions. His report is enclosed in COS(45)586(0), 24 September 1945, CAB 80/97. For American views on the future of Malaya, see three studies by James F. Green in the Notter Files: T-350, "The Problem of British Malaya: Basic Data," 20 July 1943, file "T Documents 345-351," Box 35; T-375, "The Problem of British Malaya: Possible Solutions," 13 October 1943, file "T Documents 374-381," Box 36; H-49a, "British Empire: Southeast Asia: Territorial Problems: British Malaya," 29 February 1944, file "H-Policy Summaries 40-55," Box 58.   COS views on Singapore are in COS(45)206, 9 September 1945, CAB 80/50; COS(45)229, 26 September 1945, CAB 80/50. For the continuing Cabinet deliberations about Ceylon, see WM(41)87, 28 September 1941, CAB 65/19; WM(42)166, 9 December 1942, CAB 65/28; WM(43)47, 1 April 1943, CAB 65/34; WM(43)70, 18 May 1943, CAB 65/34; WM(43)74, 21 May 1943, CAB 65/34; WM(44)77, 13 June 1944, CAB 65/42; WP(44)299, 10 June 1944, CAB 66/50.

[17]See the reports and correspondence in COS(45)580(0), 19 September 1945, CAB 80/97; COS(45)588(0), 24 September 1945, CAB 80/97; WM(43)54, 14 April 1943, CAB 65/34; WM(44)166, 4 December 1944, CAB 65/44; WM(45)58, 4 May 1945, CAB 65/50; WM(45)61, 14 May 1945, CAB 65/50; OSS memorandum, "Proposed British Policies for Post-War Burma and Probable Burmese Reactions," April (?) 1945, OSS R&A 2771; OSS memorandum 54239-C, 12 August 1943 Record Group 226, Records of the Office of Strategic Services. (Hereafter cited as RG 226.)

[18]DO(43)13, 28 June 1943, CAB 69/5; DO(43)14, 28 June 1943, CAB 69/5; Ismay, Memoirs, p. 293; Chiang Kai-shek's message (via T. V. Soong) of 28 January 1942, is quoted in Grace P. Hayes, "The War Against Japan" (2 vols.; unpublished, 1953-1954, Modern Military Branch, NA), I, 108.

Johnson is quoted in Barbara W. Tuchman, Sand Against the Wind: Stilwell and the American Experience in China, 1911-1945 (New York: Macmillan, 1970), pp. 284-86.

[19]WM(45)56, SSF, 30 April 1945, CAB 65/52; Churchill, Hinge of Fate, pp. 179-92; Churchill to Cripps and Churchill to Roosevelt, 11 April 1942, Ismay Papers, file "PM's Telegrams-1942"; WM(43)136, 7 October 1943, CAB 65/36; WP(43)435, 5 October 1943, CAB 66/42; WP(43)684, 10 December 1944, CAB 66/59; WP(44)720, 16 December 1944, CAB 66/59; WM(44)171, 18 December 1944, CAB 65/44; Charles Taussig memorandum of conversation with Cripps, 28 December 1942, Charles Taussig Papers, FDRL, file "1941-1943 inclusive," Box 52; memorandum enclosed in Nehru to Louis Johnson, 7 April 1942, Louis Johnson Papers, University of Virginia, file "1942-April-June," Box 97.

[20]Churchill-Crozier interview, 20 March 1942, Crozier Papers, file "WC, 2/10," Box 2; WM(44)20, 14 May 1944, CAB 65/41; FE(44)1, 15 November 1944, CAB 96/5; COS(44)418(0), 12 May 1944, CAB 80/83; Beaverbrook "Notes on Conversations May 15-16, 1943 in the United States," Beaverbrook Papers, file D/68; COS(44)744(0), 18 August 1944, CAB 80/86; COS(44)752(0), 19 August 1944, CAB 80/86; COS(44)763(0), 24 August 1944, CAB 80/86; Stilwell to Marshall, 28 November 1942, RG 332 Stilwell Files, WNRC, file I, Box 1; Churchill to Lord Cherwell, 11 June 1946, Cherwell Papers, Nuffield College Library, Oxford, file J62; COS(45)532(0), 14 August 1945, CAB 80/96; COS(45)535(0), 16 August 1945, CAB 80/96.

[21]See Churchill telegrams to the Viceroy and the Generalissimo, 3 February 1942, Ismay Papers, file "PM's Telegrams-1942." On 12 February, Churchill curtly rejected a proposal by the Generalissimo to meet Gandhi at Wardha. (Ibid.) Eden's presentation is in WM(42)13, SSF, 29 January 1942, CAB 65/29; see also Churchill's report from ARCADIA about American emphasis on China in WM(42)8, SSF, 17 January 1942, CAB 65/29.

[22]Chiang Kai-shek to Roosevelt, 30 July 1942, enclosed in Roosevelt to Churchill, 30 July 1942, PREM 4-45/4; Chiang Kai-shek to Churchill, 23 February 1942, PREM 3-167/1; Chiang Kai-shek to T. V. Soong, 19 April 1942, OPD Executive File 10, Item 196, Modern Military Branch, NA.

[23]Churchill to Chiang Kai-shek, 26 August 1942, Ismay Papers, file "PM's Telegrams-1942." See the 1942 correspondence in PREM 4-45/4: Roosevelt to Churchill, 30 July; Churchill to Roosevelt, 31 July; Roosevelt to Former Naval Person, 9 August; Churchill to Roosevelt, 10 August; Amery to Churchill, 12 August; Seymour to Foreign Office, 12 August; Foreign Office to Seymour, 17 August; Amery "Note of an interview with the Chinese Ambassador on 20th August

1942"; Amery to Churchill, 24 August; Martin to Resident Clerk, India Office, 23 August; C. Rolfe (Resident Clerk) to Martin, 24 August.

[24]Tuan Sheng Chien (Professor, National Peiking University) to Cripps, 3 December 1942, Lord Cripps Papers, Nuffield College Library, Oxford, 848/690. Cripps replied 17 February 1943 that the Chinese underestimated the dissension in India. He also explained that Sino-British friction in Burma arose partly because "it was too sudden and strange a fighting partnership." (Ibid.)

[25]On extraterritoriality, see WM(43)1, 4 January 1943, CAB 65/33; WM(42)171, 21 December 1942, CAB 65/28; Eden memorandum, WP(42)600, 19 December 1942, CAB 66/32; WM(42)173, 28 December 1942, CAB 65/28; WM(42)121, 7 September 1942, CAB 65/27; WM(42)131, 5 October 1942, CAB 65/28; WM(42)132, 6 October 1942, CAB 65/28; WM(42)162, 30 November 1942, CAB 65/28. Eden expressed concern about China's claims on Tibet in WM(43)94, 7 July 1943, CAB 65/35. Colonel Frank Dorn reported the markings on Chinese maps including Burma to General Thomas Hearn on 9 September 1943. (RG 332 Stilwell Files, WNRC, Vol. 2, Box 2.) The Generalissimo's comments are in Seymour to Foreign Office, 28 August 1945, FO 371,46212, F 6006/186/10. See also Raymond G. O'Connor, Diplomacy For Victory: FDR and Unconditional Surrender (New York: W. W. Norton and Company, 1971), pp. 77-79; OSS memorandum, "China's Borderlands--Criteria for Claims," 7 August 1944, OSS R&A 2420; Seymour to Eden, 26 August 1945, FO 371.46212, F 5762/186/10; Seymour to Eden, 10 April 1944, FO 371.46212, F 2126/34/10.

[26]Wallace notes of a conversation with the Generalissimo, 21 June 1944, enclosed in Ruth E. Bacon (Far Eastern Division) to Hull, 18 July 1944, SD 893.00/7-2144. Roosevelt made the proposal on several occasions during the war. See FRUS, 1943, I, 541-43; Theodore H. White, ed., The Stilwell Papers (New York: W. Sloan Associates, 1948), pp. 250-54; Lord Moran, Winston Churchill: The Struggle for Survival, 1940-1965 (Boston: Houghton Mifflin, 1966), p. 249; Halifax, Fullness, pp. 245-50. Halifax reported a story told to him by a visitor to Roosevelt's bedside immediately prior to the President's death. In some of the last words Roosevelt uttered, three times he repeated, "If Churchill insists on Hong Kong, I will have to take it to the King." Twice before, on 8 and 25 March 1945, Roosevelt had confirmed his intention "to go over Churchill's head" about Hong Kong in conversations with Patrick J. Hurley. (Hurley to Truman, 29 May 1945, SD 893.00/5-2945.) See also Berle memorandum, 24 July 1944, SD 711.41/7-2444; Beaverbrook "Notes of a Conversation," 24 July 1944, Beaverbrook Papers, file D/64; A. L. Scott (Far Eastern Department, F.O.) minute, 2 November 1943, FO 371.35834, F

5729/1591/10.   Scott inquired about having some M.P. advocate the return of Texas to Mexico if Americans continually pressed H.M.G. to return Hong Kong to China. For State Department studies of Hong Kong, see J. F. Green memorandum, "The Problem of Hong Kong: Possible Solutions," T-136, 23 October 1942, Notter Files, file "T Docs 130-170," Box 32; Robert S. Ward memorandum, "Hong Kong Under Japanese Occupation," enclosed in C. K. Moser (Chief of Far Eastern Unit, Bureau of Foreign and Domestic Commerce) to Hornbeck, 8 November 1943, SD 740.0011PW/3611; J. F. Green memorandum, "British Empire: China: Territorial Problems: Hong Kong," H-39a, 2 March 1944, Notter Files, file "H Policy Summaries 26-39," Box 57; Amry Vandenbosch memorandum, "Hong Kong," TS-169, 14 February 1944, Notter Files, file "122-183," Box 44.

[27]Colonial Office memorandum, "British Colonial Economic Interests in China," FE(E)(45)20, 28 February 1945, CAB 96/8; E. M. Gall (Secretary, China Association) to Colonial Office, 27 May 1943, FE(E)(45)4, 11 January 1945, CAB 96/8; W. B. Kennett (Chairman, China Association) to Colonial Office, 23 November 1944, FE(E)(45)4, ibid.; Colonial Office memorandum, FE(45)9, 20 February 1945, CAB 96/5; Seymour to Foreign Office, 22 December 1944, FO 371.46178, F 57/57/10; material on Hurley's visit may be found in PREM 3-159/12; Hurley's own account on 29 May for Truman is in SD 893.00/5-2945. Hurley stated, "Churchill and the British Empire will not relinquish Hongkong unless they have to do it. I suggest that we put ourselves in a trading position rather than a give-away position with Britain. You could indicate your desire for an accounting and immediate return of all used and unused equipment. . . . You could indicate an intention to sell all such equipment in the markets of the world. You could suggest that you desire strict accountability for all supplies and equipment other than lend-lease which Britain has received. You could also say that no credit or additional gifts at the expense of the American taxpayer would be given to Britain until Britain shows a more understanding attitude toward the American policy of Hongkong and towards democracy the world over. I think you would find Britain amenable to reason."

[28]Generalissimo's speech, quoted in Seymour to Foreign Office, 26 August 1945, FO 371.46212, F 5762/186/19; unsigned memorandum, "The Legal and Political Status of Certain Areas and the Resulting Consequences for United States' Occupation Forces," PWC-299a, 7 November 1944, Notter Files, file "282-302," Box 20. The Foreign Office asked the Chief of Staff to begin with the hypothesis that the Japanese surrender would precede the liberation of Singapore, and then to revise contingency plans for reoccupation as events unfolded. See COS(45)509(0), 3

August 1945, and COS(45)536(0), 16 August 1945, CAB 80/96.
See minutes of the 1945 meetings between Wedemeyer and
Chiang Kai-shek (and their respective staffs) on 15 August
(#73) and 20 August (#77), RG 332 Wedemeyer files, WNRC,
Vol. II, "G-mo's Minutes," Box 4, "MAPS." Seymour's stormy
interview with K. C. Wu, the Chinese Acting Minister for
Foreign Affairs, was reported by Bevin in FE(M)(45)1, 17
August 1945, CAB 96/9; Attlee's statement to Truman and
other pertinent correspondence may be found in FRUS, 1945,
VII, 492-513; also COS(45)549(0), 26 August 1945, CAB 80/97;
COS(45)541(0), 22 August 1945, CAB 80/96; COS(45)559(0), 2
September 1945, CAB 80/97; COS (45)606(0), 9 October 1945,
CAB 80/96.   For postwar conditions and British problems in
Hong Kong, see the private report by Rear Admiral C. H. J.
Harcourt (C-in-C, Hong Kong) to A. V. Alexander (First Lord
of the Admiralty), 25 November 1945, Alexander Papers,
Archives Center, Churchill College, Cambridge University,
file 5/10/70; also Colonial Office to COS, 21 December 1945,
COS(45)694(0), 22 December 1945, CAB 80/98.   De Wiart
described Wedemeyer's reaction in a letter to Ismay, 23
August 1945 (FO 371.46212, F 6055/186/10).   Penney
memorandum of conversation with MacArthur in Manila, 23
August 1945, Penney Papers, file 5/13. For adverse reaction
in the Chinese press about Hong Kong, see Philip D. Sprouse
(Consul, Kunming) to Secretary of State, 17 September 1945,
SD 893.00/9-1745; OSS memorandum, "The Future Status of Hong
Kong," 5 October 1945, OSS R&A 3267.   Secretary of State
James F. Byrnes revealed his concern to Bevin about the
provisions of General Order Number One and the possibility
of the Japanese forces in China surrendering to the Chinese
Communists in a letter, 24 August 1945, FO 371.46212, F
5775/186/10.

[29]Beaverbrook letters to Halifax, 25 and 29 August
1944, Beaverbrook Papers, file D/64; Stettinius memorandum,
25 February 1944, SD 740.0011PW/3792; Halifax to Eden, 2 May
1944, CAB 21/1025-14/31 Pt. I. For similar expressions by
Hornbeck in his 1943 visit to London, see Clarke to Dening,
25 October 1943, FO 371.25871, F 5460/5251/10; Hornbeck's
report of his trip is enclosed in Hornbeck to Hull, 10
November 1943, Stettinius Papers, file "S," Box 218.

[30]Stettinius to Hearn, n.d. (early January 1945), RG
332 Stilwell Files, WNRC, Vol. 3, Box 2. On instructions,
Hearn forwarded this memorandum on 11 January to Madame
Chiang but added the warning: "I trust that you or the
Generalissimo will not take offense at this informal unique
characteristic plain language." (Ibid.) See also Stilwell to
Marshall, 4 November 1942, ibid., Vol. I, Box I.   Marshall
consistently supported Stilwell in his impossible situation
but occasionally prodded his subordinate to extend more
cooperation to his Allied colleagues.   "While we here must
play God Save the King," Marshall told Stilwell, "you must

at least stand up for the ceremony." Stilwell apologized: "If I have done anything to make your job harder, put it down to ignorance rather than intent," and promised, "I will be glad to stand up for the ceremony and I will wear a monocle if necessary." See Marshall to Stilwell, 1 July 1943, and Stilwell to Marshall, 4 July 1943, ibid., Vol. II, Box 2. Mountbatten later wondered about the "unreasonable attitude" of Stilwell. (Author's interview with Louis Mountbatten, First Earl Mountbatten of Burma, 2 August 1973, London.) Admiral James Somerville dismissed Stilwell as "uninformed, obstinate and ivory-headed," and suggested that Stilwell's multilingual ability proved "no bonus since it allows officers and men of the Chinese Army to appreciate for themselves how bone-headed he is." (Somerville to Cunningham, 25 October 1943, Somerville Papers, Archives Center, Churchill College, Cambridge University, folder 8/2.

[31]Penfield to Secretary of State, 18 December 1944, SD 741.93/12-1844. See the 1944 extracts of the Chinese press sent to the Foreign Office by Seymour in FO 371.41566: 24 October, F 5374/14/10; 3 November, F 5662/14/10; 6 November, F 5707/14/10; 7 November, F 5709/14/10; 15 November, F 5656/14/10; 18 November, F 5375/14/10; 22 November, F 6069/14/10; also Tuan Sheng Chien to Churchill, 27 February 1942, PREM 4-32/14-15.

[32]Halifax to Eden, 11 February 1944, PREM 4-27/9; Eden to Halifax, 28 January 1944, ibid.; Halifax to Foreign Office, 8 June 1944, ibid.; also see in ibid.: Halifax to Churchill, 9 June 1944; Halifax to Foreign Office, 31 July 1944; Churchill to Bracken, 9 June 1944; and Bracken to Churchill, 9 June 1944. See COS(45) 453(0), 11 July 1945, CAB 80/95; WM(45)41, 9 April 1945, CAB 65/50.

[33]As quoted in Gordon Harrison, Cross Channel Attack (Washington, D.C.: Office of the Chief of Military History for the Department of the Army, 1951), p. 64. For the Greenfield and other Churchill quotations, see Kent Roberts Greenfield, American Strategy in World War II: A Reconsideration (Baltimore: The Johns Hopkins Press, 1963), pp. 45-46. Marshall's views are in the minutes of the "Meeting of the Military Experts," 29 November 1943, enclosed in COS(43)791(0) Pt. II, 28 February 1944, CAB 80/77. Michael Howard stated that the British strategy was Napoleonic: "on s'engage et puis on voit." See his Mediterranean Strategy in the Second World War (London: Weidenfeld and Nicolson, 1968), p. 22; also Samuel Eliott Morison, American Contributions to the Strategy of World War II (London: Oxford University Press, 1958), pp. 50-51; General Jacob's essay in Action This Day: Working With Churchill, ed. by John Wheeler-Bennett (London: Macmillan, 1968), pp. 200-02; Author's interview with Jacob, 26 June 1973, Woodbridge; Basil Liddell Hart essay in Churchill:

Four Faces and the Man, ed. by A. J. P. Taylor et al.
(London: Penguin, 1969). For more on the "Europe-first"
strategy, see Mountbatten to Roosevelt, 15 June 1942, Harry
Hopkins Papers, FDRL, file "Mountbatten, Louis," Box 194.

[34]Churchill memorandum, 24 July 1944, COS(44)654(O), 25
July 1944, CAB 80/85; COS(44)396(O), 4 May 1944, CAB 80/83;
Churchill to Ismay (for COS), 6 May 1944, CAB 80/83;
Churchill memorandum, "Operation ANAKIM," enclosed in
COS(T)8, 8 May 1943, CAB 80/69; Churchill minute, 26 July
1943, DO(43)16, 27 July 1943, CAB 69/5; COS(Q)6, 10 August
1943, CAB 80/73; minutes of the First Plenary Session at
Quebec, 19 August 1943, COS(43)489(O), 31 August 1943, CAB
80/73.

[35]Ismay to Pownall, 27 May 1944, Ismay Papers, file
IV/POW/3. Ismay replied on 27 May with a good-natured
request "to destroy this rather inflammable document."
(Ibid.) Churchill's comment is in COS(44)399(O), 5 May
1944, CAB 80/83. See Irwin letters to Wavell, 19 February
and 9 March 1943, Irwin Papers, Imperial War Museum, London,
file 2/1; and Irwin memorandum on Army difficulties, 28
September 1943, ibid., file 2/2; also Irwin to S. W. Kirby
(Official Historian), 21 April 1956, ibid., file 2/3.

[36]Halifax to Eden, 3 January 1945, PREM 4-27/10; Hull
memorandum of conversation with Eden and Halifax, 22 March
1943, SD 711.41/568. See also unsigned memorandum, 20 June
1942, SD 893.00/6-2042; Harry Dexter White memorandum to
Secretary of the Treasury Henry Morgenthau, Jr., 15
September 1944, SD 711.61/9-1344.

[37]The Eden-Attlee comments may be found in
COS(44)79(O), SSF, 13 March 1944, CAB 79/89. See also
Mountbatten report, COS(44)758(O), 22 August 1944, CAB
80/86; Ismay, Memoirs, p. 399; Churchill memorandum,
"Operation ANAKIM," COS(T)8, 8 May, 1943, CAB 80/69;
COS(Q)6, 10 August 1943, CAB 80/73; Churchill memorandum,
24 July 1944, COS(44)654(O), 25 July 1944, CAB 80/85;
Churchill report, COS(43)264(O), 29 October 1943, CAB 79/67;
Churchill to Ismay, 12 September 1944, as quoted in
Churchill, Triumph and Tragedy, pp. 142-43. Churchill's
reference to TORCH alluded to the successful Allied invasion
of North West Africa in November 1942. For a rich
collection of amusing poems, songs, acronymns, and other
colloquialisms, see the Frank Meservey Papers, Liddell Hart
Centre.

[38]Dening memorandum, 15 June 1945, COS(45)413(O), 23
June 1945, CAB 80/95; COS memorandum, "War Against Japan--
Summary of Various Courses," COS(44)396(O), 4 May 1944, CAB
80/83; Dening to Foreign Office, 24 January 1945, FO
371.46209, F 587/186/10; FE(45)10(Restricted), 5 March 1945,

CAB 96/5; Dening memorandum, enclosed in Eden to Churchill, 17 February 1944, COS(45)195(0), 23 February 1945, CAB 80/81. For records of the Mountbatten-Generalissimo conference, 8-9 March 1945, see AIR 23.2295, PRO. The original terms of reference for Dening are in FO 371.46328, F 4882/2984/61.

[39]COS(45)350(0), 22 May 1945, CAB 80/94; Churchill to Bracken, 9 June 1944, PREM 4-27/9; Henderson minute, 24 August 1944, attached to report by Canadian Ambassador in Moscow, L. D. Wilgress, to Ottawa of a conversation with his Chinese counterpart, Foo Ping Sheung, FO 371.41581, F 3873/34/10.

[40]Hickerson to Matthews, 28 December 1943, Hickerson Files, file "Memoranda 1943," Box 2; Davies memorandum, (?) November 1943, FRUS, Conference at Cairo and Tehran, 1943, pp. 371-72; Davies memorandum, "American Psychological Warfare in the China Burma India Theater," 17 April 1944, SD 740.0011PW/3863; Hurley to Truman, 20 May 1945, SD 740.0011PW/5-2145. Marshall described the agreed procedures in a letter to Wedemeyer, 4 February 1945. (RG 332 Wedemeyer Files, WNRC, file "C.G. In, Book #3, 79-97," Box 8.) In his 1944 report, Davies declared, "Our present military association with the imperial powers has created among the peoples of Southeast Asia suspicion of American motives and a growing hostility toward us which, if uncorrected, will impair our relations with these peoples for years to come. Moreover, this hostility and suspicion expose our troops (including Air Force personnel forced down behind enemy lines) to losses and obstruction which they would not suffer were we operating on our own terms, unassociated with the reimposition of imperial rule."

[41]Hurley to Truman, 20 May 1945, SD 740.0011PW/5-2145.

[42]Bishop memorandum, "SEAC," 6 November 1944, enclosed in Robert L. Buell (Consul, Colombo) to Secretary of State, 10 November 1944, SD 740.0011PW/11-1044; Bishop memorandum, 24 October 1944, enclosed in Buell to Secretary of State, 24 October 1944, SD 740.0011PW/10-2444. The State Department identified the Bishop memorandum of 6 November as "of exceptional interest" and included it in Roosevelt's pre-Yalta briefing book. See Record Group 43 Records of International Conferences, Comissions, Expositions and Committees: World War II, NA, file "Vincent," Tab "S.E. Asia," Box 8. (Hereafter cited as RG 43.)

NOTES ON CHAPTER V

[1]"T Minutes 56," 12 November 1943, Notter Files, file

"T Mins 50-59," Box 42; Rupert Emerson memorandum, "Regionalism in Southeast Asia," T-408, 14 September 1943, ibid., file "T Docs 401-416," Box 36. Emerson added, "The attempt to create an over-all governing body at the outset would be defeated by the lack of unity and sense of community in the region."

2Vincent explained his 20 October speech in a memorandum to Dean Acheson, Matthews, and Hickerson, 22 October 1945, Hickerson Files, file "Memoranda of Conversations April-December 1945," Box 2. See also the valuable statistical information in the OSS memorandum, 18 December 1944, OSS R&A 2589; Vandenbosch memorandum, "Regionalism in Southeast Asia: Background," T-336, 24 June 1943, Notter Files, file "T Docs 326-336," Box 34; also see his more detailed analysis of a projected regional commission under the same title and date, ibid., in folder "T Docs 337-344."

3Donovan to Secretary of State, extracted in a memorandum on Indochina by A. L. Moffat, enclosed in Stettinius to Roosevelt, 2 November 1944, SD 740.0011PW/11-2444; Wedemeyer to Marshall, 5 December 1944, RG 332 Wedemeyer Files, WNRC, file "C.G. Out Book #1, Items 1-12," Box 8; "Special Meeting" minutes, 16 January 1945, Notter Files, file "Minutes January 2-April 25," Box 55; unsigned memorandum, n.d., RG 43, file "Vincent" Tab "S.E. Asia," Box 8.

4"Security of British Commonwealth and Empire Interests in South-East Asia and the Pacific," COS(45)120(O)(PHP), 21 February 1945, CAB 80/92.

5Text of Churchill speech, 11 November 1944, PREM 4-76/2. An account of the Churchill-de Gaulle meeting 4 June 1944, is in Charles de Gaulle, War Memoirs: Unity, translated by Richard Howard (London: Weidenfeld and Nicholson, 1959). p. 227. The two leaders conferred at the Prime Minister's temporary headquarters for OVERLORD: a railroad car near Portsmouth. Perhaps the best summation of the traditional principles of British Foreign Policy may be found in the famous memorandum by Eyre Crowe, 1 January 1907. See Great Britain, Foreign Office, British Documents on the Origins of the War, 1898-1914, ed. by G. P. Gooch and Harold Temperly (8 vols.; London: HMSO, 1926-1932), III, Appendix A, 397-420.

6For a complete account of British policy decisions, memoranda, and events in Southeast Asia from November 1940 to December 1941, see the records of the Far Eastern Committee and its agencies in CAB 96/1-4. See especially the reports of the British Consuls in Haiphong and Saigon as well as the recommendations of Admiral Sir Percy Noble (C-in-C, China), all annexed to FE(40)42, 5 November 1940, CAB 96/1; Leith-Ross report, FE(40)7, 7 November 1940, ibid.; Ministry of Economic Warfare (MEW) memorandum, FE(40)59, 18 November 1940, ibid.; parent committee approval is in FE(40)9, 21 November 1940, ibid.; also C. K. Webs'er memorandum, "French Interests and Policies in the Far East," 7 March 1941, Webster Collection, Imperial War Museum, London, Vol. VIII(b)/III/i. Important French documents purloined from Governor-General Georges Catroux's files pertaining to the 1940 situation are in R. Bloom's memorandum, 27 February 1945, SD 740.0011PW/2-1545.

[7]C-in-C, China to Admiralty, 28 December 1940, FE(40)106, 30 December 1940, CAB 96/1; FE(41)1, 2 January 1941, CAB 96/2; FE(41)46, 19 February 1941, CAB 96/3; Noble telegrams to Admiralty, 9-10 August 1941, FE(41)178, 13 August 1941, CAB 96/4; Foreign Office telegram to Washington, FE(41)6, 4 January 1941, CAB 96/3; War Cabinet memorandum, "Japanese Intentions in Indo-China," WP(41)154, 6 July 1941, CAB 66/17.

[8]Butler to Foreign Office, 25 December 1940, FE(40)103, 28 December 1940, CAB 96/1.

[9]FE(41)6, 4 January 1941, CAB 96/3; FE(41)14, 23 January 1941, ibid.; FE(41)15, 30 January 1941, ibid. The treaty was finally signed in Tokyo on 9 May 1941, awarding to Thailand three rich rice-growing provinces in Cambodia (Battambang, Siemreap, Sisophong) as well as parts of Laos along the Mekong River. See James Masland, Jr. memorandum, "The Political Status of French Indo China," T-60, n.d., Notter Files, "T Docs 37-66," Box 31. For more on the military situation, see James W. Morley, ed., The Fateful Choice: Japan's Advance into Southeast Asia, 1939-1941 (NY: Columbia University Press, 1980).

[10]For a report on the Pechkoff press conference, see Seymour to Eden, 1 May 1944, FO 371.46210, F 2960/186/10. Extracts of the Brazzaville Conference may be found in unsigned memorandum, n.d., RG 43, file "Vincent," Tab "S.E. Asia," Box 8.

[11]Text of Hoppenot report, 16 October 1944, as quoted in Charles de Gaulle, War Memoirs: Salvation, 1944-1946: Documents, translated by Joyce Murchie and Hamish Erskine (London: Weidenfeld and Nicolson, 1960), pp. 48-49; Churchill to War Cabinet, 22 August 1943, PREM 3-53/4. Attlee replied for the Cabinet that same day regarding the President's position: "Cabinet fully share your views as to its unwisdom." (Ibid.)

[12]See texts of two Murphy letters to Giraud, n.d., enclosed in Eden to Churchill, 4 February 1943, FO

371.36247, L 1487/1266/69. Murphy forwarded copies of these letters carrying dates of 26-27 October 1942 in a letter to Hull on 22 March 1943 (Notter Files, file "S France," Box 78), but warned of confusion over discrepancies in the dates because the undated draft copies were shown to Giraud while the General was secretly in France. For more on the various American statements, see State Department memorandum, "Official Statements and Views Affecting the Future Status of France and the French Empire," 29 January 1944, Stettinius Papers, file "London Mission-Background Material-France," Box 250; Robert Murphy, Diplomat Among Warriors (Garden City: Doubleday and Company, 1964), pp. 119-23; Sir Ronald I. Campbell (in Washington) to Eden, 10 March 1942, PREM 4-42/9; text of 1942 Welles statement to French Ambassador Gaston Henry-Haye is in FRUS, 1942, II, 561; Eden's report of his visit to Washington, WM(43)53, SSF, 13 April 1943, CAB 65/38; Rosenman, Public Papers, XI, 455-57; Atherton to Plevin, as quoted in Eden to Halifax, 29 December 1943, FO 371.35921, F 6056/1422/61; OSS memorandum, "Territorial Conflicts Between Thailand and French Indo-China," 30 March 1945, OSS R&A 2419; Hugh Borton memorandum, "Indo-China: Military Government," T-404, 9 November 1943, Notter Files, file "T Docs 401-416," Box 36; J. Masland and A. Vandenbosch memorandum, "Indo-China: Political and Economic Factors," T-398, n.d., ibid., file "T Docs 382-400a," Box 36; Eden to Churchill, 24 December 1943, PREM 3-178/2; Halifax to Churchill, 5 February 1943, PREM 4-27/9.

[13]See the 1943 correspondence in PREM 3-178/2; Churchill to Attlee, 1 December; Churchill to Eden, 25 December; Eden to Churchill, 24 December. Eden described the Murphy letters in a telegram to Churchill (at Algiers), 4 February 1943. He preferred that the American pledges be "annulled or wholly recast." (FO 371.36247, L 1487/1266/69.) Churchill memorandum of conversation with Murphy, 4 February 1943, FO 371.36247, Z 1487/1266/69; for more on British reluctance to provide guarantees, see Borton memorandum, "Indo-China: Military Government," T-404, 9 November 1943, Notter Files, "T Docs 401-416," Box 36; C. Easton Rothwell memorandum, "British Attitude Towards the French Empire," 14 March 1943, Notter Files, file "S France," Box 78.

[14]Churchill to Attlee, 1 December 1943, PREM 3-178/2; FRUS, The Conferences at Washington 1941-1942 and Casablanca 1943, p. 514; Murphy, Diplomat, pp. 168-69; Halifax to Churchill, 5 February 1943, PREM 4-27/9; WM(43)53, SSF, 13 April 1943, CAB 65/38. Murphy believed his authority stemmed from a telegram 2 November 1942, sent by Leahy: "The decision of the President is that . . . you will do your utmost to secure the understanding and cooperation [for TORCH] of the French officials with whom you are now in contact." Murphy surmised, "This presidential directive clearly left it up to me to deal with our French allies in

whatever ways I thought best." (Murphy, Diplomat, pp. 120-21.)

[15]E. Roosevelt, As He Saw It, pp. 114-16; Roosevelt to Hull, 24 January 1944, in Elliott Roosevelt, ed., F.D.R.: His Personal Letters (3 vols.; Duell, Sloan and Pearce, 1950), III, 1489-90; White, Stilwell Papers, pp. 246-54; Rosenman, Public Papers, XIII, 563; Hull memorandum, 27 March 1943, Notter Files, file "Eden's convs. March '43, Box 284; Hull, Memoirs, II, 1597-1601; FRUS, 1943, I, 541-43; Roosevelt to Stettinius, 3 November 1944, SD 740.0011PW/11-2444, Edward R. Stettinius, Jr., Roosevelt and the Russians (Garden City: Doubleday and Company, 1949), pp.237-38; Sherwood, Hopkins, pp. 572-73. See also Christopher Thorne, "Indochina and Anglo-American Relations, 1942-1945," Pacific Historical Review, XLV (February 1976), 73-96; Walter LaFeber, "Roosevelt, Churchill, and Indochina: 1942-1945, American Historical Review, LXXX (December 1975), 1277-95; Gary R. Hess, "Franklin Roosevelt and Indochina," Journal of American History, LIX (September 1972), 353-68.

[16]See minutes of Territorial Subcommittee Meeting #55, 5 November 1943 and Meeting #56, 12 November 1943, Notter Files, file "Mins 50-59," Box 42; Rupert Emerson memorandum, "Regionalism in Southeast Asia," T-408, 14 September 1943, ibid., file "T Docs 401-416," Box 36; Bowman memorandum, T-398, 29 October 1943, ibid., file "SEA," Box 23; Masland and Vandenbosch memorandum, "Indo China: Political and Economic Factors," T-398a, n.d., ibid., file "T Docs 382-400a," Box 36.

[17]Knight memorandum, "The Economic Relations of Indo-China," T-283, 23 March 1943, Notter Files, file "T Docs 280-289," Box 34; Knight memorandum, "France's Economic Relations With Her Empire," T-251, 23 February 1943, ibid., file "T Docs 251-260," Box 33; Masland memorandum, "The Political Status of Indo-China," T-60, 3 September 1942, ibid., file "T Docs 37-66," Box 31; "C.H.O." (in Near East Division) memorandum, "Imperialism Versus an Enlightened Colonial Policy in the Area of SEAC," 6 January 1945, RG 43, "Briefing Book," Box 2; OSS memorandum, "The Degree of Japanese Control Over the French Administration of French Indo-China," 22 May 1944, OSS R&A 1677; J. Russell Andrus memorandum, "Bombing Objectives--French Indo-China," 27 June 1942, Record Group 151 Records of the Bureau of Foreign and Domestic Commerce, NA, file "Indo-China," Box 2513, 492.3.

[18]H. Ashley Clarke memorandum of conversation with Hornbeck, 18 October 1943, FO 371.35921, F 5379/1422/61. Halifax reported Roosevelt's meeting with the diplomats, 16 December 1943, in a telegram to the Foreign Office, 19 December 1943, FO 371.35921, F 6656/1422/21; also FRUS, The Conferences at Cairo and Tehran, 1943, p. 864, pp. 872-73;

Stettinius to Roosevelt, 29 October 1943, SD 740.0011PW/3648; Berle to Leahy (discussing Roosevelt's reply), 5 January 1944, SD 740.0011PW/3694. For a summary of the American attitude towards the French, see Gallman to Hull, 8 April 1943, SD 893.20/783; and Campbell telegrams to the Foreign Office on 15 October 1943, (FO 371.35921, F 5379/1422/61) and 17 October 1943 (FO 371.35921, F 5433/1422/61); unsigned memorandum, "Policy Toward Liberated States: France," PWC-175a, n.d., Notter Files, file "Policy Toward Liberated States," Box 22.

[19]De Gaulle, Unity, pp. 83-84; Bracken-Crozier interview, 1 July 1943, Crozier Papers, file "B. Bracken," Box 1; Moran, Churchill, p. 241; Murphy, Diplomat, p. 102. Hull's outburst (to an astonished Hamilton Fish Armstrong) is recorded in Michael Wright to Nevile Butler, 19 July 1943, FO 371.35994, Z 8293/2/17 (on 29 July, J. G. Tahourdin in the Foreign Office attached his comment: "Frightening!"). Stimson came to regard de Gaulle as a "psychopathic" and someone who could not be relied upon as an ally. See Stimson memorandum of conversation with Truman, 6 June 1945, Stimson Papers, file 18, Box 172, and Stimson Diary, 12 and 14 June 1944, Vol. 47, #62. See also State Department memorandum, 20 January 1944, Stettinius Papers, file "London Mission-Background Material-France," Box 250; Maurice Leon to Stimson, 20 June 1944, Stimson Papers, file 16, Box 145; Eisenhower to Marshall, 14 May 1944, Marshall Papers, file 15, Box 81; Roosevelt to Marshall, 2 June 1944, Marshall Papers, file 16, Box 81 (see Appendix E).

[20]Churchill to Eden, 11 March 1944, PREM 3-178/2; Clarke to Keswick, 21 November 1943, FO 371.35921, F 6059/1422/61; Churchill to Cadogan, 3 November 1943, FO 371.35921, F 5609/1422/61; Churchill to Eden, 17 December 1943, FO 371.35921, F 6153/1422/61; Eden memorandum, "The Future of Indo-China and Other French Pacific Possessions," WP(44)111, 16 February 1944, CAB 66/47; WM(44)25, 24 February 1944, CAB 65/41. For more on the French requests, see Pierre Vienot memorandum, enclosed in William Strang memorandum, 8 September 1943, FO 371.35921, F 5379/1422/61; Vienot memorandum, enclosed in Oliver Sargeant memorandum, 2 December 1943, FO 371.35921, F 6379/1422/61; Campbell to Strang, 8 January 1943, FO 371.35993, Z 865/2/17; Harold Macmillan (Resident Minister at Algiers) to Foreign Office, 11 December 1943, FO 371.35921, F 6513/1422/61; Clarke to Sir Maurice Peterson, 25 September 1943, FO 371.35921, F 4870/1422/61; General M. Mathenet memorandum, enclosed in COS(43)276(0), 11 November 1943, CAB 79/67; Cadogan memorandum, 23 November 1943, FO 371.35921, F 6782/1422/61; for information on proposed French naval dispositions (especially the Triomphant and Richelieu) see the several comments attached in December 1943 to FO 371.35921, F 6814/1422/61; Ambassador Henri Hoppenot to Berle, 2 January

1944, SD 740.0011PW/3630; Hoppenot to de Gaulle, in de Gaulle, Salvation, pp. 48-49; Charles Peake (British Representative to French National Committee) to Strang, 5 March 1943, FO 371.35921, F 1422/1422/61; Brooke (CIGS) memorandum, COS(43)281, considered at COS(43)253(O), 19 October 1943, CAB 79/66; Dening to Foreign Office 17 November 1943, FO 371.35921, F 5217/1422/61.

21Undated Foreign Office draft, enclosed in Richard Speight (North American Department) to F. R. Hoyer Millar, 9 January 1943, FO 371.36007, Z 2107/47/17. The Foreign Office hoped to avoid "evolving yet another species of French" and encouraged "a union of Frenchmen resolved to fight the enemy and liberate France." For Eden's persistent urgings in 1943-44, see his many memoranda in PREM 3-181/8.

22Foulds memorandum (and minutes), 7 September 1943, FO 371.35921, F 4646/1422/61.

23Unsigned Foreign Office memorandum to COS, 3 April 1944, COS(44)315(O), 3 April 1944, CAB 80/82; "The French Empire," JP(43)308(Final), 8 November 1940, considered and approved at COS(43)288(O), 25 November 1943, CAB 79/67. The Joint Planning Staff noted that former French territories then under British control included French North Africa, French West Africa, French Equitorial Africa, Syria, Lebanon, French Somaliland, New Caledonia, Antilles, Madagascar, and Reunion.

24Mack to COS, 24 June 1944, COS(44)564(O), 24 June 1944, CAB 80/84; Harvey to COS, 12 April 1944, COS(44)334(O), 12 April 1944, CAB 80/82; Duff Cooper to Foreign Office, 6 April 1944, ibid. The French division took its name from its commander, General Philippe de Leclerc.

25Smith to COS, 7 August 1944, COS(44)707(O), 7 August 1944, CAB 80/86.

26SOE memorandum, COS(44)668(O), 28 July 1944, CAB 80/86. De Gaulle's views to the Harold Stark Mission are described in Charles Peake to Strang, 5 March 1943, FO 371.35921, F 1422/1422/61. See also Strang memorandum, 8 September 1943, FO 371.35921, F 5379/1422/61; Dening to Foreign Office, 17 November 1943, FO 371.35921, F 5217/1422/61; Clarke to Peterson, 25 September 1943, FO 371.35921, F 4870/1422/61; COS(43)276(O), 11 November 1943, CAB 79/67; Cadogan memorandum, 23 November 1943, FO 371.35921, F 6782/1422/61; Mountbatten to Foreign Office, 17 March 1944, COS(44)268(O), 18 March 1944, CAB 80/81.

27Churchill to Ismay, COS(45)237(O), 4 April 1945, CAB 80/93; Cunningham memorandum, COS(44)1042(O), 20 December

1944, CAB 80/89. See also CPS memorandum, CCS 708/2, COS(44)903(0), 7 November 1944, CAB 80/89; COS(44)336(0), 23 October 1944, CAB 79/81; COS(44)207, 12 October 1944, CAB 80/45; COS(45)6, 4 January 1945, CAB 80/47; Sterndale Bennett memorandum, COS(45)320(0), 8 May 1945, CAB 80/91; Foreign Office to Halifax, COS(44)968(0), 13 November 1944, CAB 80/89; COS(44)950(0), 6 November 1944, CAB 80/89.

28"Future Relations With France," PHP(44)32(Final), 19 May 1944, CAB 81/42; also COS(44)485(0), 25 May 1944, CAB 80/84; PHP(44)28, 15 May 1944, CAB 81/40; and two FORD studies: "The Policy and Interests of France in the Far East," and "The Policy and Interests of the British Empire in the Far East," enclosed in Geoffrey Hudson to Clarke, 23 February 1943, FO 371.55917, F 1098/877/61.

29F. K. Roberts to COS, COS(44)890(0), 9 October 1944, CAB 80/88; Eden memorandum, "The Future of Indo-China and Other Pacific Possessions," WP(44)111, 16 February 1944, CAB 66/47, approved at WM(44)25, 24 February 1944, CAB 65/41; Eden memorandum, "Indo-China," WP(44)444, 13 August 1944, CAB 65/33, approved at WM(44)106, 14 August 1944, CAB 65/43; Peterson to Ismay, 11 March 1944, COS(44)249(0), 13 March 1944, CAB 80/81; Churchill to War Cabinet, 1 December 1943, PREM 4-74/2 Pt. 2; PHP(44)21, 25 April 1944, CAB 81/40; T. L. Rowan (enclosing circular letter to Dominions soliciting support for Eden's earlier memorandum) to Churchill, 13 March 1944, PREM 3-178/2.

30Cavendisch-Bentinck memorandum 30 October 1943, FO 371.35921, F 5608/1422/61; Foulds memorandum, 7 September 1943, FO 371.35921, F 4646/1422/61; Cavendisch-Bentinck memorandum, 15 September 1943, FO 371.35921, F 4871/1422/61. In his earlier memorandum, Cavendisch-Bentinck endorsed French membership in the London Pacific War Council although "we should have to dispense with the ornamental presence of a Filipino as I do not believe that we stock one here."

31PHP(44)2(0)(Final), 22 January 1944, CAB 81/45; Halifax to Eden, 19 December 1943, FO 371.35921, F 6656/1422/61 (Cavendisch-Bentinck attached his remarks about the President on 22 December 1943); Cadogan to Churchill, 25 October 1943, and Cavendisch-Bentinck minute, 30 October 1943, FO 371.35921, F 5608/1422/61. Cadogan argued that a French Military Mission to SEAC would be helpful since the only other French groups were in Chungking and "reporting wildly to Algiers." Churchill replied 19 November, "This can certainly wait." Cavendisch-Bentinck described the projected French forces as "a heterogeneous collection of black men" but warned that British forces in Europe and the Mideast might launch "a large-scale mutiny" if ordered to the Far East; therefore, "we may then be grateful for some French troops even though they be black or brown."

Cavendisch-Bentinck had served at the Foreign Office since 1919 and had never been to the United States.

[32]Stettinius to State Department, 8 May 1945, as quoted in Grew to Jefferson Caffrey (Ambassador in Paris), 9 May 1945, FRUS, 1945, VI, 307.

[33]For extracts of the Roosevelt minute, 29 February 1944 and Hull memorandum, 17 February 1944, see A. L. Moffat memorandum, "Developments--French Military Participation-- Indochina," 10 November 1944, SD 740.0011PW/11-1044; and K. P. Landon (Special Political Assistant) to Hull, 6 July 1944, SD 740.0011PW/7-644; also Roosevelt-Chiang Kai-shek and Roosevelt-Stalin conversations, FRUS, Cairo and Tehran, 1943, p. 325, pp. 485-86; Stettinius to Hornbeck 18 January 1944, Stettinius Papers, file "FE-Division of Far Eastern Affairs," Box 216; Rosenman, Public Papers, XIII, 562-63; Roosevelt to Hull, 24 January 1944, FDR Letters, III Pt.2, 1489-90; Hull, Memoirs, II, 1597.

[34]A. L. Moffat memorandum, 10 November 1944, SD 740.0011PW/11-1044. Moffat summarized the State Department memorandum (7 July) which received no presidential response. Moffat reported that Halifax delivered to the State Department a British Aide-Mémoire on 26 August, which was then forwarded to Roosevelt and Leahy (for the JCS). Roosevelt sent his reply to Hull on 28 August. Moffat made the revealing observation, "The Department was first informed of the position of the Joint Chiefs of Staff by the British Embassy." He claimed that in a letter to Hull on 28 August Leahy outlined JCS acceptance of the French requests strictly from a military point of view. Actually, the JCS disapproved any French role in political warfare and accepted the COS desire to deny French participation in strategic planning. See Sterndale Bennett memorandum, COS(45)320(0), 8 May 1945, CAB 80/94. This study indicated that the JCS never replied officially to the COS and that the State Department was told by the White House to await the pending Roosevelt-Churchill talks, but "no such opportunity ever occurred." See also Landon to Roosevelt, 7 July 1944, SD 740.0011PW/7-744; State Department memorandum to the President, 12 January 1945, RG 43, file "Vincent," Tab "Indochina," Box 8; Murphy (enclosing copy of French request to British on 24 May) to Hull, 10 June 1944, SD 740.0011PW/3967. In early July, H. Freeman Matthews warned Roosevelt that the British might try to convince the French that the United States was responsible for delaying recognition of the Provisional Government. He urged the President to extend recognition as "a step which should make difficult, if not impossible, the undermining of our position in France." Matthews to Roosevelt, n.d., Matthews Files, file "Memoranda for the President 1943-1944," Box 1.

[35]As quoted by Fénard, in de Gaulle, Salvation, pp. 39-42. See the summaries and extracts in Moffat memorandum, 10 November 1944, SD 740.0011PW/11-1044; Sterndale Bennett memorandum, COS(45)320(0), 8 May 1945, CAB 80/94; and State Department memorandum to the President, 12 January 1945, RG 43, op cit. During September the French Ministry of the Navy began registering volunteers for duty in the reconquest of Indochina, and on 22 October the French Ministry of War issued an appeal for recruits for the liberation of Indochina. See Fénard memorandum, COS(44)207, 12 October 1944, CAB 80/45. Fénard declared, "The French Government has frequently stated that the French forces would take part in the war against Japan. The French Navy, like the French Army, is anxious to participate with all its resources in the Far Eastern theatre, where French Indo-China, which is still under Japanese domination, occupies an important strategic positon. The position of the French in Indo-China would make possible a most effective underground movement. This fact plus the knowledge of the coast in Indo-China and the approaches to it, possessed by many French naval officers, permits one to believe that a wide use of French naval forces in that area would be a great asset in the pursuit of the war against Japan." The Combined Chiefs of Staff replied on 4 January 1945 that shipping limitations prevented acceptance of the French offer and that individual French vessels would be incorporated into either the British or American fleets. See the summary by Sterndale Bennett; also COS(45)6, 4 January 1945, CAB 80/47.

[36]Roosevelt to Stettinius, 24 November 1944, SD 740.0011PW/11-2444; Stettinius to Roosevelt, n.d., ibid.; also the summaries by Moffat (describing Donovan's views) and Sterndale Bennett, and the State Department cited in the previous note. The anxious Buell made inquiries on 5, 24, 28, and 30 October. He finally interpreted the French status at SEAC to be "openly and officially recognized" and equal to the Dutch and Chinese missions there. He also referred to an "Acquaint" order, apparently sent to SEAC to define the status of the French Mission, which stipulated that only military and not political questions could be discussed with the French. It was this general incorrect assumption by Buell that spurred Roosevelt's reaction on 3 November. The President ordered Stettinius to clear up the misunderstanding. On 15 November, Stettinius drafted a circular letter explaining that American policy on the French military role and on the future of Indochina had not yet been determined. Copies were also sent to Leahy, Stimson, Frank Knox, Donovan, and Elmer Davis. See Stettinius to Roosevelt, 15 November 1944, SD 740.0011PW/11-1544. The 12 January memorandum stated that on 1 January the French described liaison arrangements underway with Wedemeyer (embracing forces at Chungking and resistance forces in Indochina), and on 10 January a French advisory

group had been appointed to the SEAC Civil Affairs and Information Division to deal with questions pertaining to Indochina.

[37]Roosevelt to Stettinius, 1 January 1945, SD 740.0011PW/1-145. In his diary, Stettinius quoted this message, observing that there was much discussion at this time about French saboteurs entering Indochina on pre-operational activities by SEAC. See RG 59, Stettinius Diaries: 1 December 1944-3 July 1945, 8 Vols., NA, Vol. III, Sect. V, 2, 21-2. See also Stettinius to Hull, 22 February 1944, Stettinius Papers, file "S January-February 1944," Box 218.

[38]Stettinius memorandum of conversation with Halifax, 2 January 1945, SD 740.0011PW/1-245; Halifax to Foreign Office, 3 January 1945, COS(45)64(0), 21 January 1945, CAB 80/91.

[39]Vandenbosch memorandum, "Indo-China," TS-96, n.d., Notter Files, file "61-121," Box 44; Hull, Memoirs, II, 1595-98; Sumner Welles, Time For Decision (New York: Harper and Brothers, 1944), pp 297-303.

[40]Vincent to Stettinius, 10 November 1944, SD 740.0011PW/11-1044. For the de Gaulle-Churchill meeting in Paris (MINAUR), 11 November 1944, see PREM 4-76/2. For indications of American bureaucratic confusion about the French status in Southeast Asia, see Marshall Papers, Verifax 25, Reel 10, Item 275, especially General Joseph Hull to Wedemeyer, 4 June 1945, "Personal File C/S-I-C"; Moffat to Stettinius and J. Ballantine, 17 November 1944, Stettinius Papers, file "FE Division Far Eastern (Ballantine) Affairs," Box 216.

[41]Halifax to Foreign Office, 9 January 1945, COS(45)64(0), 21 January 1945, CAB 80/91. A month later Sterndale Bennett lamented, "It is somewhat disconcerting that this particular dog refuses to sleep." He presented a summary of British-American clashes in Southeast Asia over the presence of the French forces. See COS(45)96(0), 4 February 1945, CAB 80/91. P. J. Dixon (Foreign Office) relayed the 1944 remark by Roosevelt to J. M. Martin on 24 January. With the machinery in motion, Churchill gave his testy rebuke on 12 March. The packet of correspondence is in PREM 3-178/2. See also the excellent summary of the British problems in Eden memorandum, 11 March 1945, COS(45)172(0), 14 March 1945, CAB 80/92.

[42]SOE memorandum, COS(44)668(0), 28 July 1944, CAB 80/86; Noble to Admiralty, 28 December 1940, FE(40)106, 30 December 1940, CAB 96/1; Ellen J. Hammer, The Struggle For Indo-China, 1940-1954 (Stanford: Stanford University Press,

1966), pp. 22-26. (Hereafter cited as Hammer, Indo-China.)
Churchill inquired on 12 March, "How is it that there are
French troops and a Governor-General there now?" The
Foreign Office responded the same day with a detailed
explanation that the Japanese, short of administrative
personnel, allowed the local French army (chiefly Annamites
under French officers) to maintain order, but strictly
monitored its supply of ammunition. By 1944 Indochina was
the only French colony that had not joined with the Free
French. Many de Gaulle supporters were reported there but
no overt resistance formed because the Allies could not
provide the required support. The Japanese launched the
coup when they felt pro-Gaullist sympathies and activities
exceeded toleration. (See PREM 3-178/2.) Earlier, Eden
expressed surprise at French ships on station in the Far
East. (Eden minute, 26 December 1943, FO371.35921, F
6814/1422/61.

43Mountbatten to Roosevelt, 23 October 1943, PREM 3-
90/3; Marshall to Stillwell, 28 August 1943, RG 332,
Stilwell Files, WNRC, Vol. 2, Box 2; Mountbatten, Report to
the Combined Chiefs of Staff By the Supreme Allied
Commander, South East Asia, 1943-1945 (London: HMSO, 1951),
pp. 6-7. The text of "Agreement With the Generalissimo," 8
November 1943 is at Appendix D. For minutes of this
Chungking conference, 19 October 1943, see AIR 23/2247, PRO.
Somervell's correspondence with Marshall in October 1943 may
be found in Marshall Papers, file 54, Box 60, and file 4,
Box 81.

44Author's interview with Mountbatten, 2 August 1973,
London.

45Stettinius to Bonnet, 4 April 1945, SD 740.0011PW/3-
1245; Bonnet memorandum, 12 March 1945, ibid.; Stettinius to
Roosevelt, 16 March 1945 and Leahy (enclosing Roosevelt's
response) to Stettinius, 17 March 1945, SD 740.0011 PW/3-
1745; Air Chief Marshal Sir Charles Portal (Air Chief of
Staff) memorandum, COS(45)236(0), 14 April 1945, CAB 80/93.

46Roosevelt to Churchill, 22 March 1945 PREM 3-473;
Churchill to Roosevelt, 17 March 1945, ibid.; Hurley to
Truman, 29 May 1945, SD 740.0011PW/5-2945; also see
Marshall's lively correspondence over SEAC boundaries with
Field Marshal Sir Henry Maitland Wilson (Head, British Joint
Service Mission, Washington) in RG 332 Wedemeyer Files,
WNRC, file "Conferences, Military, Naval and others," Box
12; Wedemeyer memorandum, Policy on Indo-China," n.d., ibid,
file "Bhama Conf.," Box 2. It will be recalled that the
British decided to continue with minimum publicity the
French presence in Indochina.

47Rosenman, Public Papers, XIII, 562-63; FRUS, Yalta,

p. 770; Stettinius, Roosevelt, pp. 236-38; E. Roosevelt, As He Saw It, pp. 114-16.

[48]Gary Hess, "Franklin Roosevelt and Indochina," Journal of American History, LIX (September 1972), 365; Taussig memorandum, FRUS, 1945, I, 121-24; Taussig to Stettinius, 16 March 1945, Stettinius Diaries, NA, Vol. IV, Sect, VII, 50; Stettinius to Jefferson Caffrey, 10 April 1945, SD 740.0011PW/3-1245; Matthews to Francis Lacoste (Counsellor, French Embassy), 19 April 1945, SD 740.0011PW/5-1945; Lacoste to Matthews, 4 May 1945, SD 740.0011PW/5-445; Matthews to Lacoste, 5 May 1945 SD 740.0011PW/5-445; also George C. Herring, "The Truman Administration and the Restoration of French Sovereignty in Indochina," Diplomatic History, I (Spring 1977), 97-117. On 22 June 1944 Halifax reported one possible explanation of American policy towards France. "Pertinax" (French commentator) revealed that the French delegation in Washington possessed copies of American 1940-1942 correspondence with Vichy, urging accommodation with the Japanese demands. After Pearl Harbor, the United States feared Vichy might publish this correspondence and therefore issued an "unqualified undertaking" to support the return of Indochina to France. The British Ambassador felt that Washington was "probably unaware" that this correspondence had fallen into de Gaulle's hands (easily obtained because Vichy officials were trying to ingratiate themselves with Algiers). Churchill referred this news to Eden on 2 July. The Foreign Secretary replied the same day that he expected a Gaullist "leak" of the correspondence soon. Eden said he was unaware of any specific guarantee by the United States about Indochina, as "the President has seemed, indeed, to make little of guarantees about the integrity of the French Empire in general, but he might be somewhat more embarrassed if there is as 'Pertinax' asserts, a written specific guarantee of the return of Indo-China to France 'in all circumstances.'" (PREM 3-178/2.) In another interesting explanation, Myron C. Taylor asked during a Territorial Subcommittee meeting in late 1943 what had caused Welles to make the guarantee to France. Amry Vandenbosch replied that at the time the United States wanted to establish a consulate at Brazzaville, and Welles seized the occasion to make the statement. Taylor then inquired if Welles' statement had received prior clearance from the President, and George Blakeslee implied that it had not, answering only that earlier statements had been issued from the White House. (See Minutes of Meeting T-55, 5 November 1943, Notter Files, file "Mins 50-59," Box 42.) While it would, of course, be too simplistic to suggest that the price of the consulate at Brazzaville was the Vietnam War, this tale and the "Pertinax" story (if both could be substantiated) provide some intriguing suggestions as to the origins of American involvement there.

49Matthews to State-War-Navy Coordinating Committee, 23 May 1945, SD 740.0011PW/5-2345; Sterndale Bennett memorandum, COS(45)320(0), 8 May 1945, CAB 80/94; Grew to Truman, 16 May 1945, SD 740.0011PW/5-1645; Grew memorandum of conversation with Bonnet, 13 June 1945, SD 740.0011PW/6-1345; COS(45)352(0), 22 May 1945, CAB 80/94; COS(45)135, 24 May 1945, CAB 79/80. For more on French military plans in Southeast Asia, see de Gaulle to Truman, 15 May 1945, Grew Papers, file 13, Vol. 7; Grew memorandum of conversation with Bonnet, 13 June 1945, Grew Papers, file 30, Vol. 7. Detailed French operational proposals (including unit identifications) may be found in the Mark Clark Papers, The Citadel, Charleston, South Carolina.

50Hoppenot to Berle, n.d. [December 1944], SD 740.0011PW/3630; de Gaulle press conference in Paris, 25 January 1945, Notter Files, Black Binder "Dumbarton Oaks (II)," Box 274; de Gaulle, Salvation, pp. 58-60, pp. 202-12, pp. 281-82; Hurley to Secretary of State, 31 January 1945, FRUS, 1945, VI, 294-95; French Aide-Memoire, COS(45)473(0), 17 July 1945, CAB 80/95. On 17 August 1945 the French National Committee appointed Admiral Georges Thierry d'Argenlieu High Commissioner of France in Indochina and General Philippe de Leclerc commanding general of the troops. For details on the French complaints, see Lacoste to Grew, 6 August 1945, SD 740.0011PW/8-645; undated French Aide-Memoire (August 1944), SD 740.0011PW/8-444; SEAC correspondence and memoranda in folder "Synopsis of Bombing Effort in Japanese War," AIR 23/2428, PRO; J. R. Andrus memorandum, "Bombing Objectives--French Indo-China," 27 June 1942, RG 151, NA, file "Indo-China," Box 2513, 492.3; Atherton memorandum, 27 January 1942, FRUS, 1942, China, p 755; correspondence attached to SD 740.0011PW/8-444 and 8-1744; WM(43)56, SSF, 19 April 1943, CAB 65/38; WM(43)67, SSF, 10 May 1943, ibid.; WM (43)72, SSF, 20 May 1943, ibid.; WM(43)120, SSF, 20 August 1943, CAB 65/39; also see summaries of French complaints in Acheson to Hurley, 5 October 1945, SD 893.00/10-545; Combined China Theater Staff Meeting #43, 12 March 1945, RG 332 Wedemeyer Files, WNRC, file "Command Staff Minutes," Box 3. General J. E. Hull (Assistant Chief of Staff, OPD) provided a glimpse of French pressures in a letter to Wedemeyer 15 May 1945. Hull stated, "Hope you have not been too harassed by frequent queries from here regarding details of your aid to the French Resistance Groups. The State Department seems to be acutely concerned as to how to answer repeated queries of the French on this problem. We pass to them regularly information on your operational reports regarding tactical and supply missions into French Indo-China, but find it occasionally necessary to query your headquarters for further special information." (Ibid., file "Civil Matters," Box 12.)

[51]See de Gaulle's account of his conversation with T. V. Soong and Tsien-tai, 19 September 1945, and Pechkoff memorandum, 10 October 1944, in de Gaulle, Salvation, pp. 299-305; also editorial enclosed in William R. Langdon (Consul, Kunming) to Secretary of State, 19 May 1945, SD 893.00/5-1945; Minutes of Meeting, 2 July 1943, Notter Files, file "Minutes Security Technical Committee," Box 79; Andrus memorandum, "The Chinese in Indo-China," 27 August 1942, RG 151, NA, File "Indo-China," Box 2513, 492.3; Admiral M. E. Miles to Wedemeyer, 1 June 1945, RG 332 Wedemeyer Files, WNRC, file "Policies," Box 12. For an excellent summary of Chinese policy statements, see Masland-Vandenbosch memorandum, "Indo-China: Political and Economic Factors," T-398, 2 November 1943, Notter Files, file "T Docs 382-400a," Box 36. Chinese support for indigenous movements is described in M. Ramoin (French Consul, Kunming) memorandum, 31 January 1944, enclosed in Arthur R. Ringwalt (Consul, Kunming) to Secretary of State, 6 March 1944, SD 893.00/15315.

[52]Sterndale Bennett to COS, 25 September 1945, COS(45)598(0), 3 October 1945, CAB 80/97; this memorandum carried the notation that the COS approved the statement for Mountbatten; Mountbatten to Foreign Office, 7 January 1945, COS(45)64(0), 21 January 1945, CAB 80/91; Seymour to Foreign Office, 4 October 1945, FO 371.46214, F 7861/186/10. The COS directed the new JPS study after hearing the report of Carton de Wiart, who had returned from Chungking. See COS (45)237, 28 September 1945, extracted in FO 371.46214, F 7922/186/10. For more on the occupation of Indochina, see the AIR 23 files, PRO: 2295, 2375-77, 2741, 2881, 3221; Somerville to Mountbatten, 27 March 1945, Somerville Papers, file 9/2; Sterndale Bennett memorandum, COS(45)533(0), 14 August 1945, CAB 80/96; Prime Minister Attlee memorandum, COS(45)529(0), 12 August 1945, ibid.; Truman to Hurley, 1 August 1945, FRUS 1945, VII, 143-44; Hurley to Truman, 10 August 1945, SD 740.0011PW/8-1045; and in RG 332, Wedemeyer Files, WNRC: file "CT," Black Book #5, Vol. 2, Box 2; file "Dracula," Box 2; memorandum "CT-SEAC Bombing Agreement," 29 July 1945, file "Guam Conference," Tab 1, Box 2; file "Eyes Only," Box 2; file "Combined Staff Minutes," Book I, Box 3.

[53]Sterndale Bennett to Chief of Staff, 19 May 1945, COS(45)352(0), 22 May 1945, CAB 80/94; author's interview with Mountbatten, 2 August 1973, London; Stettinius to State Department, 8 May 1945, quoted in Grew to Caffrey, 9 May 1945, FRUS, 1945, VI, 307. The text of the Potsdam Declaration (setting the Sixteenth Parallel demarcation) is in FRUS, The Conference of Berlin (Potsdam), 1945, II, 1462-73.

[54]De Gaulle, Salvation, pp. 382-83; Hurley to Truman,

29 May 1945, SD 740.0011PW/5-2945; State Department to
Hurley, 10 June 1945, quoted in United States, Congress,
Senate, Committee on Armed Services, Military Situation in
the Far East (5 Pts.; Washington, D.C.: G.P.O., 1951), Pt.
IV, 2892-93. The State Department declared that Truman
intended "at some appropriate time to ask that the French
Government give some positive indication of its intention in
regard to the establishment of basic liberties and an
increasing measure of self-government in Indo-China." But
in the meantime, the State Department affirmed that American
policy remained as formulated by Roosevelt and agreed upon
at Yalta: "The trusteeship structure, it was felt, should
be defined to permit the placing under it of such of the
territories taken from the enemy as might be agreed upon at
a later date, and also such other territories as might
voluntarily be placed under it." The telegram admitted that
this arrangement would "preclude the establishment of a
trusteeship in Indo-China, except under the French
Government."

[55]For example, State Department officials differed over
the wisdom of decolonization. Officers on the European
desks (led by James Dunn) believed that the United States
had to cultivate close postwar relations with the European
colonial powers and pointed out that anti-colonial policies
would jeopardize prospects for U.S.-European cooperation.
Other officials, such as Abbott Low Moffat, called attention
to the emerging force of nationalism among dependent peoples
and argued that the United States, in her own best
interests, should promote these nationalist movements,
especially by blocking any attempts to restore prewar
colonial controls. For a discussion of the growing split
within the State Department, see Moffat's testimony in
United States, Congress, Senate, Committee on Foreign
Relations, Hearings Before the Committee on Foreign
Relations on the Causes, Origins and Lessons of the Vietnam
War, May 9-10 and 11, 1972 (Washington, D.C.: Government
Printing Office, 1973), pp. 161-205; see also Stettinius to
Hull, 14 February 1944, Stettinius Papers, file "S Jan.-Feb.
1944," Box 218; Stettinius to Hull, 30 March 1944,
Stettinius Papers, file "S March 1944," Box 218.

[56]State Department memorandum, "Southeast Asia," 12
January 1945, RG 43, file "Vincent," Tab "Indochina," Box 8.
A similar warning was sounded in the State Department
memorandum, "Imperialism Versus an Enlightened Colonial
Policy in the Area of South East Asia Command," 6 January
1945, RG 43, file "Briefing Books," Tab "Near East and
Africa," Box 2. For Roosevelt's determination that the
United States be consulted about Southeast Asia, see
Roosevelt to Stettinius, 3 November 1944, SD 740.0011PW/11-
2444; Hull, Memoirs, II, 1600.

NOTES ON CHAPTER VI

[1]Matthews to Hull, 31 July 1942, SD 841.00/1601. The comments by MacMillan and Creech-Jones on 24 June are in Great Britain, Parliamentary Debates, Vol. 380, pp. 2002-10, pp. 2041-42; Macdonald memorandum, "Statement of Policy of Colonial Development and Welfare and on Colonial Research," WP(G)(40)44, 13 February 1940, CAB 67/4. Later, the Cabinet authorized extension of this measure for a ten-year period beginning 1 April 1946, to include a total of 120 million pounds (with no more than 17.5 million pounds allocated for any single year). WM(44)173, 23 December 1944, CAB 65/44. For a report on the Hailey Committee, see J. H. Peck (Number Ten) memorandum, 26 May 1942, PREM 4-42/9. J. M. Martin attached his minute on 27 May: "What we want is to keep in touch without unnecessarily butting in from No. 10." Listing Churchill's qualifications of ARGENTIA, one OSS study observed, "Incidentally, some of us are beginning to wonder how many interpretations Mr. Churchill will require to interpret the Atlantic Charter out of existence entirely." OSS memorandum, 24 April 1944, OSS 71664-C, RG 226, NA.

[2]Attlee to Churchill, 16 June 1942, PREM 4-42/9; Eden to Churchill, 15 June 1943, enclosing Halifax to Foreign Office, 11 June 1943, ibid. Halifax added, "Miss Pearl Buck is making frequent and effective speeches against the attitude of United States and Britain to the colour problem, and Sumner Welles' reference to racial equality in his speech may be due to the Administration's consciousness that the issue should not be neglected." The Ambassador remarked that Thomas Dewey recently spoke "warmly in support of negroes" which may have been meant to undermine Willkie, "since Willkie is to date the most prominent American negrophile." In an attached message for Cadogan, Sir R. I. Campbell reported being told by David Scott (Foreign Office) that the Foreign Office was "studying the implications of Welles' remark that we are fighting to end Imperialism as part of the larger task of persuading Americans that the trident is not slipping from our nerveless grasp and is not being, any more than it has been in the past or will be in the future, wielded for the benefit of a handful of privileged reactionaries." (Ibid.) Shortly thereafter, Churchill privately complained to Eden about "Willkie, Luce and Co." saying "things which give profound offence here."(Churchill to Eden, 2 January 1943, FO 371.36007, Z 2101/47/17.)

[3]Stanley to Churchill, 1 December 1942, PREM 4-42/9. Stanley had replaced Lord Cranborne as Colonial Secretary on 22 November 1942. Hull's views are enclosed in Halifax to

Eden, 25 August 1942, WP(42)544, 5 December 1942, CAB 66/31. See also Appendix F; OSS memorandum, "British Colonial Policy," 28 April 1944, OSS R&A 1398. This long study quoted the Earl of Listowel: "The essential difference between Conservatives and Socialists is a difference of emphasis of focus, rather than a sharp cleavage on any matter of basic principle." The study, however, continued, "Generally British sins on colonial policy are pointed up and their virtues overlooked. . . . It should be remembered that the British themselves make available to the interested reader much more self-criticism of empire policies than can be found in other imperial systems." Describing American misconceptions, this memorandum continued, "Mr. Julian Huxley, for example, declares that "Americans generally are more hostile to empires and that when they think of empires they think of the British Empire, which presumably symbolizes all of the evil of empires in general. The British feel that Americans expect them to apologize for the existence of the empire, otherwise as Mr. [Herbert] Morrison asks, 'Why, when we say we mean to maintain our Empire--a merely defensive stabilising war aim--so many people should behave as though we had proclaimed a policy of barefaced expansion.' The British complain that . . . there are some 'who are convinced that you are lying when you tell them that Canada, Australia and South Africa are not subject states.'"

[4]Stanley, Attlee, Cripps, Eden memorandum, "Colonial Policy," WP(42)544, 5 December 1942, CAB 66/31.

[5]Ibid. Stanley submitted this draft memorandum on 4 December to Churchill, who approved it for Cabinet consideration on 6 December. (PREM 4-42/9.) Cabinet endorsement may be found in WM(42)166, 9 December 1942, CAB 65/28.

[6]WP(42)544, 5 December 1942, CAB 66/31. On 22 December Lord Chancellor John Simon wrote to Churchill: "Are you satisfied that Cordell Hull's phrase 'Parent State' is the best that can be found for the proposed declaration on Colonial Policy? It seems to me that it may hereafter be exploited by critics and agitators on behalf of 'Children' States. In what sense is Britain 'parent' to Hong Kong or Jamaica? 'Guardian States' seems to me a safer expression especially as in the future America will cast envious eyes on the West Indies." Churchill directed the next day that Simon's note be "circulated to War Cabinet & Col. Sec." This brought the prompt reply on 22 December from Amery to Churchill arguing against Simon's objections. The Secretary of State for India and Burma declared, "After all, 'parent' in that connexion implies not physical origin, but a relationship and a mutual attitude. . . . There are some famous lines in Latin poetry describing Rome as 'mother, not

mistress' of the peoples which had come under her sway. The
relationship of guardian to ward is one of duty on the one
side and on the other very often of impatience, and does not
suggest the same tie of mutual affection. Also, if we begin
to talk of ourselves as guardians of the West Indies, the
Americans might very soon retort that they are doing the
actual 'guarding.' So I hope Cordell Hull's phrase might
stand." (See correspondence in PREM 4-42/9.)

[7]See Churchill message, enclosed in Dominions Office to
Australia, Canada, New Zealand, South Africa, 11 December
1942, PREM 4-42/9.

[8]The Smuts response is enclosed in Sydney F. Waterson
(South Africa House, London) to Attlee, 16 December 1942,
PREM 4-42/9; also Fraser to Attlee, 18 December 1942, ibid.

[9]King to Attlee, 23 December 1942, ibid.

[10]Curtin to Attlee, 2 January 1943, ibid. Attlee
summarized the Dominion replies for the Cabinet at WP(43)6,
4 January 1943, CAB 66/33. Curtin continued, "An approach
arising mainly from a desire to meet current criticism in
the United States is, in our view, far too narrow. Because
it would be essentially defensive, it could hardly provide a
satisfactory basis for reaching a genuine accord of view
with the United States administration." He added, "Regional
Colonial Commissions, consisting of representatives of
trustee states or other primarily interested states,
including the Dominions in their respective areas, and of
native peoples who have reached or are approaching the stage
of self-government, to be established. This body might be
(i) regarded as the agent of the International Colonial
Commission in matters pertaining to the implementation of
agreed international policy. (ii) Co-operative and
consultative for dealing with questions of mutual concern to
all the adjacent Colonies, and for promoting regional
educational, social and economic standards."

[11]Linlithgow to Churchill, 2 January 1943, ibid. In an
attached letter to Amery the same day, the Viceroy
explained, "Great Britain is going to be pretty tightly
squeezed after the war with loss of export markets,
liquidation of foreign investments and the like, and the
importance to our trade of colonial empire is clear. . . . I
am not myself able to share the confidence of those who
appear to think by some act of faith or financial
legerdemain it will prove possible after the war to sustain
standards of living in United Kingdom from sources other
than the annual harvest of our national wealth. . . . The
[American] element which has any real understanding of
European or major colonial problems is very small: the
element which is jealous of, and prejudiced against, Great

Britain is very large. It is too easy for a great industrial country which contains its own granary and meat and milk producing areas, as well as an extensive range of natural resources, to condemn the colonial system out of which our Dominions have grown."

[12]See the two Halifax telegrams to the Foreign Office, 24 and 26 December 1942, WP(43)8, 5 January 1943, CAB 66/33; Eden to Halifax, 14 December 1942, PREM 4-42/9. Eden added, "High Commissioners suggested that proposed Regional Commission might be misunderstood as somethng like Mandated Commission which, as you know, is not at all what we have in mind and would of course be in conflict with 'parent State' idea." In his 26 December telegram Halifax stated that Roosevelt "evidently liked the idea" of regional arrangements. The President wanted to include nations on the west coast of South America because of their Pacific interests, but Halifax stated, "I think we rode him off this." Also Roosevelt observed that he did not like the phrases "backward peoples" or "parent States" and asked for alternatives. In December 1942, Lord Hailey asserted at the Mont Tremblant Conference sponsored by the unofficial International Council of Pacific Relations that the British had "always accepted the moral principle of Trusteeship" and that "the natural destiny of a dependent unit is independent and responsible self-government." He cited the Act of 1940, passed during a time of great crisis, which legislated the ruling concept of "partnership" based on the idea that "political liberties are meaningless unless they can be built up on a better foundation of social and economic progress." For accounts of this conference, see OSS report, 4 December 1942, 26217-R, RG 226, NA; J. O. Denby (Territorial Studies) memorandum, "Colonial Problems of South East Asia: Views of the Mont Tremblant Conference," CDA 118a, 22 January 1944, Notter Files, file "CDA Docs 95-120," Box 174.

[13]See "Colonial Policy: Revised Draft of Joint Declaration," WP(43)8, 5 January 1943, CAB 66/33; WM(43)4, 7 January 1943, CAB 65/33. Secretary E. E. Bridges collected the various papers on the first draft for Churchill while considering the second draft. These included the comments of Amery, WP(42)575; Bevin, WP(42)606; Cripps, WP(42)614; the four Dominions, WP(43)6, Stanley, WP(43)7; and the Viceroy of India, WP(43)9. See Bridges to Churchill, 7 January 1943, PREM 4-42/9. The responses by each of the Dominions and by Halifax to the second draft are annexed to the third draft, 19 January 1943, CAB 66/33. Cabinet approval came at WM(43)12, 20 January 1943, CAB 65/33.

[14]H. Notter, P. Mosely, C. E. Rothwell memorandum, T-15, [10] July 1942, Notter Files, file "T Docs 1-36," Box 31. This study concluded, "Any major departures from

established boundaries will tend to create more problems than are solved. . . . Whatever changes are made, large or small, probably will not accommodate all the peninsulas and islands of population." See also Hull memorandum of conversation with Halifax, 4 February 1943, Pasvolsky Files, file "Jan-March 1943," Box 4. Hull to Gauss, 21 July 1942, FRUS, 1942, China, p. 733; Shantz to Secretary of State, 25 March 1942, 841.00/1547. In addition, the State Department encouraged private organizations of experts to conduct independent studies. The Institute of Pacific Relations drew upon international scholars and statesmen to produce some valuable studies. Also the Yale Institute of International Studies, directed by Frederick S. Dunn, undertook in 1942 a continuing research project in the "study of some of the more pressing issues that threaten to come up in the immediate future and to cause dissension." See Yale President Charles Seymour to Hull, 10 November 1942, SD 711.41/555; and the attached reply by Hull, 5 December which indicated a desire that these studies be made available to the State Department.

[15]Campbell to Cadogan, 6 August 1942, PREM 4-42/9. (See Appendix C for the complete text.) See also Hassett, Off the Record, p. 104.

[16]Unsigned memorandum, "International Trusteeship," PIO-29a, 28 August 1942, Notter Files, file "PIO Docs 29-60," Box 117. For other versions of this plan, see Clarke M. Eichelburger, B. V. Cohen, James T. Shotwell memorandum, PIO 29, 28 August 1942, ibid; O. B. Gerig memoranda, PIO 30 and 30a, 4 September 1942, ibid.; Eichelburger memorandum, PIO 29e, 22 October 1942, ibid.; unsigned final draft, PIO 29i, 15 April 1943, ibid.; also ibid., file "PIO Minutes 1-40," Box 138. For more State Department studies on dependent areas, see W. R. Sharp and O. B. Gerig memorandum, "Classification of Dependent Areas," 24 September 1942, Notter Files, file "PWWPS: Dependent Areas," Box 298; Abe Fortas (Interior, Under Secretary) to Hull, 9 November 1942, SD 841.00/90-1/2; Hull to Winant," 11 November 1942, SD 841.01/88A; Gallman to Hull, 28 November 1942, SD 841.01/90; unsigned memorandum, "International Trusteeship," T-169a, 8 December 1942, Notter Files, file "T Docs 130-170," Box 32; O. B. Gerig memorandum, "Definition of Dependent Area," P-Und-1, n.d., ibid., file "P-Und-Docs 1-," Box 65.

[17]Hull to Roosevelt, 17 November 1942, Notter Files, file "AC," Box 1. Halifax reported to the Foreign Office, 6 January 1943, "Hull emphasized that his original suggestion had been made on his own responsibility and before discussion with the President." Churchill minuted two days later, "Please note how very informal and insecure is the foundation on which the 'Parent States' philosophy is being built." (PREM 4-42/9.)

[18]Notter to Welles, 15 March 1943, Notter Files, file "Documentation," Box 3; Hull to Roosevelt (enclosing memorandum of 9 March), 17 March 1943, ibid., file "AC," Box 1;   Ralph Bunche memorandum, "The Background of Recent Department Policy Regarding Dependent Areas," 3 January 1945, ibid., Black Binder I, Box 275.

[19]Hull to Roosevelt, 17 March 1943, Notter Files, file "AC," Box 1.   Hull, Memoirs, II, 1234-36, 1304-05; Bunch memorandum, op cit.; unsigned memorandum, "International Trusteeship," n.d. [late 1944], Notter Files, file "Progress Reports," Box 22.   For two similar British ideas, see George H. Blakeslee, "Report on International Foundation of the World Peace Foundation," 9 January 1943; Royal Institute of International Affairs memorandum, 11 August 1943, both in FO 371.35957, F 4015/751/25.

[20]WM(43)53, SSF, 13 April 1943, CAB 65/34.

[21]Unsigned "Memorandum of British Colonial 'Partnership,'" 29 November 1943, Notter Files, file "E Docs 216-234," Box 91; Hull memorandum, 31 August 1943, ibid., file "First Quebec," Box 284; Gallman to Hull, 11 January 1943, SD 841.00/1614; Minutes of Territorial Committee Meeting #42, 5 March 1943, Notter Files, file "Committee on Territorial Problems Minutes 36-49," Box 42; Minutes of "P" Meeting, 5 June 1943, ibid., file "Political Subcommittee Minutes (Chron.) Nos. 50-60," Box 66.   For more on British statements of colonial policy, see press reports collected in FO 371. 35917, F 1589/877/61, and PREM 4-43A/5; Gallman to Hull, 17 March 1943, SD 841.00/1633; Winant to Hull, 14 July 1943, SD 841.00/1654.

[22]Hailey memorandum, "The Future of Colonial Peoples," enclosed in Hailey to Churchill, 24 March 1944, PREM 4-42/9.

[23]Pasvolsky memorandum,"International Activities in Which the United States Must Participate," 9 August 1943, Notter Files, file "First Quebec," Box 284.

[24]Minutes of "CP" Meeting #2, 30 September 1943, Notter Files, file "CDA Mins 1-27," Box 183; Report on White House Meeting, 5 October 1943, FRUS, 1943, I, 541-43; Emerson memorandum, "Regionalism in Southeast Asia," T-408, 14 September 1943, ibid., file "T Docs 401-416," Box 36; T. Cargo memorandum, "Trusteeship: Desirability of a Trusteeship System," H-1058, n.d., ibid., Box 62; Pasvolsky memorandum, 9 August 1943, ibid., file "First Quebec," Box 284; Vandenbosch memorandum, T-428, 24 June 1943, ibid., file "T Docs 417-436," Box 36; Emerson memorandum, T-328, n.d., ibid., file "T Docs 326-336," Box 34; Pasvolsky Subcommittee memorandum, "U. S. Peace Aims," 29 March 1944,

ibid., file "PC," Box 15; Blakeslee memorandum, n.d., ibid., file "Mins I-DA Committee," Box 55. Cargo's report concluded, "For the United States the abandonment of the trusteeship idea would seem to result in the loss of one means by which American interest in commercial and air opportunities in Africa and the Pacific might be forwarded, and might require the establishment of complete control of a number of Pacific islands by the United States for security."

25Pasvolsky Subcommittee memorandum, "British Peace Aims," 29 March 1944, Notter Files, file "PC," Box 15; Minutes of "CP" Meeting #2, 30 September 1943, ibid., file "CDA Mins 1-27," Box 183.

26Stettinius report to Hull, 22 May 1944, ibid., Black Binder "Report," Box 87. See also Stettinius Papers, file "Final Report-Early draft of," Box 252; Stettinius memorandum, 17 March 1944, Stettinius Papers, file "Meeting of Group Prior to Departure," Box 254 (see Appendix D).

27Stettinius report. Stanley said that he was so optimistic about future agreement along these four points that he would bring them before the Cabinet. Bowman emphasized the informal nature of their talks, and Stettinius reserved the right of future consideration by the State Department. See Bowman to Winant, 24 April 1944, ibid., file "Int'l Org.," Box 27; State Department memorandum, n.d. [late 1944], ibid., file "Progress Report on Post-War Programs," Box 22.

28See the unsigned State Department memoranda: "Regional Advisory Councils," n.d. [August 1944], ibid., file "Progress Report," Box 22; "Trusteeship," n.d. [December 1944], ibid.; T-529, 30 August 1944, ibid., file "526-537," Box 39.

29Bunche memorandum, "Background of Recent Department Policy Regarding Dependent Areas," 3 January 1945, ibid., Black Binder I, Box 275. Bunche differentiated between (a) trusteeship controls for mandates as well as any territories detached from the enemies and (b) regional advisory councils for colonial areas. Roosevelt's desire as well as JCS pressures are described in Pasvolsky memorandum, "Questions Left Unsettled at Dumbarton Oaks," 15 November 1944, ibid., file "Int'l Org.," Box 246. See the three unsigned memoranda in previous note; also Halifax to Foreign Office, 8 October 1944, PREM 4-30/11; JCS memorandum, enclosed in Marshall to Hull, 3 August 1944; FRUS, 1944, I, 699-700; Alger Hiss memorandum, 5 August 1944, Notter Files, file "P 241-261," Box 65; William C. Johnstone (FORD) memorandum, "The Colonial Problem as an Issue in Anglo-American Relations in the Pacific Area," n.d. [August 1943], FO

371.35927, F 4767/1953/61.

[30]Halifax to Foreign Office, 8 October 1944, PREM 4-30/11. Richard Law and Harold Butler, too, made known British disappointment over American inattention to Stanley's speech. (See Taussig memorandum, September 1943, Taussig Papers, file "Miscellaneous 1939-1944," Box 52.)

[31]Halifax to Foreign Office, 30 December 1944, PREM 31/4. He added, "We can, of course, tell them politely to mind their own business but if we thus decline informal discussions with them there is nothing to prevent them from circulating their own views to other colonial powers or United Nations or even coming out with a unilateral public statement. Once they have committed themselves in this way it would be much more difficult to influence or modify their views than in informal discussions between ourselves."

[32]Churchill to Eden, 31 December 1944, PREM 4-31/4.

[33]Eden to Churchill (enclosing Stanley memorandum), 8 January 1945, PREM 4-31/4. Eden noted that the Cabinet had referred the paper to the Dominions for approval and then planned to send it on to the State Department. He also reported that Stanley, then in Jamaica, had been invited to Washington by the State Department for further discussions. Eden concluded that "such a talk would enable us to retain the initiative and possibly forestall some embarrassing American move." For a record of the Stanley visit to Washington, see O. B. Gerig memorandum, 18 January 1945, Notter Files, file "A Docs 86--," Box 3; unsigned memorandum, 19 January 1945, ibid., Black Binder "Dumbarton Oaks (III)," Box 274. Later, British planners arrived in Washington with the new colonial policy memorandum as cleared by the Dominions but, in Woodward's words, "were unable to make any progress owing to the President's death." Woodward continued, "They were told that the President had not given any ruling on the differences of view between the State Department and the Service Departments. Hence the United States Delegation did not submit their proposals to the five Powers until the opening of the Conference." (Woodward, British Foreign Policy, pp. 534-39.)

[34]See the Churchill-Martin correspondence, 10 January 1945, PREM 4-31/4. For the official paper presented to the Cabinet, see Stanley, Attlee, memorandum, "Colonial Policy," WP(44)738, 14 December 1944, CAB 66/59.

[35]See in PREM 4-31/4: Churchill to Martin, 14 January; Churchill to Eden, 18 January; and Eden to Churchill, 24 January 1945. See also Taussig memoranda of conversations, 18-19 January 1945, Taussig Papers, file "1945-January - June," Box 52. This file also contains Taussig's report of

the following Roosevelt-Stanley exchange:

Roosevelt: I do not want to be unkind or rude to the British but in 1841 when you acquired Hong Kong, you did not acquire it by purchase.

Stanley: Let me see, Mr. President, that was about the time of the Mexican War.

[36]See in FRUS, Yalta: "Draft Report By the Foreign Ministers to the Sixth Plenary Meeting," 9 February 1945 (pp. 281-85); United States Delegation [Hiss] memorandum, 8 February (p. 794); Hiss memorandum of conversation 4 February (p. 569); Charles Bohlen minutes of Roosevelt-Stalin meeting, 8 February (p. 770). At the 9 February meeting of the Foreign Ministers, Secretary of State Stettinius presented American proposals for invitations to the United Nations Conference. This draft included an agenda item to consider a statement for "the inclusion in the projected Charter of provisions relating to territorial trusteeship and dependent areas." It was agreed to omit this item. Stettinius explained that the Big Five would hold conversations on trusteeship prior to the U.N. Conference. Stettinius pointed out that "he did not contemplate any detailed discussions on particular islands or territories but wished to establish the right of the organization to deal with the problem of trusteeships and to set up some machinery." Significantly, both Eden and Vyacheslav Molotov concurred. (Ibid., p. 810, p. 817.) Also see Stettinius, Roosevelt, p. 232; Woodward, British Foreign Policy, p. 535.

[37]FRUS, Yalta, p. 856; Sherwood, Hopkins, p. 865-66; James F. Byrnes, Speaking Frankly (New York: Harper and Brothers, 1947), pp. ix-x. Lord Moran described "a rather sad scene this afternoon" as told to him by Hopkins, who reported that he could hardly follow the excited and rapid speech of the Prime Minister. (Moran, Churchill, pp. 228-29.)

[38]FRUS, YALTA, pp. 844-45, p. 856, pp. 858-59; p. 935, pp. 944-47, p. 977; Stettinius, Roosevelt, pp. 238-39; Woodward, British Foreign Policy, p. 536; Byrnes, Speaking Frankly, pp. ix-x; Earl of Avon, The Memoirs of Anthony Eden: The Reckoning (London: The Times Publishing Company, 1965), p. 595.

[39]Eden to Churchill, 5 February 1945, PREM 4-31/4; Hull, Memoirs, II, 1234-36, 1304-05; Notter, Postwar, pp. 470-72; Stettinius, Roosevelt, pp. 44-45, pp. 237-38; State Department memorandum, "Arrangements for International Trusteeship," 21 November 1944, RG 43, file "Briefing Book for Yalta Conference--1945," Box 2; Joseph Alsop to Walter Lippmann, 30 January 1945, Walter Lippmann Papers, Yale University, file 38, Box 50; Robert Hathaway, Ambiguous

Partnership: Britain and America, 1944-1947 (NY: Columbia University Press 1981), pp. 46-47; State Department draft trusteeship declaration, 19 July 1943, ibid. See in FRUS, Yalta: Stettinius to Roosevelt, 15 November 1944 (p. 54); Pasvolsky memorandum of conversation with Roosevelt, Stettinius, and Green Hackworth, 15 November 1944 (pp. 56-57); Pasvolsky-Russian Ambassador Andrei Gromyko conversation, 13 January 1945 (pp. 73-76); Briefing Book paper, "Dependent Territories," n.d. (pp. 92-93). For the text of the abortive American proposals for the Dumbarton Oaks Conference (mentioned by Stettinius to Roosevelt, 15 November 1944), see United Nations Information Organization, Documents of the United Nations Conference on International Organization, Vol III (New York: United Nations and Library of Congress, 1945), 604-8.

[40]Herbert Feis, Churchill, Roosevelt, Stalin: The War They Waged and the Peace They Sought (Princeton: Princeton University Press, 1957), p. 556. Eden cabled to Churchill on 6 February 1945: "Nevile Butler has told me what Hiss said to Cadogan about International Trusteeship. You will remember that the Colonial Secretary and I had a talk with Hopkins on this subject while he was in London. The Colonial Secretary explained the ideas which were on his mind making it clear at the same time that they were his personal ideas and had not yet been approved by the Cabinet. Hopkins said that he thought they would interest the President very much and that he would speak to the President about them. Hopkins thought that the President would not wish to press the question at ARGONAUT [Yalta] in the light of what the Colonial Secretary had said." (PREM 4-78/1 Pt. 1.)

[41]Bunche memorandum, "Arrangements for International Trusteeship," 30 April 1945, Notter Files, file "Dependent Territories," Box 273. See also State Department memorandum, "International Trusteeships," 9 April 1945, Marshall Papers, file 40, Box 88.

[42]See Minutes of Trusteeship Committee meetings, Notter Files, file "PCT Minutes," Box 273; Minutes of American Delegation meetings, ibid., file "Minutes US Delegation Meetings," Box 272; Fortas to Ickes, 10 March 1945, RG 48; "Records of the Office of the Secretary of the Interior, folder "Territories--General," NA. Ickes protested to Secretary of the Navy James Forrestal about the intentions of the Navy to administer the trusts on 1 November 1944 (ibid.). See also General E. I. C. Jacob (in San Francisco) to British Chiefs of Staff, 12 May 1945, PREM 4-31/4. Jacob reported on the American position: "It was very soon apparent that nothing could induce the American Chiefs of Staff to abandon a proposal which had evidently been arrived at after a great struggle with the State Department. The

American Chiefs of Staff feel that they acted weakly both in 1898 and in 1919, in not securing the Japanese islands for America, and they are determined not to fail again. . . . The American Chiefs of Staff would like to annex the islands but they are debarred from doing this by a decision given by President Roosevelt just before he died." Jacob believed that by placing the American trusteeship over the Pacific islands under the Security Council, the United States could then veto any future proposal to alter American control. (Jacob interview with the author, 26 June 1973, Woodbridge.)

[43]Minutes of Trusteeship Committee, Notter Files, file "PCT Minutes," Box 273.

[44]Record of the United Kingdom Delegation meetings, 8 and 12 May 1945, CAB 21-1611-16/17/1; Lord Cranborne to Stanley, 12 May 1945, PREM 4-31/4; Stanley memorandum, WP(45)300, 13 May 1945, CAB 66/65; Stanley to Churchill, 15 May 1945, PREM 4-31/4.

[45]Stanley to Churchill, 15 May 1945, PREM 4-31/4; Stanley memorandum, WP(45)300, 13 May 1945, CAB 66/65.

[46]Minutes of American Delegation meeting, 18 May 1945, Notter Files, file "US Delegation Minutes," Box 272.

[47]Taussig memorandum, 15 March 1945, Taussig Papers, Franklin D. Roosevelt Library, Hyde Park, New York, file "1945 January-June," Box 52; also Taussig's report of Roosevelt's views and the San Francisco Conference events in Taussig memorandum of conversation with Mrs. Roosevelt, 27 August 1945, Taussig Papers, file "1945 July-December," Box 52.

[48]Minutes of American Delegation meeting, 18 May 1945, Notter Files, file "US Delegation Minutes," Box 272. Significantly, at a meeting on 20 June, Nelson Rockefeller inquired if the United States had ever intended to place all dependent areas under trusteeship. Pasvolsky replied that there had never been any serious plans to do so, "although there had been some 'wild' ideas concerning a complete trusteeship system." (Ibid.) Secretary Ickes sent a plea for the Conference to support independence for colonial peoples but the American Delegation decided to have Abe Fortas tell Ickes this could not be done. See ibid.; and the pertinent correspondence in RG 126, file I-217.

[49]For a report on Stettinius' approach to Gromyko, 2 June 1945, see Notter Files, file "Stettinius Diary--S.F. Conference," Box 283. See also Minutes of Commission II meeting, 20 June 1945, ibid., file "Drafting Book--II," Box 275; Stettinius memorandum, 18 May 1945, Stettinius Papers, file "Trusteeship," Box 355; B. Gerig memorandum of

conversation with Stettinius and Stassen, 9 June 1945, Stettinius Papers, file "I-6/8/45," Box 300. It is interesting to speculate on the turn of events if Hull had not been too ill to assume direction of the American Delegation as first proposed. See Pasvolsky memorandum, 6 September 1944, Pasvolsky Files, file "July-Dec. 1944," Box 6. At the end of the Conference, someone asked Senator Tom Connally if the United Nations Charter could be passed by the Senate in two or three weeks. He replied, "You couldn't even drive a nail through the Senate in two or three weeks." (Stettinius diary entry, 25 June 1945, op. cit.)

[50]Foreign Office memorandum, 19 February 1942, enclosed in Eden memorandum, "The Four Power Plan," n.d. [October 1942], PREM 4-100/7. For Churchill's observation, see WM(42)8, SSF, 17 January 1942, CAB 65/29.

NOTES ON CHAPTER VII

[1]Hull, Memoirs, II, 1599.

[2]Willson to King, 13 March 1945, Notter Files, file "Drafting Book on Trusteeship at San Francisco," Book III, Box 275; Hull, Memoirs, II, 1706-07; Hester to Fortas, 5 October 1942, RG 126, file I-971, Pt. 2; K. Bartimo memorandum, "Guam," T-551, n.d. [November 1944], Notter Files, file "T Docs 538-558," Box 39; Bartimo memorandum, "Wake Island," T-538, n.d., ibid.; Bartimo memorandum, "American Samoa," T-535, n.d., ibid.; file "T Docs 526-537"; Paul H. Alling (Deputy Director, Division of Near Eastern Affairs) to Wallace S. Murray (Director, NEA), 1 November 1944, SD 740.0011PW/11-1444; David Harris memorandum, "Colonial Programs in the War of 1914-1918," 30 November 1942, Notter Files, file "PWWPS: Dependent Areas," Box 298; Borton memorandum, "Japan and the Issue of Racial Equality at Paris, 1919," 3 February 1943, ibid., file "T Docs 224-235," Box 33; unsigned memorandum, "Liquidation of the League of Nations," n.d. [January 1945], RG 43, "Briefing Book for the Yalta Conference--1945," Box 2; Bunche memorandum, "Arrangements for International Trusteeship," n.d., ibid., file "Dependent Territories," Box 273. The Harris memorandum concluded, "The lessons from the colonial discussions during the last war would seem to be largely negative. The governments and their spokesmen made the mistake of falling into the dilemma of publicly espousing principles hard to reconcile with their private objectives. They were finally saved from their embarrassment by the invention of the mandate system which rescued the substance of the treaties and at the same time saved the glitter of international responsibility." The Bartimo study on Wake Island pointed out that Pan American Airways supervised that

island until the Navy assumed responsibility in 1940. And
the paper on the League of Nations, after identifying the
legal troubles of official liquidation (e.g., only 28 of the
45 members were associated with the present United Nations
coalition), recommended simply establishing a new
organization "which would disregard legal continuity as
such."

[3]Hull, Memoirs, II, 1305, 1596; Blakeslee memorandum,
"Japan: United States: Disposition of the Mandated
Islands," 29 January 1945, Notter Files, file "CAC Docs
Und.," Box 53; Gerig memorandum of conversation with
Stanley, 18 January 1945, ibid., file "A Docs," Box 3;
Minutes of Inter Divisional Area Committee Meeting #176, 21
December 1944, ibid., file "CAC Reports," Box 54; House of
Representatives, Committee on Naval Affairs (Subcommittee on
Pacific Bases) report, "Pacific Bases," 1945, George
Blakeslee Papers, Clark University, Worcester,
Massachusetts, Box 10. Considering Roosevelt's instructions
to Hull, the Committee on Territorial Problems concluded in
June-July 1943 that the United States should participate
(and probably alone) in the administration of the Mandated
Islands within an International Trusteeship. See Minutes of
Territorial Committee Meetings #51 (21 June 1943) and #52
(16 July 1943), ibid., "Mins. 50-59," Box 42.

[4]FRUS, Yalta, pp. 78-81, p. 793.

[5]Ibid.

[6]Ibid., p. 57; Minutes of American Delegation meeting 1
June 1945, Notter Files, Stettinius Diaries, Vol, II, Box
283; FRUS, Cairo and Tehran, p. 197; War Department,
"Memorandum Concerning U.S. Post-War Pacific Bases," n.d.,
Marshall Papers, file 38, Box 81.

[7]FE(45)1, 17 January 1945, CAB 96/5; Halifax to Foreign
Office (reporting the Law-Roosevelt conversation), 24
December 1944, FE(45)2, 11 January 1945, CAB 96/5; FRUS,
Yalta, p. 57. Albeit unsubstantiated, Kolko is probably
correct in his allegation about Yalta: "In effect, an
operational agreement existed whereby the British would
support American claims in return for silence on the
empire." See Gabriel Kolko, The Politics of War: The World
and United States Foreign Policy, 1943-1945 (New York:
Vintage, 1968), pp. 465-66; also, Churchill, Triumph and
Tragedy, p. 333.

[8]Sherwood, Hopkins, pp. 866-68; Byrnes, Speaking
Frankly, pp. 76-77.

[9]Dulles and Ridinger, "The Anti-Colonial Policies of
Franklin D. Roosevelt," Political Science Quarterly, LXX

(March 1955), 18; Welles, Seven Decisions, pp. 178-79; Hassett, Off the Record, pp. 166-67; Halifax to Foreign Office, 19 December 1943, FO 371.35921, F 6656/1422/61; Fenard to de Gaulle, 12 October 1944, in de Gaulle, Salvation, pp. 39-42.

[10]Marshall to Hull (enclosing JCS memorandum), 3 August 194, FRUS, 1944, I, 699-700.

[11]Ibid.; also Leahy to Hull, 16 May 1944, enclosed in Hickerson to Atherton, 29 September 1944, Hickerson Files, file "A," Box 4; Minutes of Subcommittee on Security Technical Problems Meeting #20, 16 June 1943, Notter Files, file "Minutes of Subcommittee on Security Technical Problems," Box 79; Leahy to Davis, 15 September 1942, annexed to Meeting #179, 2 January 1945, ibid., file "Jan. 2-April 25, 1945," Box 55.

[12]Vandenberg to Hull, 29 August 1944, Notter Files, file "I.O. - Int'l. Discussions," Box 168; Sir Godfrey Haggard memorandum of conversation with Dewey, 7 April 1943, enclosed in Wright to Foreign Office, 8 May 1943, FO 371.34136, A 4644/57/45; Associated Press Special Survey, enclosed in Ministry of Information memorandum, 19 April 1943, FO 371.34136, A 3861/57/45; Jones memorandum, 5 March 1943, Notter Files, file "PPC-Vol. I, " Box 63. Roosevelt's remark at Yalta came during the Second Plenary Session, 5 February 1945. (FRUS, Yalta, p. 628; Churchill, Triumph and Tragedy, p. 303.) Nevile Butler suggested to the Embassy in Washington that "a pronouncement by the Chief Justice on Sovereignty, before the construction that the Isolationists are trying to put on it has crystallized into legend," might be useful. He noted that "honourable limitations of sovereignty" did exist "quite apart from the idea of selling oneself into slavery." But Campbell replied negatively, pointing out that "we may only embarrass him [Roosevelt] if we make some ambitious intervention." See Butler to Campbell, 23 October 1943, FO 371.34139, A 9560/57/45; Campbell to Butler, 8 December 1943, FO 371.34140, A 11315/57/45; also author's interview with Sir Nevile Butler, 6 June 1973, London. And John Hickerson discouraged a postwar proposal that referred to a "super organization" with the observation: "The word 'super' is generally suspect in the United States unless immediately followed by the word 'duper.'" See Hickerson to Fred Mallon (Vice-President, Pillsbury Flour Mills), 24 March 1943, Hickerson Files, file "M," Box 5; see also Mary E. Fraser to Pasvolsky, 10 March 1943, Pasvolsky Files, file "Jan.-Mar. 1943," Box 4.

[13]Churchill to Attlee and Eden, 14 September 1943, FO 371.37028, N 5412/3666/38; Eden to Churchill, 28 March 1943, PREM 4-30/3; Eden memorandum, WP(43)130, 28 March 1943, CAB

66/35; memorandum concerning the meeting of 3 May 1941, quoted in Wilson, First Summit, pp. 176-178.

[14]See two John Patterson memoranda: "Prospects for a Congressional Resolution Favoring U.S. Participation in Post War International Cooperation for Peace," and "Observations on the House of Representatives Debate on the Fulbright Resolution," 14 and 27 September 1943, Notter Files, file "Congressional Post-War Action," Box 307; Alice McDiarmid memorandum, "The Connally Resolution," n.d. [after 5 November 1943], ibid. The December 1942 results of the Gallup Poll may be found in FO 371.34163, A 57/57/45; Lippmann to Francis R. Coudert, 7 December 1943, Lippmann Papers, file 515, Box 64. On 12 January 1943 Nevile Butler attached his comment: "Congress, tho' truculent, is not very courageous. . . . it takes its line from public opinion, and the game is that the Press stirs public opinion which when stirred sends telegrams & deputations to individual Congressmen who then hastily devour their previous opinions." For the text of the two resolutions, see House Concurrent Resolution #25, Congressional Record 78th Congress, 1st Session, Vol 89, p. 7729 (21 September 1943); and Senate Resolution #192, ibid., p. 9222 (5 November 1943).

[15]Unsigned memorandum, n.d. [December 1944], Notter Files, file "Progress Report on Post-War Programs--the President," Box 22; Jones memorandum, "Towards New Responsibility in the Conduct of Foreign Affairs," 19 January 1943, Pasvolsky Files, file "Jan.-Mar. 1943," Box 4.

[16]O. B. Gerig, D. V. Sandifer, Dorothy Fosdick memorandum, 15 November 1944, Notter Files, file "Conv. B, " Box 165; Smith, American Diplomacy, p. 14. For more on State Department proposals about a world organization, see Appendix J; also I. Berlin memorandum, 5 January 1943, FO 371.34136, A 2295/57/45; J. Patterson memorandum, 12 June 1943, Pasvolsky Files, file "April-June 1943," Box 5; Postwar Committee memorandum, "Summary of Papers 60-69," 15 April 1944, Notter Files, file "60-76," Box 17. See also Robert Dallek, Franklin D. Roosevelt and American Foreign Policy, 1932-1945 (NY: Oxford University Press, 1979); Wm. Roger Louis, Imperialism At Bay: The United States and the Decolonization of the British Empire, 1941-1945 (NY: Oxford University Press, 1978); Christopher Thorne, Allies of a Kind: The United States, Britain, and the War Against Japan, 1941-1945 (NY: Oxford University Press, 1978).

[17]Smith, American Diplomacy, p. 14; E. Roosevelt, As He Saw It, p. 25, pp. 114-16. See also Moran, Churchill, pp. 241-42; OSS memorandum, "British Colonial Policy," 28 April 1944, OSS R&A 1398; Admiral King memorandum, 9 July 1944, RG 43, Files of Philip E. Mosely, NA, file "Post-War Naval

Interests," Box 22.

[18]Raymond G. O'Connor, Diplomacy, p. 81; Woodward, British Foreign Policy, pp. xxxvii-xxxviii. For comments about American idealism and foreign policy, see Lippmann to Halifax, 6 February 1945, Lippmann Papers, file 955, Box 75; Harold Laski to Max Lerner, 12 April 1942, Max Lerner Papers, Yale University, file 223, Box 5.

[19]O'Connor, Diplomacy, p. 81. Text of Roosevelt's message to Congress, 1 March 1945, RG 43, file "Report on Crimea Conference," Box 5; Rosenman, Public Papers, XIII, 610-11. See also White House memorandum, 12 February 1945, SD 740.0011PW/2-1245; Grew to Stettinius, 13 July 1945, RG 43, file "Background," Box 3; FRUS, 1945, VII, 934, 943; Sherwood, Hopkins, p. 888, p. 902; Smith, American Diplomacy, p. 147; Woodward, British Foreign Policy, xxxviii; Diane S. Clemens, Yalta (New York: Oxford University Press, 1970).

[20]John R. Colville essay in Action This Day, pp. 83-84.

[21]Eden memorandum, "The Four Power Idea," n.d. [October 1942], PREM 4-100/7; Churchill to Eden, 18 October 1942, ibid.; Eden to Churchill, 19 October, ibid. Churchill commented to Eden on 21 October, "It sounds very simple to pick out these four Big Powers. We cannot, however, tell what sort of Russia and what kind of Russian demands we shall have to face. . . . As to China, I cannot regard the Chungking Government as representing a Great Power. . . . I must admit that my thoughts rest primarily on Europe--the revival of the glory of Europe, the parent continent of the modern nations and of civilisation. It would be a measureless disaster if Russian barbarism overlaid the culture and independence of the ancient states of Europe. Hard as it is to say now, I trust that the European family may act unitedly as one under a Council of Europe. I look forward to a United States of Europe in which the barriers between the nations will be greatly minimized and unrestricted travel will be possible. I hope to see the economy of Europe studied as a whole. . . . Unhappily, the war has prior claims on your attention and on mine." (Ibid.) See also Eden memorandum, WP(42)516, 8 November 1942, CAB 66/30; Amery memorandum, WP(42)524, 12 November 1942, CAB 66/31; Cripps memorandum, WP(42)532, 19 November 1942, ibid.; Eden memorandum, WP(43)31, 16 January 1943, CAB 66/33.

[22]See Eden report to the Cabinet, WM(43)53, SSF, 13 April 1943, CAB 65/38; Eden to Churchill, 28 March 1943, WP(43)130, 13 April 1943, CAB 66/35. In his telegram Eden cited three points emphasized by Hopkins: that any plans for a European Council would arouse the Isolationists, that

there should be no attempt at Anglo-American settlement of the future of the world, and that China should not be exploited. It will be recalled that on 29 March the State Department presented Eden with Hull's memorandum of 9 March on trusteeship.

[23]Cadogan memorandum, quoted in Woodward, British Foreign Policy, p. 447; WM(43)53, SSF, 13 April 1943, CAB 65/38.

[24]Churchill memorandum, "Morning Thoughts," 31 January 1943, PREM 4-30/2; Churchill to Eden, 30 March 1943, PREM 4-30/3.

[25]Halifax memorandum of conversation, 22 May 1943, WP(43)233, 10 June 1943, CAB 66/37. For the American record of this conversation, see unsigned memorandum, 28 May 1943, Notter Files, file "Churchill's Views May 1943," Box 284. The American listeners were Wallace, Stimson, Ickes, Welles, and Connally. See Churchill memorandum, 12 April 1943, PREM 4-30/1.

[26]Stettinius memorandum, 22 May 1944, SD 711.41/5-2244; Eden (at Quebec) to Sargent, 22 August 1943, PREM 4-30/5; Campbell to Eden, 15 August 1943, ibid.; Eden memorandum, WP(43)389, 4 September 1943, CAB 66/52; memorandum of White House meeting, 5 October 1943, FRUS, 1943, I, 541-43; James C. Dunn (Assistant Secretary of State) to Campbell, 5 October 1943, SD 741.61/10-543; Dunn memorandum, 8 October 1943, Matthews Files, file "Memoranda 1943-1944," Box 1; Matthews to Ballantine, 8 October 1943, ibid.

[27]Eden to Churchill, 15 May 1944, CAB 21/854-9/7/14; Stettinius memorandum, 22 May 1944, SD 711.41/5-2244. Eden suggested an alternative policy: "By enhancing the role of the Council in which the Four Powers combine, by limiting its membership and ensuring so far as possible that the other members represent as far as practicable the different continents, an organisation will be obtained in which there will be an opportunity for the regional and ultimately continental organisations to grow up. The same objective can be kept in view in any regional organisation which may come into existence. But the offers of Cooperation which we make to the United States and the U.S.S.R. must be based on a world organisation and not on the separation of the world into continents and regions."

[28]Fraser to Eden, 18 May 1944, CAB 21/854-9/7/14. For a full account of this conference in London, see the collected documents in this file and in PREM 4-30/7; also Howard Bucknell, Jr. (in London) to Hull, 18 May 1944, SD 841.01/146.

[29]Churchill to Eden, 21 October 1942, PREM 4-100/7;
Churchill to Cranborne, 22 May 1944, PREM 4-30/7; minutes of
White House meeting, 5 October 1943, FRUS, 1943, I, 541-43.

[30]Churchill memorandum, 12 April 1943, PREM 4-30/11;
WM(43)53, SSF, 13 April 1943, CAB 65/38; Eden memorandum,
WP(43)31, 16 January 1943, CAB 66/33; Eden to Churchill, 15
May 1944, CAB 21/854-9/7/14.

[31]Churchill to Eden, 25 May 1944, PREM 4-30/7;
Churchill to Eden, 1 November 1943, PREM 4-30/5; Martin to
Churchill and Churchill minute, 4 July 1944, PREM 4-27/10;
Churchill to Eden, 22 August 1944, PREM 4-30/11.

[32]Churchill memorandum, WP(44)220, 2 May 1944, CAB
66/49. For accounts of Churchill's trips to Moscow
(including a copy of the infamous "percentages" deal) and
Paris (MINORU), see PREM 3-66/7; PREM 4-76/2; Churchill,
Triumph and Tragedy, pp. 227-28; de Gaulle, Salvation, pp.
68-78.

[33]Churchill to Stalin, 25 November 1944, PREM 4-30/8;
Churchill to Eden, 25 November 1944, ibid. See also
Ministry of Foreign Affairs of the U. S. S. R.,
Correspondence Between the Chairman of the Council of the
U. S. S. R. and the Presidents of the U. S. A. and the Prime
Ministers of Great Britain During the Great Patriotic War of
1941-1945 (2 vols.; Moscow: Foreign Languages Publishing
House, 1957). To Eden, Churchill declared, "Until a really
strong French Army is again in being, which may well be more
than five years away or even ten, there is nothing in these
countries but hopeless weakness. The Belgians are extremely
weak, and their behaviour before the War was shocking. The
Dutch were entirely selfish and fought only when they were
attacked, and then for a few hours. Denmark is helpless and
defenceless, and Norway particularly so. . . . The situation
would change if the French became noticeably friendly to us
and prepared to act as a barrier against the only other
power which after the extirpation of German military
strength can threaten Western Europe, namely Russia, and if
at the same time they built an Army comparable to that in
1914."

[34]Brian Gardner, Churchill, p. 302; Eden to Churchill,
29 November 1944, PREM 4-30/8; Churchill to Eden, 31
December 1944, ibid.; State Department memorandum, "British
Plan for a Western European Bloc," n.d., RG 43, Yalta
Briefing Book, Box 2; William D. Leahy, I Was There: The
Personal Story of the Chief of Staff to Presidents Roosevelt
and Truman Based on His Notes and Diaries Made at the Time
(New York: Whitlesey House, 1950), p. 442. For more on
regionalism and British views, see State Department
memorandum, "Unification of Europe," 2 June 1943, Hickerson

Files, file "Documents," Box 8; OSS memorandum, 25 February
1945, OSS R&A 2898; American records of Dumbarton Oaks,
Notter Files, file "I.O.-Int'l, Discussions," Box 168;
FRUS, 1944, I, 614-964; COS(44)143, 8 August 1944, CAB
80/44; COS(44)154, 17 August 1944, CAB 80/44; COS(44)194, 4
October 1944, CAB 80/45; COS(44)200, 6 October 1944, CAB
80/45; COS(44)934(0), 30 October 1945, CAB 80/88;
COS(44)955(0), 8 November 1944, CAB 80/89;
COS(44)244(Final), 30 November 1944, CAB 80/46.

[35]Bunche memorandum, "Arrangements for International
Trusteeship," 30 April 1945, Notter Files, file "Dependent
Territories," Box 273. Bunche observed, "British preference
for the use of 'partnership,' implying that dependencies
begin as junior partners and then become equal partners, is
obviously motivated by a desire to keep British colonies
within the framework of the British Commonwealth and Empire.
The British have traditionally regarded themselves as the
'trustee' of their colonial empire." See also Jessup to
Roosevelt, 29 January 1945, Notter Files, file "CDA
Documents 254-282," Box 177. A special Committee on the
Problems of Dependent Areas noted on 30 January 1945 that
the colonial issue had caused "considerable acrimony" at
this IPR Conference. See ibid., file "CDA Minutes," Box
183. On 2 May 1945, French Foreign Minister Georges Bidault
announced at San Francisco, "On the principle of
trusteeship, on the idea of entrusting backward peoples to
the guardianship of the United Nations or to one of them, I
feel that it can be done subject to consideration of each
individual case. Concerning Indo-China, I must state
unequivocally that in the plans submitted by the American
Government, and which are now under discussion, territories
such as Indo-China, which are not mandated and which have
not been taken away from the enemy, are excluded from the
discussion and will so remain." See Louise Holborn, ed.,
War And Peace Aims of the United Nations (2 vols.; Boston:
World Peace Foundation, 1943-1948), II, 892; de Gaulle,
Salvation, pp. 236-37. For the British decision to refuse
to place any of their colonial territories under
international trusteeship, see WM(45)42, 12 April 1945, CAB
65/50. It is of interest to note that Nelson Rockefeller
and Dorothy Fosdick were both members of the American
Delegation at San Francisco.

NOTES ON CHAPTER VIII

[1]Churchill memorandum, "Operation ANAKIM," 8 May 1943,
COS(T)8, CAB 80/69; Minutes of the First Plenary Meeting
(OCTAGON), 13 September 1944, enclosed in COS(44)875(0), 9
October 1944, CAB 80/88. General J. Lawton Collins wrote
that the "one great asset" of the Japanese was "their

willingness to die." (Collins to Marshall, 26 January 1943, Marshall Papers, file "The President 1943--February 1-15," Box 80.)

[2]Stimson to Colonel John S. Muirhead, 12 December 1947, Stimson Papers, file 13, Box 157. In a revealing description of the 1945 perspective, Churchill confirmed that "there never was a moment's discussion as to whether the atomic bomb should be used or not. To avert a vast, indefinite butchery, to bring the war to an end, to give peace to the world, to lay healing hands upon its tortured peoples . . . seemed, after all our toils and perils, a miracle of deliverance." (Churchill, Triumph and Tragedy, p. 639.) There is no substantiation offered for the serious-- and erroneous--charge by Gabriel Kolko: "The war had so brutalized the American leaders that burning vast numbers of civilians no longer posed a real predicament by the spring of 1945." (Kolko, Politics of War, p. 539.) More rationally, Gaddis Smith has observed, "All that can be said with assurance is that the men who decided to drop the bomb acted conscientiously and with a sense of responsibility for mankind insofar as they were able." (Smith, American Diplomacy, pp. 157-60.) For a detailed examination of the damage caused by the two bombs, see The Committee for the Compilation of Materials on Damage Caused by the Atomic Bombs in Hiroshima and Nagasaki, Hiroshima and Nagasaki: The Physical, Medical, and Social Effects of the Atomic Bombings (NY: Basic Books, 1981); "Report of Investigation of Hiroshima Air Raid Damage," 13 August 1945, Douglas MacArthur Papers, Norfolk, Virginia, RG 4, file 2, Box 1. See also unsigned memorandum, "Outline of Events Within the Japanese Government Leading Up to the Surrender," 29 June 1945, Stimson Papers, file 29, Box 153 (see Appendix I); National Security Agency memorandum, "'MAGIC' Diplomatic Extracts," 16 July 1945, as quoted in American Committee on the History of the Second World War, Newsletter No. 26 (Fall 1981), 85-113.

[3]Dening to Sterndale Bennett, 31 August 1945, Penney Papers, file 5/18; text of DOMEI broadcast, enclosed in Penney to Mountbatten, 20 August 1945, ibid., file 5/12.

[4]Seymour to Foreign Secretary Ernest Bevin (enclosing report by Major General Sir Eric C. Hayes, 13 September 1945), 18 September 1945, FO 371.46214, F 7930/186/10. The statistical information may be found in Rudolph A. Winnacher (War Department) to Stimson, 12 November 1946, Stimson Papers, file 29, Box 153; Penney memorandum, n.d. [after 14 August 1945], Penney Papers, file 5/9; CCS 300/2, "Estimate of Enemy Situation--1944," 18 November 1943, enclosed in COS(43)791(O) Pt. III, 8 March 1944, CAB 80/77; First Sea Lord Cunningham memorandum, COS(45)268(O), 17 October 1945, CAB 80/97; see also file "Guam Conference," Tab 3, n.d., RG

332, Wedemeyer Files, WNRC. William Eichelberger, the general selected to command the proposed invasion of Japan, later observed, "Having inspected the hidden defences during my period in Japan and having demobilized that great veteran Japanese Army, I am in a position looking backward, to realize what a terrific task had been assigned. Through the years I have been inclined to believe that I should have a very grateful attitude towards the atomic bomb and its use at Hiroshima and Nagasaki." See Eichelberger dictation, 10 December 1954, as quoted in Jay Luvaas, ed., Dear Miss Em: General Eichelberger's War in the Pacific, 1942-1945 (Westport, Conn.: Greenwood Press, 1972), p. 310.

[5]Mountbatten to MacArthur, 16 August 1945, Penney Papers, file 5/11. Mountbatten was convinced that he preserved order in Southeast Asia by assigning police functions to the Japanese. (Author's interview with Mountbatten, 2 August 1973, London.)

[6]A detailed analysis of events in Malaya as well as in each of the other countries to be considered falls outside the scope of this study. Rather, it is the author's intention to point out some of the regional problems associated with the abrupt termination of the war largely through the two atomic bombings and to underline the internal elements of conflict that existed to influence the course of events after the war in each country. The author is grateful to the British and Malayan Embassies for providing valuable research assistance (e.g., author's interview with General Sir George Lea, military attaché and commanding officer during the Malayan Emergency, 14 July 1969, British Embassy, Washington, D.C.) in the preparation of an unpublished study of the Malayan Emergency, 1948-1960. For more on the wartime situation in Malaya, see Ralph Bunche memorandum to O. B. Gerig, Document #28, 5 February 1945, Notter Files, file "Documents #1-#30," Box 3; H. Furber memorandum, "British Malaya," n.d., RG 43, file "Briefing Papers for Stettinius," Tab 3, Box 4; COS(45)511(0), 4 August 1945, CAB 80/96; file "Reoccupation of Malaya," n.d., AIR 23/2353, PRO. During the early 1930's Lai Teck attended communist training seminars sponsored by Moscow in Hong Kong. One of his compatriots there was Nguyen Ai Quoc--who later changed his name to Ho Chi Minh. In late 1947 Lai Teck, Head of the Malayan Communist Party, absconded with the Party's treasury. Chin Peng then ascended and is still rumored to be carrying on his revolutionary activities along the Thai-Malay border. The literature on the history of postwar Malaya is extensive. For a brief, valuable analysis of the interval immediately following the Japanese surrender, see Boon Kheng Cheah, "Some Aspects of the Interregnum in Malaya (15 August - 3 September 1945)," Journal of Southeast Asian Studies, XXXIII (March 1977), 48-74; Lee Kam Hing, "Malaya: New State and

Old Elites," in Asia-The Winning of Independence, ed. R.
Jeffrey (NY: St Martin's Press, 1981), pp. 213-57.

[7]COS(45)595(0), 29 September 1945, CAB 80/97; John
Hickerson memorandum of conversation with Dutch Counselor
Jonkheer H.F.L.K. van Vredenburch, 22 October 1945,
Hickerson Files, file "Memoranda of Conversations April-
December 1945," Box 2; Vandenbosch memorandum, "Netherlands
East Indies," T-108, 18 September 1942, Notter Files, file
"T Docs 101-129," Box 39; U.S. Congress, Senate Committee on
Foreign Relations, A Decade of American Foreign Policy
(Washington, D.C.: G.P.O., 1950), pp. 789-804; Malaysian
Department of Information Services, Indonesian Intentions
Towards Malaysia (Kuala Lumpur: Government Publications,
1964); F. C. Jones, Hugh Borton, and B. R. Pearn, Survey of
International Affairs, 1939-1946: The Far East, 1942-1946
(London: Oxford University Press issued under the auspices
of the Royal Institute for International Affairs, 1955), pp.
74-83. Anthony Reid has described the "newfound solidarity
of established Indonesian leaders" fostered among three
rival elites--nationalists, Muslims, and Pamong-Praja (an
aristocracy in transition to a bureaucracy)--by the Japanese
in his article, "The Japanese Occupation and Rival
Indonesian Elites: Northern Sumatra in 1942," Journal of
Asian Studies, XXXV (November 1975), 49-63. See also Dey
Hong Lee, "British-Dutch Relations and the Republic of
Indonesia," Asian Affairs [London], LXIII (February 1976),
35-53; Vishal Singh, "The Colonial Background of Indonesian
Politics," International Studies, XV (January-March 1976),
1-14; Joyce C. Lebra, "The Significance of the Japanese
Military Model for Southeast Asia," Pacific Affairs, XLVIII
(Summer 1975), 215-29; Robert J. McMahon, "Anglo-American
Diplomacy and the Reoccupation of the Netherlands East
Indies," Diplomatic History, II (Winter 1978), 1-24; Robert
J. McMahon, Colonialism and Cold War: The United States and
the Struggle for Indonesian Independence (Ithaca: Cornell
University Press, 1981); George M. Kahin, "Indonesian
Politics and Nationalism," in Asian Nationalism and the
West, ed. by William L. Holland (NY: Macmillan, 1953);
author's interview with Henri Warmenhoven (a civilian
internee in the NEI 1942-1945), 15 February 1978, Richmond,
Virginia. Warmenhoven, Professor of Political Science at
Virginia Commonwealth University, stressed two crucial
points: (a) Dutch war exhaustion prior to the demands of
reimposing imperial authority in the NEI; and (b) Dutch
ignorance of conditions in the NEI during the war,
especially the widespread anti-Dutch sentiment that had
developed there by 1945.

[8]Sterndale Bennett memorandum, 16 April 1945, PREM 3-
221/7; Sukarno is quoted in Malaysian Department of
Information Services, Background to Indonesia's Policy
Toward Malaysia (Kuala Lumpur: Government Publications,

1964), p. 20.

[9]Ambassador Gerbrandy's request is referred to in Churchill to Eden, 2 June 1945, PREM 3-221/7; COS(45)584(0), 21 September 1945, CAB 80/97; COS(45)595(0), 29 September 1945, CAB 80/97; von Mook to Acting Secretary of State Grew, 25 May 1945, SD 740.0011PW/5-3045. For more on the Dutch arguments, see Grew memorandum of conversation with Ambassador A. Loudon, 13 July 1945, Grew Papers, file 41, Vol. 7; Netherlands Government, "Memorandum," 25 May 1945, Grew Papers, file 19, Vol. 7 (see Appendix H).

[10]Mountbatten memorandum of conversation with Prince Bernhard, enclosed in COS(45)526(0), 9 August 1945, CAB 80/96; Matthews to State-War-Navy Coordinating Committee, 30 May 1945, SD 740.0011PW/5-3045; John Morgan (Division of Northern European Affairs) to Roosevelt, 22 March 1945, SD 740.0011PW/3-2245; Churchill to Eden, 2 June 1945, PREM 3-221/7.

[11]COS(45)683(0), 11 December 1945, CAB 80/98; COS(45)589(0), 3 October 1945, CAB 80/97. As previously noted, Mountbatten made a similar statement for Indochina.

[12]Unsigned State Department memorandum for the President, n.d. [late January 1945], RG 43, file "Vincent," Box 8. On the territorial dispute, see FE(40)103, 28 December 1940, CAB 96/1; FE(41)6, 2 January 1941, CAB 96/2; Masland memorandum, "The Political Status of French Indo-China," T-60, 3 September 1942, Notter Files, file "T Docs 37-66," Box 31. Nevile Butler reported that Sumner Welles "shared our doubts whether the Germans desired to see Japan in possession of Indo-China." See Butler to Foreign Office, 25 December 1940, CAB 96/1; also author's interview with Butler, 4 June 1973, London; War Cabinet memorandum, "Japanese Intentions in Indo-China," WP(41)154, 6 July 1941, CAB 66/71; WM(41)66, 7 July 1941, CAB 65/19. For more on the racial aspects of the Franco-German talks, see Hammer, Struggle for Indochina, pp. 19-26. See Noble's two telegrams to the Admiralty, 9-10 August 1941, FE(41)178, 13 August 1941, CAB 96/4; Foreign Office memorandum to the Prime Minister, 17 March 1945, PREM 3-178/2.

[13]Author's interview with Mountbatten, 2 August 1973, London; also see Mountbatten Final Report. Hurley described the surrender arrangements at Sino-American Staff Meeting #73, 15 August 1945, RG 332 Wedemeyer Files, WNRC, file "G-mo's Mins, Vol II," Box 4; see also Hurley to Truman, 10 August 1945, SD 740.0011PW/8-1045.

[14]See U.S. Congress, House Committee on Armed Services, United States-Vietnam Relations, 1945-1967 (12 vols.; Washington, D,C.:G.P.O., 1971); R. S. Jenys memorandum, 4

October 1945, FO 371.46214, F 8034/186/10; C. Ogburn memorandum, 23 December 1946, Matthews Files, file "Memoranda 1946," Box 2; Hickerson to James Bonright (Consul, Paris), 4 February 1947, Hickerson Files, file "Personal--1947," Box 8; correspondence-memoranda in PREM 3-178/2, 178/3, and 180/7; David Marr, "Vietnam: Harnessing the Whirlwind," in Asia, ed. R. Jeffrey, pp. 163-207.

[15]See accounts of the developing situation in Indochina in: OSS memorandum, 10 October 1945, XL 20319, RG 226, NA; Mountbatten memoranda, enclosed in COS(45)627(0), 17 October 1945, CAB 80/97; COS(45)660(0), 16 November 1945, CAB 80/98; COS(45)303, 25 November 1945, CAB 80/51; COS(45)693(0), 20 December 1945, CAB 80/98.

[16]Mountbatten memoranda cited in previous note. Also see the French request for Spitfires, enclosed in COS(45)244, 4 October 1945, CAB 80/50; British approval for the Spitfires, enclosed in COS(45)617(0), 13 October 1945, CAB 80/97; Mountbatten-Leclerc conversations to expedite the movement of the French infantry, enclosed in COS(45)619(0), 13 October 1945, CAB 80/97.

[17]For the negotiations on the British withdrawal, see Mountbatten, Final Report, and Great Britain, Secretary of State for Foreign Affairs, Documents Relating to British Involvement in the Indo-China Conflict, 1945-1965 (London: HMSO, 1965). See also Slim memorandum, COS(45)607(0), 9 October 1945, CAB 80/97.

[18]The best brief survey is Senate Committee on Foreign Relations, A Decade of American Foreign Policy, pp 860-81. See also Benedick J. Kerkvliet, The Huk Rebellion (Berkeley: University of California Press, 1977); Cesar Virata, "Philippines--Overcoming the Colonial Heritage: The Governments's View," Euromoney (August 1976), ii-vi; Carlos P. Romulo, I Walked with Heros (NY: Holt, Rinehart and Winston, 1961); C. P. Romulo, I Saw the Philippines Rise (Manila: AMS Press, 1946); Alfred W. McCoy, "The Philippines: Independence Without Decolonization," in Asia, ed. R. Jeffrey, pp. 23-65.

[19]S. D. Waley (Treasury) to E. P. Donaldson (Secretary, Far Eastern Committee), 12 October 1940, FE(40)10, 12 October 1940, CAB 96/1. See also Charles Brookhart (U.S. Commercial Attaché, Bangkok) to Division of Regional Information (Bureau of Foreign and Domestic Commerce), 12 July 1932, Record Group 151 Records of the Bureau of Foreign and Domestic Commerce, NA, file "FE-Siam," 492.2 General; Pibulasonggram (Thai Prime Minister) to Churchill, 31 August 1940, PREM 4-32/14-15.

[20]Foreign Office to Butler, 18 April 1941, FE(41)59, 22

April 1941, CAB 96/3; Ballantine memorandum, 20 October
1940, SD 711.90/59; Cadogan to Churchill, 16 January 1941,
PREM 4-32/15; Crosby to Foreign Office, 20 May 1941,
FE(41)84, 22 May 1941, CAB 96/3; Grant to Hull, 19 October
1940, SD 711.90/59.

21Churchill to Crosby, 7 December 1941, Ismay Papers,
file "PM's Tels--1941," J. M. Troutbeck (Ministry of
Economic Warfare) memorandum, 21 August 1941, FE(41)187, 21
August 1941, CAB 96/4; Crosby to Foreign Office, 17 June
1941, FE(41)116, 20 June 1941, CAB 96/3. The next day
Crosby cabled, "We must resign ourselves to paying through
the nose for any rubber or tin which we may purchase in an
open market in Thailand. Our only consolation is that our
rivals must do likewise." (Crosby telegram, enclosed in
ibid.) For some critical views of Crosby by two British
colleagues in the Far East, see Vlieland, Memoir; and
Brooke-Popham to Ismay, 3 February 1941, Brooke-Popham
Papers, file v/i/5.

22State Department Aide-Mémoire, 19 January 1942, SD
711.92/31; R. L. Smyth (SD, Far Eastern Division)
memorandum, 2 February 1942, SD 711.92/39; Pramoj
memorandum, 28 January 1942, SD 711.92/38; unsigned
memorandum, "Attitude and Policy in Regard to Thailand," 22
February 1944, Notter Files, file "FE," Box 14; text of
Pramoj's telegram to Bangkok, 11 December 1941, as quoted in
State Department Aide-Mémoire for British Embassy, 18
December 1941, SD 711.92/30A; Pramoj memorandum, 21 December
1941, SD 711.92/31; Foreign Office Aide-Mémoire, 24 December
1941, SD 711.92/33.

23Summaries of Franco-British talks on the subject are
in Cadogan memorandum, 12 November 1944, and Sterndale
Bennett memorandum, 23 February 1945, both in FO 371.46566,
F 1196/1196/40. See also FE(45)31, 10 July 1945, CAB 96/5;
FE(45)32, 11 July 1945, CAB 96/5; OSS memorandum,
"Development of Thai Cooperation With Japan," 9 June 1942,
OSS R&A 552; Masland memorandum, "Political Status of
Thailand," n.d., Notter Files, file "T Docs 37-66," Box 31;
State Department memorandum to Netherlands Legation, 17
February 1942, SD 711.92/31, describing indirect declaration
of war on the Allies by Bangkok through the Swiss Legation.
As of 30 January, the United States had still not received
notice of the Thai declaration of war. See Berle memorandum
of conversation with Swiss Minister Charles Bruggman, 30
January 1942, SD 711.92/40. Also see Welles to Vichy
Ambassador Gaston Henry-Haye, 13 April 1942, as quoted in
OSS memorandum, "Territorial Conflicts Between Thailand and
French Indochina," 30 March 1945, OSS R&A 2419; Butler to
Foreign Office, 8 January 1941, FE(41)16, 14 January 1941,
CAB 96/3.

[24]WM(45)49, SSF 23 April 1945, CAB 65/52; FE(44)20, 25 April 1944, CAB 96/5; COS memorandum, "Post War Strategic Arrangements in Siam," FE(45)18(Restricted), 5 April 1945, CAB 96/5; COS(45)31(0), 12 January 1945, CAB 80/90; Winant to Eden, 18 August 1944, FE(44)7, 25 November 1944, CAB 96/5; C. R. Price (Vice Chiefs of Staff) to Cavendisch-Bentinck, 4 December 1943, CAB 79/68; JIC(43)497(0), 3 December 1943, and COS(43)296(0), 4 December 1943, CAB 79/68; Eden memorandum, "Policy Towards Siam," WP(44)72, 3 February 1944, PREM 3-159/6.

[25]Economic Advisory Branch (FO and MEW) memorandum, "Changes in Siamese Economy," FE(E)(44)4, 21 December 1944, CAB 96/8. London later informed Washington, "If Siam were to be allowed these involuntarily hoarded stocks at the present scarcity prices, the proceeds would bring Siam's existing holdings of gold and foreign exchange to three times their present level. Even at half that price they would be doubled. In either event Siam would end the war in an incomparably better financial position than any of the other countries which were in a position to offer more serious resistance to the aggressors. His Majesty's Government feel very strongly on this point." See G. H. Hall memorandum, "Policy Towards Siam," FE(M)(45)7, 6 September 1945, CAB 96/9; also Sanderson memorandum, "Restoration of Rice Production In and Procurement of Rice for Countries At Present Occupied by the Japanese," FE(E)(45)1, 9 January 1945, CAB 96/8.

[26]FE(45)5, 13 July 1945, CAB 96/5. For detailed accounts of the Thai-Anglo-American diplomacy and the evolving Thai-British Treaty, see OSS memorandum, "Thailand's Relations With Great Britain in the Strategic Upper Malay Peninsula," 27 August 1945, OSS R&A 2954; COS(45)212, 12 September 1945, CAB 80/50; COS(45)235, 27 September 1945, CAB 80/50; FE(0)(45)6, 27 February 1945, CAB 80/50; A. L. Moffat memoranda, 24-29 September 1945, SD 741.93/9-2245 through/9-2945; OSS memorandum, 10 October 1945, XL 19969, RG 226, NA; OSS memorandum, "Progress in Discussions of British Peace Terms to Thailand," 18 October 1945, XL 23084, RG 226, NA; State Department Aide-Mémoire, 9 October 1945, enclosed in Halifax to Foreign Office, 12 October 1945, FO 371.46566, F 8238/1196/40; COS(45)653(0), 12 November 1945, CAB 80/98; OSS memorandum, "Survey of Trends in Siam," 9 December 1945 , XL 37109, RG 226, NA; COS(45)684(0), 11 December 1945, CAB 80/98; OSS memorandum tracing Bangkok instructions to Thai Delegation at Kandy, 16 December 1945, XL 30932, RG 226, NA; unsigned memorandum, "Future Status of Thailand," n.d., RG 43, Briefing Book, Box 2; COS(45)692(0), 20 December 1945, CAB 80/98; John Carter Vincent to Acheson, 25 October 1945, SD 711.92/10-2545; Acheson to Charles W. Yost (in Bangkok), 22 December 1945, SD 711.92/12-2245; A. L. Moffat memorandum, 28 August 1946,

Hickerson Files, file "1946 Files," Box 3. After protracted negotiations and a virtual state of war along the border areas with the French, the Thais finally returned the disputed territories to Indochina in October 1946 but not before the Thais arranged an extraordinary appeal to a special conciliation commission (unsuccessfully).

[27]There is the possibility of placing too much emphasis on the role of the atomic bomb in ending the war. Some key Japanese leaders, after all, favored continuing the conflict even after the bombing of Hiroshima and Nagasaki. In all likelihood, Japan would have sued for peace once the Russians entered the war--as some critics of the decision to use the atomic bomb have argued. But the chief premise of the author's analysis focuses on the sudden, unanticipated surrender by Tokyo, not the use, per se, of the atomic bomb. Even if the atomic bomb had not existed, the Russian entry would have brought about circumstances similar to those created by the use of the atomic bomb. That is, the Japanese surrender would undoubtedly have followed shortly after Stalin's declaration of war. Thus, the fact that the Allies--with inadequate capabilities and resources in the late summer of 1945--were not in a position to occupy or administer Japanese-held territories, including pre-war Western colonies in Southeast Asia, remains substantially unaltered. Those circumstances existed because of the abrupt ending of the war by Japan, regardless of whether the surrender was brought about through the use of the atomic bomb or the Russian entry into the war.

[28]This is not to suggest that the Allies should not have acted to end the war as quickly as possible. Nevertheless, any re-examination of the decision to use the atomic bomb should incorporate an analysis of the broad, unintended results of that decision.

NOTES ON CHAPTER IX

[1]Beaverbrook to Churchill, 29 February 1944, Beaverbrook Papers, file "LPS".

[2]Londonderry (M.P. from Ulster) statement, as quoted in Robert G. Hooker (Acting Secretary, Interdepartmental Committee on International Aviation) to Wayne C. Taylor (Under Secretary of Commerce), 13 March 1943, Record Group 40 Records of the Department of Commerce, NA, folder "March-May 1943," Box 955, file 102517/36.

[3]Hurley to Truman, 26 November 1945, SD 711.93/12-145.

[4]Tang Tsou, America's Failure in China, 1941-1950 (2

vols.; Chicago: University of Chicago Press, 1963), I, ix.

[5]Smith, American Diplomacy, pp. 8-9.

[6]Roosevelt is quoted as saying "Stalin would play ball if approached right" in Charles Taussig memorandum of conversation with Eleanor Roosevelt, 27 August 1945, Taussig Papers, file "1945--July to December incl.," Box 52; see also Roosevelt's air of confidence in his ability to handle the Russians in his last telegram to Churchill, 12 April 1945, Roosevelt-Churchill correspondence, FDRL.

[7]Stimson diary entry for 4 November 1943, Stimson Papers, Vol. 45, No. 59.

[8]Moran, Churchill, pp. 242-43, p. 249. At Yalta, Moran observed that "the President has gone to bits physically. . . . the shrewdness has gone, and there is nothing left. I doubt, from what I have seen, whether he is fit for his job here." Moran noted in Roosevelt "all the symptoms of hardening of the arteries of the brain in an advanced stage. . . . I give him only a few months to live." After Roosevelt died, Moran received a report from Dr. Roger Lee of Boston which stated that the President had suffered heart failure eight months before his death and had become "irascible" and "very irritable if he had to concentrate his mind for long." See also Herman Bateman, "Observations on President Roosevelt's Health During World War II," Mississippi Valley Historical Review, XL (June 1956), 82-102; James McGregor Burns, "FDR: The Untold Story of His Last Year," Saturday Review, 11 April 1970, pp. 12-15, 39; Howard G. Bruenn, "Clinical Notes on the Illness and Death of President Franklin D. Roosevelt," Annals of Internal Medicine, LXXII (April 1970), 579-91.

[9]In considering the moral attitude of Roosevelt with regard to decolonization, it might be well to keep in mind his strong racist views. Also it seems fair to add that his views about the innate inferiority of non-whites put him squarely in line with the mainstream attitudes of his contemporary white Americans. See, for example, his views on racial mixing, described in Sir Ronald I. Campbell (British Embassy in Washington) to Sir Alexander Cadogan, 6 August 1942, PREM 4-42/9 (see Appendix C); Christopher Thorne, Allies of a Kind, p. 6, pp. 8-9, pp. 158-59, pp. 167-68, p. 539, p. 695; also Roosevelt's remarks throughout the war on racial inferences, as recorded in Hassett, Off the Record.

[10]See, for example, D.C. Watt, "American AntiColonial Policy and the End of the European Colonial Empires, 1941-1962," in Contagious Conflict: The Impact of American Dissent on European Life, ed. A. N. J. den Hollander (Leiden: Brill, 1973), pp. 106-7. Watt pointed out, "It

was only after Roosevelt had invoked the extension of the
Atlantic Charter to Asia under the needling of his
Republican opponent in the 1940 election, Wendell Willkie,
that Churchill was driven to his famous public statement, 'I
have not become the King's First Minister to preside over
the liquidation of the British Empire.'"

[11]Sherwood, Roosevelt and Hopkins, p. 882.

[12]Churchill as quoted in Sir Norman Birkett, "Churchill
the Orator," in Churchill By His Contemporaries, ed. by
Charles Eade (London: Hutchinson, 1953), p. 231; Dean
Acheson, Present at the Creation: My Years in the State
Department (New York: W.W. Norton, 1969), p. 33; text of
Churchill ("roar") speech, 30 November 1945, Ismay Papers,
file II/1/26; schoolboy anecdote quoted in William T.R. Fox
memorandum, "Anglo-American Relations in the Post-War
World," 1 May 1943, FO 371.34137, A 6188/57/45.

[13]D.C. Watt, "American AntiColonial Policy and the End
of the European Colonial Empires, 1941-1962," op. cit., pp.
124-25. Watt added, "Behind all this lay, not an economic
imperialism per se, as sometimes argued by revisionists of a
Marxistic turn of views, but a moral imperialism and an
arrogance of power which has done much in its turn to induce
the growth in Western Europe of a turn of consciousness of
separateness from and lack of identity between, its own
political system and that of the United States."

[14]Roosevelt to Stettinius, 17 November 1944, Roosevelt
Papers, PSF, file "Indo-China," Box 55, FDRL.

[15]Cherwell to Churchill, 18 November 1945, Cherwell
Papers, file J57.

[16]George M. Thomson, Vote of Censure (London: Secker
and Warburg, 1968), p. 235.

[17]Tsou, Failure, I, 591.

[18]O'Connor memorandum, n.d. [late 1949], Record Group
126, Records of the Office of Territories, Department of the
Interior, NA, file 9-0-47.

APPENDIX A

LIST OF ABBREVIATIONS

CAB ....Cabinet documents and papers
CCS ....Combined Chiefs of Staff
CIGS ....Chief of the Imperial General Staff
C-in-C ....Commander-in-Chief
COS ....British Chiefs of Staff
FORD ....Foreign Office Research Department
JCS ....Joint Chiefs of Staff
JPS ....Joint Planning Staff (London)
MPAJA ....Malayan People's Anti-Japanese Army
NA ....National Archives, Washington, D. C.
NUMBER 10 ....Office of the Prime Minister (10 Downing
                  Street)
OSS ....Office of Strategic Services
OWI ....Office of War Information
PHP ....Post Hostilities Planning   Committee
                  (Subcommittee of COS)
PM ....Prime Minister
PRO ....Public Record Office, London
RG ....Record Group
SACSEA ....Supreme Allied Commander,   South East Asia
                  (Lord Mountbatten)
SD ....Department of State (State Department
                  Decimal File)
SEAC ....South East Asia Command
SSF ....(War Cabinet) Secretary's Standard File
                  (Confidential Annex)
SWPA ....South West Pacific Area
WM ....Minutes of the War Cabinet Meetings
WNRC ....Washington National Record Center,
                  Suitland, Maryland
WP ....War Cabinet (Official) Papers ("G"-
                  General, "R"-Restricted)

APPENDIX B

THE ATLANTIC CHARTER

Joint declaration of President of the United States of America and the Prime Minister, Mr. Churchill, representing His Majesty's Government in the United Kingdom, being met together, deem it right to make known certain common principles in the national policies of their respective countries on which they base their hopes for a better future for the world.

First, their countries seek no aggrandizement, territorial or other;

Second, they desire to see no territorial changes that do not accord with the freely expressed wishes of the peoples concerned;

Third, they respect the right of all peoples to choose the form of government under which they will live; and they wish to see sovereign rights and self-government restored to those who have been forcibly deprived of them;

Fourth, they will endeavor, with due respect for their existing obligations, to further the enjoyment by all states, great or small, victor or vanquished, of access, on equal terms, to the trade and to the raw materials of the world which are needed for their economic prosperity;

Fifth, they desire to bring about the fullest collaboration between all nations in the economic field with the object of securing for all, improved labor standards, economic advancement, and social security;

Sixth, after the final destruction of the Nazi tyranny, they hope to see established a peace which will afford to all nations the means of dwelling in safety within their own boundaries, and which will afford assurance that all the men in all the lands may live out their lives in freedom from fear and want;

Seventh, such a peace should enable all men to traverse the high seas and oceans without hindrance;

Eighth, they believe that all of the nations of the world, for realistic as well as spiritual reasons, must come to the abandonment of the use of force. Since no future peace can be maintained if land, sea, or air armaments continue to be employed by nations which threaten, or may threaten, aggression outside of their frontiers, they believe, pending the establishment of a wider and permanent system of general security, that the disarmament of such nations is essential. They will likewise aid and encourage all other practicable measures which will lighten for peace-loving peoples the crushing burden of armaments.

Franklin D. Roosevelt
Winston S. Churchill

APPENDIX C
A REPORT ON ROOSEVELT'S RACIAL VIEWS[*]

Dear Cadogan,

Amongst many other thoughts thrown out by the President, when I saw him on August 2, was the following:

He had set one Professor Hrdlicka of the Smithsonian Institute, to work on a private study of the effect of racial crossing. A preliminary report had been given him, with all of which he by no means agreed. But it seemed to him that if we got the Japanese driven back within their islands, racial crossing might have interesting effects, particularly in the Far East. For instance Dutch-Japanese crossings were good, and Japanese-Chinese. Chinese-Malayan was a bad mixture. Hrdlicka said that the Japanese-European cross was bad and the Chinese-European equally so. It was here he disagreed with the Professor. Experience, the President said, had shown that unlike the Japanese-European mixture, which was, he agreed, thoroughly bad, Chinese-European was not at all bad.

The President had asked the Professor why the Japanese were as bad as they were, and had followed up by asking about the Hairy Ainus. The Professor had said the skulls of these people were some 2,000 years less developed than ours (this sounds very little, doesn't it?). The President asked whether this might account for the nefariousness of the Japanese and had been told it might, as they might well be the basic stock of the Japanese.

As far as I could make it out, the line of the President's thought is that an Indo-Asian or Eurasian or (better) Eurindasian race, could be developed which would be good and produce a good civilisation and Far East "order", to the exclusion of the Japanese, languishing in coventry within their original islands.

> Yours ever,
> (Sgd.) R. I. Campbell

[* Source: Sir Ronald I. Campbell to Sir Alexander Cadogan, 6 August 1942, PREM 4-42/9, Public Record Office, London, England.]

APPENDIX D

A REPORT ON ROOSEVELT'S VIEWS ABOUT TRUSTEESHIP*

. . . .
Dr. Isaiah Bowman asked the President his wishes as to the old world issue of trusteeship.

The President said, "I have discussed this with the British many times and I have not been able to get very far with it." The President said, "This is a subject in which I have been interested for some while back. In 1936, for instance, the Secretary and I proposed it for a little island in the Pacific, Canton Island. Pan American Airways needed this for an air base in the hop to New Zealand and Australia. We sent a little group down there to establish the base when the British sent a cruiser and asked our people to get off, that the island was a British possession. The head of our group asked how they figured that out and they produced a map. 'Well' they said, 'It is shown on this map in red.'" The President said that apparently anything shown as red anywhere apparently belongs to the British.

Later, the British Ambassador to the United States, Sir Ronald Lindsay, raised the question with the President. The President imitated his English accent perfectly and quoted Sir Ronald as having said, "Well now, Mr. President, this is a British island. You simply can't do this." The President replied with a broad English accent, "But, Roney, I have done it."

The President said that he and Secretary Hull cooked up an exchange of letters by which the issue of sovereignty over the island was to be postponed for a period of fifty years until 1987. The President expressed a feeling at that time that both he and Chamberlain would be dead and that he believed the whole arrangement would be so acceptable and so harmonious by that time that the question of sovereignty would never come up again. The island was plenty large enough for both the British and the Americans to make any use they wanted of it. The system has worked beautifully and there has been no further disagreement. He indicated that it was his belief that there was no reason why the same system could not work successfully in other parts of the world with much larger areas. Dr. Bowman at this point said, "Well, Mr. President, you stated that you had not gotten very far with the British on this issue. Do you want us to bring it up here." The President said, "Yes, by all means. It is something I think we should discuss with them at every opportunity." For example, the President pointed out he had discussed the question of a trusteeship for French Indochina with General Chiang Kai-shek. As background, the President expressed the opinion that the

-286-

French had badly mismanaged the country and the people and that they had always been poor colonizers and that a trusteeship was the only practical solution. He asked General Chiang Kai-shek what he thought. The General replied that he had no designs on French Indochina, that the Chinese did not want that country because its people and the country as a whole were completely different from their people and he thought this would be an ideal arrangement.

Then the President said, "Winston, this is something which you are just not able to understand. You have 400 years of acquisitive instincts back of you and you don't understand how it is that a country does not want to accept its own land somewhere if they can get it." The President then said that the British would take land anywhere in the world even if it were only a little rock island or a sand bar.

To make certain about it, he asked General Chiang Kai-shek at Cairo whether they did not want it and Chiang assured him again that they did not want French Indochina.

Then at Tehran the President raised the question with Joseph Stalin who expressed his belief that the idea of making French Indochina a trusteeship was excellent. The President then confronted Churchill and said "Now look here, Winston, you are out-voted three to one," but we are still going to have a tough time with the British on this issue.

The President pointed out that the British suspect that if they give in on this one we will ask them to do the same with other places which are possessions of the British, for example, Burma, the Malay Peninsular [sic], and perhaps Sumatra and Java.

The British always say "What about the poor Dutch? If we take the Indies away from them they won't have anything." The President went on to say that this doesn't seem much like an argument because the Dutch are not worrying about this at all, that it is only the British who are raising this argument.

The President then pointed out how the French and the British have mulcted the people on the Western coast of Africa. He said that they had taken out ten times what they have put into it, that the people are kept poor while the country is rich. He cited as an example the cultivation of peanuts. The women are used for plowing. They use a stick that digs the soil up about two inches, that if modern mechanism were used the soil could be plowed much deeper and turned over much more often yielding a much greater and more valuable production. Then he indicated that if the peanuts have been raised they could only be sold to a British monopoly who set an artificial price ceiling instead of a price arrived at by free trade throughout the world. The President went on, "You know, back in 1940, we swapped fifty destroyers for eight naval bases in the British West Indies,

Bermuda and Newfoundland. When the Prime Minister was in Washington Christmas 1941 he said to me, "The British people are worried." When I asked what they were worried about, he said they were afraid that the United States would want to take over the entire islands on which these bases were located. The President told him that he could assure the British people that the United States had no such intention or even any possible desire to take over those islands. "As you know," he said to the Prime Minister, "I am a mixture of Scotch and Dutch ancestry and if there is one thing I won't do it is to buy a headache. The United States has no desire whatsoever to take over those islands. All we want is a small piece of property on each for bases." Then he went on to point out that the British lost $20,000,000 annually in those islands and that Newfoundland had been bankrupt for a long while.

Dr. Bowman asked the President whether we should discuss the colonial issue as a whole with the British. The President said by all means "Yes". Dr. Bowman asked, "Should we press the issue" and the President replied "Yes". Dr. Bowman pointed out that the problem of the United Nations cooperation in the administration of dependent areas was not a merely hypothetical issue, but that there was already a large sphere of such operations in the Caribbean area. The President commented that a very good job had been done there and agreed with Dr. Bowman that this was a good example of administration of dependent areas to point out to the British.

The President said that we should bear in mind various matters which he had discussed at length over the past month with the military authorities of the United States. He said that they believed that the most direct threat to the Western Hemisphere would come from the bulge of Africa directed at the bulge of Brazil. It was obvious that Brazil could not defend itself and it was also obvious that we could not get down to Brazil in time to defend her. The only way to protect this hemisphere, therefore, was to stop such an attack before it started. This would mean a United States naval and air base in one of three places--Dakar, St. Louis or the Cape Verde islands. The British do not like this idea at all. There is the alternative of Liberia, of course, but this is too far down around the bulge of Africa. In the Pacific our military were agreed that although the island of New Caledonia might remain under the French flag, Australia and New Zealand must establish a strong naval and air base there. The President said that just two years ago the Australians were in danger of being pushed into the ocean, but that since that time they seem to have forgotten how exposed their position is without adequate defenses in such a place as New Caledonia.

The President said that a third area in which the

United States was interested was the Tuomotu archipelago, or alternatively the Marquesas Islands just to the north. The United States needs landing rights in these islands for postwar air routes to the Western Pacific area. . . .

[*Source: Stettinius memorandum, 17 March 1944, Edward R. Stettinius, Jr., Papers, Alderman Library, University of Virginia, Charlottesville, VA, file "Meetings of Group Prior to Departure," Box 254.]

APPENDIX E

SOME OF ROOSEVELT'S VIEWS ABOUT DE GAULLE*

MEMORANDUM FOR GENERAL MARSHALL

When you get over there, tell General Eisenhower that I have read his memorandum to you but that I still think he does not quite get the point.

He evidently believes the fool newspaper stories that I am anti-deGaulle, even the kind of story that says that I hate him, etc., etc. All this, of course, is utter nonsense. I am perfectly willing to have deGaulle made President, or Emperor, or King or anything else so long as the action comes in an untrammeled and unforced way from the French people themselves.

But it is possible in an election so to influence it, so to restrict the vote, so even to count the vote, that the people in power can swing it overwhelmingly their way.

Let me cite an example which I happen to know about. In a town of four or five hundred people in German-occupied France, the Mayor, now about sixty, was first chosen about 1917 because he could not go to the front on account of a club foot. He has been a magnificent success as Mayor, has been reelected every couple of years since then. The people in the village learned through the underground that the French National Committee for Liberation had picked another man to be imposed on them, even though there was nothing against the present Mayor, who had had no dealings with Vichy but has merely administered his own arrondissement. The man chosen by the Committee is well described as an unsuccessful politician and, in all probability, a porch-climbing robber.

I want Eisenhower to do what we have done in Italy -- i.e., have a British and American representative go to the community and talk with a number of leading citizens, such as the cure, the doctor, the avocat, the leading merchants, some leading farmers and see who should be installed, if anybody. As a matter of fact, most of these arrondissement officials are not pro-Vichy. They have gone about their local duties and kept out of the other problem altogether.

I do not agree when Ike says that there are only two major groups in France today -- the Vichy gang, and the other characterized by unreasoning admiration for deGaulle. I wonder how he knows this because nobody else knows anything really about the international situation in France. Most of the people who get out come out with the help of the French National Committee, and they are rightly grateful.

Tell Ike that it is my thought, based on talks with many people who have come out of France recently, that he has overlooked the biggest group of all -- bigger than the

-290-

Vichy group and bigger than the deGaulle group. It consists of those people who do not know what it is all about. Probably the great majority of them are anti-Laval and, by now, anti-Petain. Probably most of them like the symbol of deGaulle and his early actions in 1940, but they have not made up their minds as to whether they want deGaulle and his Committee as their rulers.

It is awfully easy to be for deGaulle and to cheer the thought of recognizing that Committee as the provisional government of France, but I have a moral duty that transcends "an easy way". It is to see to it that the people of France have nothing foisted on them by outside powers. It must be a French choice--and that means, as far as possible, forty million people. Self-determination is not a word of expediency. It carries with it a very deep principle in human affairs.

As a matter of practical fact, Ike has plenty of time because for some time every square kilometer under his control will be a part of the military zone. I count on his good judgment in case Germany collapses or in case he can move his armies toward Germany at the rate of ten miles a day.

Good luck to him. We shall be thinking much of him and his problems.

F. D. R.

[*Source: Roosevelt To Marshall, 2 June 1944, George C. Marshall Papers, George C. Marshall Foundation, Lexington, VA, file 16, Box 81.]

APPENDIX F

SOME BRITISH VIEWS ABOUT COLONIALISM*

. . . .

Since, to many Americans, "imperialism" is typified by
British holdings and British colonial policy, and since the
end of imperialism is tied up in many American minds with
British policy toward India, it is possible that if a
reasonable agreement on Indian independence could be
reached, American interest in colonial problems and in the
end of "imperialism" would diminish. But it is also true
that Americans will tend to be critical of post-war colonial
arrangements that do not seem to involve a definite ending
of the pre-war colonial system, or, at the very least, a
substantial modification of it.

The above relates to popular opinion in the United
States. The very small group which has given any close
study to colonial problems recognizes that as conditions
differ from colony to colony, no single over-all formula
provides a satisfactory answer to the colonial
problem. . . .

Directly related to the question of imperialism in
American thinking, is the American belief in and support of
"independence" as a goal for colonial areas, which seems in
contrast to British support of full "self-government" as a
pattern of colonial progress. The difference is not merely
one of terminology, but has a real historical background.

The development of the British Commonwealth of Nations
has provided for Britain, the Dominions and the British
colonies an approximation to an international organisation
in the absence of any working collective security system.
Thus the status of complete self-government within the
framework of the Commonwealth is taken for granted by the
British as being the most reasonable goal for a colony.
Such a status, in British thinking, possesses obvious
economic and political advantages over that of complete
severance of Commonwealth ties.

The United States has developed no comparable system.
Although it would be theoretically possible to bring
colonies into the American Federal system as states or
territories, there has been little support for inclusion of
overseas possessions within this American framework.

On the contrary, in the early 19th century, Americans
supported complete independence for the colonies in the
Western Hemisphere partly because it was compatible with
American traditions of then recent origin and partly because
America was too weak to expand outside North America and
expansion within North America offered many opportunities.

This attitude continued because it was in accord with
an American tradition against assumption of colonial

responsibilities. The tradition was continued in the 20th century because it was advantageous to the United States. We preferred to deal with independent countries, and as a great power were in a position to press for such economic or political advantages as we desired in a given area, without assuming any responsibility for its administration. This American point of view has provided support for such policies as the Monroe Doctrine, the Open Door, the maintenance of China's independence and the promise of independence for the Philippines. This attitude underlies present American interest in the independence of India and the eventual independence of other colonies in southeast Asia.

It should be noted, however, that this American point of view raises certain difficulties in relation to the colonial problem. Colonial progress, economic and political development, are dependent upon the integration of colonial areas within a world-wide system of economic and political relations. The American desire for independence of former colonies will have to be made compatible with such a system and with the operation of whatever international agencies and organs are evolved to make it workable. . . .

The difficulties, mainly political, in the way of inaugurating any international administration for any of the colonial areas of southeast Asia are likely to prevent the adoption of such schemes. On the other hand, there is a general reluctance to see the colonies revert to their previous status without some attempt to realize a cooperative effort toward improving the life of the colonial peoples. Progress made toward this end before 1939 by the colonial governments is recognized, but regarded as insufficient in the light of war-time changes in the colonial picture.

The United States is committed to restore the Philippines to scheduled independence and seems committed to the protection of that independence. It is likely that Burma will progress to the status of a self-governing unit within the British Commonwealth. Realization of self-government in other colonies has been a stated goal of the British and Dutch governments. In terms of the Atlantic Charter and other war aims of the United Nations, as well as the future good relations between Eastern and Western nations, a more specific program of political, economic and social development in southeast Asia seems to be required.

For this purpose, it is suggested that the principle of "accountability" be accepted and be made effective through the operation of an international agency. Each colonial government, for these areas not yet fully self-governing, would agree to be accountable to an international agency for orderly political, economic and social development within its area. The international agency would have the responsibility for surveying progress in existing colonies, making suggestions for improvement, and providing a channel for cooperative action on common problems, and assistance to the colonies wherever needed. Its reports and activities would be made public and would serve as a stimulus to fulfilment of specific measures in each area. It is recognized that the creation of such a system raises a number of problems. The nations with Pacific interests would have to be given representation. Some provisions would have to be made for native representation and for the hearing and adjustment of grievances voiced against the colonial government.

In any such plan, success would be directly dependent upon the operation of a world-wide, or, at the very least a Far Eastern, collective security system. And the league of international co-operation already attained in the field of the immediate problems of reoccupation, relief and reconstruction will have an important bearing on the measures taken to deal with the problem of the colonies.

[*Source: Foreign Office memorandum, August 1943, FO
            371.35927, F 4767/1953/61, PRO.]

APPENDIX G

BRITISH ECONOMIC PRESSURES ON JAPAN, 1940-1941*

I CIRCULATE for the information of my colleagues a memorandum on our economic restrictions on Japan. . . .

Our policy is based on the inescapable fact that Japan has allied herself with our enemies, and in present circumstances there is no alternative to this policy. It is not true, however, as the Japanese Ambassador has tried to contend (see paragraph 11), that the policy is one of vindictiveness. The measures of restriction involved are conceived as precautions taken in the interests of prosecuting the war against the Axis and of self-defence. Their purpose is threefold, namely (1) to conserve for our own use vital raw materials necessary to the war effort, (2) to prevent such materials from reaching our enemies, and (3) to prevent Japan from accumulating stocks of these materials and thus to strengthen her power to make war on ourselves, the Netherlands East Indies and the United States of America.

That our restrictions should produce some reactions in Japan is inevitable. In so far as such reactions indicate a realisation on the part of the Japanese of the disadvantages of their allying themselves with the Axis, they are not necessarily undesirable; indeed, it is our hope that we may bring home to an increasing number of Japanese the solid advantages to be gained by renewing Japan's former relations with us and renouncing her connexion with the Axis. Meanwhile, constant care and vigilance is being exercised by the Far Eastern Committee, in the prosecution of their policy, not to push restrictions to the point of provoking Japan to war either by reducing too drastically and suddenly supplies, e.g., of oil, considered vital by the Japanese Government or by striking too brusquely at Japanese enterprises within British territory. It must be realized, however, that if and when Japan judges--for whatever reasons--that the moment has come to strike at Malaya and the Netherlands East Indies she will in all probability seize on our restrictions as a justification for her action.

The closing of the Siberian route by the outbreak of the Russo-German war has provided Japan with a plausible pretext for demanding the relaxation of our restrictions. But in the first place, no one can deny that there is at any rate a possibility that the route may be reopened at no distant date under German control and with increased capacity. It would, therefore, be undesirable to allow Japan to accumulate stocks which could be rapidly transported across this railway if that occurred. Apart from this, so long as Japan remains tied to the Axis, she remains our potential enemy; the third main purpose of our economic restrictions retains its force, and until there are

signs of a radical reorientation of Japanese policy away
from the Axis and towards ourselves, it would be premature
to make any change in the policy described in the
accompanying memorandum.

Recent indications of Japanese intentions reinforce the
above.

ECONOMIC RESTRICTIONS AGAINST JAPAN

Memorandum by the Minister of Economic Warfare. [Hugh
Dalton]

DURING the first year of war there was no systematic
policy throughout the Empire of restricting supplies to
Japan, though in the case of key commodities steps were
usually taken to limit exports to normal proportions. In
addition, certain commodities largely controlled in the
Empire, for example, nickel, jute and mica, were more
drastically restricted. These restrictions were imposed
partly to avoid the danger of important commodities being
sent across the Siberian Railway, and partly to put pressure
on Japan to induce her to sign a War Trade Agreement. The
United States of America had also taken certain measures.
Thus they had imposed a moral embargo on a small range of
exports and entirely prohibited exports of aviation spirit
and scrap iron under the Defence Act; on the other hand,
other exports, e.g., copper, were completely unrestricted.

2.   After the collapse of France the situation rapidly
altered. Japan signed the Tripartite Pact, and so publicly
ranged herself on the side of the Axis, while the security
of British possessions in the Far East became directly
threatened by Japan's declared intention of setting up a new
order in Eastern Asia. It became necessary, therefore, to
regard Japan not merely as a potential source of supply to
the enemy but as herself a potential enemy, and to take
steps to weaken her economy and prevent her from
accumulating stocks which might make her invulnerable to
blockade in the future. At the same time, the strategical
situation made it essential to avoid any measures which
might drive her to violent reactions.

3.   Accordingly, an approach was made in October 1940
to the Governments of the Empire and at the same time to the
United States and Netherlands Governments with a view to the
institution of a co-ordinated policy of limitation of
exports to Japan. This approach was favourably received by
the Empire countries, though certain of them emphasised the
danger of marching ahead of the United States.
Nevertheless, the export licensing system was extended
throughout the Empire, and the general policy accepted of
limiting exports to Japan to normal figures of all
commodities which are regarded as German, Italian or
Japanese deficiencies. Where stricter embargoes were

already in force, these were, of course, maintained.

4.   The United States maintained and extended its specific embargoes, imposed haphazard, but showed much hesitancy in adopting a general system of rationing, being impressed by the danger of "encircling" Japan.   The Japanese were thus able during several crucial months materially to increase their reserves of many vital commodities, with the result that (apart from a few important exceptions) they probably now hold about a year's stocks.   Our objective can, therefore, no longer be merely to prevent the accumulation of stocks, but to force Japan to draw on her reserves, which obviously creates a greater risk of violent reactions.

5.   After the Presidential election, the United States became more ready to co-operate.   By now, they have subjected the majority of important commodities to export licence, and in practice when they place a commodity on the licensing list they normally refuse all licences to Japan. Their practice is, therefore, more drastic than ours, though certain important commodities, such as cotton and mineral oils (with the exception of aviation spirit and lubricants), are subject to no restriction at all.   They have also extended their licensing system to goods transhipped in the United States, which seriously affects Japanese imports from Latin America.   Finally, they have recently extended it to cover the Philippines, which had become a large supplier to Japan of such commodities as copra, iron ore, chrome, &c., and it is expected that there will be severe restrictions on most of these exports.

6.   Apart from restricting Japanese supplies from or via the United States, the United States Government have also, largely at the instance of His Majesty's Government, embarked on a comprehensive policy of purchases in Latin America.   Their primary motive was to safeguard their own supplies, but the economic warfare aspect, which has always been stressed by His Majesty's Government, is coming increasingly to the fore, so that large-scale purchases, particularly of minerals, are now being made in Latin America with the partial object of denying goods to Japan and to the enemy.

7.   The Netherlands Government have shown themselves, in principle, anxious to co-operate in restricting exports to Japan.   In practice, however, they have found it impossible, in the absence of any assurance of assistance from the United States, entirely to resist the Japanese demands for increased supplies. In particular, after the United States embargo on aviation spirit, the Japanese brought strong pressure to bear to secure increased quantities of mineral oil for the Netherlands East Indies, and this pressure was largely successful.   In September 1940 the Japanese Government sent a special delegation to Batavia to discuss the whole complex of economic relations between Japan and the Netherlands Indies.   This delegation appeared to have no instructions from its Government, and the

preponderance of service personnel in an ostensibly economic mission gave grounds for suspicion that the Japanese were more interested in infiltration than negotiation. After a good deal of pressure from the Dutch side the delegation eventually produced an agenda, a feature of which was a demand for astronomic quantities of raw materials. Final Japanese demands were delivered on the 14th May, and the Dutch said their last word in a memorandum of the 6th June. While firmly resisting every suggestion that the N.E.I. forms part of the "co-prosperity" sphere, the Dutch found it necessary to offer supplies of important materials (including rubber, copra and nickel ore) on a more generous scale than we had wished. Their offers did not go far enough to satisfy the Japanese who, after a violent press campaign which failed to move the Dutch, then withdrew their delegation. It is understood, however, that the Governor-General has agreed to regard the quotas offered as constituting a gentleman's agreement if the Japanese will accept Dutch desiderata on the same basis.

8. The Free French have also introduced quotas (on a somewhat generous scale) for their exports to Japan from the French Pacific Islands, and this has led to somewhat acrimonious complaints from the Japanese accompanied by radio propaganda to the inhabitants of the territories.

9. Meanwhile, in the Empire itself restrictions have been gradually tightened. A certain number of commodities are embargoed entirely on supply grounds (e.g., nickel and ferro-alloys). Other embargoes, e.g., on scrap iron, have been imposed to conform with United States policy. In other cases restrictions have been increased for purely economic warfare reasons. Thus, no further licences are to be granted for rubber and tin from Malaya this year, owing to the excessive quantities which Japan is now obtaining from other sources. Similarly, an embargo has been placed on exports of copra from most parts of the Empire in view of Japan's abnormal imports, particularly from the Philippines, and of the evidence that she has been sending copra and other fats to Germany. In fact, 80 percent of the commodities sent across the Siberian Railway is believed to have consisted of fats of one kind or another. Additional restrictions have also recently been placed on other exports to Japan, e.g., pig iron, lead and zinc, and proposals are under consideration to tighten the restrictions on manganese, jute and other commodities. India and the Colonial Empire have been co-operating closely with us in these restrictions. The policy of the Dominions has not been so easy to co-ordinate; Canada, for example, has imposed some embargoes against our advice, while Australia and South Africa have, on occasion, been reluctant to restrict their exports even to normal quantities.

10. Apart from our restrictions upon exports, Japan's difficulties have been aggravated by the withdrawal of British and Allied shipping from Japanese charter, and she

is now suffering from an acute shortage of shipping.

11.   It is inevitable that our restrictions should produce some reactions in Japan. But care is being exercised not to impose such restrictions to the extent of provoking Japan to war. Thus, with the exception of copra and an embargo placed by the Canadian Government on wheat, little has been done to interfere with Japan's food supplies. For example, Burmese rice is open to her to buy at will. Japanese reactions to date may be summed up as follows: The Canadian embargo on wheat was followed by a veiled threat to withdraw the Japanese Diplomatic Mission in Canada. The embargo on copra led to urgent appeals and protests in Tokyo, Canberra and London. An embargo imposed in Hong Kong on exports of scrap iron, wolfram and gall nuts caused a similar outburst and the Japanese intimated that Hong Kong should be regarded as having some special relationship in economic matters with the Japanese Empire. This suggestion was firmly rejected. Again an appeal was made to His Majesty's Ambassador at Tokyo to bring pressure to bear on the Netherlands Government to allow larger quantities of rubber to be sent to Japan. Finally, the Japanese Ambassador, in conversation with Mr. R. A. Butler on 30th May, endeavoured to adopt the attitude that our economic policy towards Japan was vindictive and that our future relations could not hope to improve.

12.   These complaints, coupled with the threatening attitude of the Japanese press to the Netherlands East Indies, make it legitimate to assume that our policy over the past eight months has begun to bear fruit. The Japanese are, it may be hoped, finding it more and more difficult to avoid drawing on their reserves. In every part of the world they are meeting with obstruction ultimately caused either by British or United States action. In British and Allied territories direct embargoes or restrictions are imposed; in the United States licences are usually refused altogether; in Latin America the Japanese find a comprehensive policy of United States and United Kingdom purchases of the more important war materials; in Thailand they find us doing what we can to baulk their plans. By their control of Indo-China and by their pressure on Thailand they have countered our efforts to restrict supplies of rubber and tin; but they have had to share their loot with Germany and are not satisfied with the position. While it would be foolish to claim that they are as yet seriously weakened, it would be equally foolish to deny that they are becoming increasingly alarmed.

[*Source: Anthony Eden memorandum, 7 July 1941, CAB 96/4,
             PRO.]

APPENDIX H

THE DUTCH ARGUE TO PARTICIPATE IN THE WAR AGAINST JAPAN*

During the year 1943 the Netherlands Government considered plans and proposals for the increased participation of Netherland forces in the war against Japan as soon as these forces could be recruited after the liberation of the Netherlands. At the same time the organization of the necessary units for the administration of civil affairs in the Netherlands Indies was taken in hand. The necessary personnel for these units would also have to be recruited, to a large extent, in the liberated Netherlands as the available manpower outside occupied territory was limited by other war commitments.

It must be obvious that both projects are of the highest importance for the future of the Kingdom. Participation in the war with all available resources up to the final defeat of Japan has always been considered an immutable obligation of the Kingdom from the moment it declared war upon Japan, at the moment of the attack upon Pearl Harbor, Manila and Singapore. The liberation of the Netherlands Indies and the elimination of Japanese pockets of resistance in those islands are obviously, within the general framework of this war, of such specific concern to the Netherlands Government that they want to take the greatest possible part in those operations. The restoration of orderly government and the relief and rehabilitation of the territory and its inhabitants are the primary task of that government after liberation.

The military proposals covered the two first objectives. They comprised the reinforcement and completion of the navy and the airforce and the establishment of an expeditionary force of one to three divisions, of a brigade of marines, and of fifteen battalions specially equipped for local operations in the Netherlands Indies. For the administration of civil affairs agreements were concluded with the Commanders-in-Chief of the areas covering the Netherlands Indies (S.W.P.A. and S.E.A.C.) which would ultimately call for some 5,000 personnel, mostly militarized during the first or military phase of liberation.

The proposals with regard to the armed forces were generally approved by the Combined Chiefs of Staff. It was decided at the same time that, with the exception of the marines, the training and equipment should be British; only the marines were to be trained and equipped in the United States.

It is obvious that speed was going to be of essential importance in the execution of these plans. The unexpected slowness of the liberation of the Netherlands and the rapid developments in the war with Japan have emphasized this factor. The response to the call for service overseas in the liberated parts of the Netherlands has been very

gratifying. It is therefore with a sense of grave
disappointment and concern that the Netherlands Government
draw attention to the fact that they have met with serious
delay, which hamper the timely realization of these
proposals and, in consequence, endanger the situation of the
Kingdom.

The first delay occurred as a result of the
simultaneous demands upon the available manpower in the
Southern part of the Netherlands for the requirements of
S.H.A.E.F. and for service overseas. Although that part was
liberated in September/October 1944, an agreement in this
respect was only reached in the beginning of March 1945,
when some 15,000 men were released for the war against
Japan.

After that new negotiations were necessary for the
transportation of these men to the countries where they
could be most effectively be [sic] trained for their future
duties. This could not be done in the Netherlands because
the necessary facilities for these purposes were lacking.
Therefore the Netherlands proposals indicated:

a) the training of the marines in the United States;
b) the training of the expeditionary force and of the
naval and air forces in Great Britain, with the exception of
the ground staff for the already existing air squadrons in
the Far East;
c) the training of the last named ground staff and of
the light battalions in Australia;
d) the training of the civil affairs personnel at the
provisory Netherlands Indies government center in Australia.

These arrangements were in accordance with the
available facilities and with the necessity of a rapid and
effective completion of the training period.

Meanwhile the execution of this program was again
delayed by the lack of sufficient provision for
transportation of the recruits. Little headway was made
with respect to the transportation of marines to the United
States, hardly any in the case of that of troops and civil
affairs personnel to Australia. As these three categories
are those which offer the best prospects of being ready for
action after a comparatively short period of training the
situation has become very critical.

In the middle of April 1945 the Combined Chiefs of
Staff agreed to the transportation of approximately 5,600
personnel to Australia on the proviso that it would depend
on other requirements of higher priority. It was added that
this amount of transportation could probably be made
available up to the end of the war in Europe. When that end
came, however, in May next the already low priority was
apparently completely extinguished after transportation for
not more than 600 personnel had actually been arranged.

It must be obvious that the Netherlands Government

cannot possibly acquiesce in this state of affairs. It may
have the result that, although the necessary manpower is
available, it will be impossible to take an adequate part in
the liberation of the Netherlands Indies and to fulfil the
obligations of the Netherlands, both as the sovereign state
and under the existing agreements with regard to civil
affairs, relief and rehabilitation. It need not be pointed
out how serious the consequences would be for the Kingdom
and for the inhabitants of the Netherlands Indies.

There are two circumstances which further accentuate
the unacceptability of the position. It is impossible to
keep tens of thousands of volunteers waiting indefinitely
for the beginning of active training without sapping their
morale and creating a general unrest among the population of
the Netherlands. An explanation of the cause of this delay
would be inevitable, but such an explanation could hardly
seem satisfactory to the people concerned.

In the second place it is a well known fact that the
Netherlands have, ever since 1940, placed at the disposal of
their allies all their transports, of which they possessed a
considerable number and which have carried large numbers of
troops across the seas to every theatre of war. Grievous
losses have been incurred in this work but yet the capacity
of the remaining transports is far in excess of what would
be needed for our own requirements. The realization of this
fact would make it even less acceptable to the nation that
transportation, even by their own ships and in the most
vital interests of the Kingdom, remains denied to them.

Under these circumstances the Netherlands Government
must press for an urgent reconsideration of the matter and
for an early and satisfactory answer to the question how
this problem can be solved and the present deadlock can be
broken.

[*Source: Government of the Netherlands memorandum, 25 May
          1945, Joseph C. Grew Papers, Houghton Library,
          Harvard University, Cambridge, MA, file 19, Vol.
          7.]

APPENDIX I

OUTLINE OF EVENTS WITHIN THE JAPANESE GOVERNMENT LEADING UP TO THE SURRENDER*

29 June 1946

The appointment of Admiral Baron Suzuki as Premier of Japan on 7 April 1945 was the first major success of the leaders within the Japanese government who ever since the fall of Saipan in July 1944 had felt certain that the war was lost and that an early peace was necessary. This group found its major strength in the Elder Statesmen, or Jushin, whose failure to support Premier Tojo had led to the latter's overthrow on 19 July 1944. However, Tojo's successor, Koiso, an old soldier who had been very critical of his predecessor, did not fulfill the expectations of the Elder Statesmen, who had sponsored his appointment. He contented himself with peace feelers at Chungking. He did not create a cabinet of peace-minded men and proved unable to overcome Army opposition to a change in policy. Any action independent of the Army, which in 1944 still exercised great influence over the Emperor, was impossible. Army reaction to peace proposals was likely to take the form of wholesale assassinations. Nevertheless, the Elder Statesmen, dissatisfied with the all-out continuation of the war, worked for Koiso's overthrow, which was finally accomplished in April 1945.

Suzuki was selected as Premier because he was considered "a man of deep sincerity and enormous courage", and the current problem required that the man chosen "stake his life in pursuing his task". Suzuki recalls that in his first audience with the Emperor he received no direct order to end the war, but was given to understand that it was the Emperor's desire for him to make every effort to bring the war to a conclusion as quickly as possible. He realized that his mission required the utmost discretion, because he would undoubtedly be assassinated if those opposed to the new policy, specifically the Army officers, should learn of his mission. Accordingly, while publicly advocating an increase in the war effort, he undertook secretly to carry out the Emperor's desire.

His first move was to direct his Chief Cabinet Secretary, Sakomizu, to survey Japanese fighting power and report whether it justified continuation of the struggle. Sakomizu reported early in May in the negative. About the middle of May, Suzuki, having approved Sakomizu's conclusions, had another audience with the Emperor and on his return told Sakomizu "We must start some steps toward peace." His first step was to have former Premier Hirota privately sound the Russian Ambassador, Malik, regarding the possibility of USSR mediation with the United States. The

-303-

ensuing conversations, which started promisingly, led to no conclusion. Meanwhile the collapse of Germany made the Minister of War, Anami, ask for a meeting of the Supreme War Guidance Council, or Inner Cabinet, to be held in the presence of the Emperor to consider whether or not to continue the war. The six members of this Council were the Prime Minister, the Ministers of War, Navy, and Foreign Affairs, and the Chiefs of Staff of the Army and the Navy.

A preparatory meeting, which included lower officials in addition to the six regular members, was held on or about 6 June. So many persons were present that opinions were not freely expressed, but the report for the Emperor, prepared by Sakomizu, indicated doubt of the possibility of military success. Two or three days later, on 8 or 9 June, the Inner Cabinet met in the presence of the Emperor, who listened to the report but said nothing. Other unofficial meetings of those members of the Inner Cabinet who were cognizant of the conversations with Ambassador Malik were held from time to time. The Army Chief of Staff was apparently not included in this group or informed of its activity, but presumably the Minister of War, Anami, was at least informed. Discussions apparently centered around the terms of capitulation which would be acceptable. It was hoped that through Russian mediation terms more favorable than unconditional surrender might be obtained. Since the Russian Ambassador in Tokyo was reported to be ill and great difficulty was experienced in maintaining contact with Moscow through him, it was decided to send a special envoy to the Soviet Capital, and Japanese Ambassador Sato was instructed to prepare the way for the visit.

By 20 June no tangible results had been achieved and the Emperor, doubtless on the advice of the Elder Statesmen, took the unusual step of calling the Inner Cabinet to meet in his presence. He called the conclusion of the 9 June report "paradoxical" and concluded: "I think it necessary for us to have a plan to close the war at once as well as one to defend the home islands". This for the first time made it clear to all present, including Army representatives, that the Emperor was definitely on the side of those who were trying to bring the war to an end. The statement gave new courage to Suzuki and the Navy representatives, who apparently felt that their lives would thereafter be in less peril. The War Minister, Anami, also was believed to approve the new policy, since he refrained from breaking up the cabinet by resigning. He did not dare, however, to let his opinion be known to his subordinates.

Following this meeting Prince Konoye was selected as special envoy to the USSR and Ambassador Sato in Moscow discussed the proposed mission with the Vice Commisar for Foreign Affairs. The Russians asked for a specific statement of the Prince's mission. The reply stated that the Japanese wanted:

        1.   To effect an improvement in Russo-Japanese

relations required in consequence of Russian denunciation of the neutrality pact.

       2. To ask the USSR to mediate between Japan and the United States in order to end the war.

The Emperor meanwhile had shown his impatience over the slow progress of negotiations by asking the Foreign Minister on 10 July directly why the envoy had not yet been sent.

On or about 13 July the Russians stated that Stalin and Molotov were just leaving for the Potsdam Conference and that no serious attention could be given to the Japanese proposal until their return. Prince Suzuki and his colleagues felt very pessimistic after this reply. Nothing further could be done but wait for the return of Stalin and Molotov to Moscow.

On 26 July came the Potsdam Declaration and 6 August the first atomic bomb. Suzuki at once realized that the chance had come to end the war: "Even the military know that if President Truman's announcements were true no country could carry on war. Without the atomic bomb it would be impossible for any country to defend itself against a nation which had the weapon". He and the Foreign Minister reported the new situation to the Emperor on 7 August and gave their opinion that the time had come to accept the Potsdam Declaration. On the following day, 8 August, before any further move could be made, the USSR declared war on Japan effective 9 August. Suzuki saw the Emperor in the early morning of the 9th and received authority to take the necessary measures for ending the war at once on the basis of the Potsdam Declaration. This involved obtaining the agreements of both the Inner Cabinet and the full cabinet.

The Inner Cabinet met at 10:00 that same morning, and the meeting lasted for three hours. The Premier, the Navy Minister, and the Minister of Foreign Affairs proposed to accept the Potsdam Declaration with the sole proviso that the Emperor's legal position should not be effected. The Minister of War and the two Chiefs of Staff proposed conditional acceptance: (1) none of the main Japanese islands to be occupied; (2) forces abroad to be withdrawn and demobilized by Japan; (3) all war crimes to be prosecuted by the Japanese government. No decision was reached by 1:00, when the full cabinet was called in. Sixteen members were present. Foreign Minister Togo reported on the Inner Cabinet. Nine members were for unconditional acceptance of the Potsdam Declaration, four favored the conditional acceptance proposed by the War Minister, and three suggested variant conditions. The meeting lasted until 8:00 p.m. without reaching a decision. During the recess the Prime Minister, Foreign Minister, and Chief Cabinet Secretary in private conference decided to have the Inner Cabinet meet in the Emperor's presence, to express their differing views and, if possible, to obtain a decision from the Emperor. This was arranged for 11:30 p.m.

The session began with a reading of the Potsdam

Declaration. Each minister then expressed his opinion, taking exactly the same positions as in the previous Inner Cabinet meeting. Baron Hiranuma, President of the Privy Council, was also present by invitation and sided with the unconditional acceptance group. Still no agreement could be reached. Finally about 3:00 in the morning of the 10th, Suzuki made the unprecedented move of requesting the Emperor to break the deadlock by expressing his wish. The Emperor at once stated clearly that he agreed with the opinion of the Prime Minister and Foreign Minister on both humanitarian grounds and those of military hopelessness.

The Inner Cabinet then left the Palace and reconvened with the full cabinet. The Emperor's decision was reported by the Prime Minister. All the members agreed with the conclusions and signed a document "advising" the Emperor to accept unconditionally the Potsdam Declaration.

By 7:00 a.m. of the 10th the cable accepting surrender was dispatched through the Swedish and Swiss legations. About 4:00 am on the 12th the American answer was received by broadcast, but the official reply did not arrive through neutral diplomatic channels until 7:00 a.m. on the 13th. Delay in delivery of the official American reply led to fears, fostered by the San Francisco radio, of further atomic bombing, and Domei was authorized in spite of Army objections to broadcast on the 12th that the text had not reached Tokyo. Following receipt of the official text on the morning of the 13th a full cabinet meeting was held at 1:00 p.m. The main subject of debate was the post-war position of the Emperor. By 6:00 p.m. an intermission had to be declared, since no agreement could be reached between the thirteen members willing to accept the American terms and the military members who refused either to accept the American terms or agree to request a session in the Emperor's presence. The whole night was spent in further discussions by small informal groups.

On the morning of the 14th Suzuki went to the Palace to suggest that the Emperor himself summon the cabinet to meet in his presence. The suggestion was approved and shortly after 10:00 a.m. the sixteen cabinet ministers, the two Chiefs of Staff, and the directors of the Bureaus of Naval and Military Affairs assembled at the Palace. Baron Hiranuma was again present as representative of the Privy Council. Suzuki urged all to express openly their opinions of the American terms. Anami, the War Minister, Umezu, Army Chief of Staff, and Toyada, Navy Chief of Staff, held that a more concrete and specific answer should be requested of the United States, or if this was impossible, that the war be continued. All the others present favored acceptance of the American terms.

Then the Emperor spoke. He first expressed his hope that all would agree with his opinion. "My opinion", he said, "is the same as the one I expressed the other night. The American answer seems to me acceptable." He restated his reasons for the opinion, spoke of the reconstruction of Japan, urged general cooperation, ordered the cabinet to draft an Imperial Rescript ending the war, and finally offered to broadcast to the nation. The cabinet then met without the Emperor and took formal action advising the Emperor to do as he had already ordered. About noon a message accepting the American terms was sent off. At 11:00 p.m. the Imperial Rescript ending the state of war was issued, at midnight the Emperor's speech was recorded, and at noon on the 15th was broadcast to the nation. The war was over.

[*Source: unsigned memorandum, 29 June 1946, Henry L. Stimson Papers, Sterling Library, Yale University, New Haven, CT, file 29, Box 153.]

APPENDIX J

WHY NAME THE ORGANIZATION "UNITED NATIONS?"*

The "United Nations" seems the best designation for the organization for the following reasons:

1. It is the designation favored by President Roosevelt and accepted in the Dumbarton Oaks proposals by the four powers.

2. It has been the designation of the military coalition against the Axis declared on January 1, 1942, is easy to say, and has become familiar to millions of people throughout the world.

3. It emphasizes the continuity of the permanent organization to maintain international peace and security with the military coalition which fought and won the war making such an organization possible. The permanent organization will have a much firmer foundation if it rests, not upon a mere contract of governments but upon actual and effective collaboration in the great task of destroying the greatest of aggressions. Beginning with a great success in the application of international sanctions the organization will command more confidence than if it began merely with paper pledges and future expectations. In this respect the United Nations resembles the United States which originated not in the Articles of Confederation or in the Constitution but in the Declaration of Independence and the fact of collaboration of the states to realise this declaration in the Revolutionary War.

4. It appropriately describes the organization set forth in the Charter as a "union" not a league or alliance, and a union of "nations" not of rulers or of governments. The organic and popular character of the organization are thus emphasized.

5. It is different from the name of any past international organization thus emphasizing the distinctiveness of the organization and the beginning of a new epoch in history.

6. It has been employed in the title of several voluntary groups organized to support the general international organization and appears in numerous books and pamphlets constituting a literature about that organization. A public opinion has developed about the name "United Nations" and if a different name were subject this momentum would be lost and the public would be confused.

Opposition to the name "United Nations" seems to flow from the feeling that a permanent and eventually universal organization for peace and security ought to be differentiated from the military coalition which constituted one side in the war and that the present enemy states might find it difficult later to enter an organization reminiscent of their victorious enemies and of their own defeat.

These arguments are answered by the general recognition
that the present war is not a "war" in the old sense that
the belligerents are equally entitled to pursue their
interests by force, but is a vast sanctioning operation
supported by most of the states of the world against a small
group of aggressors which resorted to hostilities in
violation of their international obligations. The United
Nations are not one side in a war but those states which
have assumed responsibility "on behalf of the community of
nations" to maintain international peace and security.
Continuity of the organization with this first successful
action to maintain its principles is far more important than
consideration for the sentiments of that small number of
states guilty of aggression. Instead of being a detriment
to the organization, the use of the name should benefit it
by permanently recalling both to the aggressors and to the
other states that aggression does not pay.

[*Source: Quincy Wright memorandum, 7 June 1945, Record
          Group 59, Harley A. Notter Files, file "Name,"
          Box 246, National Archives, Washington, D. C.]

SELECTED BIBLIOGRAPHY

I. PRIMARY SOURCES

A. UNPUBLISHED SOURCES

1. OFFICIAL DOCUMENTS AND PUBLIC RECORDS

Most of the appropriate British records are deposited in the Public Record Office, London. Beginning with the central direction of the war effort, the minutes (CAB 65, WM Series, 55 volumes) and memoranda (CAB 66, WP Series, 67 volumes) of the War Cabinet are well indexed and replete with cross-references to additional material. Researchers would be well advised to begin working through CAB 65 in reverse chronological order because the British Secretariat under E. E. Bridges provided in the margins an accompanying reference to the next previous discussion of each subject item. Citation to the Secretary's Standard File, or SSF, should be considered the same as references to the Confidential Annex. This particularly secret material is separately classified within the CAB 65 minutes according to the appropriate Cabinet meeting number. These two files also include the minutes (CM Series) and papers (CP Series) of the Caretaker Government from May 1945 until the announcement of the results of the General Election on 26 July 1945. Two other categories of Cabinet papers of great value are the WP(G) Series in CAB 67 and the WP(R) Series in CAB 68. The former were less secret than those in CAB 66 and received a wider distribution, while the latter consist of reports from various governmental departments to the Cabinet.

Miscellaneous papers of the Prime Minister's Office are contained in the PREM 1 file, conveniently arranged by subject. There is no PREM 2 category. Operational material dealing with defense and the conduct of the war in each theater may be found in PREM 3. This file also contains the bulk of the Roosevelt-Churchill correspondence, arranged chronologically in volumes 467-473. Other valuable papers kept at Number Ten Downing are catalogued in the PREM 4 files, especially those pertaining to important domestic and foreign political issues.

Eight volumes of minutes and memoranda relating to the War Cabinet Defence Committee directly under the supervision of the Prime Minister are in the CAB 69 Series. Moreover, there are 91 volumes for the minutes of the meetings of the Chiefs of Staff (CAB 79) as well as 106 volumes of accompanying COS memoranda (CAB 80). The staff at the Public Record Office could not explain the COS system whereby some minutes and papers carried the "(O)" (Official?) designation and were separately indexed; however, that label was dropped for the designation of

FO meetings after December 1944. The COS records are
indispensable for studies of World War II because the
Cabinet, Foreign Office, Colonial Office, Dominions Office
and other governmental organizatons constantly referred to
the British Chiefs for advice from the military point of
view about a wide range of subjects. The records of various
COS subcommittees are contained throughout CAB 81; see
especially the minutes and memoranda of the Post Hostilities
Subcommittee in volumes 40-46. Because of the British
system of parallel documentation, each of the Services
maintained a complete file of records. Thus, the Command
and Theater documents of the South East Asia Command are
contained in the AIR 23 file. This important collection
includes SEAC minutes and memoranda, Mountbatten's
directives, and minutes of Mountbatten's meetings with
Chiang Kai-shek, Stilwell, Wedemeyer, and visiting
officials.

Of special note is the miscellaneous collection in CAB
21. This extensive file holds records for a wide range of
subjects and is well worth combing. Also, there are 108
volumes of material relating to the correspondence and
papers of Lord Hankey in CAB 63, which cover many various
issues. Hankey maintained periodic six-month
"Appreciations" of the war situation which are extremely
helpful.

CAB 96 comprises 10 volumes of the minutes and
memoranda of the interdepartmental Far Eastern Committee.
The first four volumes deal with the period October 1940 to
December 1941. The documents of a special Far Eastern
Economic Subcommittee in this period are in volume 7, while
the records of a special 1941 Far Eastern Propaganda
Subcommittee are in volume 10. Volume 6 contains material
of the short-lived Far Eastern (Official) Committee in
February-April 1942. The records of a revised main
committee and a corresponding economic subsidiary may be
found in volume 5 and volume 8 respectively. Finally, the
important developments in 1945 after the surrender of Japan
are traced in the documents of the Far Eastern (Ministerial)
Committee in volume 9.

Complete records of the Foreign Office, Colonial Office
(CO 323) and Dominions Office (DO 35) also proved very
helpful. The general political correspondence of the
Foreign Office after 1906 in file FO 371 totals over 18,500
volumes, which, fortunately, are extremely well indexed.
The records of each of the war years are separately
catalogued with an extensive cross-reference system. This
series is particularly valuable apart from the diplomatic
correspondence itself because of the marginalia inscribed by
the Prime Minister and Foreign Secretary as well as the
attached comments of the various departmental officials.
Inexplicably, a convenient special collection of Foreign
Office Confidential Prints (FO 401-FO 438) for the war years
remains closed despite the fact that FO 371 contains not

only these memoranda but also most of the material
pertaining to the evolution of such statements. The Foreign
Office collection of private papers boasts a significant
list of luminaries but is disappointingly sparse in
substantive content.

Perhaps the most important source for the researcher in
steering through the bewildering array of material in the
Public Record Office is the special handbook: Public Record
Office, <u>The Second World War: A Guide to Documents in the
Public Record Office</u> (London: HMSO, 1972).

American archival material relating to this study is
divided between the National Archives in Washington, D.C.
and the Washington National Record Center in Suitland,
Maryland.

At the National Archives, the most important documents
for this study are in the records of the Department of State
(RG 59). The many files for each country and for various
combinations of international relations are well indexed.
This study relied heavily on the records pertaining to the
United States, Great Britain, China, Russia, France,
Thailand, and Indochina. In addition, RG 59 contains
important segregated material under the general file heading
of 740.0011, such as EW (European War), PW (Pacific War),
Potsdam, Moscow, Stettinius Mission (1944), and Control (by
enemy country). Other special collections in RG 59 include:
"Byrnes Briefing Book" (5 volumes grouped under file
740.0011PW9 Potsdam/5-2446), "Records of the Office of
European Affairs, 1934-1947: Files of John D. Hickerson" (8
boxes), "Records of the Office of European Affairs, 1942-
1947: Files of H. Freeman Matthews" (2 boxes), Harley
Notter Files (307 boxes), Leo Pasvolsky Files (7 boxes), and
the "Stettinius Diaries: December 1, 1944-July 3, 1945" (8
volumes). The Notter Files are indispensable for tracing
the development of postwar policies. File 123 of RG 59
holds material relating to various individual Foreign
Service Officers (Hurley, Gauss, Stuart, Davies, Service,
Ringwalt, Winant, Atcheson, etc.,). Finally, all available
OSS Research and Analysis studies may be found in RG 59.

In addition, the Diplomatic Branch at the National
Archives contains the records of the Marshall Mission to
China (LOT 121.893) and the unclassified portions of RG 43:
"Records of International Conferences, Commissions and
Expositions: World War II Conferences." Also see especially
in RG 43 the files of Philip E. Mosely, the records of the
Far Eastern Commission (RG 59), and the records of the
Office of War Mobilization and Reconversion (RG 250).

Pertinent Joint Chiefs of Staff and Combined Chiefs of
Staff documents are deposited in the Modern Military Branch
at the National Archives, as are the records of the Office
of Strategic Services (RG 226). See also on file there the
extremely valuable unpublished manuscripts: Vernon E. Davis,
"The History of the Joint Chiefs of Staff in World War II,"
2 vols., 1953; Grace P. Hayes, "The War Against Japan," 2

vols., 1953-1954 (published in 1982 by the U.S. Naval Institute); and Tracy Kitteridge, "Evolution of Global Strategy in World War II," n.d. These studies are based on primary documents but because the JCS never considered them, the works cannot be described as "Official Histories." Nevertheless, these important manuscripts have been examined and unofficially approved by "officers who had participated in the events." Intra-governmental difficulties and rivalries about the trusteeship administration of the Pacific islands surfaced in the records of the Office of the Secretary of the Interior (RG 48) and the records of the Office of Territories (RG 126). In particular, see the correspondence contained in the Abe Fortas files in RG 48.

Other material consulted at the National Archives included the records of the Commerce Department (RG 40), the Bureau of Foreign and Domestic Commerce (RG 151), the Justice Department (RG 60), and the Treasury Department (RG 39, RG 56).

Important military files are housed at the Washington National Record Center in Suitland, Maryland. Valuable documents relating to the C-B-I Theater and SEAC may be found in RG 332 "Records of United States Theaters of War, World War II," and RG 332 "Records of United States Army Commands, 1942-." Moreover, RG 332 also contains the Stilwell Files (4 boxes) and the Wedemeyer Files (12 boxes), both of which are particularly helpful for both personal and professional information.

Official United States attitudes on a variety of subjects emerge in the records of the Office of War Information (RG 208). OWI policy guidelines sent to field representatives (e.g., John K. Fairbank in China) reveal some of the reasons why certain items were or were not publicized. Information on key economic issues and policies may be found in the records of the Federal Economic Administration (RG 169), an organization which caused great concern among British observers in the Far East.

Finally, the diplomatic post papers (RG 108) are in accession at Suitland. These documents include the correspondence among the American consulates in each country; see especially those in the United Kingdom and in China.

2. MANUSCRIPT COLLECTIONS

Cambridge, England. Churchill College Library. Cambridge University.

> Alexander, Albert V. First Lord of the Admiralty.
> Attlee, Clement R. Correspondence with Churchill traces the growing political divergence and includes the famous letter of complaint about Churchill and Beaverbrook monopolizing the meetings of the War

Cabinet.
Bevin, Ernest. A sparse collection.
Cockroft, Sir John.
Edwards, Admiral Sir Ralph. Chief of Staff, Eastern
    Fleet.
Godfrey, Admiral J. H. Commander-in-Chief, Indian
    Navy.
Hankey, 1st Baron.
Keyes, Baron.
Kilmuir, Earl. Chairman Conservative Party Committee on
    Postwar Reconstruction.
Margesson, 1st Viscount. Chief Whip Conservative
    Party.
Somerville, Admiral Sir James. Valuable
    correspondence, especially with Mountbatten,
    Ismay, and Pound.
Vansittart, 1st Baron.
Weir, 1st Viscount.

Cambridge, England. University Library. Cambridge
University.

Templewood, Viscount (Samuel Hoare).

Cambridge, Massachusetts. Houghton Library. Harvard
University.

Fischer, Fred. Typescript.
Greene, Roger Sherman.
Grew, Joseph C.
Moffat, Jay Pierrepont.
Phillips, William.

Charleston, South Carolina. Archives-Museum. The Citadel.

Clark, Mark. Valuable for Clark's contacts with the
    French.

Charlottesville, Virginia. Alderman Library. University of
Virginia.

Johnson, Louis. Valuable correspondence on the
    situation in India.
Stettinius, Edward R., Jr.
Watson, General Edwin. Sparse.

Hyde Park, New York. Franklin D. Roosevelt Library.

Berle, Adolph A., Jr.
Cox, Oscar.
Field, Henry.
Hopkins, Harry.
Morgenthau, Henry.

Records of the President's Rubber Survey Committee.
Roosevelt, Franklin D.
     Map Room
     Official File
     President's Personal File
     President's Secretary's File
     Roosevelt-Churchill Correspondence
Taussig, Charles.
Thomas, Elbert D.
Wallace, Henry A.
War Production Board. Records of the War Production
     Board Mission to China.
Wehle, Louis B.

Lexington, Virginia. George C. Marshall Foundation.

     Butterworth, W. Walton.
     Marshall, George C.

London. Beaverbrook Library.

     Balfour, Herbert Harrington.
     Beaverbrook, Lord.
     Crozier, William R. Many valuable interview
          transcripts.

London. British Museum.

     Cunningham, Admiral of the Fleet Sir Andrew B. Much
          remains restricted. See especially the corres-
          pondence with Pound.
     Goodall, Sir Stanley Vernon. See the report of the
          Bucknill Committee on the sinkings of the Repulse
          and the Prince of Wales; Goodall correspondence as
          Director of Naval Construction; and the diary of
          his private secretary, F. O. Bamford.

London. Imperial War Museum.

     Hilken, Captain T. J. N.
     Irwin, Lieutenant General M. S.
     Johnstone, Major General T.
     McClure, Lieutenant Commander J. A. Narrative on the
          end of the British China Squadron.
     Webster, C. K. Far Eastern Research Committee Papers.
     Wynn, Colonel G. C.

London. Liddell Hart Centre for Military Archives. King's
College. University of London.

     Brooke-Popham, Air Chief Marshal Sir Robert. Valuable
          for events in late 1941 and early 1942.
     Davidson, F. H. N.

Ismay, General the Lord Hastings. Extremely signifi-
cant collection of revealing correspondence.
Lindsell, Lieutenant General Sir William.
Meservey, Frank. SEAC Public Relations.
Miksche, Captain F. O.
Penney, Major General Sir Ronald C. Valuable
correspondence.
Vlieland, C. A. Unpublished memoir sharply critical of
British Far Eastern policies, especially with
regard to the strategic emphasis on Singapore.

London. Privately Held.

Craigie, Sir Robert L. In care of his son, Robert.

New Haven, Connecticut. Sterling Library. Yale University.

Baldwin, Hanson. See file on Wedemeyer and the
situation in East Asia.
Bowles, Chester.
Byas, Hugh.
Gabriel, Ralph H.
Hartford and Connecticut Chapters of the Committee to
Defend America by Aiding the Allies. Files.
Kent, Tyler G.
Lane, Arthur Bliss.
Lerner, Maxwell A.
Lippmann, Walter
MacMurray, John.
Paxton, John H. See his secretary's journal.
Stimson, Henry L.
Stokes, Harold Phelps.

Oxford. Nuffield College Library. Oxford University.

Cherwell, Lord. Prior permission required. Covers a
wide range of topics.
Cripps, Lord and Lady.

Washington, D. C. Manuscript Division. Library of
Congress.

Alsop, Joseph. Valuable correspondence.
Bradley, Omar.
Chennault, Claire L.
Connally, Tom.
Davies, Joseph E.
Davis, Norman H.
Feis, Herbert.
Frankfurter, Felix. Extensive and important
correspondence.
Green, Theodore F.
Hull, Cordell.

Ickes, Harold.
Johnson, Nelson T.
Jones, Jesse H.
Knox, Frank.
Leahy, William D.
Long, Breckinridge.
Pasvolsky, Leo
Patterson, Robert P.
Steinhardt, Laurence A.

Woodbridge, Suffolk. Privately Held.

Jacob, General Sir E. I. C.

Worcester, Massachusetts. Library. Clark University.

Blakeslee, George H. Papers relating to the Far East.
Dennis, Alfred L. P.
Jordan, H. Donaldson.
Lee, Dwight S.
Maxwell, James A.

3. INTERVIEWS

Batterbee, Sir Harry. London. 3 August 1973. British High Commissioner in New Zealand.

Butler, Sir Nevile. London. 4 June 1973.

Jacob, General Sir E. I. C. Woodbridge, Suffolk. 26 June 1973.

Larsen, Emmanuel. Washington, D. C. 21 August 1974. China Desk, Naval Intelligence and State Department. Involved in the loyalty investigations after the war; see his testimony in Congressional Record, 81st Cong., 2nd sess., pp. 7441-49.

Lea, General Sir George. Washington, D. C., 14 July 1969.

Matsui, Itsuko. Norfolk, Virginia. 22 October 1982. Japanese Ministry of Foreign Affairs.

Mountbatten, Earl of Burma. London. 2 August 1973.

Warmenhoven, Henri. Richmond, Virginia. 15 February 1978. Interned by the Japanese in NEI.

B. PUBLISHED SOURCES

1. OFFICIAL DOCUMENTS AND PUBLIC RECORDS

British Supply Council in North America. History of the British Supply Organization in the United States. Washington, D. C.: n.p., 1943

Congressional Quarterly Service. China and U.S. Far East Policy, 1945-1966. Washington, D.C.:

Congressional Quarterly Service, Inc., 1967.

Great Britain. Chiefs of Staff Committee. Diagrammatic Representation of Certain Phases of the War. London: HMSO, 1946.

Great Britain. Parliament. Parliamentary Debates.

Great Britain. Secretary of State for Foreign Affairs. Documents Relating to British Involvement in the Conflict in the Indo-China, 1945-1965. London: HMSO, 1965.

Ministry of Foreign Affairs of the U.S.S.R. Correspondence Between the Chairman of the Council of the U.S.S.R. and the Presidents of the U.S.A. and the Prime Ministers of Great Britain During the Great Patriotic War of 1941-1945. 2 vols. Moscow: Foreign Languages Publishing House, 1957.

Mountbatten, Earl of Burma. Report to the Combined Chiefs of Staff by the Supreme Allied Commander, South East Asia, 1943-1945, Vice-Admiral the Lord Mountbatten of Burma. London: HMSO, 1951.

Office of War Information. Information Guide. Washington, D.C.: G.P.O., 1943.

Preparatory Commission of the United Nations. Committee 4: Trusteeship, Summary Record of Meetings. London: Church House, Westminster, 1945.

Public Record Office. The Second World War: A Guide to Documents in the Public Record Office. London: HMSO, 1972.

United States. Congress. Congressional Record.

United States. Congress. House. Committee on Armed Services. United States-Vietnam Relations, 1945-1967. 12 vols. Washington, D.C.: G.P.O., 1971.

United States. Congress. House. Committee on Foreign Affairs. World War II: International Agreements and Understandings Entered Into During Secret Conferences Concerning Other Peoples. Washington, D.C.: G.P.O., 1953.

United States. Congress. House. Committee on International Relations. Select Executive Session Hearings of the Committee, 1943-1950. 8 vols. Washington, D.C.: G.P.O., 1976. See especially "U.S. Policy in the Far East," vols. VII-VIII; "Problems of World War II and Its Aftermath," vols. I-II.

United States. Congress. Joint Committee on the Investigation of the Pearl Harbor Attack. Investigation of the Pearl Harbor Attack. Washington, D.C.: G.P.O., 1950.

United States. Congress. Senate. Committee on Armed Services. Military Situation in the Far East. 5 pts. Washington, D.C.: G.P.O., 1950.

United States. Congress. Senate. Committee on Foreign Relations. A Decade of American Foreign Policy. Washington, D.C.: G.P.O., 1950.

United States. Congress. Senate. Committee on Foreign Relations. Causes, Origins, Consequences of the Vietnam War. Washington, D.C.: G.P.O., 1972.

United States. Congress. Senate. Committee on the Judiciary. The "Amerasia" Papers: A Clue to the Catastrophe of China. 2 vols. Washington, D.C.: G.P.O., 1970.

United States. Congress. Senate. Committee on the Judiciary. Institute of Pacific Relations. Washington, D.C.: G.P.O., 1952.

United States. Congress. Senate. Committee on the Judiciary. Morgenthau Diary (China). 2 vols. Washington, D.C.: G.P.O., 1965.

United States. Department of State. The Axis in Defeat: A Collection of Documents on American Policy Toward Germany and Japan. Washington, D.C.: G.P.O., 1946.

United States. Department of State. Foreign Relations of the United States. Washington, D.C.: G.P.O., 1939-1948.

For information on the wartime conferences, see:

The Conference at Washington, 1941-1942, and Casablanca, 1943, Washington, D.C.: G.P.O., 1968.

The Conferences at Washington and Quebec, 1943. Washington, D.C.: G.P.O., 1970.

The Conferences at Cairo and Tehran, 1943, Washington, D.C.: G.P.O., 1961.

The Conference at Quebec, 1944. Washington, D.C.: G.P.O., 1972.

The Conferences at Malta and Yalta, 1945. Washington, D.C.: G.P.O., 1955.

The Conference of Berlin (The Potsdam Conference), 1945. 2 vols. Washington, D.C.: G.P.O., 1960.

United States. Department of State. Peace and War: United States Foreign Policy, 1931-1941. Washington, D.C.: G.P.O., 1943.

United States. Department of State. United States Relations with China. Washington, D.C.: G.P.O., 1949.

United States. Strategic Bombing Survey. The Campaigns of the Pacific War. Washington, D.C.: Naval Analysis Division, 1946.

United States. Strategic Bombing Survey. Interrogations of Japanese Officials. Washington, D.C.: G.P.O., 1946.

United States. Strategic Bombing Survey. Japan's Struggle to End the War. Washington, D.C.: G.P.O., 1946.

United States. Superintendent of Documents. World War II: National Defense, Post-War Planning, Washington, D.C.: G.P.O., 1944.

War Reports of General of the Army General George C. Marshall, Chief of Staff, General of the Army H. H. Arnold, Commanding General, Army Air Forces [and] Fleet Admiral Ernest J. King, Commander-in-Chief, United States Fleet and Chief of Naval Operations.

Philadelphia: J. B. Lippincott, 1947.

2. MEMOIRS, DIARIES, PAPERS, AND SPEECHES

Acheson, Dean. Present at the Creation: My Years in the State Department. New York: W. W. Norton, 1969.

Arnold. H. H. Global Mission. New York: Harper and Brothers, 1949.

Attlee, Clement R. A Prime Minister Remembers: The War and Post-War Memoirs of Rt. Hon. Earl Attlee. London: Heinemann, 1961.

Barrett, David D. Dixie Mission: The United States Army Observer Group in Yenan, 1944. Berkeley: Center for Chinese Studies, University of California, 1970.

Blum, John M., ed. From the Morgenthau Diaries: Years of Decision, 1939-1941. Boston: Houghton Mifflin, 1964.

Bond, Brian, ed. Chief of Staff: The Diaries of Lieutenant-General Sir Henry Pownall. 2 vols. Hamden, CT: Shoestring Press, 1974.

Bryant, Arthur. Triumph in the West: A History of the War Years Based on the Diaries of Field-Marshal Lord Alanbrooke, Chief of the Imperial General Staff. Garden City, NY: Doubleday,1959.

_____. The Turn of the Tide. Garden City: Doubleday, 1957.

Byrnes, James F. Speaking Frankly. New York: Harper and Brothers, 1947.

Cameron, Alan W., ed. Vietnam Crisis: A Documentary History, 1940-1956. Ithaca: Cornell University Press, 1976.

Chiang Kai-shek. China's Destiny and Economic Theory. New York: Roy Publishers, 1947.

Chinese Ministry of Information, comp. The Collected Wartime Messages of Generalissimo Chiang Kai-shek, 1937-1945. 2 vols. New York: The John Day Company, 1946.

Churchill, Winston. The Second World War. 6 vols. New York: Bantam Books, 1962. Paperback edition.

Clubb, O. Edmund. The Witness and I. New York: Columbia University Press, 1975.

Cunningham, Andrew B. A Sailor's Odyssey. New York: Dutton, 1951.

De Gaulle, Charles. War Memoirs: Salvation, 1944-1946: Documents. Translated by Joyce Murchie and Hamish Erskine. London: Weidenfeld and Nicolson, 1960.

_____. War Memoirs: Unity. Translated by Richard Howard. London: Weidenfeld and Nicolson, 1959.

Dilks, David, ed. The Diaries of Sir Alexander Cadogan, 1938-1945. New York: Putnam, 1972.

Dorn, Frank. Walkout With Stilwell in Burma. New York: Thomas Y. Crowell Company, 1971. See pp. 74-

79 for the formation of plans to assassinate Chiang Kai-shek based on orders to Stilwell from "the very highest level."

Eade, Charles, comp. Secret Speeches by the Rt. Hon. Winston S. Churchill. London: Cassell and Company, 1946.

Eden, Sir Anthony. The Reckoning: The Memoirs of Anthony Eden, Lord of Avon. Boston: Houghton Mifflin, 1965.

Grew, Joseph. Ten Years in Japan. New York: Simon and Schuster, 1944.

_____. Turbulent Era: A Diplomatic Record of Forty Years, 1904-1945. Boston: Houghton Mifflin, 1952.

Groves, Leslie. Now It Can Be Told: The Story of the Manhattan Project. New York: Harper, 1962.

Hachey, Thomas E., ed. Confidential Dispatches: Analysis of America by the British Ambassador, 1939-1945. Evanston, IL: New University Press, 1974.

Halifax, Earl of. The American Speeches of the Earl of Halifax. London: Oxford University Press, 1947.

_____. Fullness of Days. New York: Dodd, Mead and Company, 1957.

Hankey, Lord. Politics, Trials and Errors. Oxford: Pen-in-Hand, 1950.

Harvey, Oliver. The Diplomatic Diaries of Oliver Harvey, 1937-1940. London: Collins, 1970.

Hassett, William D. Off the Record with F.D.R., 1942-1945. London: George Allen and Unwin, Ltd., 1960.

Hollis, Leslie. One Marine's Tale. London: A. Deutsche, 1956.

Hull, Cordell. The Memoirs of Cordell Hull. 2 vols. New York: Macmillan, 1948.

Ismay, General the Lord. The Memoirs of the Lord Ismay. London: Heinemann, 1960.

Israel, Fred L., ed. The War Diary of Breckinridge Long: Selections From the Years 1939-1944. Lincoln: University of Nebraska Press, 1966.

Kase, Toshikazu. Journey to the Missouri. New Haven: Yale University Press, 1950.

Kennedy, Sir John. The Business of War: The War Narrative of John Kennedy. New York: Morrow, 1958.

King, Ernest J. and Whitehall, Walter M. Fleet Admiral King: A Naval Record. New York: W. W. Norton, 1952.

Leahy, William D. I Was There: The Personal Story of the Chief of Staff to President Roosevelt and Truman, Based on His Notes and Diaries Made at the Time. New York: Whitlesey House, 1950.

Leaser, James. The Clock With Four Hands: Based on the Experiences of General Sir Leslie Hollis. New York: Reynal, 1959.

_____. War at the Top: Based on the Experiences of General Sir Leslie Hollis. London: M. Joseph, 1959.

Lowenheim, Francis L.; Langley, Harold O.; and Jonas, Manfred; eds. Roosevelt and Churchill: Their Wartime Correspondence. New York: Saturday Review Press, 1975.

Luvaas, Jay, ed. Dear Miss Em: General Eichelberger's War in the Pacific, 1942-1945. Westport, CT: Greenwood Press, 1972.

MacArthur, Douglas. Reminiscences. New York: McGraw-Hill Book Company, 1964.

Maisky, Ivan. Memoirs of a Soviet Ambassador: The War, 1939-1943. London: Hutchinson and Company, 1967.

Millis, Walter, ed. The Forrestal Diaries. New York: Viking Press, 1951.

Moran, Lord. Winston Churchill: The Struggle for Survival, 1940-1965. London: Constable, 1966.

Nicholas, H. G., ed. Isaiah Berlin's Washington Despatches, 1941-1945. Chicago: University of Chicago Press, 1981.

Nicolson, Nigel, ed. Harold Nicolson Diaries and Letters, 1945-1962. London: Collins, 1968.

North, John, ed. The Memoirs of Field-Marshal Earl Alexander of Tunis, 1940-1945. London: Cassell and Company, 1962.

Pawle, Gerald. The War and Colonel Warden: Based on Recollections of Commander C. R. Thompson. London: George G. Harrup, 1963.

Publishing Committee for Children of Hiroshima. Children of Hiroshima. Cambridge, MA: Oelgeschlager, Gunn, and Hain, 1981; reprint ed., 1951. Children's accounts of the day of the atomic bombing.

Richardson, James O. On the Treadmill to Pearl Harbor: The Memoirs of Admiral James O. Richardson. Washington, D.C.: G.P.O. (Naval History Division, Department of the Navy), 1973.

Roosevelt, Elliot, ed. F.D.R.: His Personal Letters. 3 vols. New York: Duell Sloan and Pearce, 1950.

Roosevelt, Franklin D. On Our Way. New York: The John Day Company, 1934.

Rosenman, Samuel I., comp. The Public Papers and Addresses of Franklin D. Roosevelt. 13 vols. New York: Random House, 1938-1950.

Sherwood, Robert, ed. The White House Papers of Harry L. Hopkins: An Intimate History. 2 vols. London: Eyre and Spottiswood, 1948-1949.

Stettinius, Edward R., Jr. Roosevelt and the Russians. Garden City: Doubleday and Company, 1949.

Stimson, Henry L. and Bundy, McGeorge. On Active Service in Peace and War. New York: Harper and Brothers, 1948.

Stuart, John L. Fifty Years in China: The Memoirs of John Leighton Stuart, Missionary and Ambassador. New York: Random House, 1954.

Thompson, Walter H. Assignment: Churchill. New York: Farrar, Straus, and Young, 1955.

_____. I Was Churchill's Shadow. London: Christopher Johnson, 1951.

Truman, Harry S. Memoirs. 2 vols. Garden City: Doubleday and Company, 1956.

Wedemeyer, Albert C. Wedemeyer Reports! New York: Holt and Company, 1958.

Wheeler-Bennett, Sir John, ed. Action This Day: Working With Churchill. London: Macmillan, 1968.

White, Theodore, ed. The Stilwell Papers. New York: W. Sloan Associates, 1948.

Wilson, Henry M. Eight Years Overseas, 1939-1947. London: Hutchinson, 1950.

Winant, John G. A Letter From Grosvenor Square: An Account of a Stewardship. London: Hedder and Stoughton, 1947.

II. SECONDARY SOURCES

Space limitations preclude the offering of even a representative list of secondary sources (including the so-called "Official Histories") dealing with World War II. For a preliminary yet selective guide, see the works cited in the Endnotes. See also a full, annotated bibliography, John J. Sbrega, editor, The War Against Japan (Richard L. Blanco, editor, The Wars of the United States series, Garland Publishing, Inc.).

INDEX

ABDA, 15
Acheson, Dean, 43, 62, 202
Africa, 98, 105
Akyab, 81
Allies, 22, 66, 69, 73, 75, 79,
    81, 85, 87-88, 90, 95, 113-21,
    138, 162, 164, 167, 169, 178-
    88, 190, 194-98, 205
American Samoa, 155
Amery, Leo, 3, 20, 21, 69-70, 73,
    208
Anglo-American Psychological War-
    fare Division, 77
Annam, 119, 187, 189-90
Anti-Fascist People's Indepen-
    dence League (Burma), 67
ANZAC, 65
Appleby, Paul, 62-63
ARCADIA, 11-12
ARGENTIA (See Atlantic Charter)
Asama Maru, the, 51
Asia, 88, 105, 113, 154, 161,
    184, 187, 198, 200
Associated Press, the, 163
Atherton, Ray, 96
Atlantic Charter, 17-32, 58, 119,
    124, 125, 129-30, 134-35, 152,
    156, 519-60, 166, 199, 202, 207
Atomic bomb (see U. S., atomic
    bomb)
Attlee, Clement, 18-19, 30, 76,
    126-27, 131, 206
Australia, 14, 64, 129, 174, 184-
    85, 191
Axiom, 77
Axis Powers, 96, 187, 193, 201,
    203, 206
Azores, 211

Baltic, the, 138
"Baltic Munich", 29
Bangkok, 94, 192
Banque de l'Indo-Chine, 92
Bao Dai, Emperor, 188
Barkley, Senator Alben, 41
Bay of Bengal, 86
Beaverbrook, Lord, 8, 38, 69, 77,

198
Belgium, 151, 174, 270
Bennett, John Sterndale, 57, 120,
    121, 159
Berle, Adolph, Jr., 29, 59, 89
Berlin, 175, 185
Bevin, Ernest, 76, 186
Bidault, Georges, 108
Big Four Nations, 132, 169, 171,
    173-74
Big Three Powers, 167
Bishop, Max, 87-88, 110
Blaizot, General Roger, 104-05,
    109
Blakeslee, George H., 156
Boatner, General Haydon, 77
Bohlen, Charles, 146-47
Bonnet, Henri, 116, 118
Borneo, 83
Bowman, Isaiah, 37, 98, 137, 140
Bracken, Brendan, 130
Brazzaville, 94, 249
Brewster, Ralph O., 39
Briggs, Ralph, 222
British China Association, 75
British Force 136, 190
British Rice Unit, 196
Bromley, Thomas E., 23-24
Brooke, General Sir Alan, 187
Brooke-Popham, General Sir
    Robert, 13-14
Buell, Robert Lewis, 110
Bulgaria, 158
BULLFROG, 81, 83
Bunche, Ralph, 142, 150
Burma, 14-15, 18, 20, 22, 55, 67-
    69, 73-74, 79, 81, 84, 116-17,
    124, 180, 182, 185, 196
Burma Road, 73, 80
Butler, Nevile, 93-94
Byrnes, James F., 146, 160

Cadogan, Sir Alexander, 31, 51,
    107, 170, 192
Cairo Conference, 97-98, 109,
    148, 161
Cairo Declaration, 27

-324-